THE COMPLETE ILLUSTRATED GUIDE TO
CHINESE COOKING

THE COMPLETE ILLUSTRATED GUIDE TO
CHINESE COOKING

TECHNIQUES, INGREDIENTS & RECIPES

ORATHAY SOUKSISAVANH
PHOTOGRAPHS BY PIERRE JAVELLE
ILLUSTRATIONS BY YANNIS VAROUTSIKOS

Hardie Grant
NORTH AMERICA

CONTENTS

THE BUILDING BLOCKS

Flours & starches 10

Rice. 12

Dim sum dough 14

Noodles & pancakes. 22

Techniques 34

Broths. 38

Ingredients. 42

THE RECIPES

Dim sum 54

Meat 100

Fish & seafood 142

Tofu. 164

Vegetables 170

Noodles & rice 194

Street food. 242

Desserts 254

ILLUSTRATED GLOSSARY

Equipment 278

Essential techniques 280

Ingredients. 282

HOW TO USE THIS BOOK

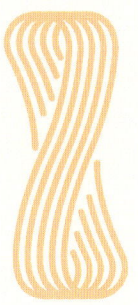

ESSENTIALS

In this section, you will discover all the recipes and essential ingredients of Chinese cuisine. For each item there is an infographic and detailed explanation of the technique and preparation.

THE RECIPES

In this section, you will use the building blocks and essential ingredients to create the recipes. For each recipe there are references to the essential ingredients and techniques, an infographic to understand the concept of the recipe, and step-by-step photos for making each item.

ILLUSTRATED GLOSSARY

The ingredient and equipment details and illustrated techniques in the glossary will help deepen your knowledge of the recipes.

CHAPTER 1
ESSENTIALS

FLOURS & STARCHES

Wheat flour 10
Starches 11

RICE

Rice (jasmine) 12

DIM SUM DOUGH

Translucent dumpling dough 14
Wheat-flour dumpling dough 16
Bao dough 20

NOODLES & PANCAKES

Rice-flour noodles 22
Egg noodles 26
Biang biang noodles 28
Steamed wheat-flour pancakes 32

TECHNIQUES

Deboning a chicken thigh 34
Preparing shrimp 36

BROTHS

Basic broth .38
Vegan broth 40

INGREDIENTS

Baking soda .42
Kansui 43
Lye water 43
Chile oil 44
Rice vinegar 46
Soy sauce 47
Oyster sauce 48
Wine and spirits 49
Fermented Products 50

Understanding

WHEAT FLOUR

WHAT IS IT?

The powder obtained after milling the wheat kernel.

COMPOSITION OF A GRAIN OF WHEAT

Bran (the outer coating): 20 to 25 percent of the kernel. It is rich in minerals.
Endosperm: 70 to 75 percent of the kernel. It contains 70 percent starch and about 12 percent gluten.
Germ: 3 percent of the kernel. It contains vitamins. The whiter a flour is the less bran it has, and consequently the more gluten it has.

FROM WHEAT TO FLOUR

The wheat kernel is ground, sifted, sorted, and ground again until a more (or less) refined powder is obtained according to the desired quality (white, whole wheat, etc.).

WHAT IS PROTEIN CONTENT?

Flour contains two types of proteins that, once hydrated and kneaded, combine to form gluten which gives the dough two properties: elasticity, the ability to return to its initial shape, and extensibility, which allows you to stretch the dough without tearing it.

WHAT PROTEIN CONTENT SHOULD YOU CHOOSE?

Low-protein flour (between 8 and 10 percent), such as for the baos (page 20). This flour forms less gluten, therefore a less dense structure, lending a lighter and softer texture.

Flour rich in protein (between 12 and 14 percent), such as for noodles. This flour offers a strong gluten network. The dough obtained is more resistant and can be stretched without breaking, such as for biang biang noodles (page 28). It maintains a pleasant and chewy texture after cooking.

LOW-GLUTEN BLEACHED WHEAT FLOUR

Wheat flour (such as organic pastry flour, with a protein level between 9 and 10 percent) once cooked will always have a slightly yellow color. If you want to make white baos, use a low-protein bleached flour. The most well-known brand in Chinese recipes is Purple Orchid.

10

Understanding

STARCHES

1 WHEAT STARCH
What is it?
A fine white powder obtained from a mixture of wheat flour and water from which the starch has been extracted.
Uses
Once cooked, it becomes translucent with a slightly elastic texture. It is used for dim sum since it allows the filling to be partially visible.

2 TAPIOCA STARCH
What is it?
A fine white powder obtained from cassava pulp from which the starch has been extracted. It has a strong thickening and gelling power.
Uses
Once mixed with hot water, it turns into a viscous clear gel. Its flavor is almost neutral. It is used to thicken soups and sauces and to make them smooth and glossy. It is also used with other flours and starches to create a perfect combination of textures (dim sum, rice noodles, etc.).

3 SWEET POTATO STARCH
What is it?
A powder obtained from sweet potatoes from which the starch has been extracted. There are fine sweet potato starches and granular sweet potato starches.
Uses
For a golden-brown breading that remains brown and crisp, even after refrigeration. The granules give items an irregular appearance, resembling popcorn (page 250).

4 RICE FLOUR AND GLUTINOUS RICE FLOUR
What is it?
Made from ground rice and then dried. Long grain rice is used for rice flour (Asian) and round and opaque glutinous rice is used for glutinous rice flour.
Uses
Rice flour is slightly more sticky than wheat flour and is used to make noodles, pancakes, balls, and desserts. Glutinous rice flour, which is extremely sticky, is mainly used in desserts for which its gooey texture is most appreciated. In savory recipes, it is combined with other flours for balanced textures.

Understanding
RICE

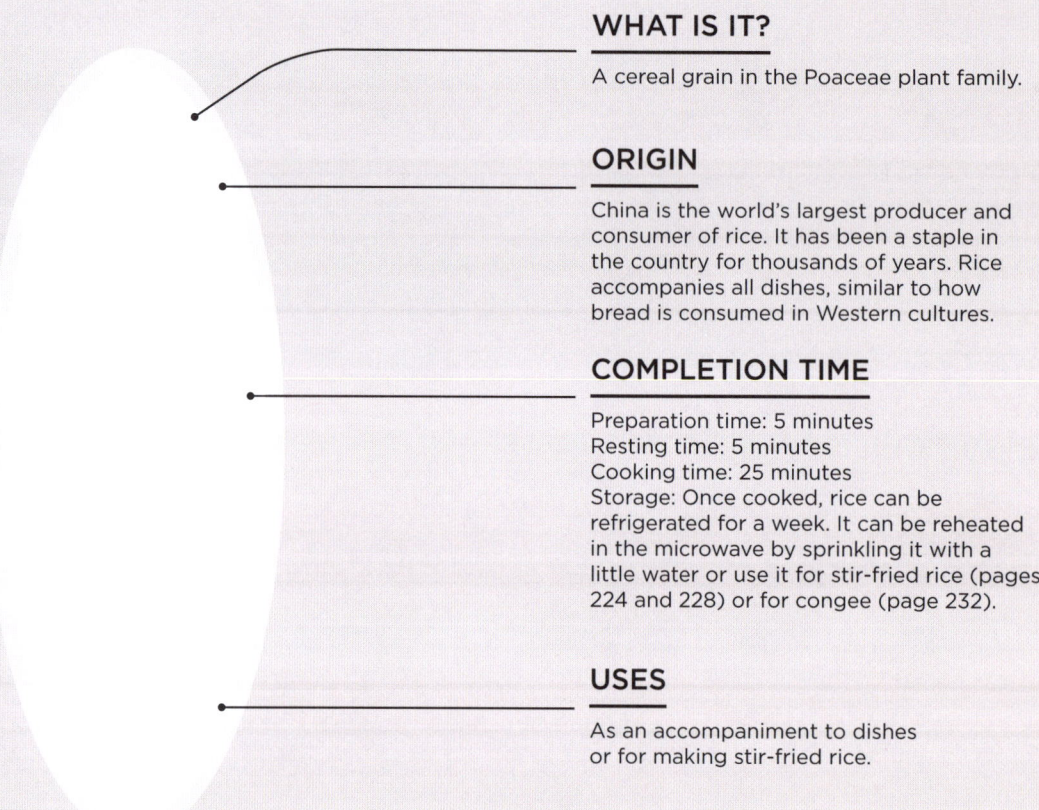

WHAT IS IT?
A cereal grain in the Poaceae plant family.

ORIGIN
China is the world's largest producer and consumer of rice. It has been a staple in the country for thousands of years. Rice accompanies all dishes, similar to how bread is consumed in Western cultures.

COMPLETION TIME
Preparation time: 5 minutes
Resting time: 5 minutes
Cooking time: 25 minutes
Storage: Once cooked, rice can be refrigerated for a week. It can be reheated in the microwave by sprinkling it with a little water or use it for stir-fried rice (pages 224 and 228) or for congee (page 232).

USES
As an accompaniment to dishes or for making stir-fried rice.

SPECIAL EQUIPMENT
Rice cooker or lidded saucepan

USEFUL TIP
Cook at a low boil, covered.

VARIETIES
There are three main varieties of rice grown and widely consumed in China:

Indica rice (*Oryza sativa*)
Grown in the subtropical and temperate regions of China. It is a long-grain, low-starch rice that absorbs little water when cooked, allowing it to remain light and not sticky. Among this variety, there are two families: long-grain rice, neutral in flavor, also used for "nonsticky" rice, and naturally flavored rice, which is very popular, such as jasmine rice.

Japonica rice (*Oryza sativa japonica*)
Grown mainly in the northern regions of China. Japonica rice has a grain of various shapes, from short to medium. It absorbs a great deal of water when cooking and releases starch, which makes it stickier.

Glutinous (sticky) rice (*Oryza sativa glutinosa*)
Grown in southern China, it has a characteristic sticky texture after cooking. It is most often eaten in festive or seasonal dishes, or in desserts.

Learning

WHY RINSE RICE?
Traditionally, rice was washed to remove dust, insects, small pebbles, and pieces of stems left behind by the process of husking. Today, rinsing rice has been shown to remove up to 20 percent of the microplastics present. Rinsing also removes some of the starch on the surface of the rice grains, which are responsible for the cloudy water when it is rinsed. Rinsing promotes separation of grains, making them less likely to stick together.

WHICH RICE SHOULD YOU CHOOSE?
Jasmine rice is the most popular rice to accompany Chinese dishes. The best rice within this category comes from Thailand and can be found easily in markets. At the beginning of the year, you can find it in Asian grocery stores as rice from the new harvests (Heavenly Birds brand). The beginning year is written in red on the packages and guarantees freshly harvested, tender, soft, and slightly glutinous rice with a delicate floral fragrance that fades over time. This rice can be enjoyed on its own or as an accompaniment to dishes. As rice ages, the grains will separate better and be drier. At this stage, the rice is perfect for stir-fried rice.

PER 2 POUNDS 7 OUNCES / 1,100 G OF COOKED RICE

2⅔ cups / 500 g Thai rice (jasmine)
2¾ cups / 650 ml cold water

1 Rinse the rice twice with cold water, rubbing it between your hands to remove excess starch.

2 Drain, and add it to a pot or saucepan. Add the cold water.

3 Cover, and bring to a low boil over medium heat for about 5 minutes. The water level should reach the surface of the rice. Reduce the heat and cook at a gentle boil, without stirring, until the water has evaporated, about 10 minutes. Reduce the heat to the lowest possible temperature and continue cooking for 15 minutes. Turn off the heat, cover, and set aside for 15 to 20 minutes without removing the lid.

Understanding

TRANSLUCENT DUMPLING DOUGH

WHAT IS IT?
A starch-based dough that, once cooked, becomes translucent, allowing the filling to show through.

COMPLETION TIME
Preparation time: 10 minutes

USES
To make dim sum and, in particular, the wrappers for ha kao shrimp dumplings (page 54).

SPECIAL EQUIPMENT
Large mixing bowl
Small rolling pin
Round cookie cutter between 4 and 4¾ inches / 10 and 12 cm in diameter

CHALLENGES
Preventing the dough from drying out.
Rolling it out evenly.

USEFUL TIPS
Wrap scraps in plastic wrap to keep for rolling out again. Knead the dough well to restore its suppleness.
To obtain perfect discs, cut each one with a round cookie cutter 4 to 4¾ inches / 10 to 12 cm in diameter.

VARIATIONS
Combine 3½ ounces / 100 g of spinach leaves with 1 scant cup / 230 ml water. Measure out just over ¾ cup / 200 ml of the green water and bring it to a boil. Pour it over the starches according to the directions in the recipe. The result will be a green dough.

Learning

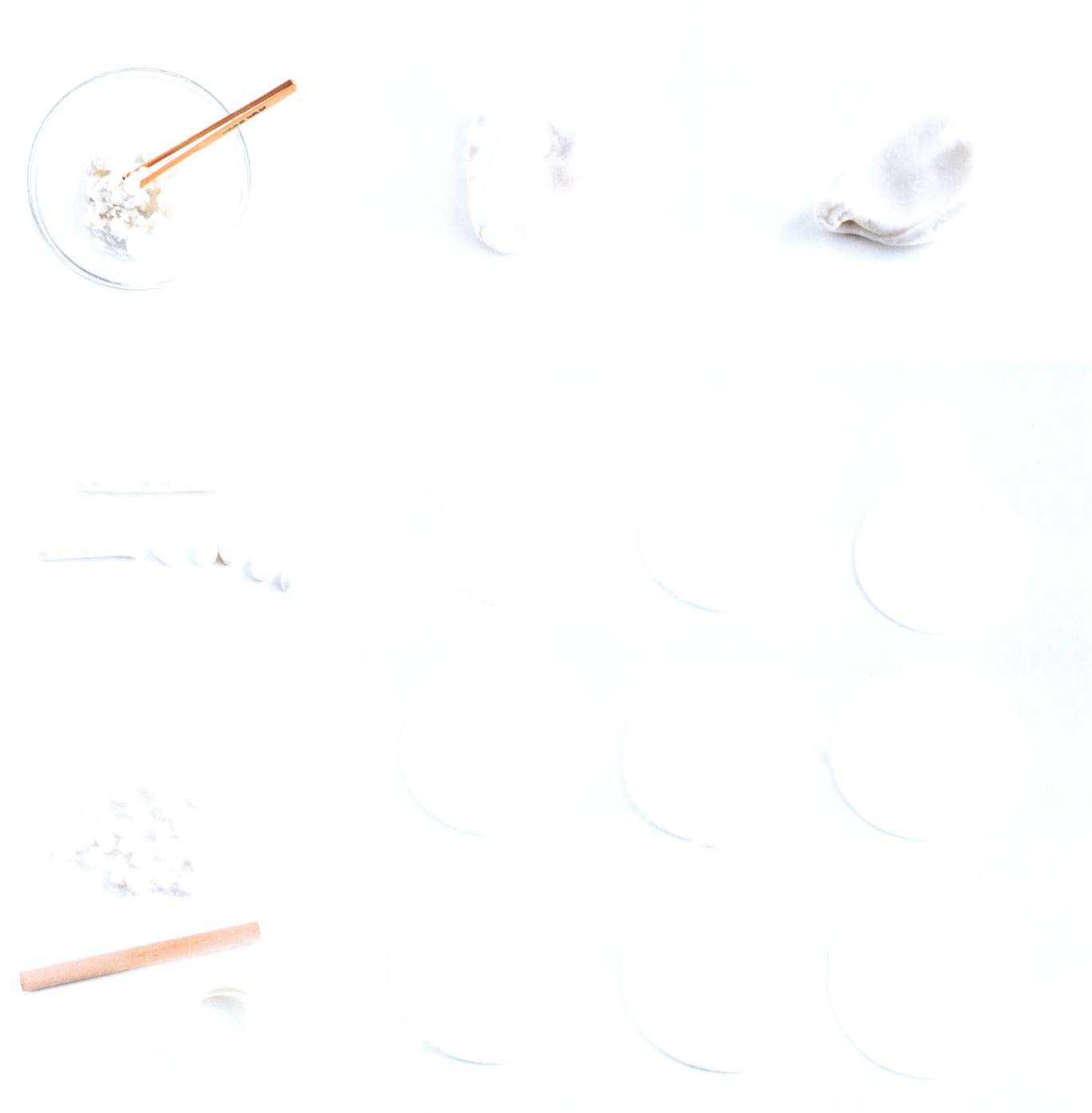

MAKES 20 WRAPPERS ABOUT 4 INCHES / 10 CM IN DIAMETER

1½ cups / 145 g wheat starch
¼ cup / 35 g tapioca starch
1 level teaspoon salt
2 tablespoons neutral-flavor oil (sunflower, peanut)
Just over ¾ cup / 200 ml boiling water

1 In a bowl, combine the starches and salt. Make a well in the center. Add the oil to the center, then add the boiling water, stirring briskly with chopsticks or a wooden spoon.

2 When the flour begins to combine, scrape the dough out onto a work surface and knead for about 5 minutes using your palm while the dough is still hot; the dough will be hot but not burning. The dough must be perfectly smooth, elastic, and soft and should not stick to your hand.

3 Roll the dough into three sausage shapes and cut them widthwise into sections about ½ ounce / 15 to 17 g each.

4 Roll out each section to a disc 4 to 4¾ inches / 10 to 12 cm in diameter. While rolling each one, keep the others wrapped in plastic wrap to prevent them from drying out.

Understanding

WHEAT-FLOUR DUMPLING DOUGH

WHAT IS IT?
A wheat-flour dough made with boiling water.

COMPLETION TIME
Preparation time: 10 minutes
Resting time: 30 minutes
Storage: The dough discs can be frozen by dusting them with flour and coating them generously with cornstarch. If wheat flour is used to dust them, it will be absorbed by the dough. Once thawed, use immediately.

USES
Guō tiē dumplings (page 64), xiǎo lóng bāo (page 60).

SPECIAL EQUIPMENT
Small rolling pin
Round cookie cutter 4 inches / 10 cm in diameter

CHALLENGES
Mixing briskly, then kneading it while still hot.
Weighing the dough pieces to create uniformly sized discs.

USEFUL TIPS
Wrap scraps in plastic wrap to keep for rolling out again.
To obtain perfect discs, cut each disc with a round cookie cutter 4 inches / 10 cm in diameter.

VARIATIONS
Flavor the dough by adding spices (paprika, chile powder, five-spice powder, etc.) or chopped herbs (cilantro, parsley, chives, etc.). You can also color it by adding beetroot juice to the water or mixed spinach, as is done when making Italian pastas.

WHY USE BOILING WATER?
Gluten is formed from two proteins in wheat flour (page 10), one of which is shaped like a spring. In dry flour, proteins are immobile. By adding cold water, proteins are unlocked, and when the dough is kneaded these proteins bind together to form an elastic gluten network with an ability to return to its original shape. The same thing happens in dough made with boiling water, but the high temperature of the water denatures the gluten-forming proteins, causing them to lose their shape. Without shape, the proteins cannot bind together well, and the gluten network is fragmented and dispersed. The dough using boiling water, therefore, becomes less elastic and is easier to roll out. Once cooked, the texture of this dough is also more tender and moist than those made using cold water.

Learning

**MAKES 20 TO 30 WRAPPERS
ABOUT 4 INCHES / 10 CM
IN DIAMETER**

2⅓ cups plus 1 tablespoon /
300 g all-purpose flour
½ teaspoon salt
Just over ⅔ cup / 170 ml boiling water

Making

WHEAT-FLOUR DUMPLING DOUGH

1 In a bowl, combine the flour and salt. Make a well in the center. Add the boiling water to the center, stirring with a spatula or chopsticks.

2 When the dough begins to form in clumps, knead it until all the flour is incorporated (about 5 minutes).

3 Scrape the dough out onto a work surface and continue kneading for several minutes. The dough should be smooth and pliable.

4 Cover with plastic wrap, and let rest at room temperature for 30 minutes.

5 Portion the dough in thirds and roll each portion into sausage shapes. Roll out the wrappers, keeping the other pieces under plastic wrap between each step to prevent them from drying out.

6 TO MAKE GUŌ TIĒ: Cut sections of about ½ ounce / 17 g each. Dust the work surface with flour and roll out each section to obtain a disc 4 inches / 10 cm in diameter.

TO MAKE XIĂO LÓNG BĀO: Cut sections of about ⅓ ounce / 10 g. Dust the work surface with flour and roll out each section to obtain a disc 4 inches / 10 cm in diameter.

Understanding
BAO DOUGH

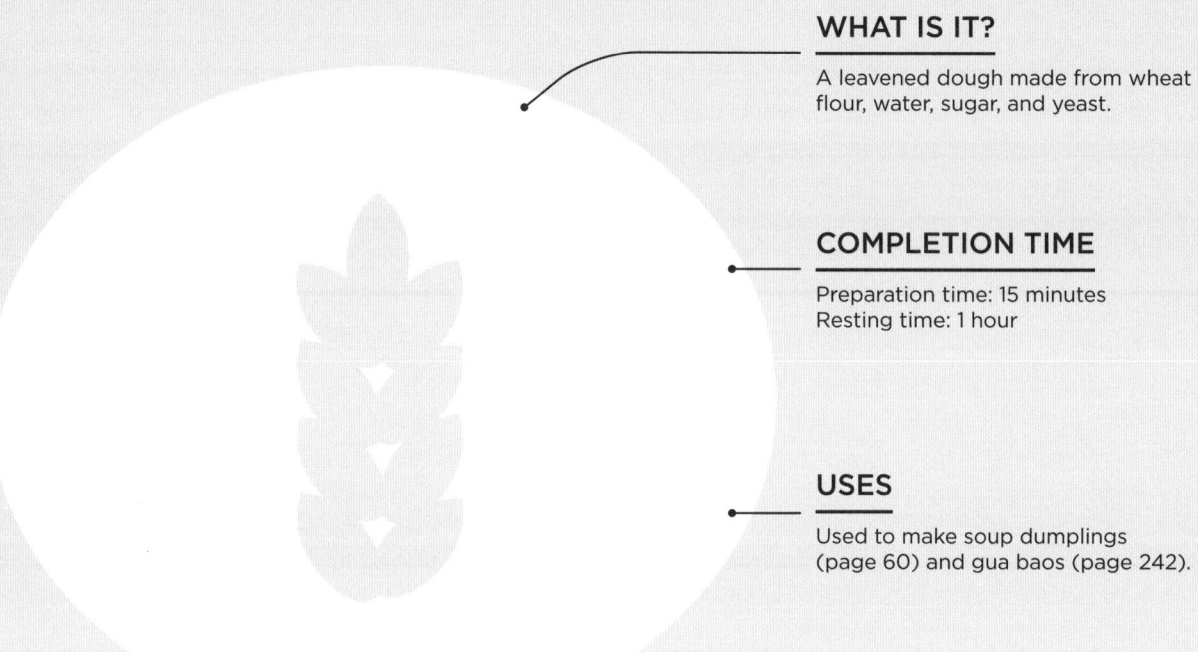

WHAT IS IT?
A leavened dough made from wheat flour, water, sugar, and yeast.

COMPLETION TIME
Preparation time: 15 minutes
Resting time: 1 hour

USES
Used to make soup dumplings (page 60) and gua baos (page 242).

SPECIAL EQUIPMENT
Stand mixer + dough hook

CHALLENGES
Kneading the dough with a dough hook until it is smooth and homogeneous. Without an electric mixer, this will have to be done by hand.

USEFUL TIPS
Use bleached or unbleached flour with a low protein level of around 9 to 10 percent for very soft baos, or 10 to 11 percent protein for a good balance between softness and elasticity. With higher protein levels, you will lose softness. Although the dough will be more elastic in this case, it will be more flavorful. For the gua baos, use medium-protein flour. Since the dough is filled like a sandwich, it needs to hold up to the filling and will have a little chewiness. It is all a matter of taste and personal preference!

USEFUL TIP
For the gua baos (page 242), you can add 1 teaspoon of salt to the dough with the other ingredients.

VARIATIONS
As with dumpling dough, you can customize it by adding chopped herbs or spices (paprika, chile powder, etc.) when kneading. You can also replace the water with the juice from vegetables to make a colored dough (spinach, carrot, beetroot, etc.).

WHY DOES THE DOUGH OMIT SALT?
This dough ideally has a light texture and a somewhat neutral flavor to highlight the flavor of the filling instead. Adding salt to the dough would tighten the gluten structure and slow down the action of the yeast. The result would be a firmer and less airy dough.

Learning

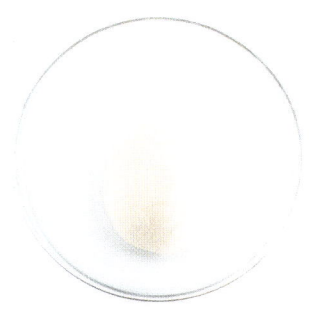

MAKES 10 TO 12 BAOS

2¾ cups / 350 g low-gluten Chinese flour or pastry flour
1¼ teaspoons / 5 g active dry yeast
3 tablespoons / 40 g sugar
1 tablespoon lard,
or 1½ tablespoons vegetable oil
Just over ⅔ cup / 170 ml water

1 Preheat a warming drawer or bread proofer to 86°F (30°C). In the bowl of a stand mixer fitted with the dough hook, combine the flour, yeast, and sugar. Make a well in the center, add the fat, then add the water.

2 Mix for 3 to 5 minutes to form a smooth dough. The dough should not feel sticky.

3 Shape the dough into a ball.

4 Cover the dough with a cloth and place it in the proofer or set it in a warm place for 1 hour. The dough should double in size.

Understanding

RICE-FLOUR NOODLES

WHAT IS IT?
Sheets of dough made from rice flour and tapioca starch, steam cooked, then layered and cut into noodles.

COMPLETION TIME
Preparation time: 1 hour
Resting time: 5 minutes after baking, to be able to easily peel off the dough.
Cooking time: 2 minutes per sheet
Storage: 3 to 4 days. Once cooked and well-oiled, wrap the entire stack of sheets in plastic wrap. It is best to cut them just before cooking them instead of in advance. Peel off the noodles one by one. If the noodles tend to break, heat them in the microwave for a few seconds to soften them.

USES
In stir-fried beef noodles (page 220), or in the broth of 5-flavored braised duck (page 104)

SPECIAL EQUIPMENT
Steamer
Two 9½ by 7-inch / 24 by 18 cm rectangular baking sheets
Ladle
Plastic bowl scraper or spatula
Pastry brush

CHALLENGE
Distributing the dough evenly in the baking sheet.

USEFUL TIPS
Always mix the dough while adding the water because the flour and starch tend to clump together in the bottom of the bowl. Let the dough cool well before you peel it off. Do not oil the baking sheet too much, as the dough will have difficulty adhering to it. Heat the baking sheet before adding the dough. If you don't have a large enough steamer, you can use a large wok or pot. Use a rack with legs so that you can raise the baking sheet above the water to avoid touching it.

WHAT DOES THE TAPIOCA STARCH DO?
It lends transparency and shine and improves cooking resistance by preventing the noodles from disintegrating or becoming too sticky when cooked (in a wok or in broth).

Learning

**MAKES ABOUT
1 POUND 2 OUNCES / 500 G
(6 SHEETS)**

1 cup / 150 g rice flour
¼ cup plus
2 tablespoons / 65 g tapioca starch
½ teaspoon salt
1½ cups / 360 ml water
Neutral-flavor oil of your choice
(sunflower, peanut)

Making

RICE-FLOUR NOODLES

1 Before you begin, make sure you have two identical rectangular or square baking sheets that fit in the steamer. Lightly oil the baking sheets using a pastry brush. The thickness of each baking sheet should ideally be about 1/16 inch / 1.5 mm. Use a ladle or a small container to add a consistent quantity of dough to the pans.

2 Combine the flour, starch, and salt in a large bowl. Stir in the water and 1 tablespoon of oil.

3 Prepare an ice water bath to help cool the pan. Bring the water in the steamer to a boil. Place the first baking sheet in the steamer basket for 2 minutes.

4 Stir the dough to smooth it out, then pour a ladle of dough into the hot baking sheet, tilting the steamer basket handles to distribute the dough evenly. Cover, and cook for 2 minutes over high heat. The dough should bubble.

5 Remove the baking sheet and soak it in a pan of ice water. While the first baking sheet is cooling, heat the second baking sheet and stir the dough well before ladling it into the baking sheet.

6 Grease a cutting board. Loosen the edges of the cooked dough using a plastic bowl scraper or spatula. Grab the dough and gently peel it off the baking sheet. If it has trouble coming off, it is still too hot. Place it on the cutting board and generously oil the top.

7 When the second noodle sheet is cooked, layer it on top of the first and apply more oil. Repeat to make a layer of six noodle sheets.

8 Cut strips about ¾ inches / 2 cm wide. If you want to enjoy them in broth, it is best to cut them narrower (⅔ inch / 1.5 cm maximum). Loosen the noodles one at a time before cooking them.

Understanding EGG NOODLES

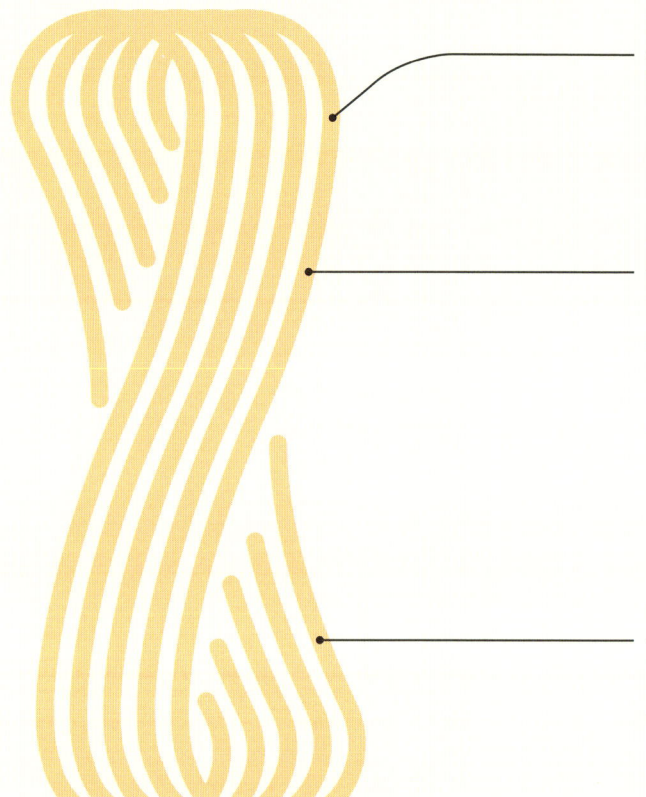

WHAT IS IT?
Noodles made from wheat flour, enriched with eggs.

COMPLETION TIME
Preparation time: 1 hour
Resting time: 1 hour
Storage: 1 day maximum, beyond that, they will develop a gray hue. You can freeze the noodles. Frozen noodles can be added to boiling water without thawing them. Stir them well using chopsticks to unstick them.

USES
Stir-fried noodles (Stir-Fried Noodles with Vegetables, page 198; Seafood Noodles page 194) but also in a broth (5-Flavor Braised Duck, page 104, Beef Noodle Soup page 206), or simply mixed with sesame oil, black or white rice vinegar, and sweet soy sauce.

SPECIAL EQUIPMENT
Stand mixer + dough hook
Pasta roller

CHALLENGE
Once the noodles are made, flour them well and let them dry for 30 to 40 minutes on a kitchen towel without overlapping them to prevent them from sticking together.

USEFUL TIPS
After kneading, the dough is dry and cracked. But once it has rested, it will become supple and easy to work with. Remember to flour the dough regularly before passing it through the pasta roller. The role of kansui (page 43) is to firm up the texture of the noodles.

VARIATIONS
Vary the thickness and size of the noodles according to your preferences.

MAKES
1 POUND 10 OUNCES / 740 G OF NOODLES

4 cups / 500 g type '00' or pastry flour
4 medium / 180 g eggs
¾ teaspoon salt
½ teaspoon kansui (optional)
1 tablespoon plus 1 teaspoon / 20 ml water

Learning

1. In the bowl of a stand mixer fitted with the dough hook, add the flour. Make a well in the center and add the eggs to the well. Add the salt and kansui, if using. Mix on low speed for 5 minutes. Add the water. The mixture should form a slightly dry ball. If necessary, add 1 tablespoon of water so that the dough can be gathered together. Cover the dough with plastic wrap and let rest at room temperature for 1 hour.

2. Have a bowl with flour and a strainer ready so that you can apply flour as you go. Set up the pasta roller. Divide the dough into six portions. As you work with each portion, keep the other portions wrapped in plastic wrap.

3. Set the pasta roller to the first notch. Flatten the first portion of dough using the palm of your hand. Lightly dust it with flour. Roll it through the machine.

4. Fold each dough portion in half and roll it again through the machine, repeating this four to five times, always folding it before rolling it. Dust with flour, if necessary. As soon as the dough is smooth, change the roller setting to the next notch, repeating this operation until you end on the second to last notch.

5. Flour the dough on both sides. Attach the noodle blade to cut noodles. Place the noodles flat on a kitchen towel and dust them lightly with flour. Be careful not to layer the noodles on top of each other. Repeat these same steps with the other portions of dough. Use them immediately, or let them dry for 30 minutes on the towel. Dust them again with flour, and then shape them into nests and store them in an airtight container for up to 1 day.

Understanding

BIANG BIANG NOODLES

WHAT IS IT?
Long, wide wheat-flour noodles stretched by hand and slapped against the work surface.

ORIGIN
These noodles originated from the northeastern province of Shaanxi, of which Xi'an is the capital. The Chinese character *biang* is an onomatopoeia, intended to imitate the sound made when slapping the dough against the counter. This is the most complex character of the Chinese language, composed of fifty-seven strokes. It is not defined in dictionaries and is learned as a linguistic curiosity. Legend has it that a young scholar of the Qin Dynasty (221–207 BC) invented this character as payment for his bowl of noodles.

COMPLETION TIME
Preparation time: 45 minutes
Resting time: 30 minutes +
20 minutes + 6 hours
Cooking time: About 3 minutes
Storage: Once stretched, the noodles should be consumed immediately. The dough pieces can be kept for 2 days in the refrigerator. The color will become slightly gray, but the flavor will not be altered.

USES
They are suitable for all recipes. Noodle stir-fries, in soups, seasoned with hot oil (a traditional recipe), etc.

SPECIAL EQUIPMENT
Stand mixer + dough hook

CHALLENGES
Intense kneading in a stand mixer. Relaxing the gluten. The more the dough rests, the more it can be stretched. Traditionally, once a noodle is stretched, it is added to boiling water and the next one is stretched. Until you have more experience with them, it is best to lay the noodles flat without overlapping them, then cook them all at once. This avoids uneven cooking, and you can complete the recipe more easily.

USEFUL TIPS
Use a flour with at least 12 percent protein (page 10). Before cooking them, rinse them with cold water to remove excess starch.

Learning

SERVES 4

3¼ cups / 400 g all-purpose or bread flour (12% protein)
Just over ¾ cup / 200 ml water
Neutral-flavor oil of your choice (sunflower, peanut)

Making

BIANG BIANG NOODLES

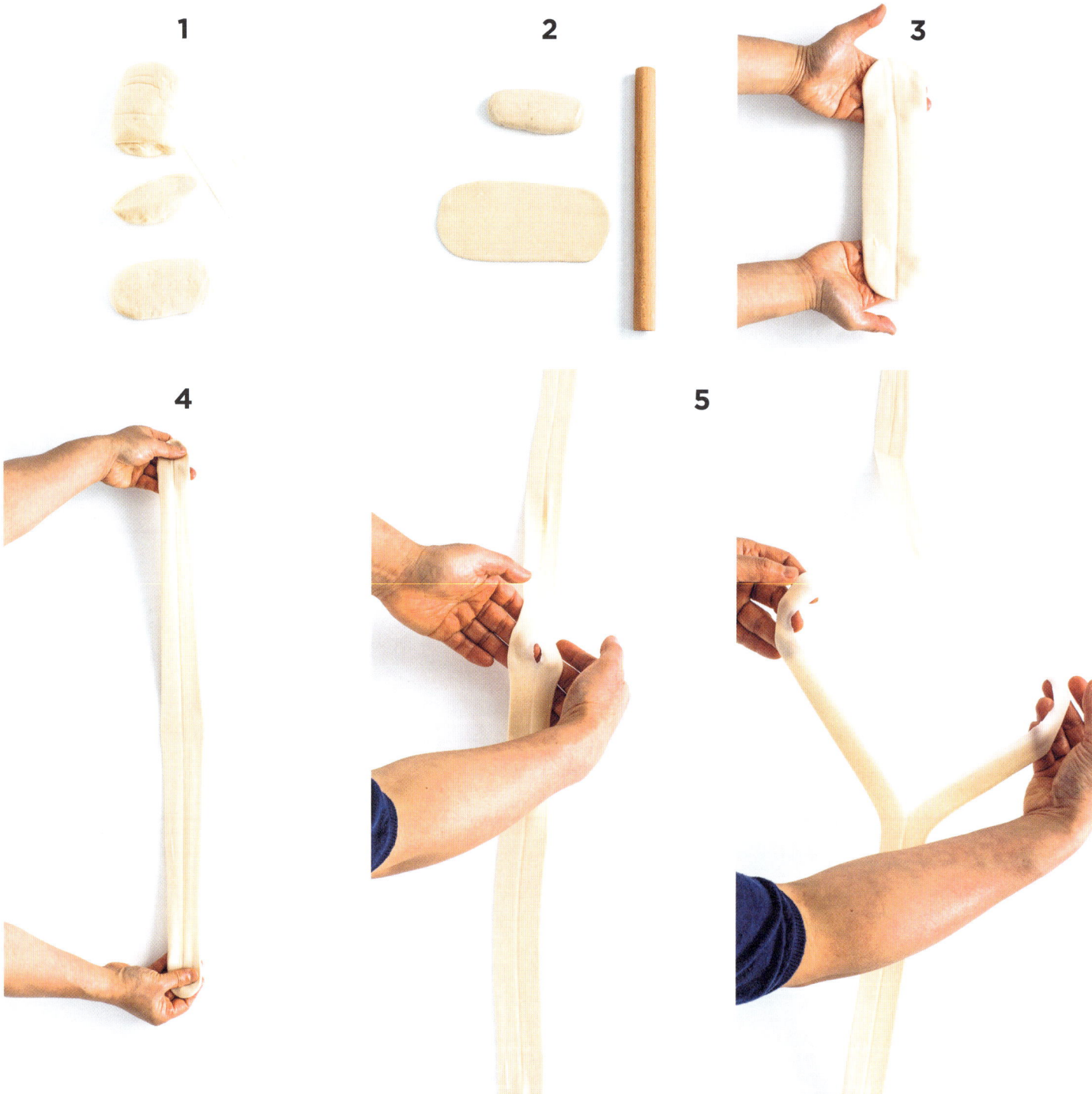

1 In the bowl of a stand mixer fitted with the dough hook, combine the flour and water and knead for 10 minutes to form a smooth dough. Shape the dough into a ball and cover the bowl with plastic wrap. Let rest for 30 minutes. Place the dough back on the stand mixer and knead again for 10 minutes. Set aside for 20 minutes. Weigh the dough (about 1 pound 5 ounces / 600 g) and divide it into six portions. Shape the portions into sausage shapes and flatten them slightly using your hand. Thoroughly oil both sides. Place them on a baking sheet lined with plastic wrap and set aside in the refrigerator at least 6 hours, ideally overnight, and up to 3 days.

2 Remove the dough portions 30 minutes prior to cooking them. Dust the work surface with flour, if necessary. Roll out one of the portions into a rectangle about 7 by 3 inches / 18 by 8 cm. Place a chopstick on its side in the center of the rectangle and press down to create an indentation.

3 Grab the two ends of the dough from underneath, as if holding an open book. Stretch the dough.

4 When the dough is about shoulder-width in length, start slapping the dough on the work surface while stretching it (slap it hard enough to bounce the dough off the work surface). The thickness should be adjusted according to taste.

5 Pull the dough in half by tearing it at the indentation to create a wide ring. Transfer to a baking sheet. Repeat these steps with the other dough pieces, avoiding overlapping the noodles once they are formed.

Understanding

STEAMED WHEAT-FLOUR PANCAKES

WHAT IS IT?
Thin wheat-flour pancakes cooked by steaming.

COMPLETION TIME
Preparation time: 1 hour 15 minutes
Resting time: 40 minutes
Cooking time: 8 minutes

USES
Served with lacquered duck (page 100), traditionally Peking, or with various vegetable, meat, and egg fillings to celebrate the beginning of spring (Lichun).

SPECIAL EQUIPMENT
Stand mixer + dough hook

CHALLENGE
Enlarging the diameter of the pancakes by pressing and spreading the stack of dough with your hands.

USEFUL TIPS
Oil the pancakes well to prevent them from sticking together. If the dough shrinks, cover it with plastic wrap and let rest. Once cooked, separate the pancakes quickly by peeling them apart.

Learning

MAKES 16 PANCAKES

2¼ cups / 285 g all-purpose flour
1 teaspoon salt
¾ cup / 180 ml water at 158°F / 70°C
Neutral-flavor oil of your choice (sunflower, peanut)

1 In the bowl of a stand mixer fitted with the dough hook, combine the flour and salt. Add the water and knead until the dough is soft and no longer sticking to the bowl. Cover with plastic wrap and set aside for 30 minutes.

2 Shape the dough into a sausage shape and cut it into sixteen pieces ¾ ounce / 20 g each. Flour the dough balls. Set aside under plastic wrap or under a clean towel.

3 Roll out each ball into a 5-inch / 13 cm disc. As you work with each disc, keep the remaining ones wrapped in plastic wrap or a cloth to prevent them from drying out too quickly. They can also be placed between two sheets of parchment paper.

4 Oil the work surface. Place a disc on the work surface, oil the top, then place another disc on top. Apply a little oil between each disc and make two stacks of eight discs each.

5 Using your fingers, press on the stack, moving from the center outward, to enlarge the diameter of the discs. Turn the stack over and repeat on the other side. Repeat this twice more. Set aside for 10 minutes, covered with plastic wrap.

6 Roll out the two stacks to obtain discs approximately 9 inches / 23 cm in diameter. Bring the water in a steamer to a boil. Oil the top of a stack again and overlap the two stacks. Place them in a steamer basket lined with parchment paper and steam for 8 minutes.

7 Remove the pancakes. Let cool a little before gently peeling them apart. If the pancakes get too cold, they will not be able to be peeled apart. Fold them into quarters.

Understanding

DEBONING
A CHICKEN THIGH

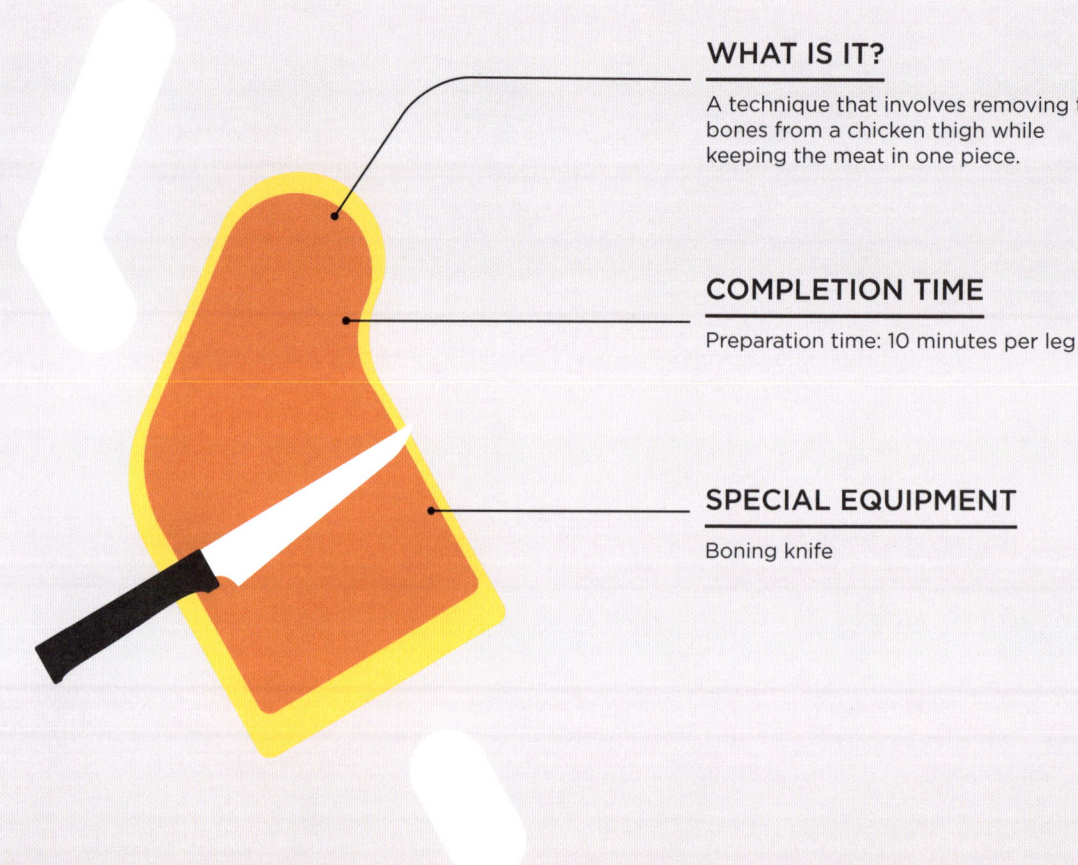

WHAT IS IT?
A technique that involves removing the bones from a chicken thigh while keeping the meat in one piece.

COMPLETION TIME
Preparation time: 10 minutes per leg

SPECIAL EQUIPMENT
Boning knife

USES
Only drunken chicken (page 114) requires the thigh to be boneless and whole. For most recipes, the meat can be cut into pieces.

Learning

FOR 1 CHICKEN THIGH

Remove fat and excess skin from the sides, if needed.

WHOLE BONELESS

1 Using a sharp boning knife, cut the meat at the back of the thigh along the bone. Gradually release the femur, still sliding along the bone and along the joint. Run the knife underneath the bone to detach the meat.

2 Remove this first bone by cutting it at the joint.

3 Cut through the center of the leg following along the bone. Remove the meat on each side, still following the bone, then go underneath it so the second bone can be removed.

DEBONING INTO PIECES

1 Cut the thigh in half at the joint.

2 Remove the meat following along the bone.

3 Cut the meat into pieces.

4 Reserve the bones to make broth.

Understanding
PREPARING
SHRIMP

WHAT IS IT?
A technique that makes it possible to obtain firm and crunchy shrimp after cooking with the use of baking soda.

COMPLETION TIME
Preparation time: 15 minutes
Resting time: 1 to 2 hours
Storage: 2 days in the refrigerator, once salted

USES
All recipes based on whole or chopped shrimp.
For recipes where shrimp are blended, this technique is not useful.

USEFUL TIPS
Adjust the proportions according to the weight of the shrimp. The sugar is added to essentially balance the flavors, but will allow better caramelization in stir-fried dishes. The salt will keep the inside of the shrimp moist.

Learning

MAKES 9 OUNCES / 250 G ONCE PREPARED (ABOUT 10½ OUNCES / 300 G BEFORE PREPARED)

10½ ounces / 300 g thawed shrimp
1 level teaspoon baking soda
1 teaspoon sugar
Just over ¾ cup to 1¼ cups / 200 to 300 ml water
½ teaspoon salt

1 Peel the shrimp. Depending on the recipe, leave the tail on or remove it.

2 Cut down the back of each shrimp and remove the shell.

3 Combine the baking soda, sugar, and water. Add the shrimp and combine. The shrimp should be fully submerged in the liquid.

4 Refrigerate for 1 to 2 hours.

5 Rinse and drain the shrimp thoroughly. Add the salt, stir to combine, and set aside in the refrigerator until ready to cook.

6 They can be refrigerated for 2 days once they have been salted.

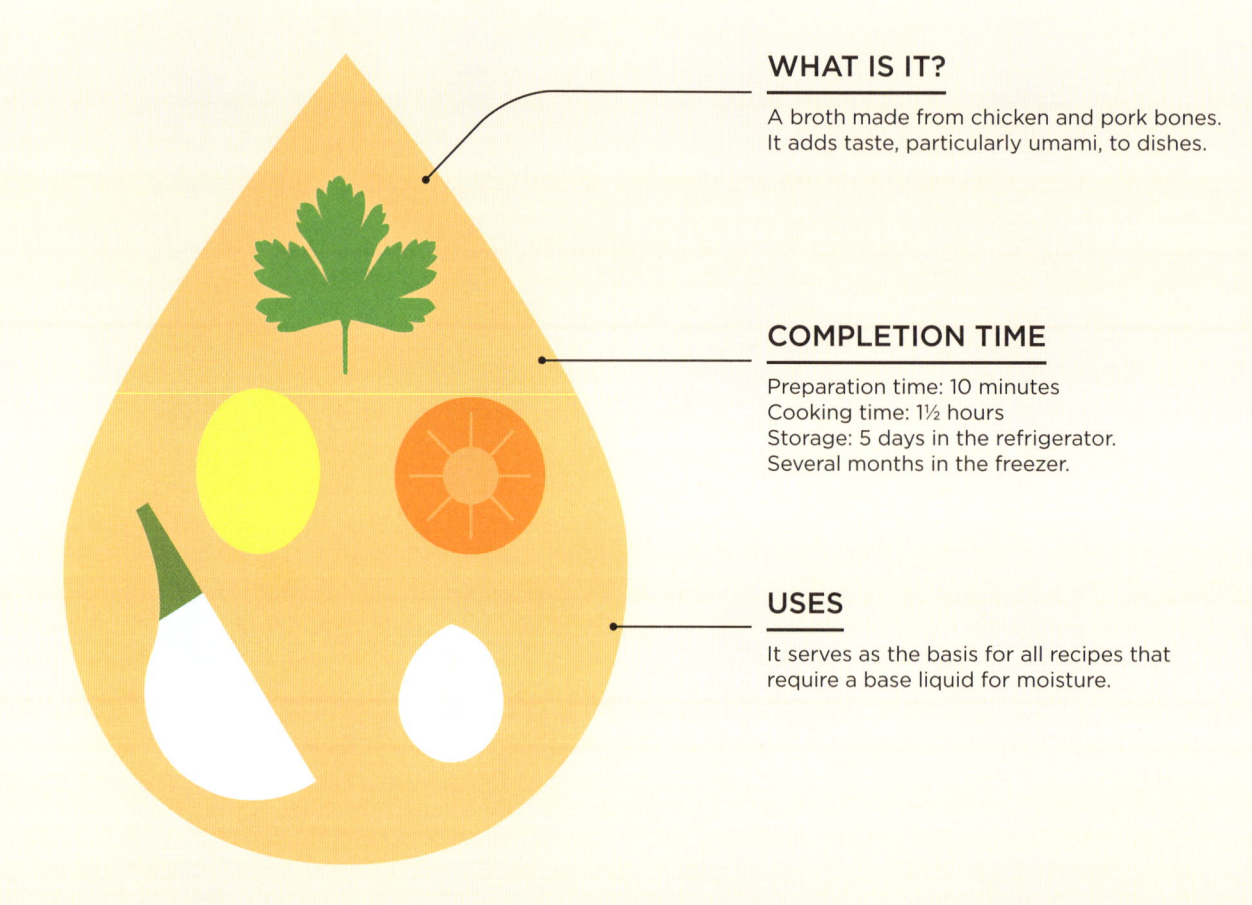

Understanding
BASIC BROTH

WHAT IS IT?
A broth made from chicken and pork bones. It adds taste, particularly umami, to dishes.

COMPLETION TIME
Preparation time: 10 minutes
Cooking time: 1½ hours
Storage: 5 days in the refrigerator. Several months in the freezer.

USES
It serves as the basis for all recipes that require a base liquid for moisture.

CHALLENGES
Making broth is a fundamental technique in Chinese cuisine. This is why bones can be found for sale in all Asian markets. You can also ask your butcher for any that might be intended for throwing away.

USEFUL TIP
To make soup dumplings (xiǎo lóng bāo, page 60), reduce the amount of bones by half to make a lighter broth that is less rich in collagen, but will be more fluid when serving.

VARIATIONS
You can replace the bones with a chicken, chicken wings, or even the leftover bones of a roasted chicken or lacquered duck. Using a mixture of chicken and pork lends a richer, deeper flavor, but you can make the broth with what you have on hand.

Learning

MAKES 6 CUPS / 1.5 L OF BROTH

2 large onions
3 carrots
3 stalks celery
¾ ounce / 20 g fresh ginger
1 head of garlic
½ bunch of cilantro, or the stems of 1 bunch
3 quarts / 3 L water
1 teaspoon salt
1 teaspoon sugar
1 tablespoon black peppercorns
4 pounds / 1.8 kg chicken and pork bones

1 Cut the onions into quarters and the carrots and celery into sections. Wash the ginger and cut it into strips with the skin still on. Crush the garlic cloves or cut the entire head in half. Tie the cilantro with a string to prevent the leaves from coming loose.

2 In a large saucepan, combine the onions, carrots, celery, ginger, garlic, cilantro, water, salt, sugar, peppercorns, and bones and bring to a boil.

3 Reduce the heat, skim off any impurities from the surface, and simmer for 1½ hours.

4 At the end of the cooking time, the broth should be well concentrated. Strain, and let cool before using or storing in the refrigerator. As it cools, the broth will gelatinize because of the collagen in the bones. Reheat it to liquefy it again.

Understanding

VEGAN BROTH

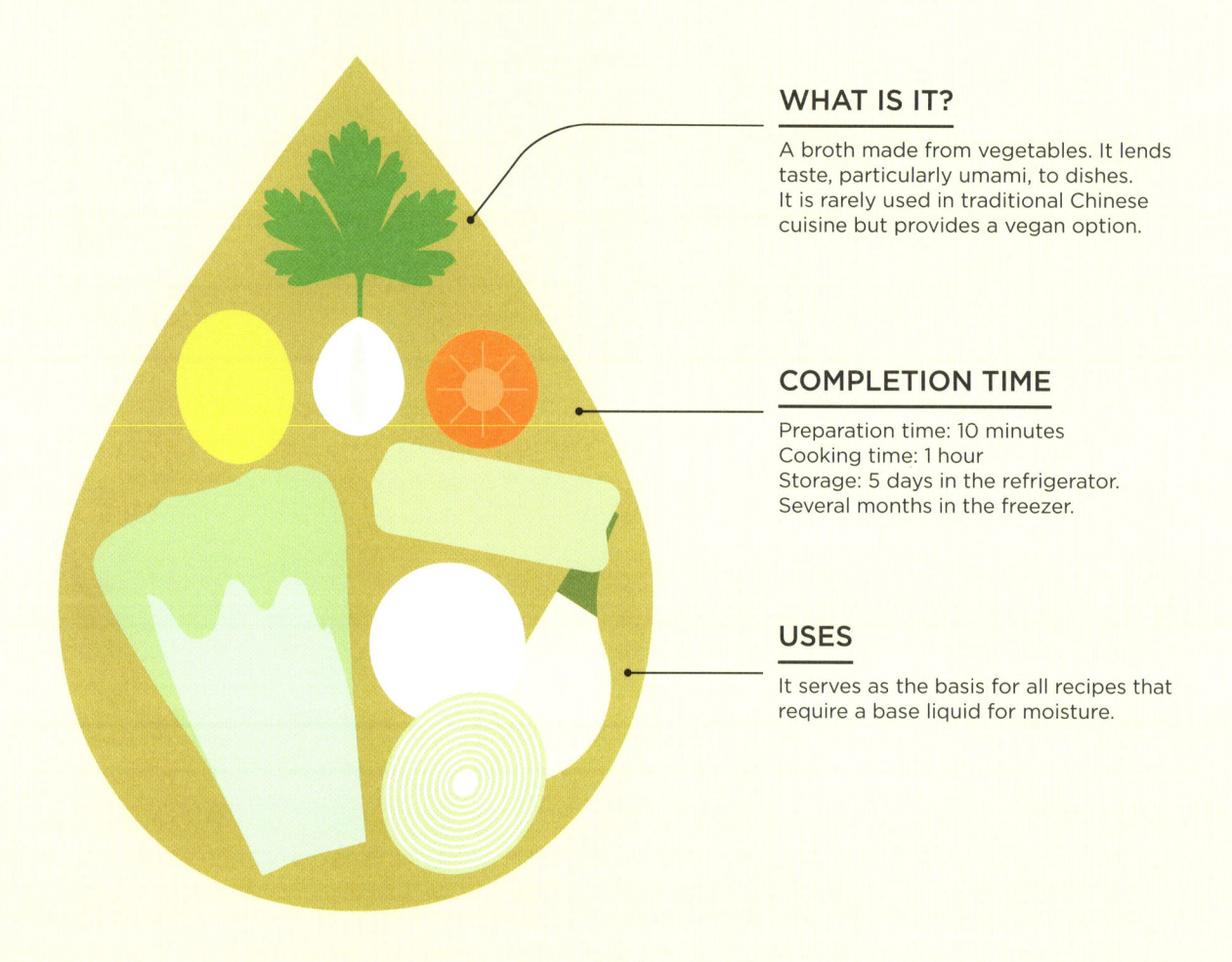

WHAT IS IT?

A broth made from vegetables. It lends taste, particularly umami, to dishes. It is rarely used in traditional Chinese cuisine but provides a vegan option.

COMPLETION TIME

Preparation time: 10 minutes
Cooking time: 1 hour
Storage: 5 days in the refrigerator. Several months in the freezer.

USES

It serves as the basis for all recipes that require a base liquid for moisture.

Learning

MAKES 6 CUPS / 1.5 L OF BROTH

2 large onions
3 carrots
1 leek
3 stalks celery
1 ounce / 30 g fresh ginger
1 head of garlic
½ bunch of cilantro, or 1 bunch of cilantro stems
4 to 5 outer leaves from various cabbages (bok choy, Chinese, white or green cabbages)
12 ounces / 350 g daikon radish
5 to 6 dried shiitake mushrooms (or the unused stems of button mushrooms)
⅓ ounce / 10 g kombu seaweed
¾ ounce / 20 g cubes white fermented tofu (or white miso)
1 teaspoon sugar
1 teaspoon salt
1 tablespoon black peppercorns

1 Quarter the onions. Cut the carrots, leek, and celery into sections. Wash the ginger and cut it into strips with the skin on. Cut the garlic head widthwise in half. Tie the cilantro with a string to prevent the leaves from coming loose. Roughly chop the cabbage leaves.

2 In a large saucepan, combine the onions, carrots, leek, celery, ginger, garlic, cilantro, cabbage, radish, mushrooms, seaweed, tofu, sugar, salt, and peppercorns and bring to a boil.

3 Reduce the heat, skim off any impurities from the surface, and simmer for 1 hour.

4 Strain, and let cool before using or storing in the refrigerator.

Understanding

BAKING SODA

WHAT IS IT?
A mineral powder in the form of an odorless, water-soluble white powder.

USES
It is the secret ingredient to perfecting some Chinese dishes. It is used especially to tenderize meats or to make shrimp crunchy.

HOW DOES IT WORK?
Baking soda acts on proteins by changing their pH.

For meat, it prevents the muscle fibers from tightening and contracting during cooking, resulting in more moisture and therefore juicier and more tender meat after cooking.

For shrimp, the same principle applies as with meat but with the addition of creating a crunchy texture. The high pH promotes a more pronounced Maillard reaction, forming an outer crust after cooking while keeping the meat moist.

QUANTITY
⅜ teaspoon per 1 pound 2 ounces / 500 g marinated meat
1 teaspoon per 9 ounces / 250 g peeled raw shrimp rinsed in a bowl of water then rinsed under running water (page 36)

Understanding
KANSUI

WHAT IS IT?
An alkaline salt, with a high pH.

USES
For making ramen and other noodles.

HOW DOES IT WORK?
Increasing the pH changes the interactions between gluten proteins, forming a more elastic and resilient structure, which gives the noodles a firmer texture and a slippery character when eaten. Adding kansui turns the noodles yellow and gives them a typical ramen mineral taste. Kansui makes dough more difficult to work with and less stretchy, so it is not suitable for biang biang noodles (page 28).

BASIC PRINCIPLE
When baking soda is heated to a pH of 8.5, the water and CO_2 are evaporated. Losing one-third of its weight, sodium bicarbonate turns into sodium carbonate (soda ash) at a pH of 12.5. This makes kansui. To make kansui: Preheat the oven to 250°F / 120°C. Spread 3 tablespoons / 50 g of baking soda onto a baking sheet lined with parchment paper. Bake for 1 hour. Let cool, and store in a jar.

LYE WATER

WHAT IS IT?
An alkaline solution.

USES
To improve the texture of the crust of mooncakes by giving them an amber color while also prolonging their shelf life (by inhibiting the growth of certain microorganisms). It can be purchased in bottles in Asian grocery stores or made at home.

BASIC PRINCIPLE
Calculate a ratio of 1 to 4. Mix ¼ teaspoon kansui with 1 teaspoon water.

Understanding

CHILE OIL

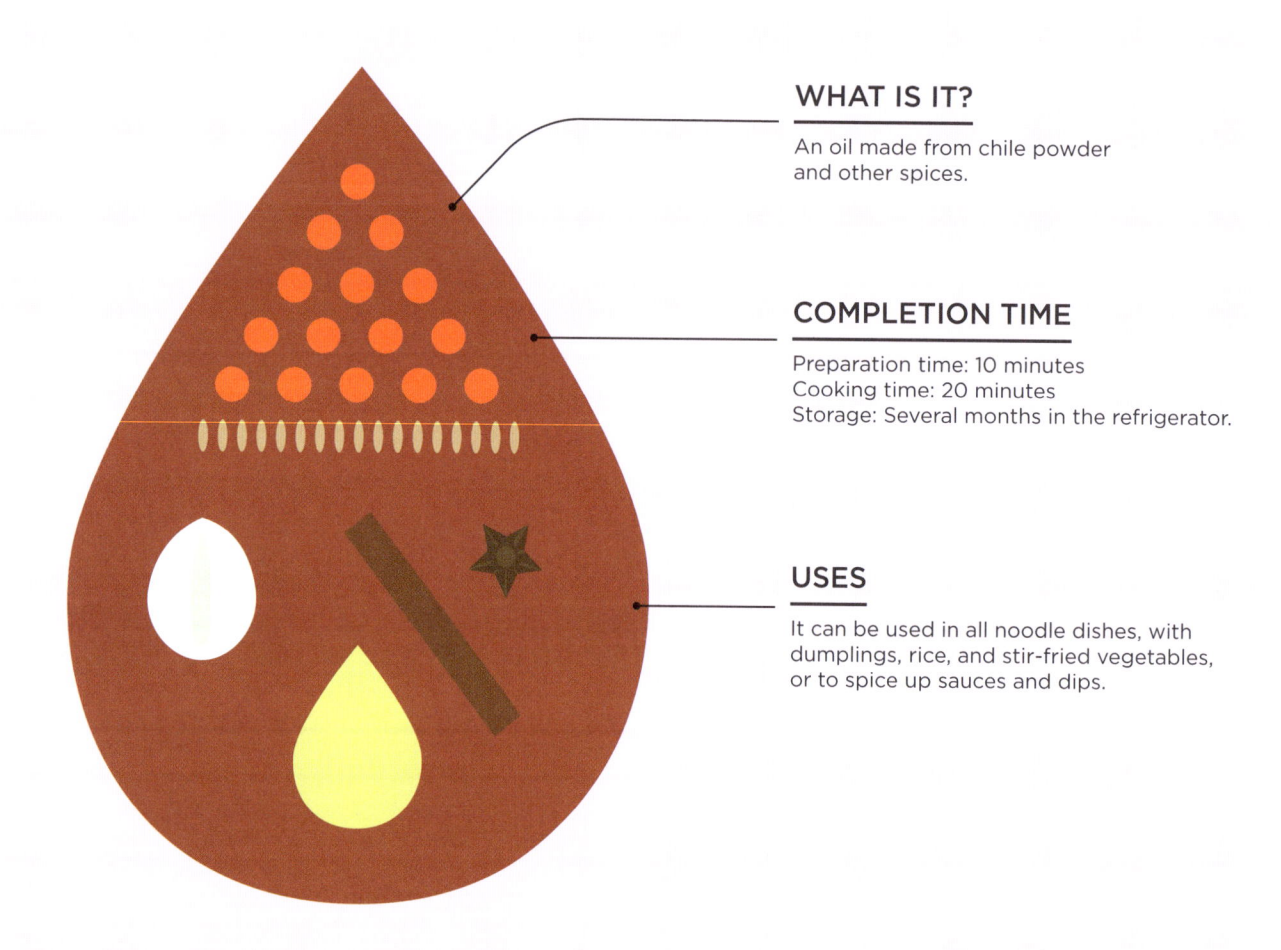

WHAT IS IT?
An oil made from chile powder and other spices.

COMPLETION TIME
Preparation time: 10 minutes
Cooking time: 20 minutes
Storage: Several months in the refrigerator.

USES
It can be used in all noodle dishes, with dumplings, rice, and stir-fried vegetables, or to spice up sauces and dips.

VARIATIONS
There is a commercial alternative, Lao Gan Ma chile oil, recognizable by its packaging depicting an old woman (lao gan ma means "old grandmother").

Add 2 tablespoons black vinegar and 1 tablespoon soy sauce to give the oil even more flavor.

Learning

**MAKES ONE
1¼-CUP / 300 ML JAR**

3 tablespoons / 10 g Szechuan pepper
2 tablespoons coriander seeds
1½ teaspoons fennel seeds
½ teaspoon salt
1½ tablespoons white sesame seeds
3 large cloves garlic, pressed
½ cup plus 1 tablespoon /
45 g red pepper flakes
1 stick cinnamon
3 star anise pods
2 bay leaves
1 cup / 240 ml neutral-flavor oil of your choice (peanut, rapeseed)

1 Using a mortar and pestle, crush the Szechuan pepper, coriander seeds, and fennel seeds.

2 Add half this mixture to a small saucepan and the other half to a bowl with the salt. Add the sesame seeds, freshly pressed garlic, and the red pepper flakes to the bowl. To the saucepan, add the cinnamon stick, star anise pods, and bay leaves.

3 Add the oil to the saucepan over very low heat and let infuse for 20 minutes. Strain the oil into the bowl with the spices; beware of bubbling up. Set aside to cool completely, then store in a jar.

Understanding

RICE VINEGAR

WHAT IS IT?
Rice vinegar is a staple of Chinese cuisine. It is used as a seasoning and for marinades.

VARIETIES
There are many varieties of vinegar in Chinese cuisine, but here are the three most commonly used:

1. Chinkiang Black Rice Vinegar
This is a vinegar made from glutinous rice, wheat bran, and sugar. It originated in Zhenjiang City (Chinkiang) in Jiangsu province. It has a mild acidity and is almost sweet and smoky, with hints of malt. It is used to season salads and noodles, for dipping dumplings, and to bring a subtle balance to meat dishes.

2. Yongchun Laogu Black Vinegar
This is a vinegar made from glutinous rice and red yeast rice. It is originally from the county of Yongchun in Fujian province. It has a pronounced acidity and is slightly alcoholic. Its uses are similar to Chinkiang vinegar, plus it is used to season spicy (Peking) soups.

3. White Vinegar
This is a vinegar made from glutinous rice. It has a sharp acidity (4.6 percent). It is used for sweet-and-sour sauce and pickled foods. It provides a boost and freshness to salads.

Understanding

SOY SAUCE

WHAT IS IT?

It is made from fermented soybeans, wheat, water, and salt. It comes in two main varieties: light (shēngchōu) and dark (lǎochōu). It is an essential condiment and inseparable from Chinese cuisine.

CHARACTERISTICS

Rich in umami amino acids, it is dark brown in color with a salty and pronounced taste.

VARIETIES

1 LIGHT SOY SAUCE

Ingredients: soybeans, wheat, water, and salt.
Characteristics: salty, light. It has a short fermentation of 3 to 6 months.
Uses: As a seasoning and in marinades.

2 DARK SOY SAUCE

Ingredients: same as light soy sauce but with the addition of molasses or caramelized sugar.
Characteristics: thick, even syrupy, slightly sweet, and more complex flavor. It has a fermentation lasting 6 months to 2 years.
Uses: Mainly used to provide color and flavor to dishes.

Understanding

OYSTER SAUCE

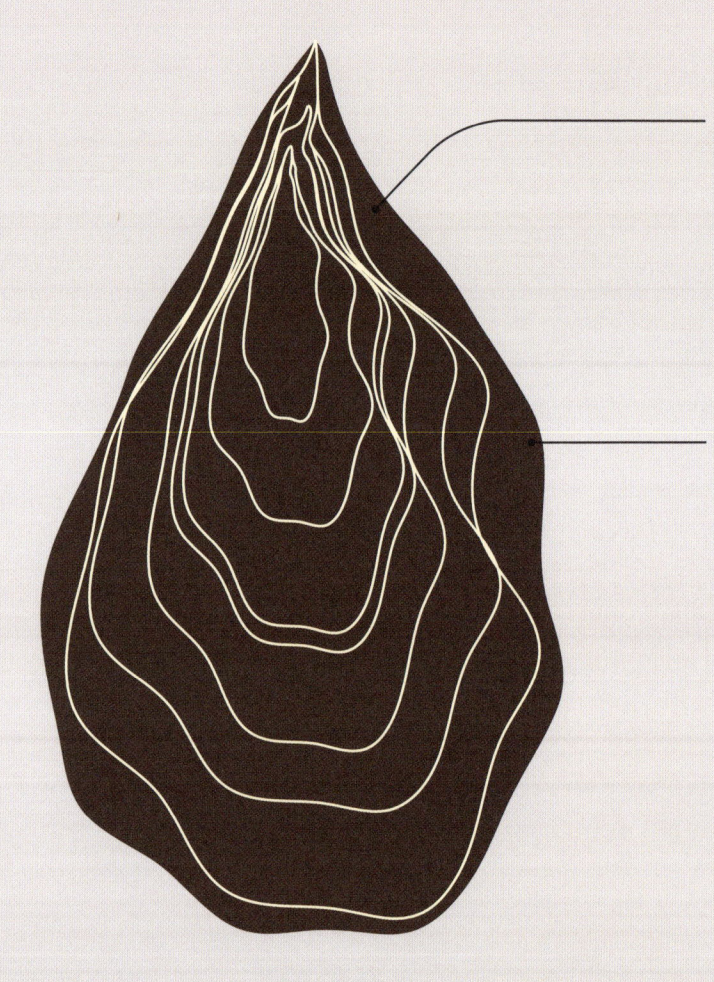

WHAT IS IT?
It is referred to as oyster "oil" or "milk" in Chinese *(hao you)*. It is a thick, brown sauce with a salty-sweet flavor that lends dishes the famous fifth taste of umami. Like soy sauce, oyster sauce is a staple of Chinese cuisine.

ORIGIN
This sauce was invented accidentally in 1888 by Lee Kum Sheung, a restaurateur in the Guangzhou area. The cook was simmering oysters to make soup, but he forgot about them on the fire. When he remembered, the oysters had turned into a dark broth with a rich and savory flavor.

INGREDIENTS
Commercial sauces consist of an oyster reduction to which soy sauce, sugar, thickeners, and flavor enhancers are added. Depending on the brand, the percentage of oysters can vary between 3 and 45 percent. The Lee Kum Kee company, founded by the family of the sauce's creator, is the historic brand (1). Some brands, such as Megachef (2), offer a sauce without flavor enhancers with 45 percent oysters.

USES
Oyster sauce can be used in all wok-sautéed dishes (vegetables, meat, noodles, rice), but also in marinades, sauces, or as seasoning for stews and braised dishes.

SHELF LIFE
Once opened, the bottle will keep in the refrigerator for several months.

VARIATIONS
There is a vegetarian version in which the oysters are replaced with shiitake mushrooms.

1   **2**

Understanding
WINE AND SPIRITS

1 **2** **3**

1 SHAOXING RICE WINE (OR SHAO HSING)
What is it?
An amber-colored wine, originating from the city of the same name in Zhejiang province in eastern China. It has been made for over two thousand years from fermented glutinous rice, wheat, yeast, and spring water from Lake Shaoxing. Once fermented, it is filtered and then stored in earthenware jars to age from three months to a year.
Which one should you choose?
Pagoda brand, with the blue label, 17 percent alcohol.
Taste
It has notes of nuts, caramel, and earthy aromas of mushrooms. It lends umami to dishes.
Uses
For deglazing, marinating, and flavoring. It is essential for making drunken chicken (page 114) or dong po pork (page 128).

2 CANTONESE RICE WINE (GUĂNGDŌNG MĬJIŬ OR KWANGTUNG MIJIU)
What is it?
A clear alcohol (29 percent alcohol) originating from the Canton province in southern China. It is made from glutinous rice, water, and *qū* (a mold and yeast culture). The region's hot and humid climate is conducive to the fermentation of rice, developing a distinct flavor that has been appreciated for more than a thousand years.
Which one should you choose?
Zhong Qiao brand.
Taste
A sweet and rounded, fresh flavor.
Uses
It is used to deglaze, marinate, and flavor. Its mildness goes well with shrimp, chicken, and desserts. It can be replaced with sake.

3 MEI KUEI LU CHIEW (OR MÉIGUĪ LÙJIŬ)
What is it?
A liquor made from sorghum cane (a grain with a neutral taste) in which rose petals are infused. The alcohol is then filtered, and honey or sugar is added to sweeten it. Its name literally translates to "rose petal dew alcohol." The petals grown in northern China are picked covered in dew before sunrise.
Which one should you choose?
Golden Star brand, 54 percent alcohol.
Taste
A very pronounced floral aroma.
Uses
It is consumed neat in small shot glasses during celebrations or at parties. In cooking, it adds a sophisticated note to rotisseries (lacquered pork, lacquered duck, crispy pork, etc.). It can also be used to flavor desserts and syrups.

Understanding

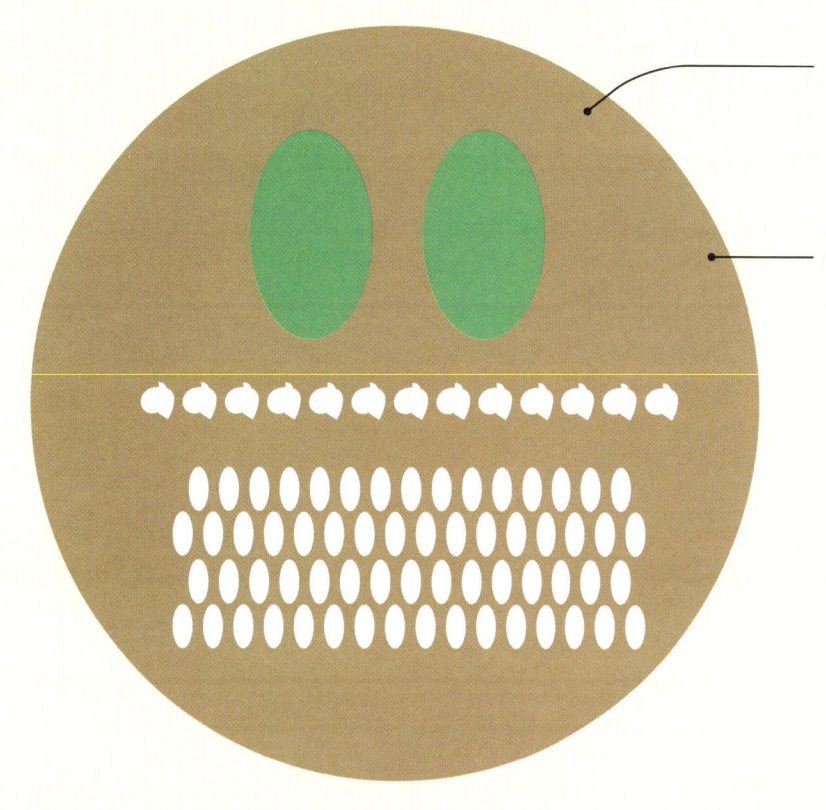

FERMENTED PRODUCTS

WHAT IS IT?
Pastes, sauces, or other fermented products.

USES
An essential ingredient in Chinese cuisine used mainly as a condiment or in marinades.

1 DÒUBÀNJIÀNG
What is it?
A spicy bean paste native to the Sichuan province and especially the Pidu District, renowned for its quality paste and local ingredients.
Production
The beans are soaked, steamed, then mixed with wheat flour and water. They are then left to ferment in earthenware jars for several months. Crushed red peppers and salt are added to the mixture, which then ferments for another one to three years.
Taste
Salty, tangy, a little earthy, and rich in umami.
Uses
It is essential for making mapo tofu (page 164), Szechuan poached fish (page 144) and beef noodle soup (page 206). It can also be used to sauté vegetables and meats.

2 TIÁN MIÀN JIÀNG
What is it?
A wheat paste, often translated as "sweet bean sauce." It is believed to have been created in Peking (Beijing) during the Ming Dynasty (1368–1644) to accompany the imperial lacquered duck.
Production
Flour, and possibly soybeans, are mixed with water to form a thick paste. A ferment is added, and the dough is left to ferment for several days. During or after fermentation, sugar and salt are added. The fermented paste is then cooked, which caramelizes the sugars, giving it a dark brown color.
Taste
Rather mild and salty.
Uses
It is used in sauce on steamed dumplings to accompany Peking duck, but tián miàn jiàng is the essential ingredient for the recipe for zhájiàng miàn (page 210), a Beijing specialty. It is often sold vacuum-packed. If you have difficulty finding it, you can replace it with chunjang, which is the Korean version.

50

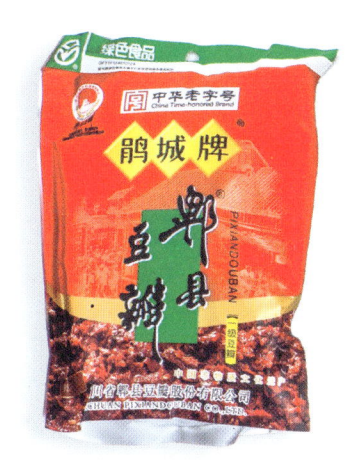

Learning

1   **2**   **3**   **4**

3 HOISIN SAUCE (HĂIXIĀN JIÀNG)

What is it?
A sauce made from fermented soybeans, originally from Guangzhou. Contrary to what its Chinese name suggests ("seafood sauce"), it does not contain seafood.

Taste
Sweet, salty, slightly acidic, with pronounced umami notes. It is often referred to as Chinese barbecue sauce.

Uses
It lends an exotic touch to dishes. It is used to marinate meats, such as lacquered pork, or as a condiment to accompany certain rotisserie meats. It is also used as a sauce for rice pancakes and spring pancakes. It is very common to see it served with spring rolls or as a dip for pho.

4 TOFU - PRESERVED/FERMENTED BEANCURD (FŬRŬ)

What is it?
Widely consumed since the Han Dynasty (206–220 AD), tofu cubes are cut and seeded with mold spores. They are left to ferment until they develop a layer of mold. They are then salted and undergo a second fermentation lasting several weeks to several months. At this stage tofu acquires its creamy texture. Some types of *fŭrŭ* are then cured in earthenware jars or pots where they continue to develop their flavor.

Varieties
-Red. Fermented with red koji (rice yeast). Powerful and very salty.
-White. Fermented with light rice wine. Milder and less salty.
-Spiced. Freshly ground black peppers, and sometimes sesame oil, are added.

Uses
Fŭrŭ has a thick, creamy consistency. It is eaten plain with rice or with congee. It is also used as a marinade for meat (lacquered pork), as a seasoning for stews and braised meats, and also with vegetables, such as Buddha's delight (page 172).

CHAPTER 2
RECIPES

DIM SUM

Ha kao / Shrimp dumplings 54
Fun guo / Vegetable dumplings . . . 58
Xiǎo lóng bāo / Soup dumplings . . 60
Guō tiē / Grilled pork dumplings . . 64
Shu mai / Pork and shrimp bites . . 68
Char siu bao 72
Mama's bao 76
Lo bak go / Daikon cake 80
Wu gok / Taro dumplings 84
Cheung fun /
Rice noodle rolls with shrimp 88
Jiǔcài hézǐ / Flat steamed garlic chive dumplings 92
Lo mai gai / Glutinous rice
with chicken in lotus leaf 96

MEAT

Kǎoyā /
Cantonese lacquered duck 100
Lor ark / 5-flavor braised duck . . . 104
Zhāngchá yā /
Tea-smoked duck 108
Jiàohuā jī / Beggar's chicken 110
Zuì jī / Drunken chicken 114
Gōng bǎo jī dīng /
Kung pao chicken 118
Sān bēi jī / Three-cup chicken 120
Char siu / Lacquered pork 122
Siu yuk / Crispy pork 124
Dōng pō ròu / Dong po pork 128
Gūlǔ ròu /
Sweet and sour pork 132
Chǐ zhī niúròu / Stir-fried beef
with black soybeans 136
Yàngròu bao /
Braised lamb casserole 138

FISH & SEAFOOD

Jiāng cōng yú / Steamed turbot with ginger and scallion sauce 142
Shuǐ zhǔ yú /
Szechuan poached fish 144
Yú shēng / Prosperity salad 148
Sōngshǔ yú /
Sweet and sour fish 152
Jiāoyán xiā /
Salt and pepper shrimp 156
Steamed prawns, vermicelli
noodles, and fried garlic 158
Chǎo lóngxiā /
Sautéed langoustine 162

TOFU

Mápó dòufu / Mapo tofu 164
Jiāng chǎo dòufu /
Stir-fried tofu with ginger 168

VEGETABLES

Háoyóu jiè lán /
Gai lan in oyster sauce 170
Luóhàn zhāi / Buddha's delight . . . 172
Pāi huángguā /
Pressed cucumber salad 176
Hóngshāo qiézi /
Braised eggplant 178
Shǒu sī bāo cài /
Cabbage stir-fry in vinegar 180
Dìsānxiān /
Three treasures from the earth . . . 182
Suān là tāng /
Hot and sour soup 186
Chūn bǐng / Spring pancake 190

NOODLES & RICE

Hǎixiān chǎomiàn /
Seafood noodles 194
Sùcài chǎomiàn / Stir-fried noodles with vegetables 198
Yóu pō chě miàn / Biang biang
noodles with spicy oil 200
Yángròu miàn / Biang biang
noodles with lamb 202
Niúròu miàn /
Beef noodle soup 206
Zhájiàng miàn 210
Dàndàn miàn / Dan dan noodles . . 214
Jiǎndāo miàn /
Scissor-cut noodles 216
Gon chow ngau ho /
Stir-fried beef noodles 220
Yángzhōu chǎofàn /
Yangzhou stir-fried rice 224
Bāo zǎi fàn / Clay pot rice 228
Pídàn jīròu zhōu /
Century egg chicken congee 232
Zòngzi / Stuffed glutinous rice . . . 234
Xián yú chǎofàn /
Salted fish fried rice 238

STREET FOOD

Gē bāo /
Dong po pork gua bao 242
Cōng yóubǐng /
Fried scallion pancake 244
Yè er bā / Stuffed dumplings
wrapped in leaves 248
Yán sū jī / Popcorn chicken 250

DESSERTS

Ma lai go / Steamed sponge cake 254
Dan tat / Egg tarts 256
Yuèbǐng / Mooncakes 260
Tāngyuán with black sesame 264
Liúshā bāo / Lava bao 268
Máhuā / Black sesame twists 272

Understanding

HA KAO
SHRIMP DUMPLINGS

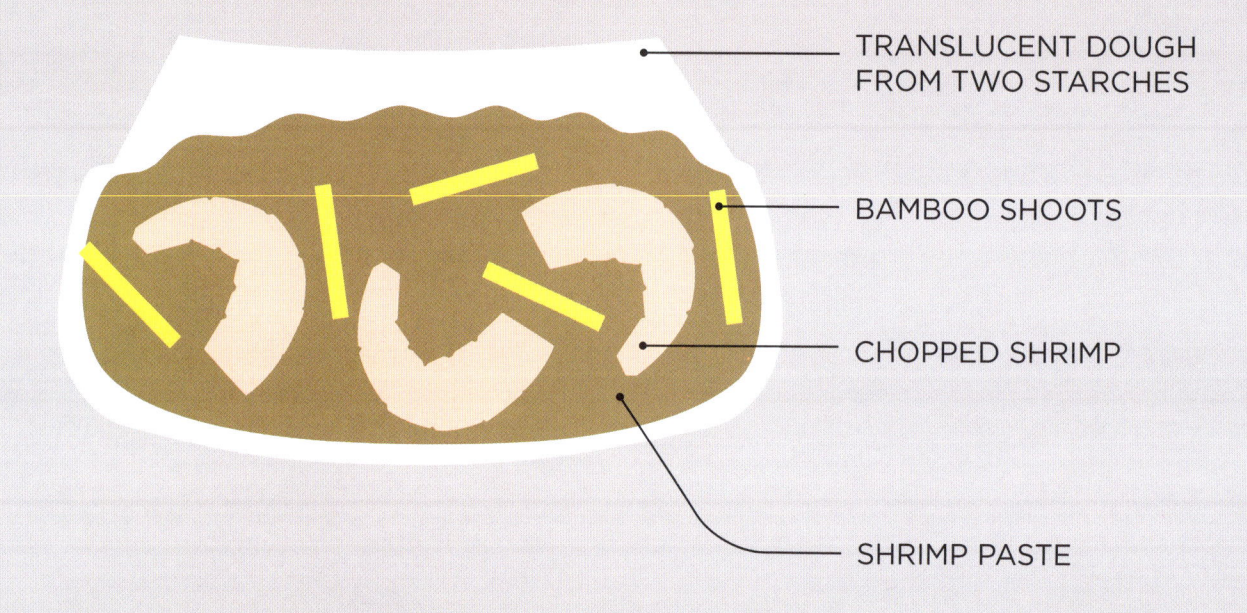

- TRANSLUCENT DOUGH FROM TWO STARCHES
- BAMBOO SHOOTS
- CHOPPED SHRIMP
- SHRIMP PASTE

WHAT IS IT?
A filling made of mixed and chopped shrimp and bamboo, wrapped in a translucent starch-based dough. It is probably the most emblematic dumpling in dim sum.

ORIGIN
Ha kao, *Xiā Jiǎo* in Mandarin, originated in a tea house in the 1920s and 1930s in the village of Wucu (Canton province). The owner had access to a nearby river where the shrimp were caught to make the filling. The dumpling has between seven and thirteen pleats. The number of pleats and their symmetry reflect the skill and mastery of the chef.

COMPLETION TIME
Preparation time: 1 hour 20 minutes
Resting time: 20 minutes
Cooking time: 7 minutes
Storage: You can freeze ha kao uncooked. Place them flat on a sheet of parchment paper. Once frozen, you can store them in an airtight container. Cook them without thawing for about 10 minutes.

SPECIAL EQUIPMENT
Steamer basket
Steamer

SKILLS TO MASTER
Blanching bamboo shoots (page 281)
Preparing shrimp (page 36)

USEFUL TIPS
If making the pleats seems too tedious, make half-moon fun guo (page 58). You can make the filling the day before, stored in plastic wrap. Cut using a cookie cutter for a perfect round. Set the scraps aside wrapped in plastic wrap to roll them out again.

Learning

TAPIOCA STARCH
Made from cassava starch. It is a strong thickening and gelling agent.

WHEAT STARCH
It becomes translucent when cooked.

RICE WINE (KWANGTUNG MIJIU)
Alcohol made from fermented glutinous rice. Similar to sake.

BAMBOO SHOOTS
Canned bamboo shoots. Boil them in water before using them to remove the pungent smell.

MAKES 20 DUMPLINGS

FILLING
- 1¾ ounces / 50 g canned bamboo shoots

  9 ounces / 250 g peeled shrimp (10 to 10½ ounces / 280 to 300 g unpeeled)
- 1 tablespoon tapioca starch

  1 heaping tablespoon oyster sauce

  1 tablespoon soy sauce

  1 tablespoon sesame oil
- 2 tablespoons rice wine (kwangtung mijiu)

  1 teaspoon organic cane sugar

  ½ teaspoon salt

  White pepper or ground Szechuan pepper

TRANSLUCENT DOUGH
- 1½ cups / 145 g wheat starch
- ¼ cup / 35 g tapioca starch

  Just over ¾ cup / 200 ml boiling water

  1 level teaspoon salt

  2 tablespoons neutral-flavor oil of your choice (sunflower, peanut)

Making

HA KAO SHRIMP DUMPLINGS

1 Blanch the bamboo shoots (page 281). Cut them into about 1/16- to 1/8-inch / 1 to 4 mm pieces. Chop half the shrimp into small pieces of about 1/3 inch / 8 mm. Combine the remaining shrimp with the starch, oyster sauce, soy sauce, sesame oil, rice wine, sugar, salt, and pepper. Combine the seasoned shrimp mixture with the bamboo and chopped shrimp. You can taste the seasoning by cooking a little filling in the microwave, then adjust the seasoning as needed. Refrigerate for 20 minutes.

2 Make the dough (page 14): Roll the dough into two or three identical sausage shapes. Place them under plastic wrap to prevent them from drying out. Cut each one into sections weighing about 1/2 ounce / 15 to 17 g. Set the sections aside wrapped in plastic wrap. Roll out the dough pieces into 4-inch / 10 cm discs. Place a teaspoon of filling in the center of each.

3 Pick up an edge of the dough from the top of the disc using your thumb and forefinger.

4 Form a pleat with the index finger of the other hand. Pinch the dough together.

5 Make eight more pleats in the same way, always turning in the same direction.

6 Close the dumpling by folding the smooth part of the dough against the pleated part.

7 Press and pinch the dough to close it.

8 Place the dumplings spaced apart in a steamer basket lined with perforated parchment paper. Repeat these steps until all the ingredients are used. Bring the water in a steamer to a boil. Once the water is boiling, cook the dumplings for 7 minutes. Serve hot.

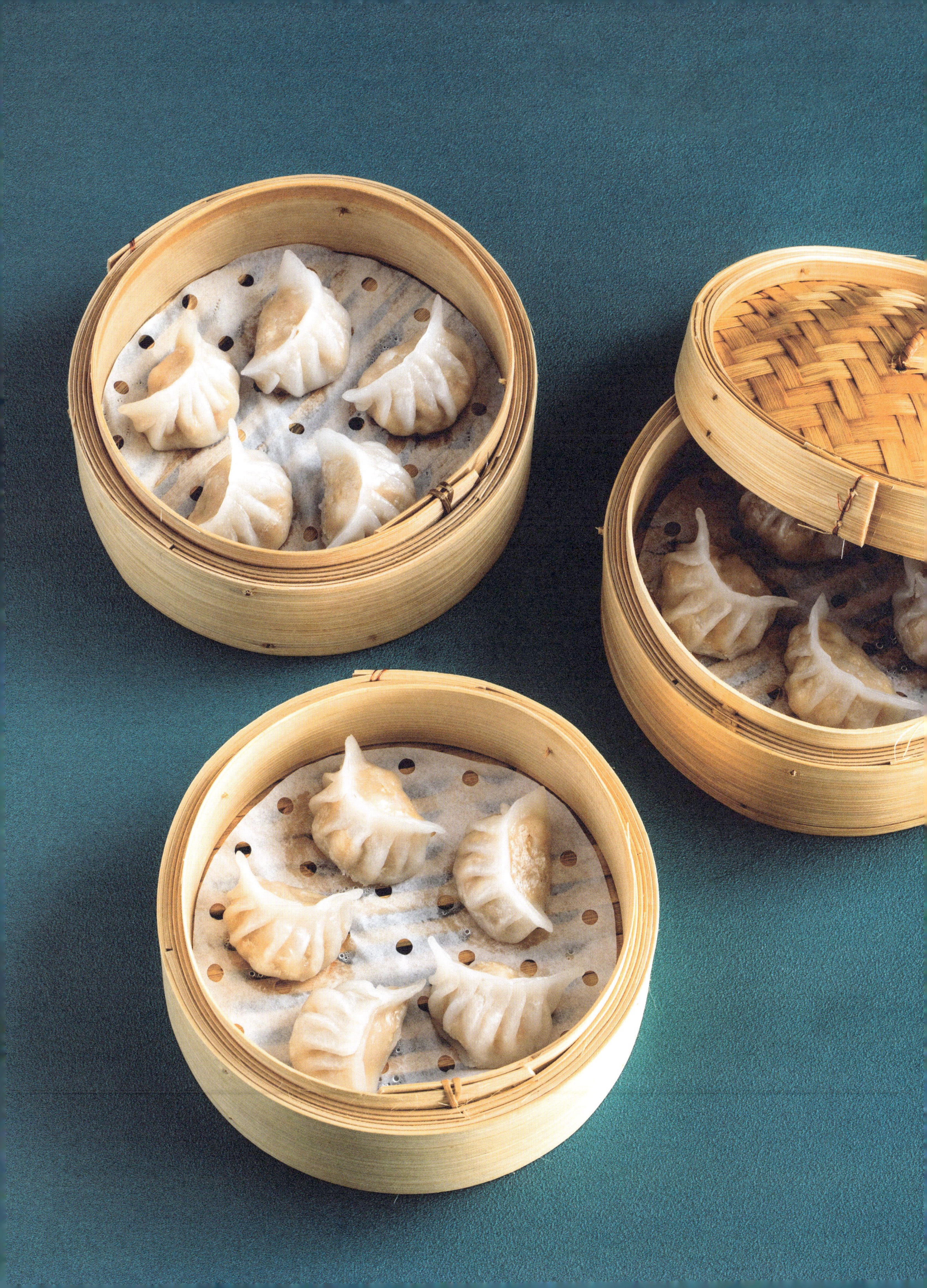

Understanding

FUN GUO
VEGETABLE DUMPLINGS

TRANSLUCENT DOUGH FROM TWO STARCHES

VEGETABLE FILLING

WHAT IS IT?
A vegetable filling wrapped in a translucent starch-based dough, native of Chaozhou in the province of Canton.

COMPLETION TIME
Preparation time: 45 minutes
Cooking time: 8 minutes
Storage: Freeze raw, flat, then store in a container once frozen. Cook without thawing for about 10 minutes.

SPECIAL EQUIPMENT
Steamer basket
Steamer

SKILL TO MASTER
Rehydrating mushrooms (page 280)

USEFUL TIP
Use a cookie cutter to make perfect dough discs.

MAKES ABOUT 30 DUMPLINGS

TRANSLUCENT DOUGH
1½ cups / 145 g wheat starch
¼ cup / 35 g tapioca starch
Just over ¾ cup / 200 ml boiling water
1 level teaspoon salt
2 tablespoons neutral-flavor oil of your choice (sunflower, peanut)

FILLING
⅓ ounce / 10 g dried shiitake mushrooms

Learning

⅓ ounce / 10 g dried black mushrooms
½ onion
3½ ounces / 100 g carrots
3½ ounces / 100 g water chestnuts (or kohlrabi)
3½ ounces / 100 g tofu of your choice
2 cloves garlic
⅓ ounce / 10 g fresh ginger
½ bunch of cilantro
3 tablespoons / 45 ml vegetable oil
1 teaspoon organic cane sugar
2 tablespoons soy sauce
2 tablespoons oyster sauce
White pepper

1 Make the translucent dough (page 14).

2 Make the filling: Rehydrate the mushrooms (page 280). Peel and chop the onion. Cut the carrot, chestnuts, and tofu into about ⅛-inch / 4 mm cubes. Press the garlic, grate the ginger, and chop the cilantro.

3 Heat the oil in a skillet. Sauté the onion and shiitake mushrooms for 3 to 4 minutes. Add the black mushrooms, onion, carrot, chestnuts, tofu, garlic, ginger, sugar, soy sauce, and oyster sauce. Continue cooking for 1 to 2 minutes. The vegetables should remain slightly crunchy. Taste, and adjust the seasoning, if necessary. Let cool, then add the cilantro.

4 Cut the dough into sections of ½ ounce / 15 g. Set the sections aside wrapped in plastic wrap to prevent them from drying out. Roll out each section into a disc of about 3½ to 4 inches / 9 to 10 cm.

5 Place a spoonful of filling in the center of the dough disc and fold the dough in half, pushing out any air, to form a half moon. Press the edges of the dough down well to seal them. Repeat these steps until all the ingredients are used.

6 Place the dumplings spaced apart in a steamer basket lined with parchment paper. Bring the water in a steamer to a boil, place the basket in the steamer, and cook for 8 minutes.

Understanding

XIĂO LÓNG BĀO
SOUP DUMPLINGS

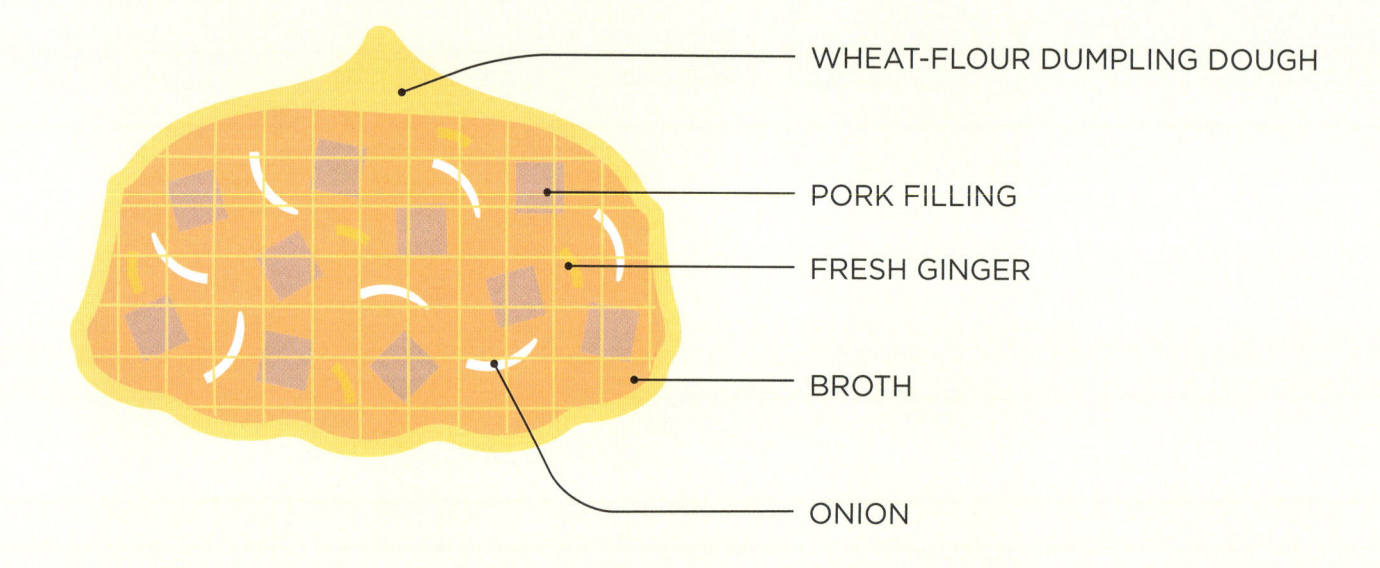

- WHEAT-FLOUR DUMPLING DOUGH
- PORK FILLING
- FRESH GINGER
- BROTH
- ONION

WHAT IS IT?
A pork and gelatinous broth filling, wrapped in a thin wheat-flour dough. Once cooked, the broth liquefies but remains enclosed in the wrapper, resulting in a juicy and tasty dumpling.

ORIGIN
It was created in 1870 by a Shanghai restaurateur who wanted to stand out from the fierce competition of tea houses. Xiăo lóng bāo has been inscribed on the list of Chinese national treasures since 2006.

COMPLETION TIME
Preparation time: 1½ hours
Resting time: Overnight + 30 minutes
Cooking time: 8 minutes
Storage: The dumplings can be frozen raw and then cooked for about 11 minutes without thawing, but it is best to consume them quickly once cooked.

SPECIAL EQUIPMENT
Steamer basket
4-inch / 10 cm round cookie cutter
Rolling pin

SKILL TO MASTER
Cutting into julienne (page 281)

SERVING
Grab a dumpling delicately with chopsticks. Place it in a spoon. Make a hole in the dumpling using the chopsticks. Let the broth run into the spoon. Blow on it a little to cool it. Add a little vinegar with strips of ginger, then eat the dumpling in one bite.

USEFUL TIP
The delicacy of this dumpling lies in the finesse and meticulous folding of the dough. Weigh the dough pieces without exceeding ⅓ ounce / 10 g each. This allows you to make even dumplings and gives you a reference point when rolling them out.

Learning

BLACK RICE VINEGAR
Made from glutinous rice and red yeast rice. It has a sharp acidity and is slightly alcoholic.

SESAME OIL
Choose an Asian sesame oil (Chinese, Japanese, or Korean) that was roasted before being pressed. It is amber to dark brown in color. It has a nutty flavor with an intensely pronounced aroma.

SOY SAUCE
Choose bottles that state "natural fermentation."

MAKES ABOUT 32 DUMPLINGS

GEL
Just over ¾ cup / 200 ml Basic Broth (page 38)
1 teaspoon agar-agar

FILLING
10½ ounces / 300 g finely chopped pork belly
3½ tablespoons / 30 g finely chopped onion
1 tablespoon grated fresh ginger
¼ cup / 60 ml Basic Broth (page 38)
- 2 tablespoons soy sauce
- 1 tablespoon sesame oil
1 tablespoon Shaoxing wine (optional)
1 level teaspoon salt
1 level teaspoon organic cane sugar

DOUGH
1⅔ cups / 200 g all-purpose flour
½ cup / 120 ml boiling water
½ teaspoon salt

SAUCE
⅓ ounce / 10 g fresh ginger, cut into julienne (page 281)
- Black rice vinegar

Making

XIĂO LÓNG BĀO

1 The day before, make the gel: Whisk together the broth and agar-agar and bring the mixture to a boil in a pot for a full minute. Transfer it to a small bowl and set aside overnight, covered. Make the filling: Combine the pork belly, onion, ginger, broth, soy sauce, sesame oil, wine, if using, salt, and sugar. Stir until the mixture has absorbed the broth and becomes slightly sticky. Cover with plastic wrap, and set aside in the refrigerator.

2 The next day, chop the gelled broth mixture into small cubes and combine them with the filling. Set aside in the refrigerator.

3 Make the dough (page 16): When the dough has rested, shape into two identical sausage shapes and cut into sections 1/3 ounce / 10 g each. Cover the sections with plastic wrap to prevent them from drying out.

4 Dust the work surface with flour and roll out the dough pieces to obtain a thin wrapper. Using a cookie cutter, cut out 4-inch / 10 cm discs. Place a teaspoon of filling in the center of each disc.

5 Grab the edge of the dough with the thumb and forefinger of both hands. Form a pleat and pinch it to stick together. Make another pleat and seal it at the first pleat, a bit like gathering paper.

6 Continue to create pleats by turning the wrapper.

7 Gather all the pleats in the center.

8 Pinch and twist to close the dumpling. Be sure to seal the center well so that the broth will not seep out during cooking.

9 Gently place the dumplings well spaced in a steamer basket fitted with perforated parchment paper. Bring the water in a steamer to a boil. Once the water is boiling, cook for 8 minutes. Combine the julienned ginger and black rice vinegar. Serve the sauce with the dumplings.

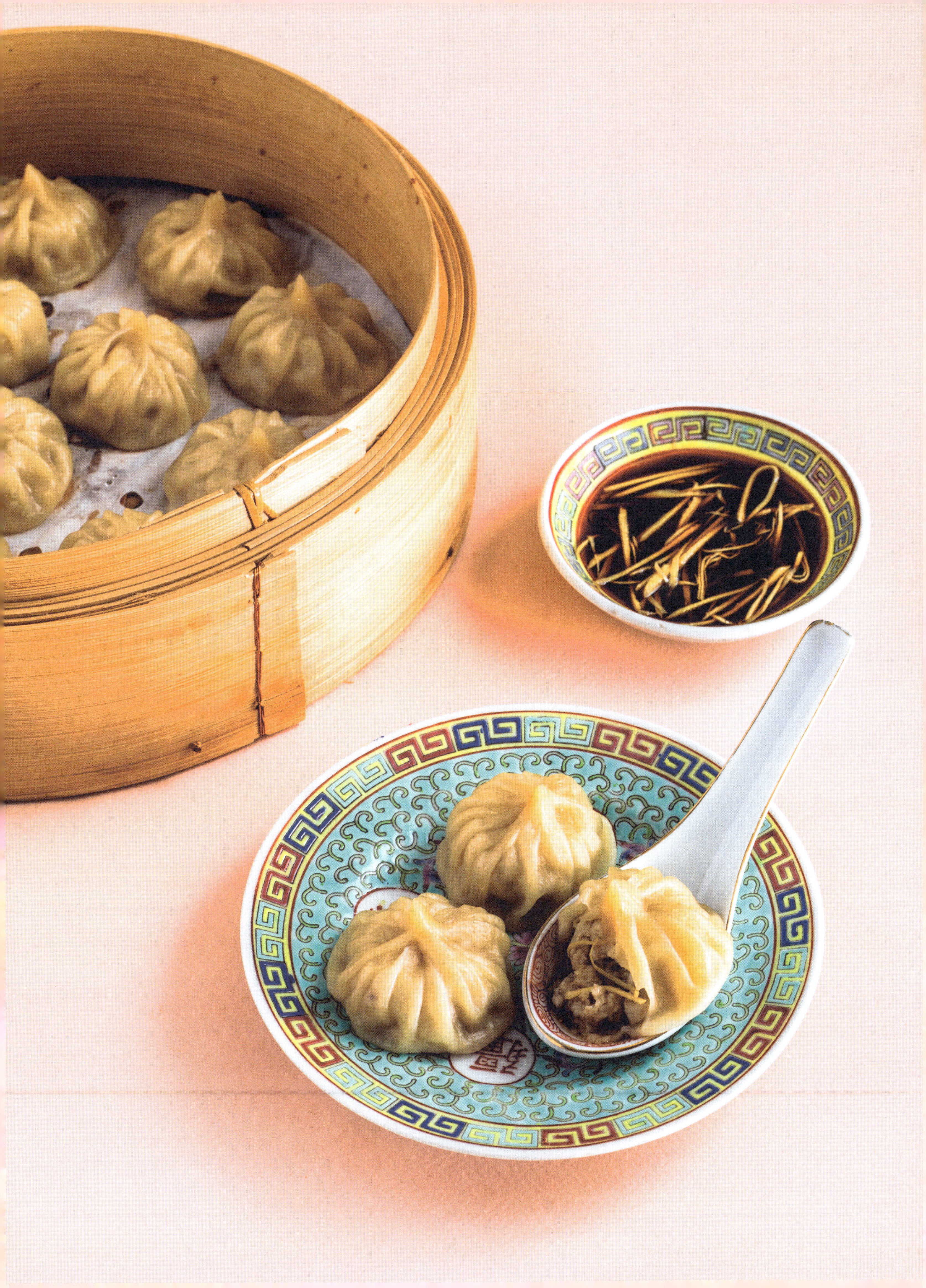

Understanding

GUŌ TIĒ
GRILLED PORK DUMPLINGS

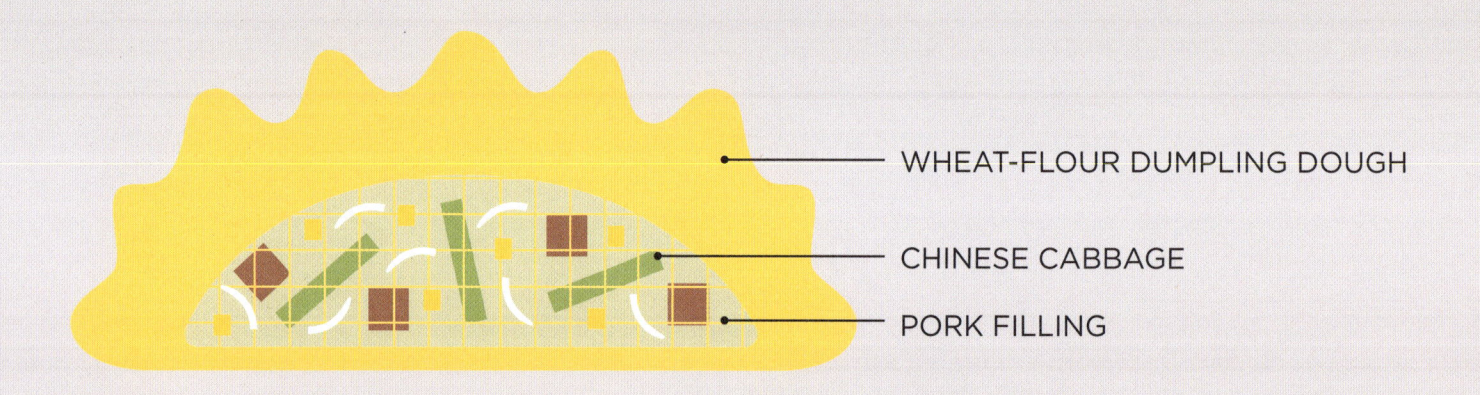

WHEAT-FLOUR DUMPLING DOUGH

CHINESE CABBAGE

PORK FILLING

WHAT IS IT?
A pork and Chinese cabbage filling, wrapped in a wheat-flour dough, cooked in water, then panfried.

ORIGIN
Like many wheat-based specialties, this one originates from northern China, where wheat is cultivated. Guō tiē literally means "attached to the pot." It is cooked in a pan, covered, with water and oil. When the water has evaporated, the lid is removed, and it is cooked until the bottom browns. The top of the dumpling remains soft, as if steamed, but the underside is crisp. The dumpling is similar to Japanese gyoza. Traditionally, guō tiē have a simpler folding technique, and the ends are left open and the juice from the filling escapes, making the dumpling drier.

COMPLETION TIME
Preparation time: 1 hour
Resting time: 30 minutes
Cooking time: 15 minutes
Storage: Freeze flat on a baking sheet, then transfer to a container.

SERVING
Serve the dumpling with a black vinegar of your choice (chinkiang or yongchun), embellished with julienned ginger.

SKILL TO MASTER
Cutting into julienne (page 281)

USEFUL TIPS
Check the seasoning level by cooking a little of the filling in the microwave. Taste, and adjust the seasoning, if necessary. You can cut the wrapper with a cookie cutter for a perfectly round disc. Save the scraps wrapped in plastic wrap to roll them out again. To make a crispy lace: Combine 1 tablespoon of flour into the water to be used to cook the dumplings. Replace the Chinese cabbage with 4¼ ounces / 120 g finely chopped garlic chives or wild garlic.

Learning

CHINESE CABBAGE
This is a tender and mild cabbage. It is eaten cooked in Chinese cuisine but is also very suitable raw in salads.

SOY SAUCE
Choose bottles that state "natural fermentation."

MAKES ABOUT 30 DUMPLINGS

FILLING
- 5¼ ounces / 150 g Chinese cabbage (3 leaves)
- 1 small onion
- ¾ ounce / 20 g fresh ginger
- 14 ounces / 400 g finely chopped pork belly or pork loin
- 1 level teaspoon organic cane sugar
- 2 tablespoons soy sauce
- ½ teaspoon salt
- Freshly ground black pepper

DOUGH
- 2¾ cups / 350 g all-purpose flour
- ½ teaspoon salt
- Just over ¾ cup / 200 ml boiling water
- Neutral-flavor oil of your choice (sunflower, peanut)

Making

GUŌ TIĒ

1 Make the filling: Cut the cabbage leaves into large pieces and blanch them for 3 minutes in boiling salted water. Drain, and let cool. Peel and chop the onion. Cut the ginger into very small cubes. Squeeze the cabbage firmly between your hands to remove excess water. Combine the cabbage, onion, ginger, pork, sugar, soy sauce, and salt with the meat. Season with pepper. Set aside in a cool place.

2 Make the dough (page 16). When the dough has rested, roll it into three sausage shapes. Cut small sections of about ½ ounce / 15 to 17 g each and set them aside under a piece of plastic wrap or a cloth to prevent them from drying out. Dust the work surface with flour and roll out the sections into discs of about 4 to 4¾ inches / 10 to 12 cm. Place a spoonful of filling in the center of each disc. Join two opposite edges of the disc in the center. Pinch the edges together lightly to close them. Make three to four folds on the right from the center, then three to four folds on the left. Pinch the edges each time to seal the dumpling well.

3 Set aside on a baking sheet lined with parchment paper.

4 Cook the dumplings in two batches or freeze some of the dumplings. Heat 2 tablespoons of oil in a nonstick pan. Arrange half the dumplings without placing them too snuggly together; they should not touch each other. Let cook for several minutes until they begin to sizzle, then add more water to about one-third the height of the dumplings (about 1 cup / 240 ml). Cover, and cook until the water has evaporated.

5 Remove the lid and cook until the bottoms brown, keeping an eye on the cooking. They are cooked when the bottom is golden brown. Repeat for the remaining dumplings, cleaning the pan after each batch. Serve hot with black rice vinegar. The vinegar can be enhanced with a little julienned (page 281) fresh ginger.

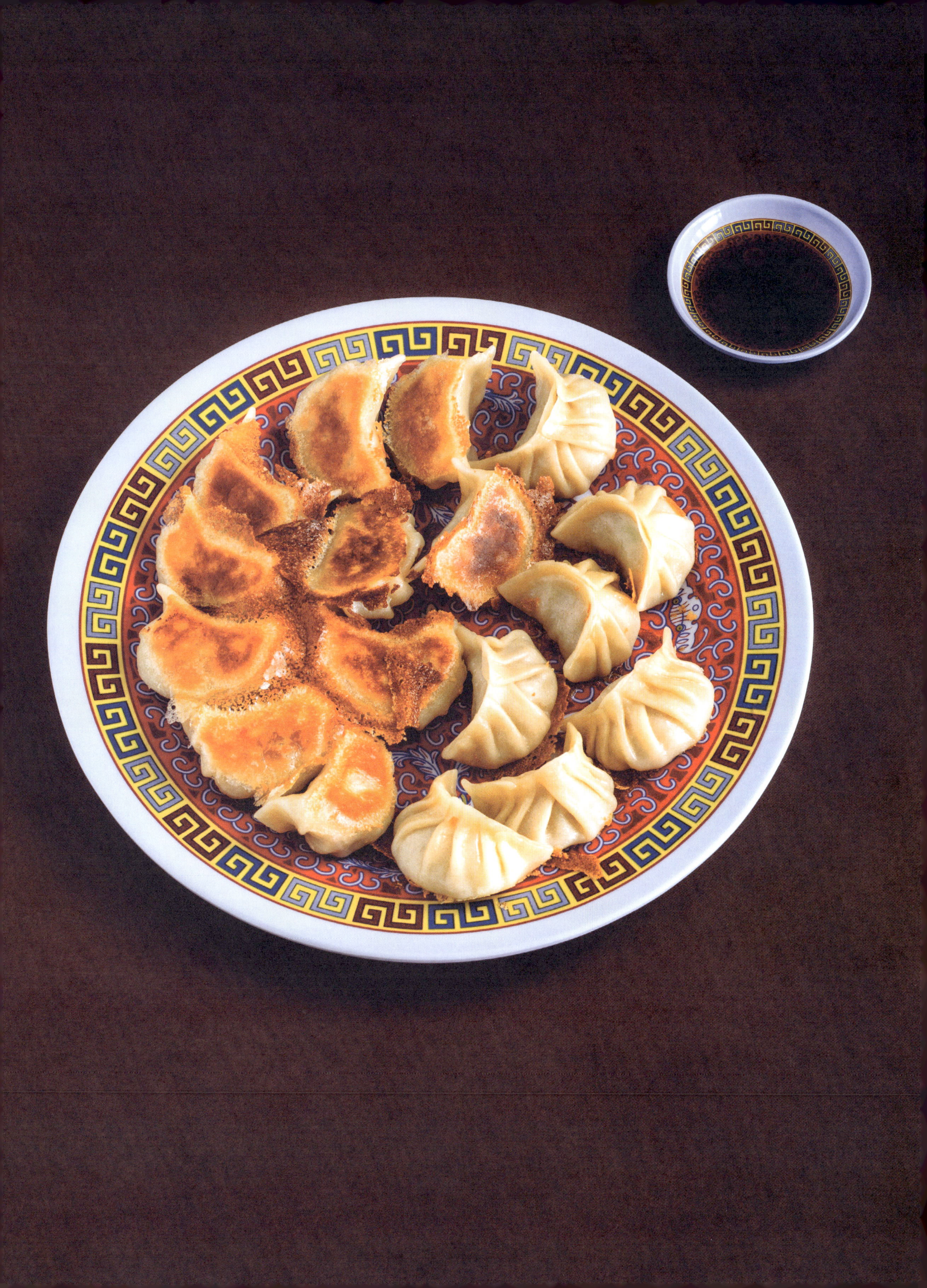

Understanding

SHU MAI
PORK AND SHRIMP BITES

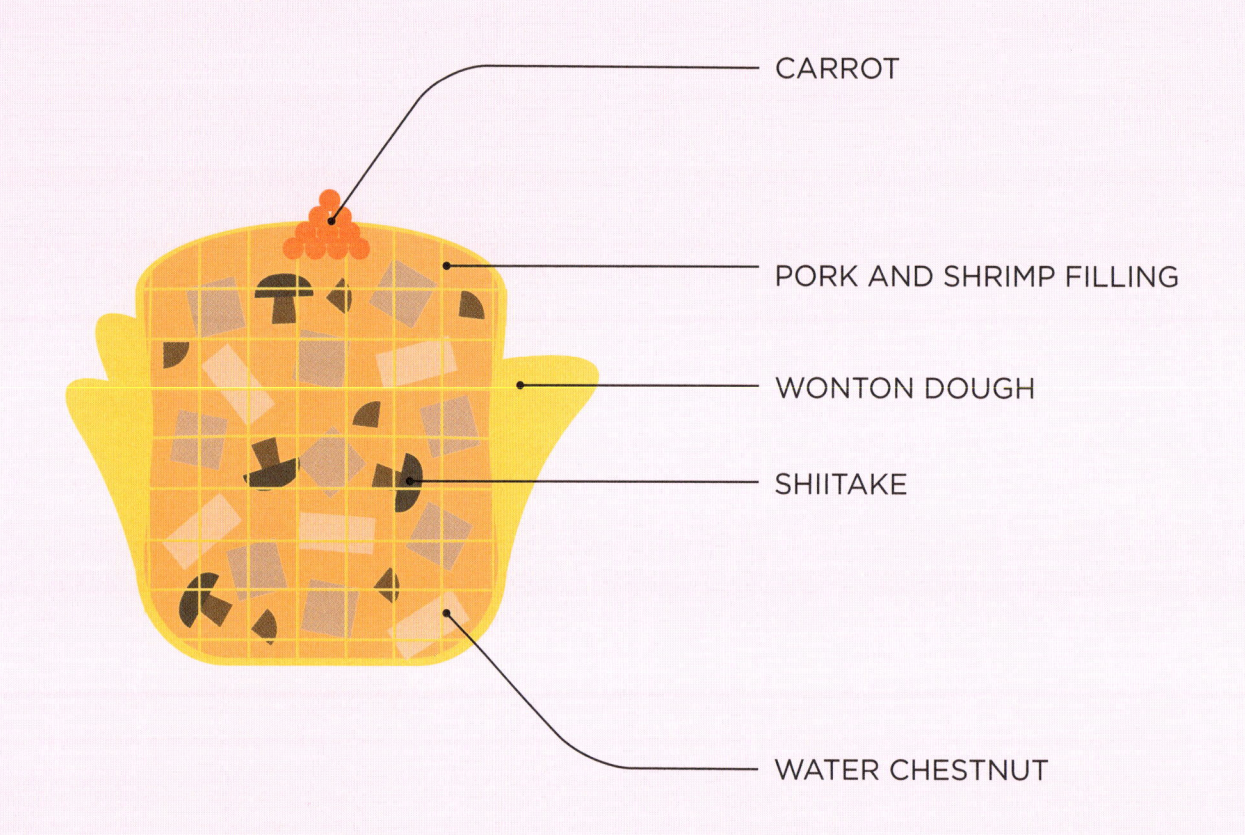

- CARROT
- PORK AND SHRIMP FILLING
- WONTON DOUGH
- SHIITAKE
- WATER CHESTNUT

WHAT IS IT?
A pork, shrimp, and shiitake mushroom filling encased in a wheat-flour dough. They are left open at the top.

ORIGIN
The dumpling is said to have originated in Inner Mongolia under the name *suumai* ("without being cooled") to indicate that it should be eaten hot. The filling was made of lamb, scallion, and ginger. Thanks to its popularity, the dumpling became more widespread, and its filling was changed according to local preferences. It is one of the most popular dim sums.

COMPLETION TIME
Preparation time: 1 hour 20 minutes
Resting time: 1 hour
Cooking time: 8 minutes
Storage: Like all dim sum, they can be frozen raw. Cook for 10 to 12 minutes without thawing.

SPECIAL EQUIPMENT
Stand mixer + paddle attachment
Silicone spatula
4-inch / 10 cm diameter cookie cutter
Perforated parchment paper
Steamer
Steamer basket

SKILLS TO MASTER
Rehydrating mushrooms (page 280)
Preparing shrimp (page 36)

USEFUL TIP
The quality of a good shu mai lies in its texture, which is springy to the bite, even a little crunchy. This texture is obtained by mixing the meat for a long time. They are more concentrated and have a more umami taste than fresh ones.

Learning

SHAOXING RICE WINE
Fermented glutinous rice wine. Choose the Pagoda brand (blue label).

SOY SAUCE
Choose bottles that state "natural fermentation."

DRIED SHIITAKE
Depending on their size, rehydrate them for at least 2 hours before use.

OYSTER SAUCE
Choose the Megachef or Lee Kum Kee (Premium) brands.

CANNED WATER CHESTNUTS
They have a soft, crunchy texture. After opening, freeze leftovers in small freezer bags.

WONTON WRAPPERS
Squares of wheat-flour dough, used to make dumplings.

MAKES 20 SHU MAI

- 4 to 5 small dried shiitake mushrooms (about ⅓ ounce / 10 g)
- 2 ounces / 60 g canned water chestnuts (optional)

  10½ ounces / 300 g finely chopped pork belly

  9 ounces / 250 g peeled shrimp
- 1 package of wonton wrappers

  ¼ carrot

SEASONING

- 2 tablespoons Shaoxing rice wine
- 1 tablespoon oyster sauce
- 1 tablespoon soy sauce

  1 tablespoon cornstarch

  1 level teaspoon organic cane sugar

  ½ teaspoon salt

  Freshly ground black pepper

Making

SIU MAI

1 Rehydrate the mushrooms (page 280). Cut off the rough ends of their stems, then cut the mushrooms into small cubes of just less than ⅛ inch / 3 mm. Cut the chestnuts in cubes of the same size, if using. Slice the carrot into thin wide strips, then into narrow strips, and then into small cubes that are smaller than those of the mushrooms and chestnuts.

2 In the bowl of a stand mixer fitted with the paddle attachment, combine the pork, wine, oyster sauce, soy sauce, cornstarch, sugar, and salt. Season with pepper. Mix for about 5 minutes; the meat should become slightly sticky. Continue as needed. Add the whole shrimp and mix until they are well incorporated.

3 Add the mushrooms and water chestnuts. Mix for several minutes. Take a little filling, heat it in the microwave, taste, and adjust the seasoning, if necessary. Refrigerate for at least 1 hour, ideally overnight.

4 Stack the wonton wrappers and cut them out with a cookie cutter, or just cut off the corners to make them rounded and have less scraps.

5 Place a generous teaspoon of filling in the center of a disc. Make a "C" shape by joining the tips of your thumb and forefinger and place the dough disc in the hollow of your hand to form a cup. Press in the filling using the back of a spoon while keeping your hand constricted. The goal is to make a small open "purse" shape. Place the dumpling on the work surface to test that it stands upright on its own.

6 Repeat until all ingredients are used.

7 Place the dumplings in a steamer basket lined with perforated parchment paper. Place a little of the diced carrot on the top center of each. Bring the water in a steamer to a boil, place the basket in the steamer, and cook for 7 to 8 minutes. Serve hot.

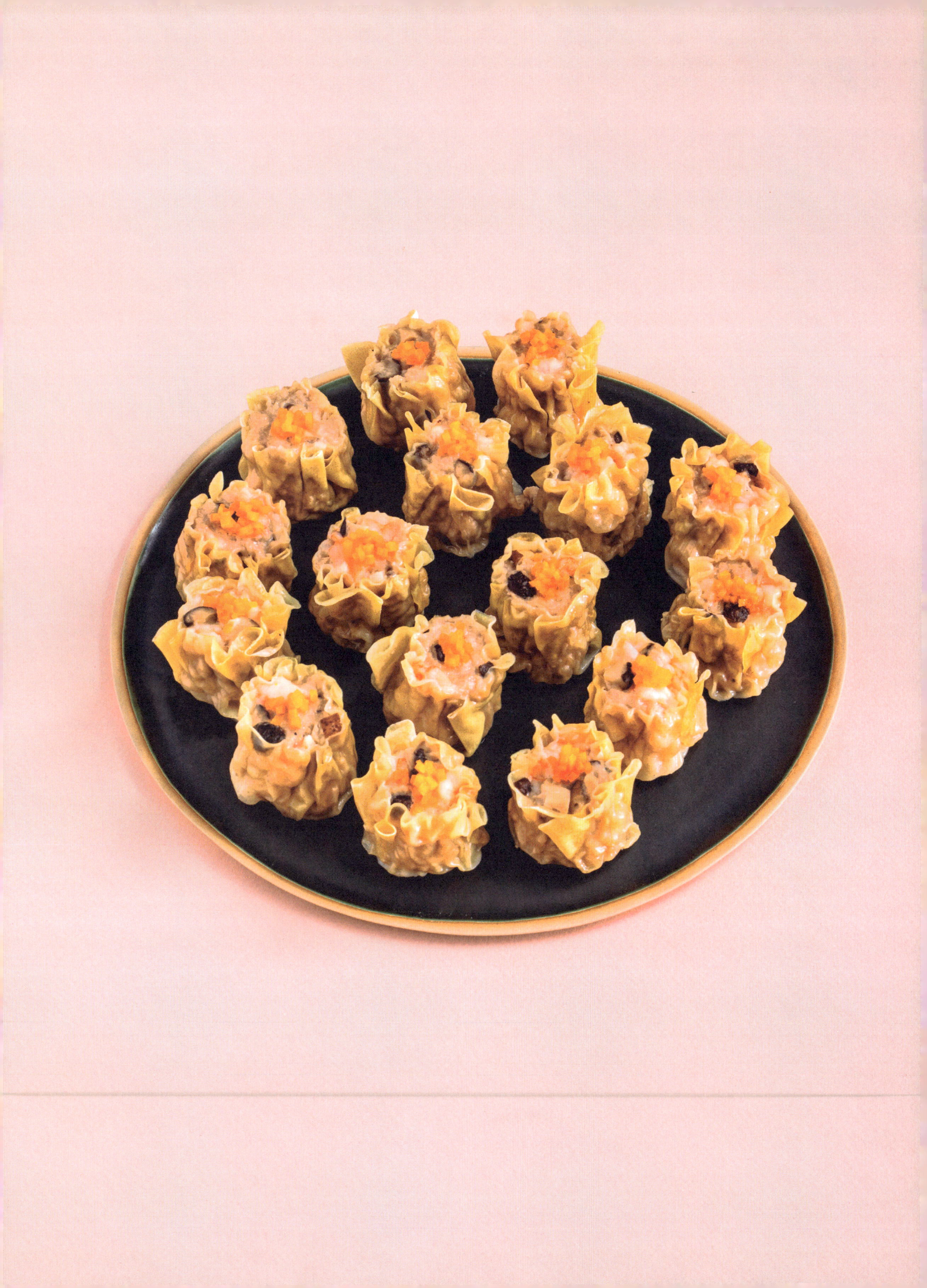

Understanding
CHAR SIU BAO

- BAO DOUGH
- SAUCE
- CHAR SIU PORK

WHAT IS IT?
A stuffed steamed bun. The lacquered pork filling (char siu) or pork is coated in a sweet-and-savory sauce.

ORIGIN
This is a great classic of dim sum. It is also available in a baked bun version with a shiny glaze, or with a sweet craquelin topping that accentuates the sweet and savory side even more.

COMPLETION TIME
Preparation time: 1½ hours
Resting time: 2 hours
Cooking time: 15 minutes
Storage: Once cooked, they can be refrigerated for 5 days. Reheat for 8 minutes by steaming.

SPECIAL EQUIPMENT
Steamer basket
Steamer

SERVING
Enjoy slightly warm.

USEFUL TIP
If you make lacquered pork, you can reserve 1 pound 2 ounces / 500 g of it with its marinade. Boil the marinade before adding the cubed lacquered pork. Add the flour and starch mixture to thicken the sauce.

Learning

FIVE-SPICE POWDER
A powdered mix containing coriander seeds, fennel, anise, cinnamon, black or Szechuan pepper, and cloves.

HOISIN SAUCE
A Chinese barbecue sauce. It is brown, thick, and salty-sweet.

OYSTER SAUCE
Choose the Megachef or Lee Kum Kee (Premium) brands.

CHINESE LOW-GLUTEN FLOUR
A bleached wheat flour with a low protein content (9–10 percent). It can be replaced with a pastry flour near the same percentage.

MAKES 14 BAOS

FILLING
1 pound 2 ounces / 500 g pork loin

1 heaping tablespoon organic cane sugar

- 1 tablespoon oyster sauce
- 2 tablespoons hoisin sauce

1 tablespoon soy sauce

2 tablespoons mei kuei lu chiew (sorghum liquor)

2½ tablespoons / 40 ml water

- 1 level teaspoon five-spice powder

White pepper

1½ tablespoons all-purpose flour

1½ tablespoons potato starch

1 teaspoon beetroot powder, or 1 drop of red food coloring (optional)

BAO DOUGH
- 2¾ cups / 350 g Chinese low-gluten or pastry flour

1¼ teaspoons / 5 g active dry yeast

2 tablespoons plus 2 teaspoons / 40 g organic cane sugar

¾ cup / 180 ml lukewarm water

½ teaspoon salt

1 tablespoon neutral-flavor oil of your choice (sunflower, peanut) or lard

Making

CHAR SIU BAO

1 Make the filling: Cut the pork into cubes (about ⅓ inch / 1 cm).

2 In a saucepan, combine the sugar, oyster sauce, hoisin sauce, soy sauce, alcohol, and water. Add the beetroot powder or red food coloring, if using. Bring to a boil. Add the pork and five-spice powder and season with pepper. Cook for 7 to 10 minutes, stirring occasionally. Mix the flour and potato starch with a little water. Add this mixture to the pan, and stir continuously until thickened. Let cool completely.

3 Make the bao dough (page 20). When the dough has risen, weigh it and divide it into about fourteen balls of 1½ ounces / 40 g each. Set aside under plastic wrap or a clean kitchen towel. Lightly flour the work surface, and roll out a ball of dough into a disc of about 4¾ inches / 12 cm. Roll out the edges more so that the center is thicker.

4 Place a tablespoon of filling (about 2 ounces / 30 to 33 g) in the center. Take up an edge of dough with the thumb and index finger (on the right if you are right-handed) and make a pleat.

5 With the index finger of the other hand, form a second pleat. Seal the second pleat to the first, pinching with your right index finger. The thumb of the right hand does not move and must always hold the first pleat.

6 Continue by creating pleats by turning the bao. At the end, all the pleats are held between the right thumb and index finger.

7 Seal the bao by turning and pinching the center. Form a small ball to seal.

8 Place the baos well-spaced in a steamer basket lined with perforated parchment paper and let rise again for 1 hour under a clean kitchen towel ora lid. Bring the water in a steamer to a boil. Reduce the heat slightly. Place the dumplings in the basket and cook for 15 minutes. Serve slightly warm.

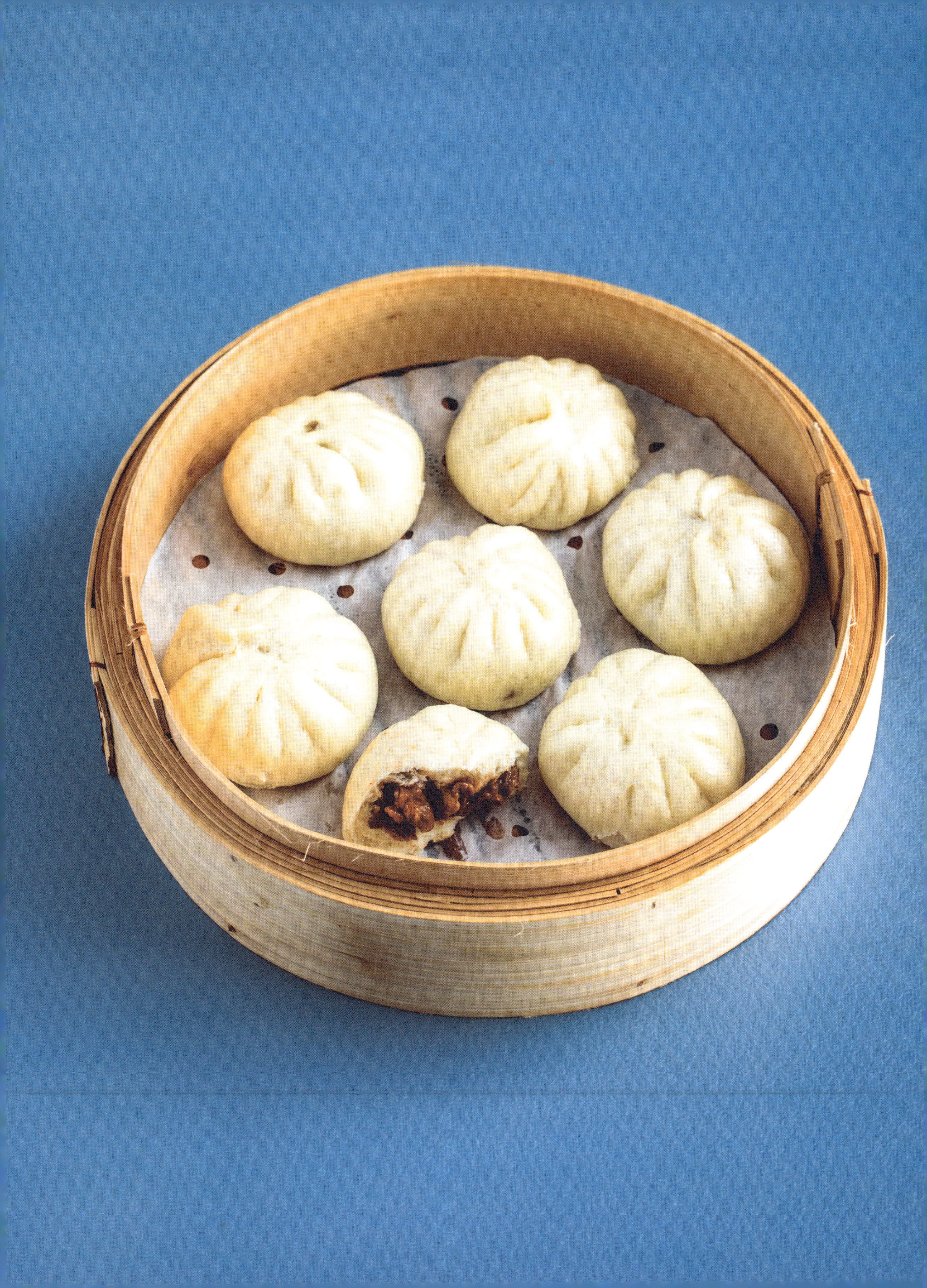

Understanding
MAMA'S BAO

BAO DOUGH IN TWO MIXTURES

MEAT AND VEGETABLE FILLING

WHAT IS IT?
A steamed bun, stuffed with pork, vegetables, and cilantro. This is our family's version of the meat-based bao.

ORIGIN
Meat bao (ròu bāo zi) is more of a street snack than dim sum. It is eaten for breakfast or as a snack.

COMPLETION TIME
Preparation time: 1½ hours
Resting time: 2 hours
Cooking time: 15 minutes

Storage: You can prepare the filling the day before. The buns can be refrigerated for 5 to 7 days. Steam them for 10 minutes.

SPECIAL EQUIPMENT
Steamer basket
Steamer
12 squares of parchment paper, 2⅓ to 2¾ inches / 6 to 7 cm

SKILL TO MASTER
Rehydrating mushrooms (page 280)

USEFUL TIPS
Taste the seasoning by cooking a little filling for 15 seconds in the microwave. Adjust the seasoning, if necessary. The wrapper does not have to be perfectly round when you roll it out.

CHALLENGE
In this recipe, the dough used is more difficult to handle than the classic bao dough. The pleats will not be as pronounced. However, the dough will be extremely soft and light, with a slight taste of butter.

VARIATIONS
The recipe can be made with classic bao dough (page 20).

Learning

SESAME OIL
Choose an Asian sesame oil (Chinese, Japanese, or Korean) that was roasted before being pressed. It is amber to dark brown in color. It has a nutty flavor with an intensely pronounced aroma.

CANNED WATER CHESNUTS
They have a soft, crunchy texture. After opening, freeze leftovers in small freezer bags.

DRIED BLACK MUSHROOMS
Rehydrate them 20 to 30 minutes before use. They have a crunchy, slightly gelatinous texture. Their taste is subtle rather than neutral. They absorb the flavors of other ingredients and provide a textural contrast.

FIVE-SPICE POWDER
A powdered mix containing coriander seeds, fennel, anise, cinnamon, black or Szechuan pepper, and cloves.

DRIED SHIITAKE
Depending on their size, rehydrate them for at least 2 hours before use. They are more concentrated and have a more umami taste than fresh ones.

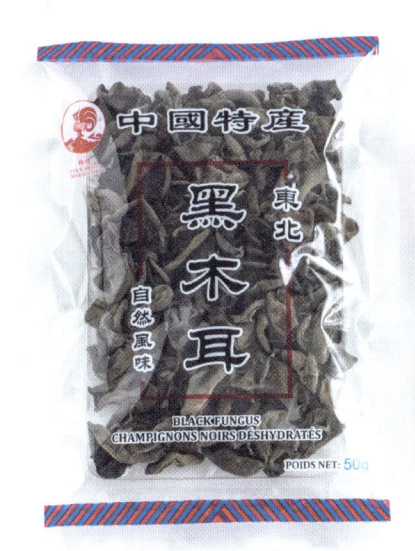

MAKES 12 BAOS

FILLING
- ⅓ ounce / 10 g dried shiitake mushrooms (3 small)
- ⅓ ounce / 10 g dried black mushrooms
- 1 ounce / 30 g onion (½ small)
- 2 ounces / 60 g carrot (1 medium)
- 1¾ ounces / 50 g canned water chestnuts (optional)
- ½ bunch of cilantro
- 1 tablespoon neutral-flavor oil of your choice (sunflower, peanut)
- 1 clove garlic, pressed
- 3 tablespoons / 45 ml soy sauce
- ½ teaspoon five-spice powder
- 1 pound 2 ounces / 500 g finely chopped pork belly
- 1 large / 50 g egg
- 1 heaping tablespoon potato starch
- 1 tablespoon sugar
- 1 tablespoon sesame oil
- 1 level teaspoon salt
- Freshly ground black pepper

DOUGH

Mix 1

2 cups plus 2 tablespoons / 265 g all-purpose flour, sifted

2 teaspoons / 8 g active dry yeast

1 cup minus 1 tablespoon / 225 ml warm water (95°F / 35°C)

Mix 2

1 cup / 125 g all-purpose flour, sifted

2½ teaspoons / 11 g baking powder

5 tablespoons / 75 g organic cane sugar

3 tablespoons / 40 g melted butter, allowed to cool but remain fluid

Making

MAMA'S BAO

1 Rehydrate the shiitake mushrooms for 2 hours and the black mushrooms for 40 minutes. Drain. Dice the shiitake mushrooms and roughly chop the black mushrooms. Chop the onion. Dice the carrot and water chestnuts, if using. Chop the cilantro. Heat the neutral-flavor oil. Sauté the garlic and shiitake mushrooms for 2 minutes. Add 1 tablespoon of the soy sauce, the five-spice powder, and ¼ cup / 60 ml water. Cook until the water has evaporated. Let cool.

2 Combine the shiitake mushroom mixture, onion, carrot, chestnuts, cilantro, pork belly, remaining soy sauce, egg, potato starch, sugar, sesame oil, and salt. Season with pepper. Divide the filling into twelve balls. Set aside in the refrigerator.

3 Preheat a warming drawer or bread proofer to 86°F / 30°C. Combine the flour and yeast from the mix 1. Add the warm water while whisking. Cover the mixture with a clean kitchen towel and set it aside for 1 hour in a warming drawer; the dough should bubble and double in size. Combine the flour, baking powder, and sugar from mix 2. Gradually add mix 2 to mix 1 while stirring. Stir in the cooled melted butter.

4 When the dough is smooth, scrape it out onto a floured work surface and knead until it no longer feels sticky. Roll it into a sausage shape and divide it into twelve balls. Roll out a ball of dough. When the ball starts to take on a round shape, concentrate on the edges so that the center is a little thicker. The disc should be about 6 inches / 15 cm in diameter.

5 Place a ball of filling in the center of a dough disc. Grab an edge of dough with the thumb and forefinger to make a pleat.

6 With the index finger of the other hand, form a new pleat and pinch it with the thumb and index finger of the right hand to seal the first pleat. The thumb of the right hand does not move and must always hold the first pleat.

7 Continue creating pleats by turning the bao and always keeping your thumb on on the first pleat. Close the bao by turning and pinching the center. Transfer them to squares of parchment paper to rise.

8 Place the baos well-spaced in steamer baskets and let rise for 1 hour under a clean kitchen towel. Bring the water in a steamer to a boil. Once the water is boiling, place the basket in the steamer, and cook for 15 minutes per batch. Serve hot.

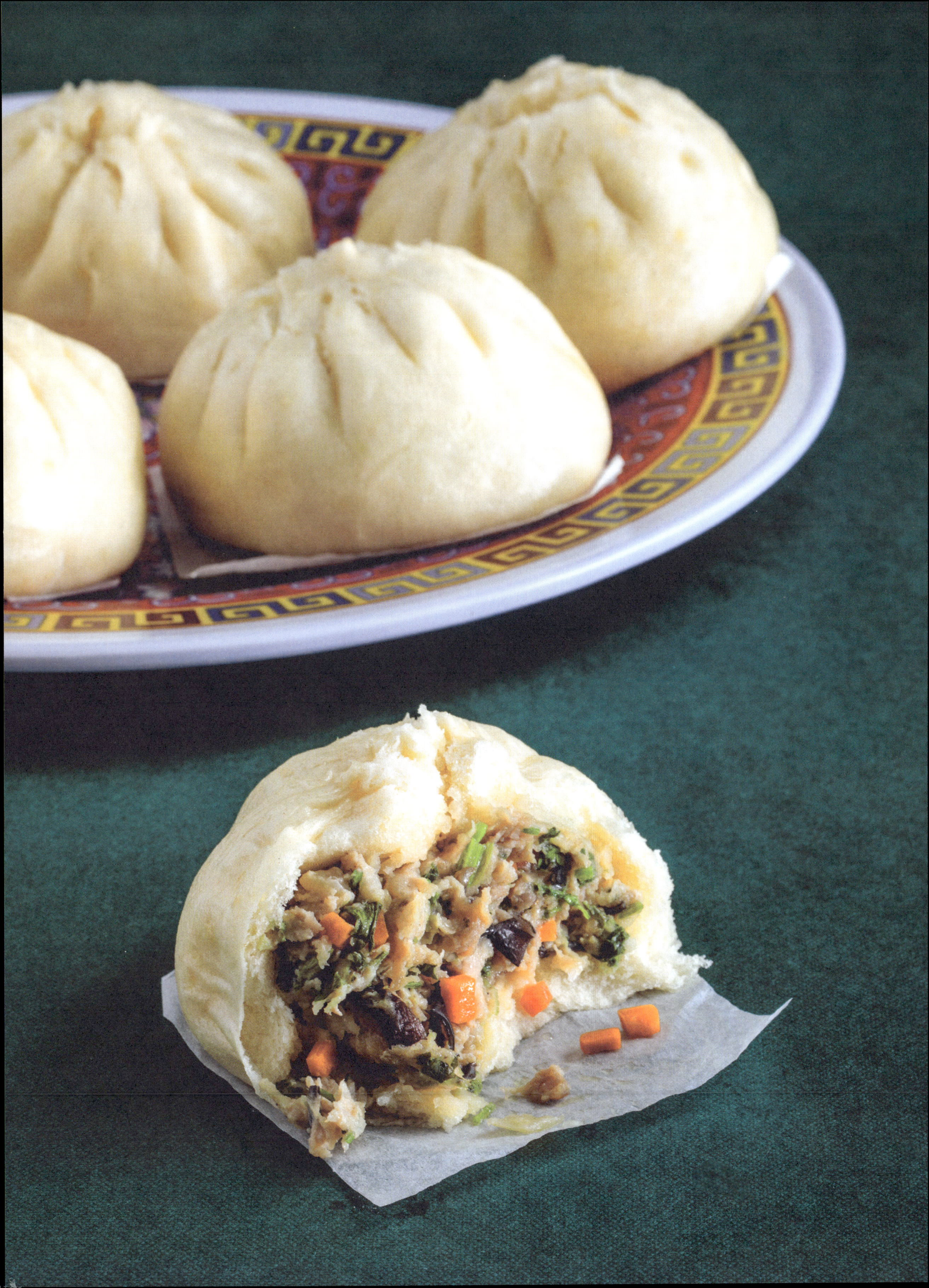

Understanding

LO BAK GO
DAIKON CAKE

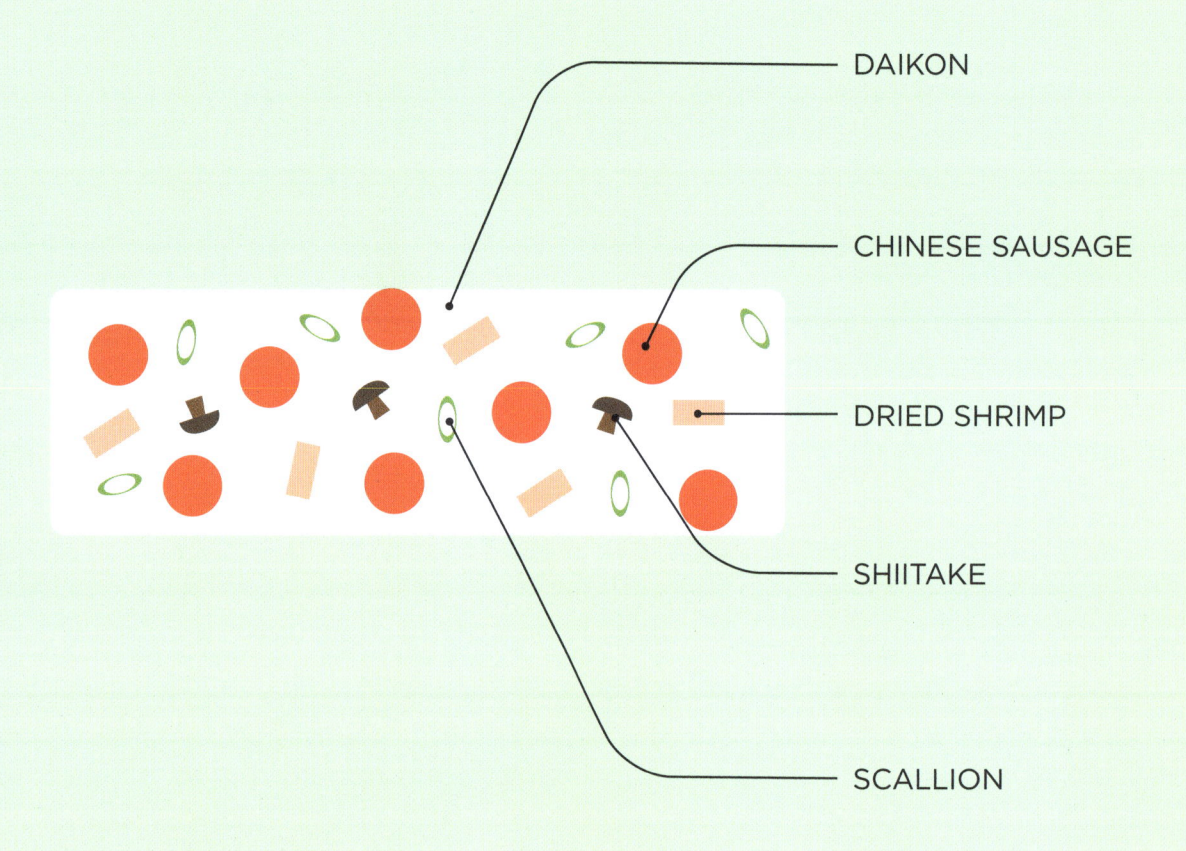

- DAIKON
- CHINESE SAUSAGE
- DRIED SHRIMP
- SHIITAKE
- SCALLION

WHAT IS IT?
A grated white radish and rice flour cake to which various toppings are added (sausage, shiitake mushrooms, dried shrimp, etc.). The cake is steamed, then cooled before being sliced and panseared until golden brown and crispy on the outside and tender on the inside.

ORIGIN
This is a great classic of dim sum. The cake is also enjoyed on Chinese New Year because it symbolizes luck and prosperity.

COMPLETION TIME
Preparation time: 40 minutes
Resting time: Overnight
Cooking time: 48 minutes
Storage: Once steamed, the cake will keep refrigerated, well wrapped, in plastic wrap.

SPECIAL EQUIPMENT
A bamboo basket or mold about 7½ inches / 19 cm in diameter.

SKILL TO MASTER
Rehydrating shiitake mushrooms (page 280)

VARIATIONS
You can also enjoy the cake right after steaming, but traditionally it is browned in oil.

Learning

DAIKON
A juicy and mildly sweet white radish.

CHINESE SAUSAGE (LAP CHEONG)
Dried pork sausages with mei kuei lu chiew (sorghum liquor) and spices. It has a salty-sweet taste.

DRIED SHRIMP
Sold in the refrigerated section. Choose size XL (about ¾ to 1⅛ inches / 2 to 3 cm). Soak them for 30 minutes in lukewarm water before use. They lend an umami taste to dishes.

DRIED SHIITAKE
Depending on their size, rehydrate them for at least 2 hours before use. They are more concentrated and have a more umami taste than fresh ones.

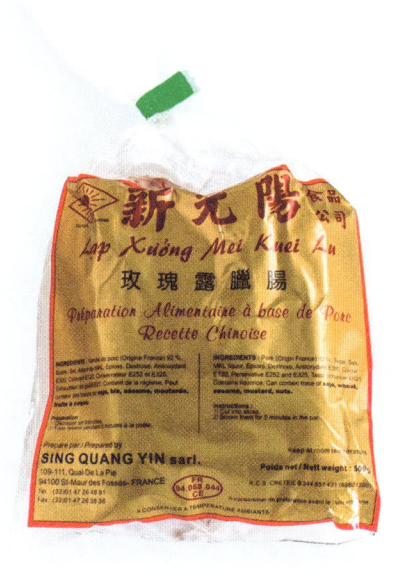

SERVES 4 TO 6

- 4 dried shiitake mushrooms (¾ ounce / 20 g)
- 1¾ ounces / 50 g dried shrimp
- 1¾ pounds / 800 g white daikon radish
- 2 Chinese sausages (lap cheong)

Neutral-flavor oil of your choice (sunflower, peanut)

1 level teaspoon salt

1 level tablespoon organic cane sugar

White pepper

1¼ cups / 190 g rice flour

2 tablespoons cornstarch

4 scallions, finely chopped

Sriracha as garnish if desired

Making

LO BAK GO

1

2

3

4

5

6

1 Rehydrate the shiitake mushrooms (page 280) and soak the shrimp in a bowl of cold water. Peel and grate the daikon. In a wok or large skillet, dry fry the daikon for 10 minutes, stirring occasionally to evaporate some of the water. Transfer to a bowl and let cool.

2 When the shiitake mushrooms are rehydrated, remove the rough sections and finely chop the mushrooms. Finely chop the sausages. Chop the scallions.

3 In the same pan, heat 2 tablespoons of oil. Sauté the mushrooms and sausage for 5 minutes. Set aside. Season the radish with the salt and sugar. Season generously with pepper. Add the rice flour and cornstarch and stir well to combine. Add the mushrooms, sausages, drained shrimp, and scallions, and stir to combine.

4 Wet a cheesecloth. Line a bamboo steamer basket with the cloth. Scrape the batter into the basket and steam for 40 minutes once the water begins to boil. Check for doneness by inserting a toothpick into the center; the cake should be firm. Let cool, then invert the basket to unmold the cake. Let cool completely. Ideally, cover with plastic wrap and set aside overnight in the refrigerator.

5 The next day, in a skillet, heat a little oil. Cut slices of the cake about ⅓ inch / 1 cm thick.

6 Brown for 3 to 4 minutes on each side. Serve with a little sriracha, if desired.

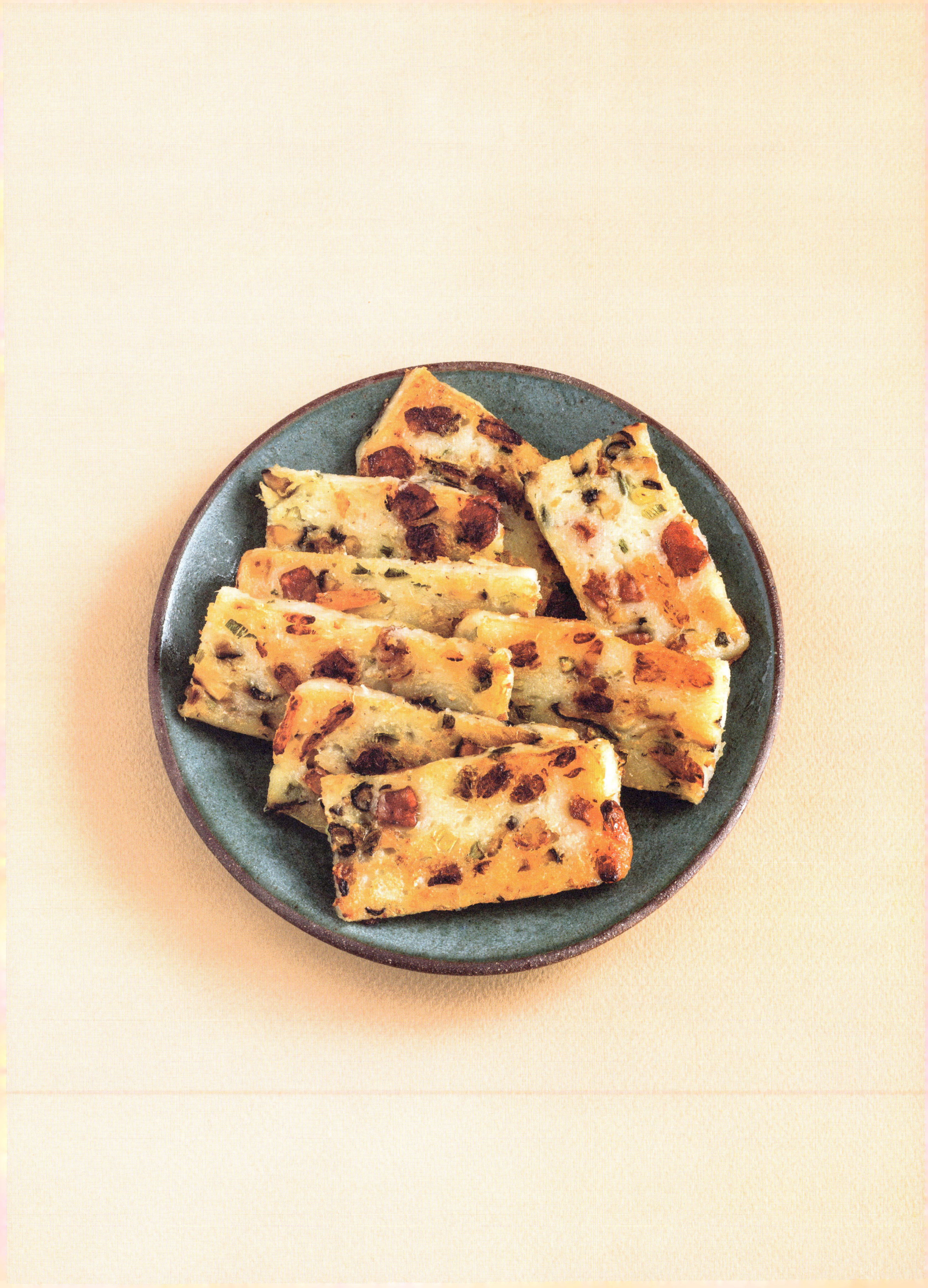

Understanding

WU GOK
TARO DUMPLING

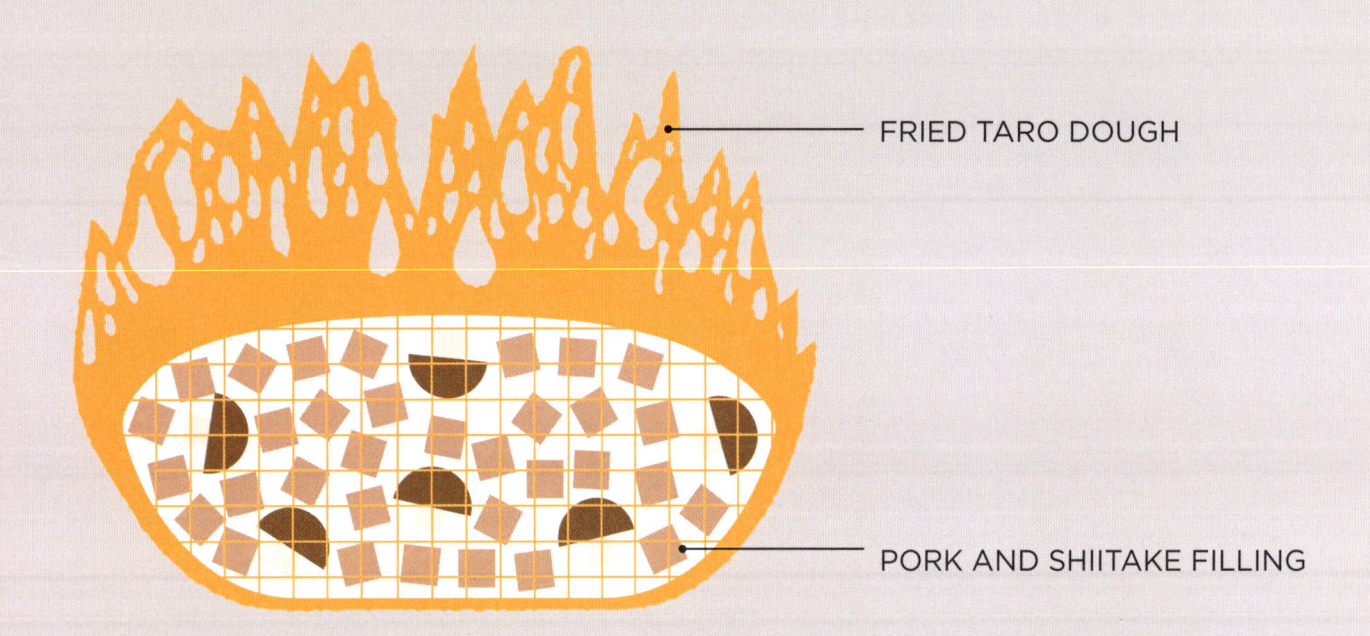

FRIED TARO DOUGH

PORK AND SHIITAKE FILLING

WHAT IS IT?
A pork and shiitake mushroom filling enrobed in a taro purée and wheat starch, shaped into a dumpling and then fried.

ORIGIN
This is a Cantonese specialty, served in dim sum restaurants.

COMPLETION TIME
Preparation time: 1 hour 20 minutes
Resting time: 1 hour
Cooking time: 25 minutes
Storage: The filling can be prepared the day before and stored in the refrigerator in an airtight container.

SPECIAL EQUIPMENT
Stand mixer + paddle attachment
Wok

SKILL TO MASTER
Rehydrating mushrooms (page 280)

USEFUL TIPS
Be careful, as the temperature of the oil is essential for this recipe. If the oil is not hot enough, the starch lace will spread and the dumpling will fall apart. If the oil is too hot, the lace will not form. If the oil is at the right temperature, but the dumpling still disintegrates, it means there are holes in the dumpling.

Learning

SHAOXING RICE WINE

Fermented glutinous rice wine. Choose the Pagoda brand (blue label).

TARO

A slightly sweet, starch tuber. It is toxic when consumed raw. Choose the dasheen variety from Asia. It has a characteristic walnut/hazelnut taste.

WHEAT STARCH

It becomes translucent when cooked.

MAKES ABOUT 14 DUMPLINGS

FILLING

⅓ ounce / 10 g dried shiitake mushrooms (about 4 small ones)

2 tablespoons neutral-flavor oil of your choice (sunflower, peanut)

5¼ ounces / 150 g finely chopped pork belly

1 tablespoon Shaoxing wine

1 tablespoon oyster sauce

1 tablespoon soy sauce

1 tablespoon organic cane sugar

1 level tablespoon five-spice powder

1 teaspoon cornstarch

3 tablespoons / 45 ml water

TARO DOUGH

10½ ounces / 300 g peeled taro (about 12 ounces / 350 g raw)

¼ cup / 60 ml boiling water

⅔ cup / 60 g wheat starch

½ teaspoon salt

1 teaspoon organic cane sugar

½ teaspoon five-spice powder

1 teaspoon / 4 g baking powder

2 ounces / 60 g lard, finely chopped

2 quarts (2 L) oil, for frying

85

Making

WU GOK

1 Make the filling: Rehydrate the mushrooms (page 280), then remove the rough ends of the stems. Cut the mushrooms into small cubes of just less than ⅛ inch / 3 mm. Heat the oil in a wok or skillet. Sauté the mushrooms for 1 minute, then add the pork, wine, oyster sauce, soy sauce, sugar, and five-spice powder. Stir well. When the meat is cooked (about 3 to 4 minutes), combine the cornstarch and water. Add the mixture to the wok and stir. As soon as the mixture thickens, set aside off the heat. Let cool.

2 Make the taro dough: Peel and cut the taro into slices. Place them in a steamer basket and cook for 12 to 15 minutes; the taro should be soft enough to mash with a fork. Transfer the taro to the bowl of a stand mixer fitted with the paddle attachment and beat to a smooth purée.

3 Pour the boiling water into the wheat starch. Mix with chopsticks until a paste forms. Knead using your hands. Transfer small pieces of the paste to the mixer bowl. Add the salt, sugar, and five-spice powder and beat until the wheat starch is completely incorporated and the mixture forms a smooth dough. Add the baking powder and lard pieces. Mix until combined. Cover with plastic wrap and refrigerate for 40 minutes.

4 Divide the dough into fourteen balls (about 1¼ ounces / 35 g each). Flatten a ball with your thumbs while twisting it to form a disc of about 2¾ inches / 7 cm.

5 Place a tablespoon of filling in the center (½ ounce / 15 g).

6 Fold the dumpling in half to close it and seal it closed by pinching the edges together.

7 Repeat these steps and transfer them to a parchment paper–lined baking sheet. Refrigerate for 20 minutes.

8 Heat the oil to between 350° and 375°F / 180° and 190°C. Place two dumplings on a slotted spoon and gently submerge them in the hot oil. Once a crust forms on the bottom, slide the slotted spoon out from underneath them. Cook for 3 to 4 minutes. A lace should form and the dumpling should be golden brown. Set aside on paper towels to drain. Serve barely warm.

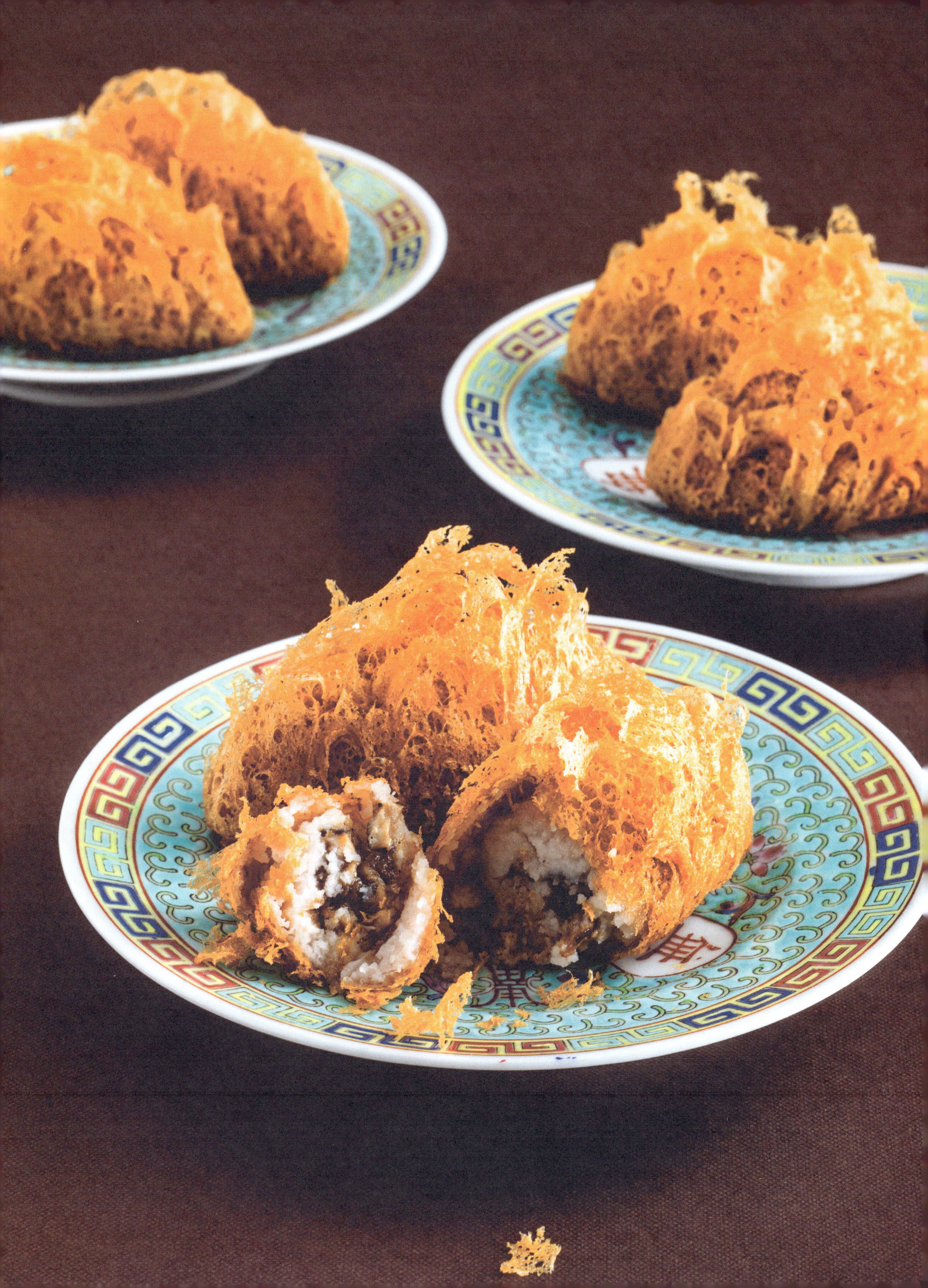

Understanding

CHEUNG FUN
RICE NOODLE ROLLS WITH SHRIMP

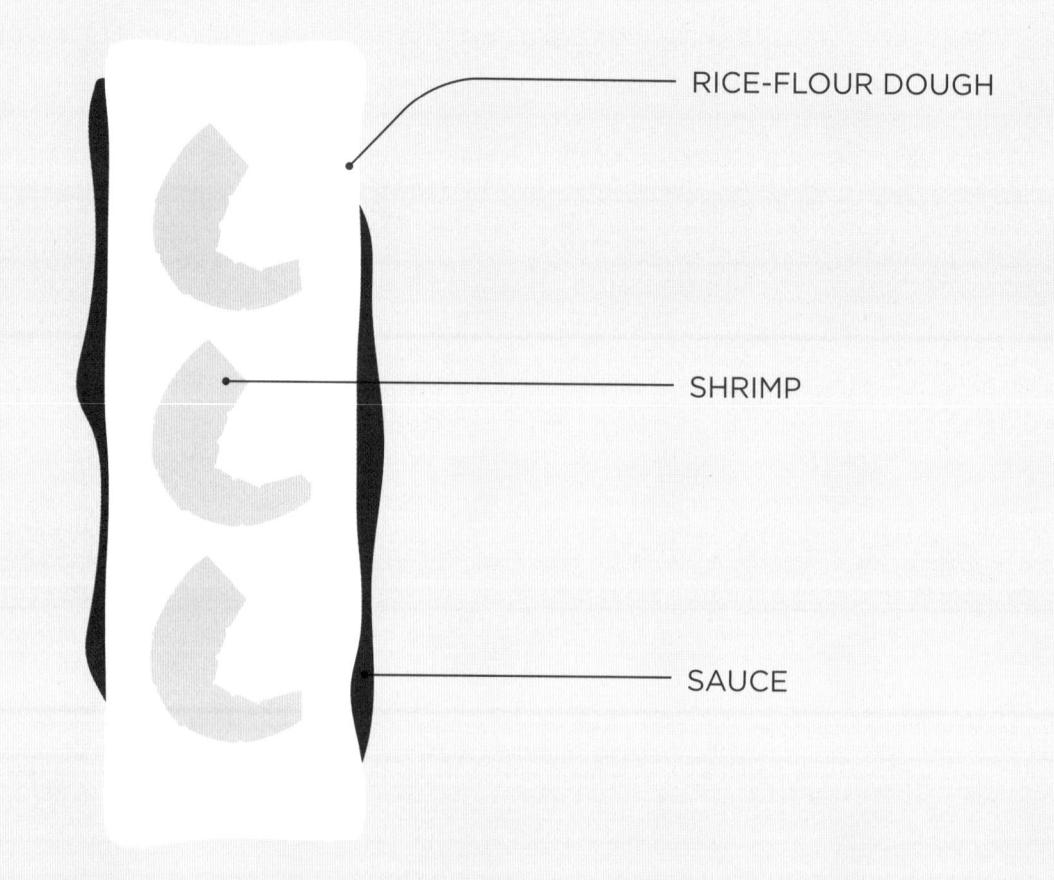

— RICE-FLOUR DOUGH

— SHRIMP

— SAUCE

WHAT IS IT?
Rice noodle rolls that have been steamed, then rolled around shrimp and served with a sweet sauce.

ORIGIN
This is a dim sum of Cantonese origin. The shrimp version is enjoyed at dim sum brunches at restaurants. The scallion and fried versions are more for street snacks.

COMPLETION TIME
Preparation time: 45 minutes
Cooking time: 15 minutes
Storage: The rolls should be eaten immediately after preparation.

SPECIAL EQUIPMENT
Baking dish
about 9½ by 7 inches / 24 by 18 cm
Steamer
Plastic bowl scraper or spatula

SKILL TO MASTER
Preparing shrimp (page 36)

USEFUL TIPS
Always stir the dough to homogenize it before pouring it into the baking sheet. You can reheat a plate of the rolls by steaming them for 3 to 4 minutes just before serving.

VARIATIONS
You can replace the shrimp with diced char siu pork. For a vegetarian version, sprinkle the roll with finely chopped scallions before cooking it. You can also wrap the roll around a yóutiáo (a strip of deep-fried dough) sold in the frozen food sections of Asian markets.

Learning

SESAME OIL
Choose an Asian sesame oil (Chinese, Japanese, or Korean) that was roasted before being pressed. It is amber to dark brown in color. It has a nutty flavor with an intensely pronounced aroma.

RICE FLOUR
Made from Asian long rice. Choose varieties from Asia to give the dough a very different texture.

WHEAT STARCH
It becomes translucent when cooked.

MAKES 8 ROLLS

SAUCE

½ onion
3 tablespoons / 45 ml water
3 tablespoons / 45 ml soy sauce
1 tablespoon dark soy sauce
1 tablespoon oyster sauce
1⅔ tablespoons organic cane sugar
1 tablespoon sesame oil

FILLING

1 tablespoon cornstarch
24 shrimp, size 21/25, prepared (page 36)
- 1 tablespoon sesame oil

DOUGH

- 1 cup / 150 g rice flour
  5 tablespoons / 60 g potato starch
- ⅓ cup / 30 g wheat starch
  1 teaspoon salt
  1 tablespoon neutral-flavor oil of your choice (sunflower, peanut)

Making

CHEUNG FUN

1 Make the sauce: Cut the onion in half again. In a saucepan, combine the onion halves, water, soy sauces, oyster sauce, and sugar. Bring to a low boil, and stir to dissolve the sugar. Cook for 2 minutes. Let cool. Remove the onion halves and add the sesame oil.

2 Make the filling: Combine the cornstarch with a little water to dilute it, then add it to the prepared shrimp. Toss to coat. Place the shrimp on a plate or small dish, without overlapping them, and steam them for 3 to 4 minutes.

3 Remove the shrimp from the steamer and drizzle them with the sesame oil and set aside.

4 Make the dough: In a large measuring cup, combine the flour, potato and wheat starches, and salt. Add twice their volume in water. Stir to combine. Bring the water in a steamer to a boil. Grease a 9½ by 7-inch / 24 by 18 cm baking sheet and heat it for 2 minutes in the steamer. Add approximately 3 ounces / 80 g of the dough and tilt the steamer basket handles to distribute the batter evenly over the baking sheet. Cover, and cook for 2 minutes, in the same manner as when cooking rice noodles (page 22). Remove the baking sheet and immerse it in an ice water bath.

5 Cut the dough in half. Arrange three shrimp in the center of each half, about 1 inch / 3 cm from one edge. Using a bowl scraper or spatula, fold the edges over the shrimp, then flip the roll. Place the roll on an oiled work surface. Repeat these same steps for the remaining dough and rolls.

6 Brush the tops of the rolls with a little oil. Trim off the ends. Serve with the sauce on the side.

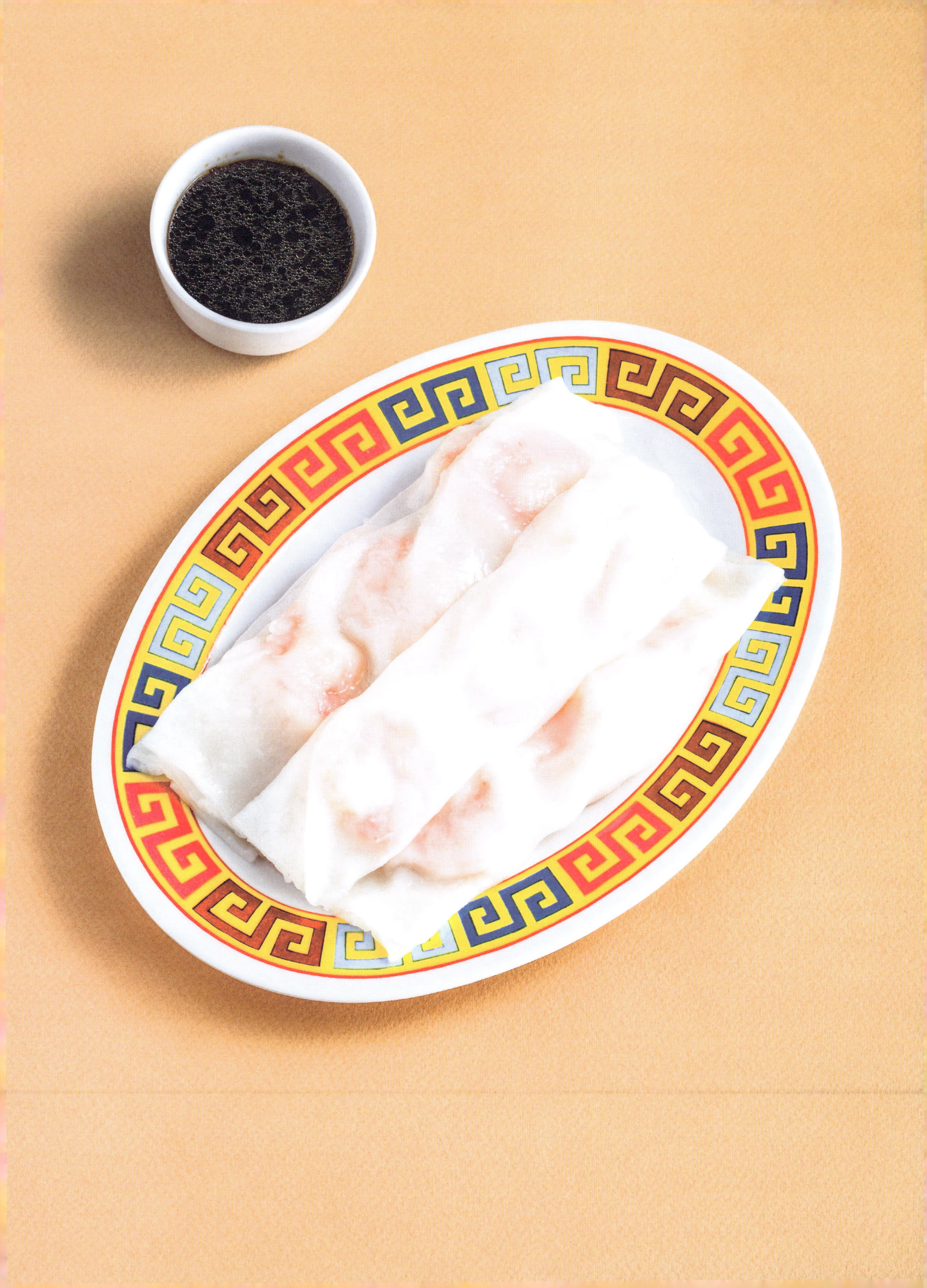

Understanding

JIŬCÀI HÉZĬ
FLAT STEAMED GARLIC CHIVE DUMPLINGS

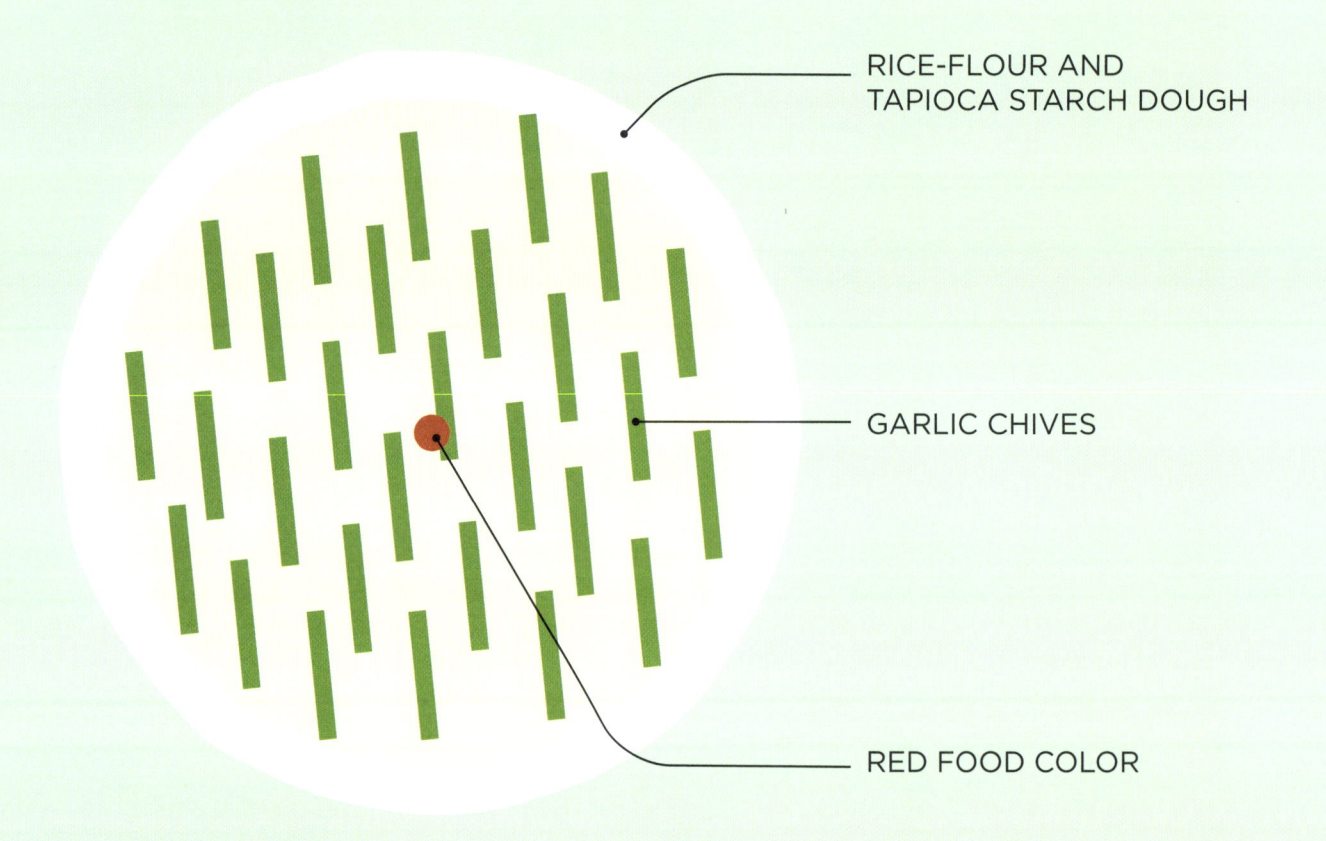

- RICE-FLOUR AND TAPIOCA STARCH DOUGH
- GARLIC CHIVES
- RED FOOD COLOR

WHAT IS IT?
A flat dumpling. The wrapper is made from rice flour and tapioca starch. It is filled with garlic chives, then steamed.

ORIGIN
This dumpling originated in Chaozhou at the far eastern end of the province of Canton. The community and dialect of this region is referred to by the term *teochew*. These cakes are made for special occasions, holidays, or religious ceremonies. The red dot symbolizes happiness and fortune. At funerals, the red dot is not used.

COMPLETION TIME
Preparation time: 1 hour 20 minutes
Resting time: 15 minutes
Cooking time: 12 minutes
Storage: Once cooked, the dumplings can be refrigerated for 5 days. Steam them for 5 minutes or brown them in a pan with a little oil to serve them again.

SPECIAL EQUIPMENT
Steamer basket

SERVING
Eaten slightly warm. In dim sum restaurants, they are served hot, lightly browned in a pan.

USEFUL TIP
Baking soda helps preserve the chives' green color.

Learning

GARLIC CHIVES
Also called Chinese chives. They are an aromatic plant with a garlic flavor and can be eaten whole.

TAPIOCA STARCH
Made from cassava starch. It is a strong thickening and gelling agent.

RICE FLOUR
Made from Asian long rice. Choose those from Asia so that the dough will have a very different texture.

GLUTINOUS RICE FLOUR
Made from round glutinous rice with opaque grains. It becomes very sticky after cooking.

MAKES 20 DUMPLINGS

DOUGH

- 1⅔ cups / 250 g rice flour
- ¼ cup plus 1 tablespoon / 50 g glutinous rice flour
- ⅔ cup / 100 g tapioca starch
- 1 level teaspoon salt
- 1 tablespoon neutral-flavor oil of your choice (sunflower, peanut)
- 2 cups / 480 ml boiling water

FILLING

- 1 pound 2 ounces / 500 g garlic chives
- 3 tablespoons / 45 ml neutral-flavor oil of your choice (sunflower, peanut), plus more for brushing
- 1 slightly heaping teaspoon salt
- 1 slightly heaping teaspoon powdered broth of your choice, or ½ broth cube crushed in oil
- 1 level teaspoon sugar
- 1 level teaspoon baking soda
- Beetroot powder or red food color (optional)

Making

JIŬCÀI HÉZĬ

1 Make the dough: Combine the rice flours, starch, and salt. Add the oil, then add the boiling water. Mix with a spatula until the mixture begins to form a dough. Knead to a supple, smooth, and homogeneous dough. If the dough feels sticky, add a little rice flour to your hands. Cover, and set aside at room temperature for 15 minutes.

2 Make the filling: Wash and thoroughly dry the chives in a clean kitchen towel. Cut them into sections about ⅛ inch / 4 mm long. Combine the chives, oil, salt, broth, sugar, and baking soda. Stir well to combine.

3 Weigh the dough, then divide it into twenty balls (about 1½ ounces / 40 to 45 g each). Roll the balls out with a rolling pin to form 4¾-inch / 12 cm diameter discs.

4 Place each dough disc in a small bowl, working with only one at a time. Add a generous spoonful of the garlic chives in the center (about ¾ ounce / 25 to 28 g). Fold the edges toward the center. Pinch the dough together. Invert the dumpling.

5 Work the dumpling gently between your hands to form a rounded shape.

6 Place the dumplings in a steamer basket lined with perforated parchment paper. Once the water in the steamer is boiling, place the dumplings in the basket and cook for 12 minutes.

7 Place the dumplings on a parchment paper–lined baking sheet or greased serving plate. Brush the tops with a little oil to prevent the dough from forming a crust.

8 Break a toothpick, dip the broken side in the beetroot powder, if using, and make a red dot in the center of each dumpling. Serve warm, or let cool then brown them in a pan in vegetable oil, about 2 minutes on each side.

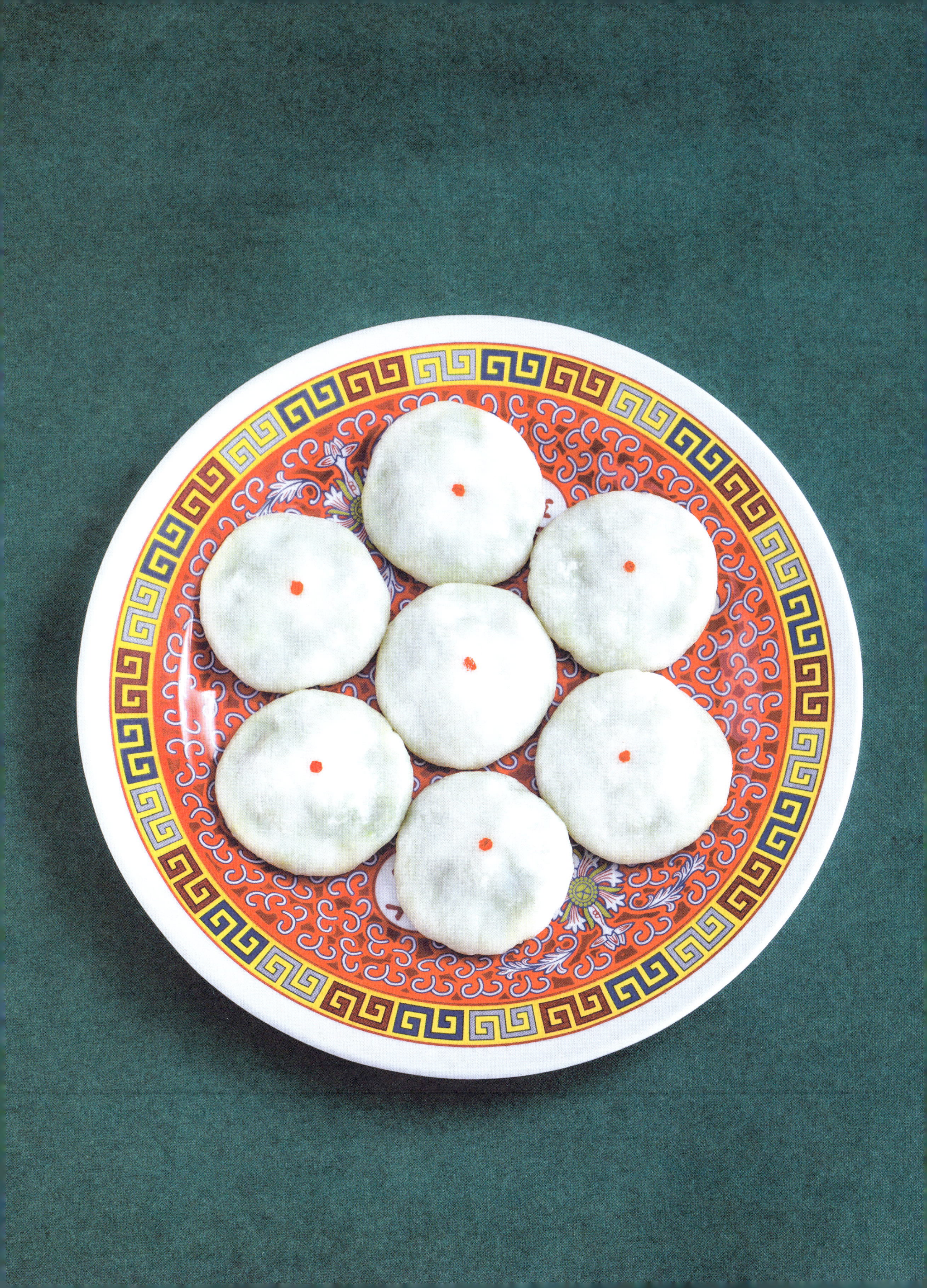

Understanding

LO MAI GAI
GLUTINOUS RICE WITH CHICKEN IN LOTUS LEAF

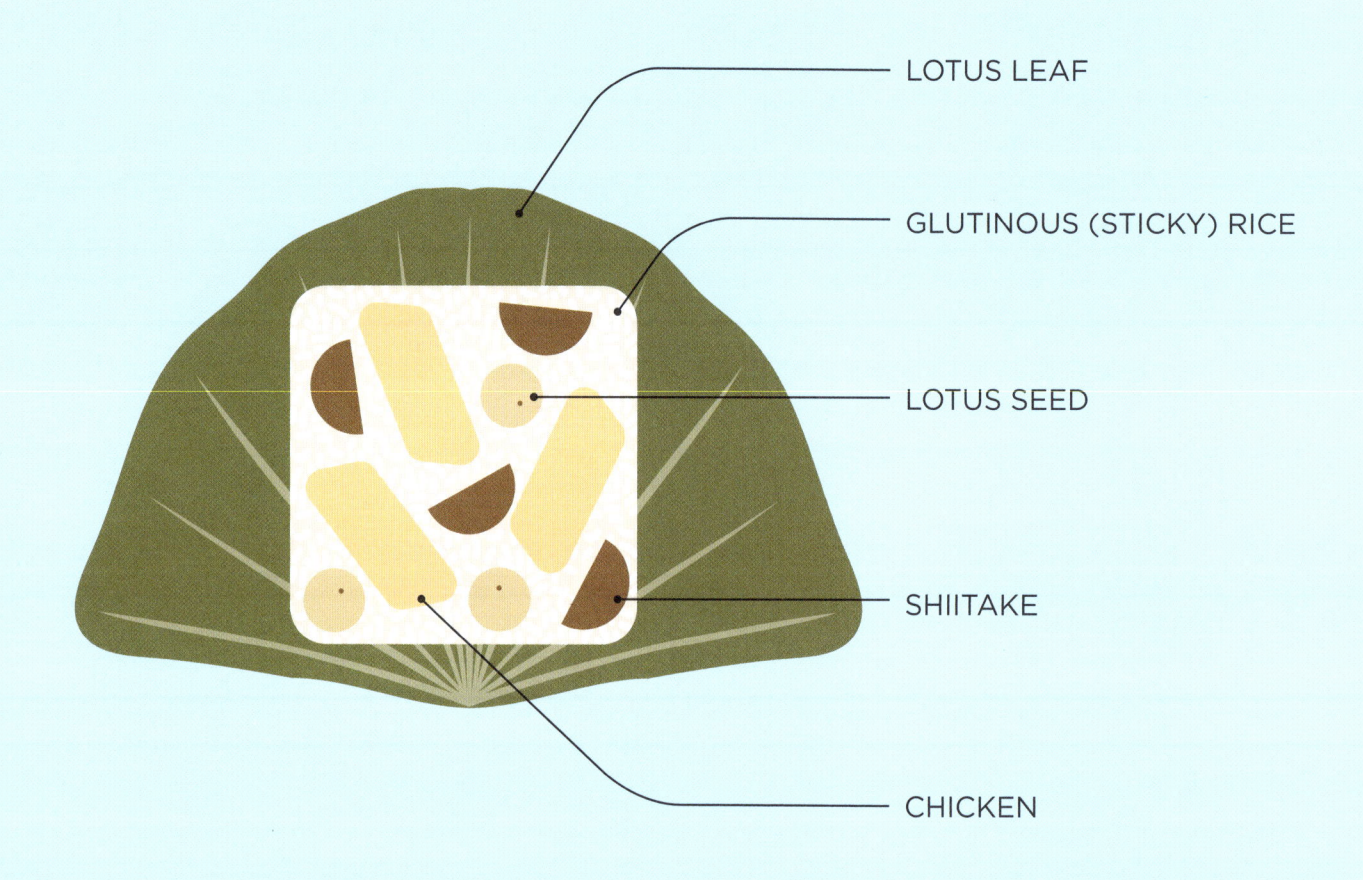

- LOTUS LEAF
- GLUTINOUS (STICKY) RICE
- LOTUS SEED
- SHIITAKE
- CHICKEN

WHAT IS IT?
A glutinous rice filling (marinated chicken, lotus seeds, shiitake mushrooms, sometimes sausage, and salted duck egg yolk) wrapped in a lotus leaf and steamed.

ORIGIN
This is a Cantonese specialty served in dim sum restaurants. Originally, street vendors at the Guangzhou night market prepared this rice in porcelain bowls. The bowls have been replaced by lotus leaves which, in addition to being practical for carrying, flavor the rice and give it its signature flavor.

COMPLETION TIME
Preparation time: 45 minutes
Cooking time: 50 minutes
Storage: Once cooked, the rice can be kept for a week in the refrigerator. Steam for 20 minutes.

SKILLS TO MASTER
Rehydrating mushrooms (page 280)
Softening lotus leaves (page 280)

USEFUL TIP
As a precaution, soak an extra lotus leaf or choose your leaves carefully before soaking them (they should not have too many holes or tears).

VARIATIONS
Replace the lotus seeds with 8 chestnuts cooked sous vide. Replace the chicken with the same amount of pork loin.

Learning

LOTUS LEAVES

A hydrophobic leaf, which allows for airtight cooking. Used to flavor mixtures (it contributes a little earthiness). Sold dried. They must be rehydrated before use.

DRIED SHIITAKE

Depending on their size, rehydrate them for at least 2 hours before use. They are more concentrated and have a more umami taste than fresh ones.

GLUTINOUS RICE

It should be soaked between 4 hours to overnight, depending on the recipe. Without soaking, the rice will remain firm, even after prolonged cooking.

DRIED LOTUS SEEDS

Rehydrate them in 4 cups / 1 L water, then remove the bitter germ from the center before use.

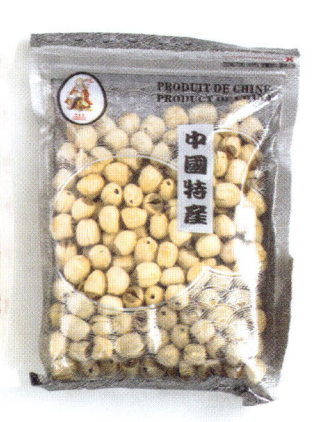

SERVES 4

- 3 cups / 500 g glutinous rice
- 8 small dried shiitake mushrooms
- 2 or 3 lotus leaves
- 24 to 32 lotus seeds

2 free-range chicken thighs, deboned (14 ounces / 400 g; page 34)

3 tablespoons / 45 ml neutral-flavor oil of your choice (sunflower, peanut)

1¾ teaspoons salt

2 tablespoons soy sauce

2 teaspoons organic cane sugar

½ teaspoon pepper

Scant ½ cup / 100 ml shiitake soaking water

CHICKEN MARINADE

1 tablespoon oyster sauce

1 tablespoon soy sauce

1 teaspoon organic cane sugar

½ teaspoon five-spice powder

Making

LO MAI GAI

1 Soak the glutinous rice in cold water for at least 4 hours. Rehydrate the mushrooms (page 280). Soften the lotus leaves (page 280). Soak the lotus seeds for 1 hour in a bowl of cold water (page 280).

2 Drain the lotus seeds and cook them in a pot of water for 20 minutes. Drain, and let cool. Break them in half to remove the bitter germ.

3 Prepare the chicken and marinade: Remove the skin from the chicken and cut the meat into even pieces. Combine the oyster sauce, soy sauce, sugar, and five-spice powder. Add the chicken and stir to coat. Set aside for 20 minutes.

4 Drain the rice. Squeeze the excess moisture from the mushrooms and cut off the rough ends of the stems. Halve or quarter the mushrooms (depending on their size). Heat the oil in a wok or skillet. Fry the mushrooms for 30 seconds, then add the marinated chicken pieces. When the chicken begins to brown, add the drained glutinous rice. Sauté for 1 minute. Add the salt, soy sauce, sugar, pepper, lotus seeds, and the scant ½ cup / 100 ml of shiitake soaking water. Bring to a boil and cook over low heat for 5 minutes. The rice should absorb all the liquid.

5 When the lotus leaves are well hydrated, cut them in half following the fold to obtain what looks like two fans. If the leaf has too many holes, overlap another cut piece from another leaf.

6 Divide the rice into four portions. Place a portion of the rice in the center of one of the leaf halves. Fold the bottom over the rice.

7 Fold over the sides toward the center. Turn the package over and tie with string to secure them. Repeat with remaining leaves and rice.

8 Arrange the rice packets in a steamer basket and cook for 40 to 45 minutes. Serve hot.

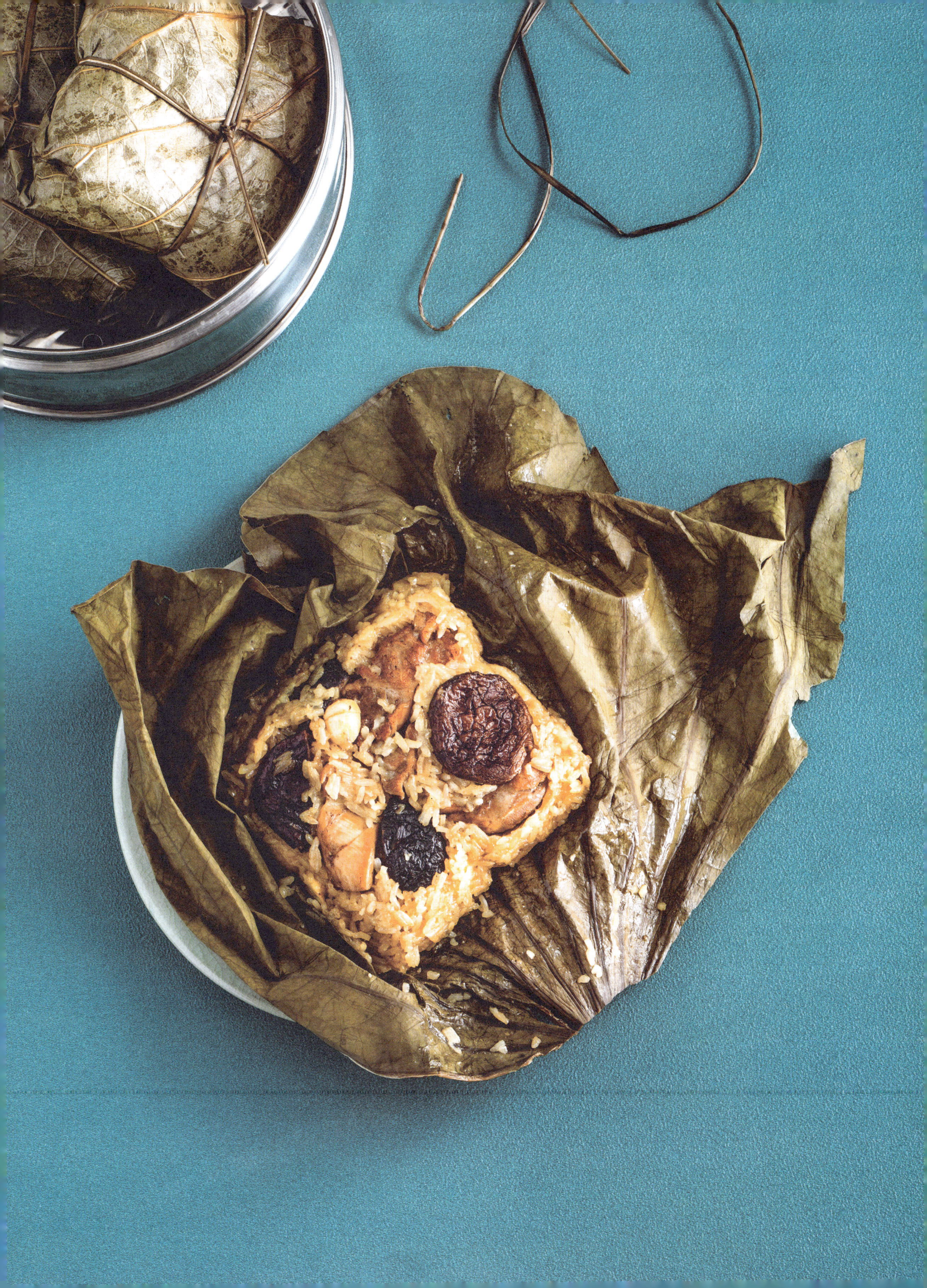

Understanding
KǍOYĀ
CANTONESE LACQUERED DUCK

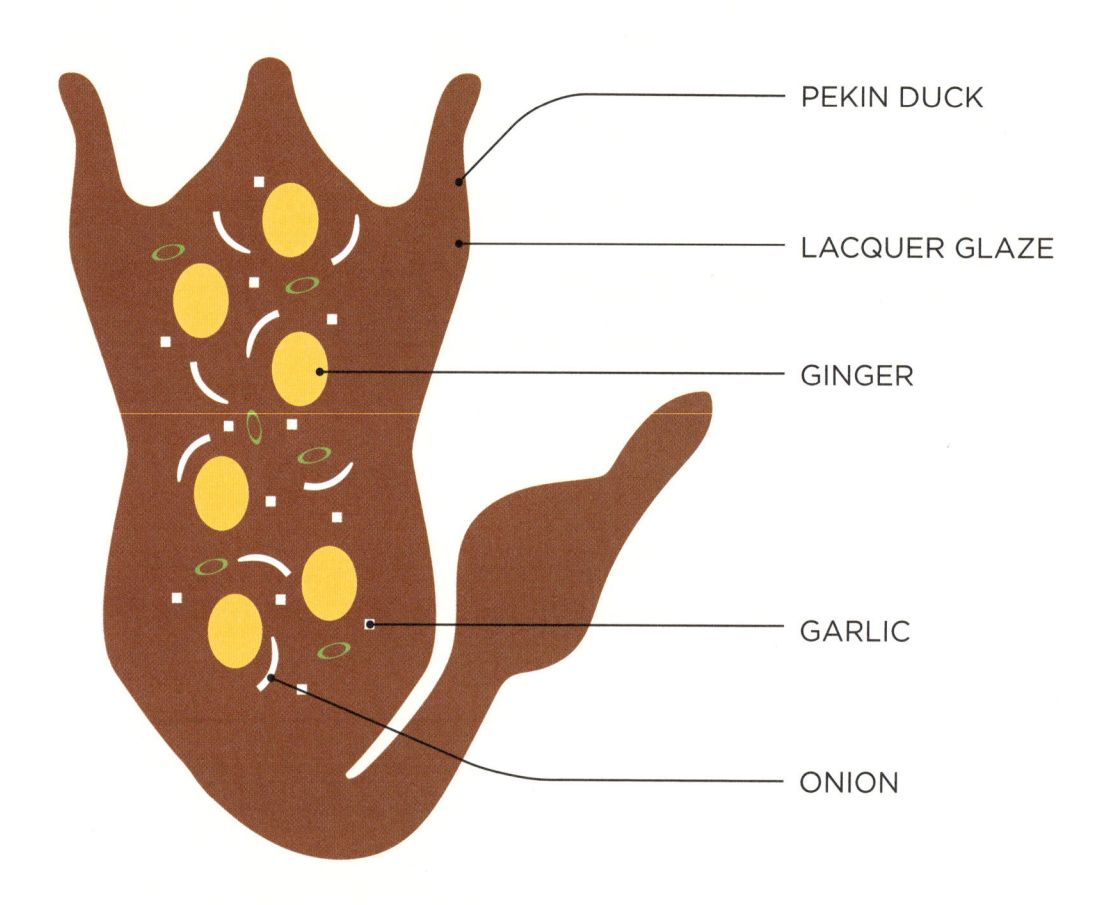

- PEKIN DUCK
- LACQUER GLAZE
- GINGER
- GARLIC
- ONION

WHAT IS IT?
A duck stuffed with spices and marinated, dried for 48 hours in the refrigerator, then roasted.

ORIGIN
Lacquered duck is one of the Cantonese rotisserie dishes. It should not be confused with the sophisticated Peking duck that requires many more techniques and is impossible to reproduce at home. However, Cantonese lacquered duck can be served with steamed pancakes (page 32), hoisin sauce, and a julienne of cucumber and scallions, which are the traditional accompaniments to Peking duck.

COMPLETION TIME
Preparation time: 40 minutes
Resting time: 50 hours
Cooking time: 1 hour 20 minutes
Storage: Once cooked and carved, the duck can be kept for 5 days in the refrigerator. Reheat in the oven at 350°F / 180°C for 15 minutes, skin side up. Pour a little marinade into the bottom of the dish to prevent the meat from becoming too dry.

SPECIAL EQUIPMENT
Large sewing needle or small trussing needle
Air compressor
Basting brush

SKILL TO MASTER
Detaching skin using a small air compressor (page 281)

VARIATIONS
You can replace the two fermented soybean pastes with hoisin sauce in the same proportions (1½ ounces / 40 g). You can add 1¼ cups / 300 ml mei kuei lu chiew (sorghum liquor) to the marinade.

Learning

PEKIN DUCK

A duck breed of Chinese origin, large in size and fleshy, with a thick skin and thick layer of fat. Cook the skin to make it crispier. Sometimes they are found in the frozen food section.

TIAN MIAN JIANG OR SWEET BEAN PASTE

A paste made of wheat flour and sometimes soy, fermented. It is essential for zhájiàng miàn sauce. It is often sold in small vacuum packs.

CHU HOU PASTE

A paste made from fermented soybean paste, sesame, garlic, ginger, and spices.

MALTOSE

A sugar made from the starch of barley or corn in the form of a viscous liquid. It lends shine, facilitates caramelization, and stabilizes certain pastry preparations.

SERVES 4 TO 6

MARINADE

½ onion, or 2 scallions
¾ ounce / 20 g fresh ginger
4 cloves garlic
1¾ teaspoons salt
1 tablespoon plus 2 teaspoons / 20 g organic cane sugar
1 tablespoon soy sauce
- 1 tablespoon chu hou paste
- 1 tablespoon tián miàn jiàng (sweet bean paste)
1 tablespoon oyster sauce
2 tablespoons five-spice powder
1 teaspoon black pepper

LACQUER GLAZE

3 tablespoons / 45 ml hot water
- ½ ounce / 15 g maltose
2 tablespoons white vinegar or wine vinegar
1 tablespoon beetroot powder, or 1 drop of red food color (optional)

- 1 Pekin duck (about 5½ pounds / 2.4 kg) thawed, with neck and head attached

Making

KĂOYĀ

1 Two days before, make the marinade: Cut the onion into quarters and thinly slice the ginger. Crush the garlic cloves with the flat side of a knife blade (page 281). Combine the onion, ginger, garlic, salt, sugar, soy sauce, chu hou paste, tián miàn jiàng, oyster sauce, five-spice powder, and pepper.

2 Make the lacquer glaze: Combine the hot water, maltose, vinegar, and beetroot powder, if using. Stir to fully dissolve the maltose. Set aside at room temperature.

3 Cut off the flippers from the duck. Remove the fat, if needed, and rinse the cavity to remove any bloody parts. Pat the duck dry using paper towels.

4 Fill the cavity with the marinade. Using a trussing needle, sew up the cavity to close it.

5 Detach the skin from the meat using a small air compressor (page 281). This will allow the skin to crisp during cooking.

6 Bring a large pot of water to a boil. Ladle the boiling water over the duck. The skin will retract. Pat the duck dry.

7 Using a basting brush, cover the skin on both sides with the lacquer glaze. Set aside on a wire rack for 2 hours in the refrigerator to dry. Apply the lacquer glaze again. Refrigerate on a rack for 24 hours to dry. Turn the duck over and let dry for another 24 hours. The skin should be absent of any moisture and should look like leather.

8 Preheat the oven to 325°F / 160°C. Place the duck breast side down on a rack placed on a baking sheet. Add a little water to the baking sheet to prevent the fat from burning as it drips. Bake for 40 minutes.

9 Turn the duck over. Protect the browned area (thighs and legs) by covering them with foil. Continue cooking for an additional 30 to 40 minutes, keeping an eye on the browning. Set aside for 15 to 20 minutes. Cut the trussing string to remove it and empty the juice from the cavity into a bowl. Serve with rice (page 12) or with steamed pancakes (page 32).

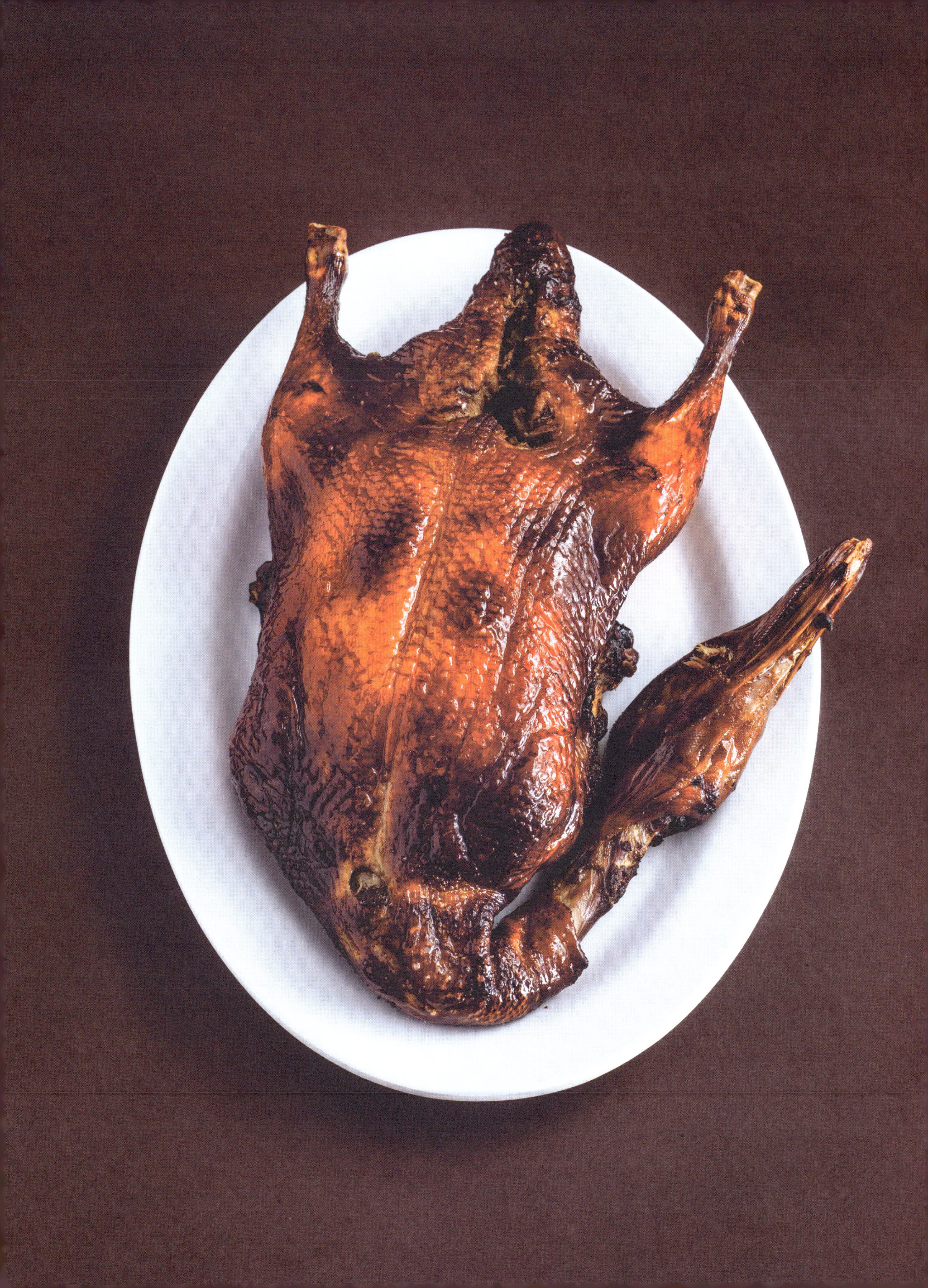

Understanding

LOR ARK
5-FLAVOR BRAISED DUCK

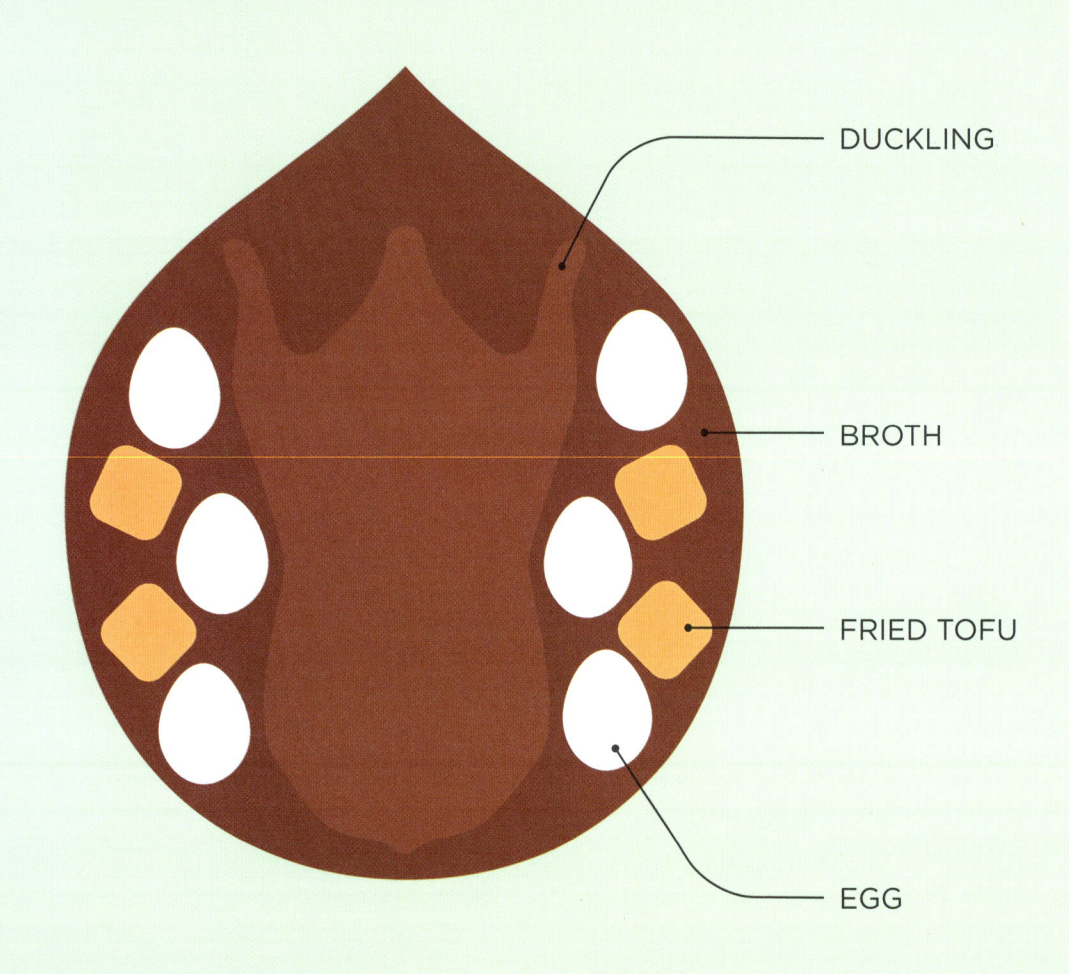

- DUCKLING
- BROTH
- FRIED TOFU
- EGG

WHAT IS IT?
Duckling (or duck) slow braised in a spicy broth made of soy sauce. At the end of the cooking time, hard-boiled eggs and cubes of tofu are added to soak up the flavors of the broth.

ORIGIN
This is a traditional dish of *teochew* cuisine (originating from Chaozhou at the eastern end of Canton province).

COMPLETION TIME
Preparation time: 45 minutes
Cooking time: 2½ hours
Storage: 4 days. Reheat the duck in its broth for 10 to 15 minutes over low heat.

SERVING
Serve this dish with rice. Reduce a little broth and combine with starch mixed with a little liquid to obtain a sauce with a coating consistency. It can also be served with egg noodles or rice noodles (pages 22 and 26). The broth can then be enjoyed as a soup. Arrange the pieces of duck, a halved egg, and two cubes of tofu in the noodles. Add the broth, fried garlic, cilantro, and scallions as a topping. If the broth is too strong, add a little water.

USEFUL TIP
If you cannot find galangal, replace it with the same amount of ginger.

Learning

SHAOXING RICE WINE
Fermented glutinous rice wine. Choose the Pagoda brand (blue label).

FRIED TOFU CUBES
They have a porous interior. Used in stews and dishes to act as a sponge for soaking up flavors. Sold vacuum-packed in the refrigerated section of Asian supermarkets or in bulk in Chinese supermarkets.

DRIED MANDARIN PEEL
It can be replaced with fresh organic orange or mandarin zest.

FIVE-SPICE POWDER
A powdered mix containing coriander seeds, fennel, anise, cinnamon, black or Szechuan pepper, and cloves.

DARK SOY SAUCE
Less salty than classic soy sauce and thicker and slightly sweet. It is mainly used to lend more color and flavor to dishes.

SERVES 4 TO 6

SAUCE
1 onion
1 head of garlic
1¾ ounces / 50 g fresh ginger
1¾ ounces / 50 g galangal (optional)
1 bunch of cilantro (stems or stems and leaves)

1 cleaned duckling (about 3½ pounds / 1.6 kg net weight)
3 tablespoons / 50 g organic cane sugar or unrefined brown sugar
1¾ ounces / 50 g rock sugar
2½ tablespoons / 15 g salt
- ¼ cup / 60 ml dark soy sauce
Scant ½ cup / 100 ml soy sauce
- Scant ½ cup / 100 ml Shaoxing wine
3 bay leaves
2 sticks cinnamon
3 star anise pods
6 cloves
1 teaspoon peppercorns of your choice

- ⅓ ounce / 10 g dried mandarin peel or organic orange peel
- 1 level teaspoon five-spice powder
6 eggs
- 7 ounces / 200 g fried tofu cubes or firm tofu

Making

LOR ARK

1   Prepare the sauce: Peel and quarter the onion. Cut the garlic head lengthwise in half. Rinse the ginger and galangal, if using, then thinly slice them. Tie the cilantro in a bundle using kitchen twine.

2   Place the duck on a large baking sheet. Bring 6 cups / 1.5 L water to a boil and ladle the boiling water over the duck, turning it over while doing so. Drain, and remove any visible feathers.

3   In a large heavy pot, melt the sugars. Once they begin to caramelize, add the salt and deglaze with the soy sauces and wine. Stir to combine. Add bay leaves, cinnamon sticks, star anise pods, cloves, peppercorns, mandarin peel, and five-spice powder. Add 2 quarts / 2 L water.

4   Add the duck and cook for 2½ hours at a low boil, turning the duck over from time to time.

5   Meanwhile, cook the eggs in boiling water for 7 minutes. Immerse them in cold water, then carefully peel them. After 2 hours of cooking the duck, add the cooked eggs and the tofu to the pot. Continue cooking for 30 minutes.

6   Test the doneness of the duck by using a chopstick to pierce the leg. The chopstick should sink into the meat with no resistance. Remove the duck and aromatics from the pot. Strain the broth. Skim off any fat from the surface of the broth using a spoon. Serve with tofu and eggs on the side.

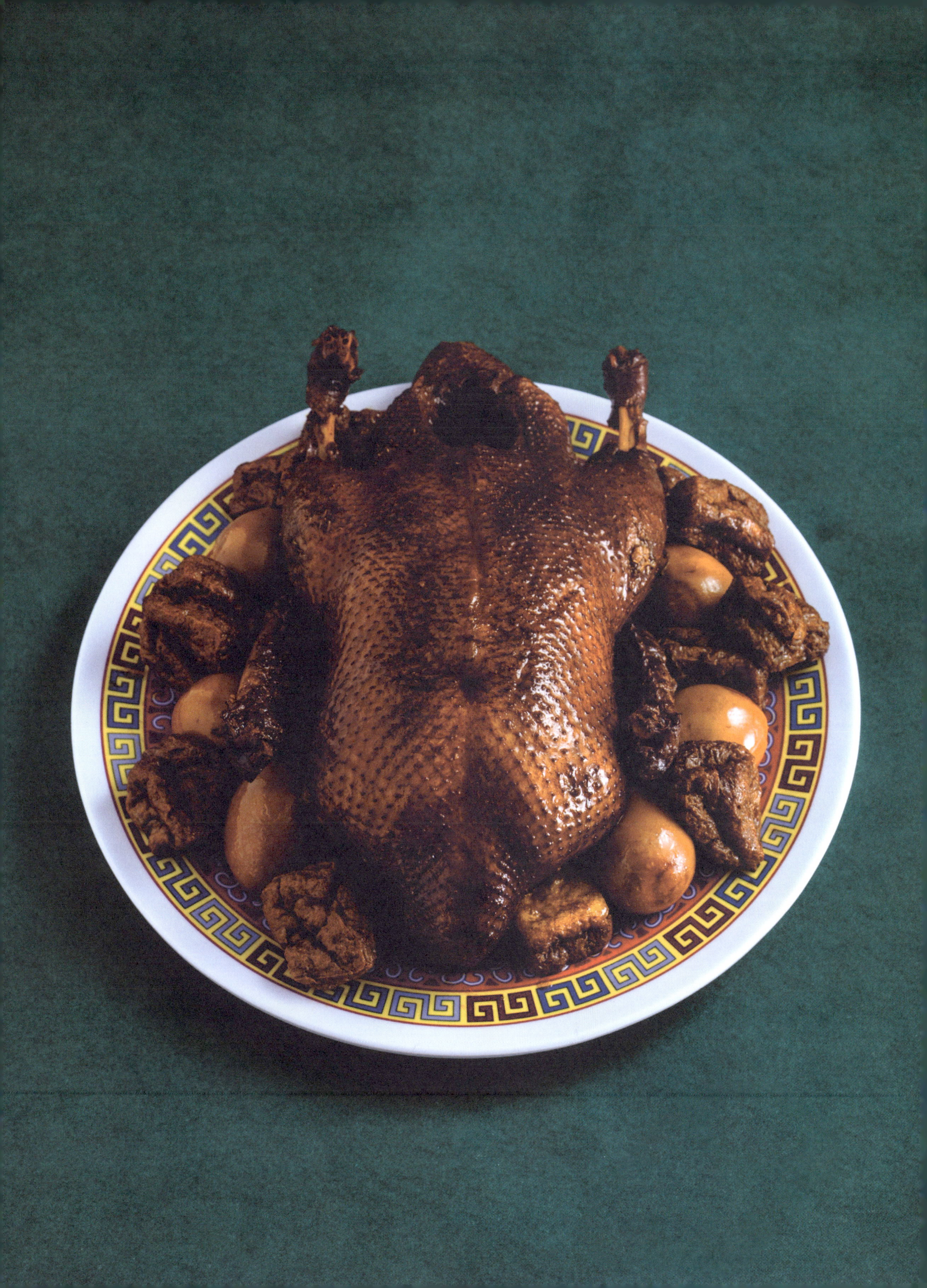

Understanding

ZHĀNGCHÁ YĀ
TEA-SMOKED DUCK

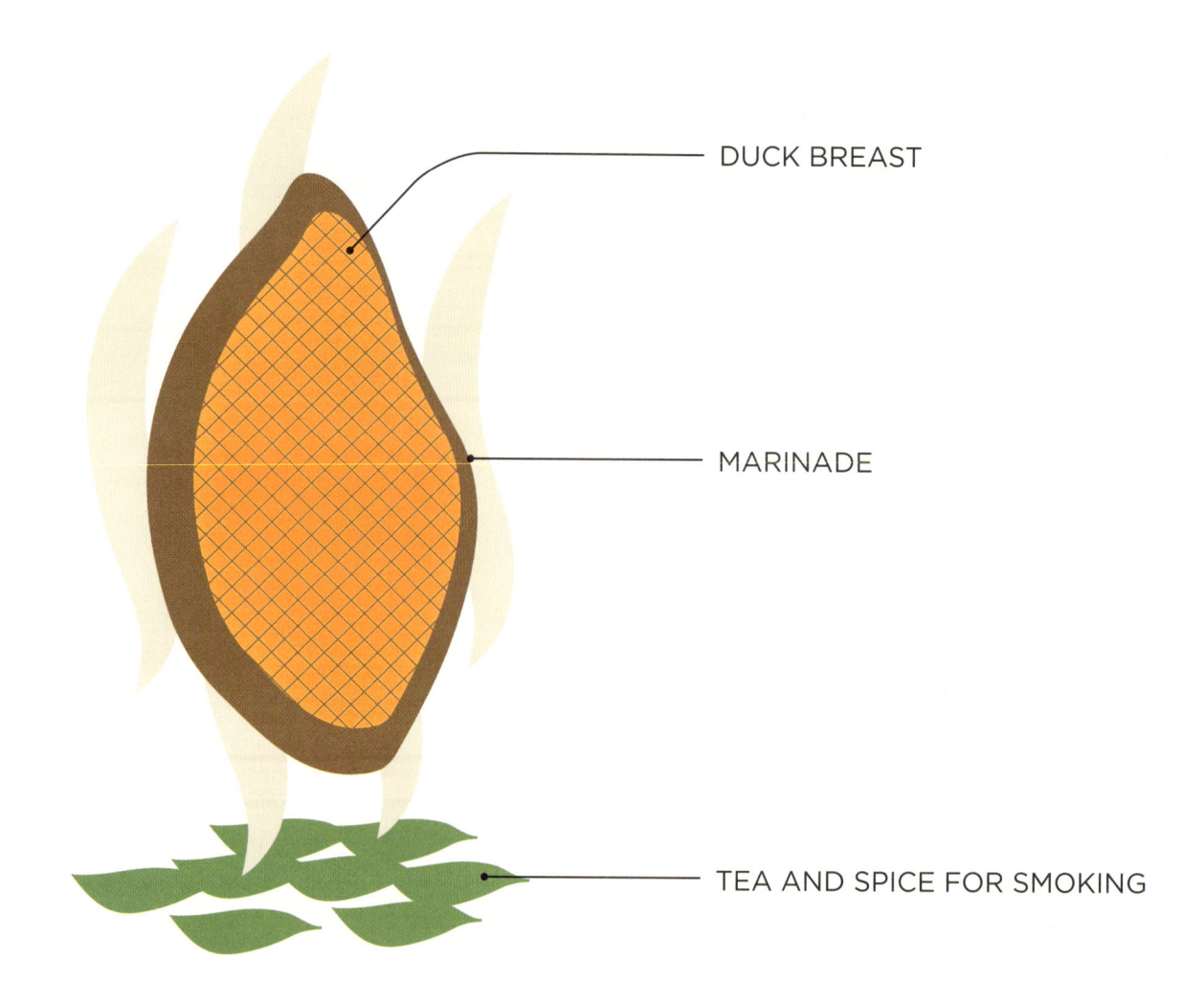

- DUCK BREAST
- MARINADE
- TEA AND SPICE FOR SMOKING

WHAT IS IT?
A marinated duck breast smoked with tea leaves and spices.

ORIGIN
Tea-smoked duck is associated with the Sichuan region. Smoking was once used to preserve food.

COMPLETION TIME
Preparation time: 10 minutes
Resting time: Overnight
Smoking time: 20 minutes
Storage: 3 to 4 days in the refrigerator, wrapped in plastic wrap.

SPECIAL EQUIPMENT
Dutch oven
A grilling rack the same dimensions as the Dutch oven

SERVING
Serve as charcuterie, as a starter with cucumber salad (page 176), or as a filling for spring pancakes (page 190).

Learning

SERVES 2 TO 4

1 duck breast (about 1 pound 2 ounces / 500 g)

MARINADE

2 tablespoons mei kuei lu chiew (sorghum liquor) or Shaoxing wine

½ teaspoon five-spice powder

½ teaspoon ground Szechuan pepper

3 teaspoons organic cane sugar

1 teaspoon salt

1 ounce / 30 g black or green tea leaves

¼ cup / 50 g rice

¼ packed cup / 50 g brown sugar

4 sticks cinnamon, crushed

1 tablespoon Szechuan pepper

5 star anise pods

6 strips orange peel

1 Trim the duck breast if necessary, removing excess fat. Score the skin in a crisscross pattern. Do not cut all the way through the skin.

2 Make the marinade: Combine the mei kuei lu chiew, five-spice powder, Szechuan pepper, sugar, and salt. Coat the duck breast with the marinade, then place it on a plate skin side up and refrigerate overnight to marinate.

3 Place a skillet over medium heat and place the duck breast skin side down in the skillet. Do not add any additional fat. Cook for 3 minutes. Transfer the duck breast to a rack.

4 Cover the bottom of a Dutch oven or lidded wok with foil. Combine the tea leaves, rice, brown sugar, cinnamon sticks, Szechuan pepper, star anise pods, and orange peels for the smoke mixture, and place the mixture in the bottom of the pot. Place the rack and duck skin side up on top, and cover with the lid. Heat over high heat. When smoke begins to appear, reduce the heat a little. Let smoke for 10 minutes. Turn off the heat, and let stand for an additional 10 minutes without opening the lid. Serve the breast sliced.

Understanding

JIÀOHUĀ JĪ
BEGGAR'S CHICKEN

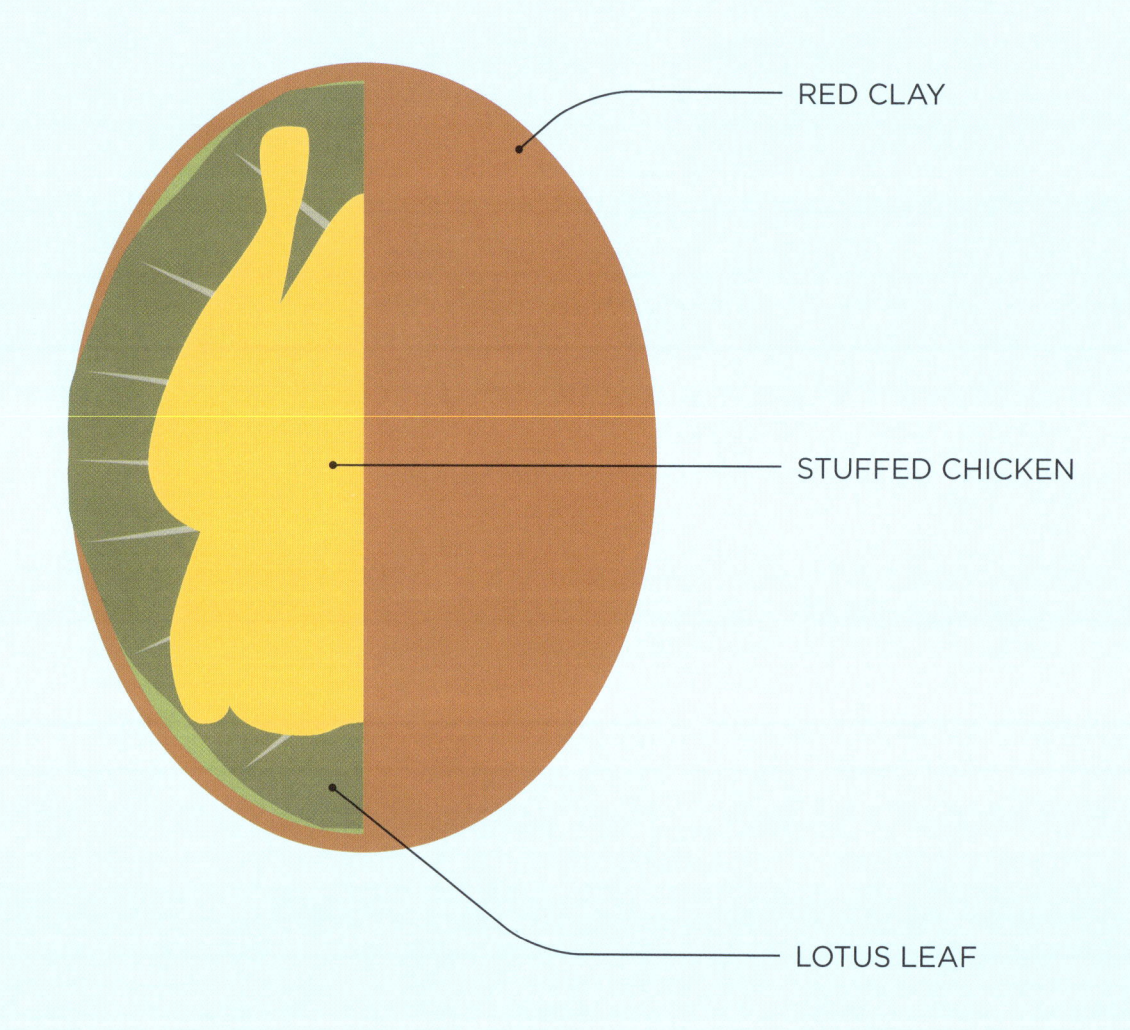

- RED CLAY
- STUFFED CHICKEN
- LOTUS LEAF

WHAT IS IT?

A whole chicken, marinated and stuffed, then wrapped in lotus leaves and encased in a clay crust. It is then baked for a long time in the oven until tender and juicy.

ORIGIN

The dish is native to eastern China (Jiangsu and Zhejiang provinces). Legend has it that during the Qing Dynasty (1644–1911), a hungry beggar stole a chicken. He was chased by the farmer to the edge of a river where he hid the chicken in the mud. When he returned to collect his spoils, he placed the chicken, still covered in mud, directly on the fire. A solid clay crust formed around the chicken. Once broken open, the feathers fell off, revealing a tender, fragrant meat.

COMPLETION TIME

Preparation time: 1 hour 20 minutes
Resting time: 48 hours
Cooking time: 3½ hours
Storage: 3 days in the refrigerator

SPECIAL EQUIPMENT

Large freezer bag

SKILLS TO MASTER

Rehydrating mushrooms (page 280)
Softening lotus leaves (page 280)

VARIATION

Replace the clay with 4½ pounds / 2 kg of bread dough or make a salt crust by mixing 2¼ pounds / 1 kg of flour with 2¼ pounds / 1 kg of coarse salt and 3 large / 150 g eggs. Add 1⅔ cups / 400 ml water little by little and knead to form a dough. Adjust the amount of water until the dough is somewhat soft. Set aside in the refrigerator to chill slightly to make it easier to roll out.

Learning

LOTUS LEAVES

A hydrophobic leaf, which allows for airtight cooking. Used to flavor mixtures (it contributes a little earthiness). Sold dried. They must be rehydrated before use.

DARK SOY SAUCE

Less salty than classic soy sauce and thicker and slightly sweet. It is mainly used to lend more color and flavor to dishes.

CHINESE BACON

Pork belly marinated in spices and soy sauce, cut into strips. Sold vacuum-packed in the refrigerated section.

SERVES 4

MARINADE

7 large cloves garlic
Scant ½ cup / 100 ml Shaoxing wine
1 tablespoon five-spice powder
8 tablespoons / 120 ml soy sauce
2 tablespoons dark soy sauce
- 1 tablespoon oyster sauce
1 teaspoon salt

1 whole chicken
(about 3¾ pounds / 1.7 kg)

FILLING

9 small dried or fresh shiitake mushrooms
1 small onion
10 cloves garlic
¾ ounce / 20 g fresh ginger
- 3½ ounces / 100 g Chinese bacon or classic smoked slab bacon
4 tablespoons / 60 ml neutral-flavor oil of your choice (sunflower, peanut)
3½ ounces / 100 g cooked chestnuts
½ teaspoon organic cane sugar
Freshly ground black pepper

- 4 lotus leaves
4½ pounds / 2 kg untreated clay

Making

JIĀOHUĀ JĪ

1 Two days before, make the marinade: Press the garlic. Combine the garlic with the wine, five-spice powder, soy sauces, oyster sauce, and salt. Fill the chicken with half the marinade. Add the remaining marinade to a large freezer bag. Place the chicken in the bag, massage the bag to distribute the marinade over the chicken, and place the bag on a large platter. Refrigerate for 48 hours.

2 On the day of cooking, make the filling: Rehydrate the mushrooms (page 280). Chop the onion, press the garlic, and cut the ginger into very thin sticks up to about ¼ inch / 5 mm long. Remove the rough ends of the shiitake stems, then slice the shiitake. Cut the bacon into thin strips.

3 Remove the chicken from the bag, place it on a large rimmed baking sheet, and set it aside at room temperature. Collect the marinade in a bowl. Heat 2 tablespoons of the oil in a wok or skillet. Sauté the onion and bacon for 1 to 2 minutes. Add the shiitake, garlic, ginger, chestnuts, and sugar. Add ¼ cup / 60 ml of the marinade, and cook for 2 minutes. Taste, and adjust the seasoning, if necessary. Set aside at room temperature.

4 Soften the lotus leaves (page 280). Stuff the chicken with the filling and rub the skin with the remaining oil. Place the chicken breast side down in the center of an open lotus leaf. Wrap the chicken in the lotus leaf.

5 Place the wrapped chicken on another lotus leaf, with the folded side facing down. Wrap with the lotus leaf. Repeat with the remaining leaves. Using kitchen twine, tie the leaves tightly to secure them around the chicken.

6 Roll out the clay to about 12 by 14 inches / 30 by 35 cm. Place the wrapped chicken on top, breast side down. Fold the clay over the chicken and tightly seal it using wet hands.

7 Preheat the oven to 325°F / 160°C. Place the chicken seam side down on a parchment paper-lined baking sheet. Bake for 3½ hours. Set aside for 15 minutes. Break open the clay crust using a small mallet or hammer. Serve with rice.

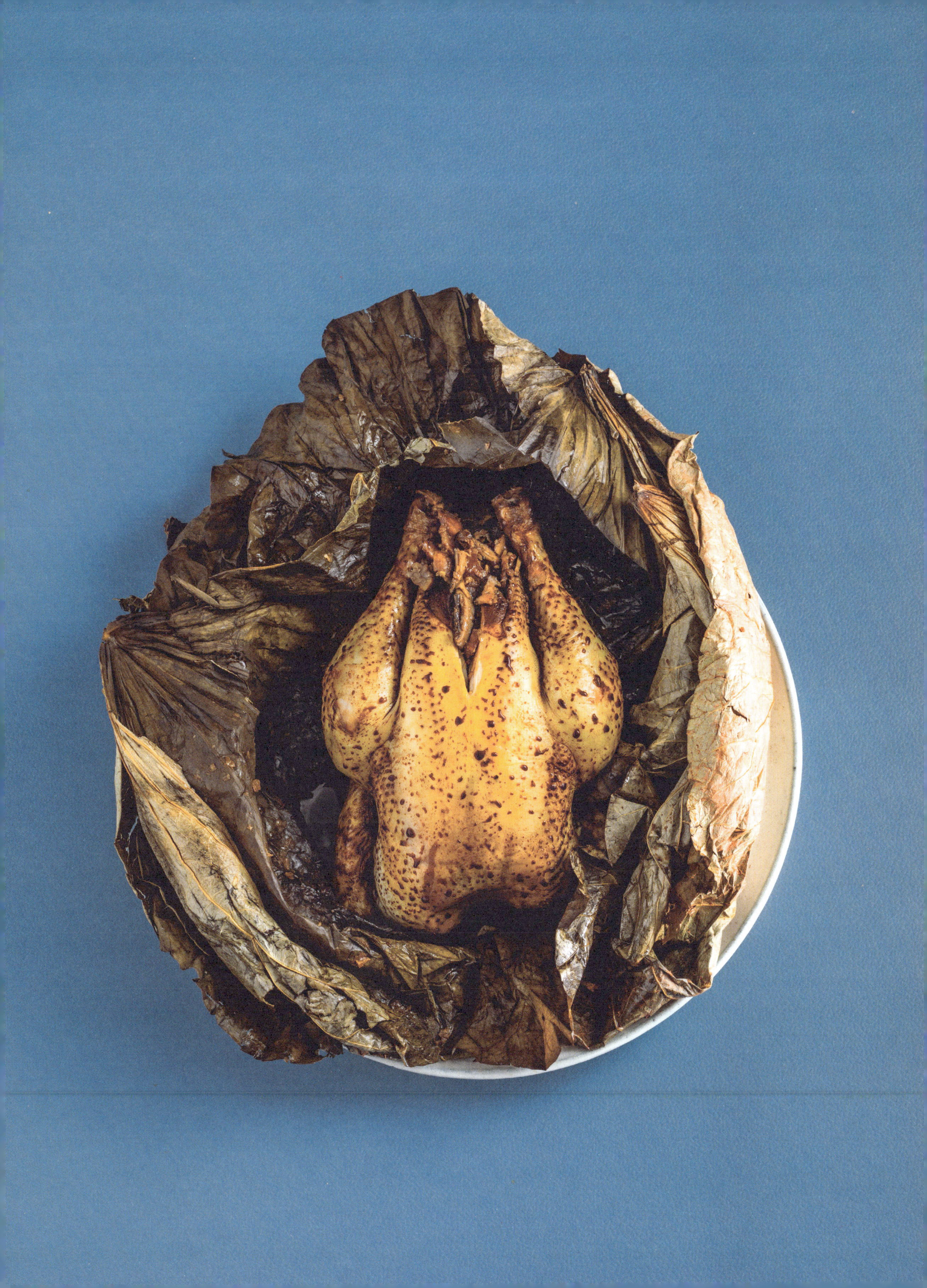

Understanding

ZUÌ JĪ
DRUNKEN CHICKEN

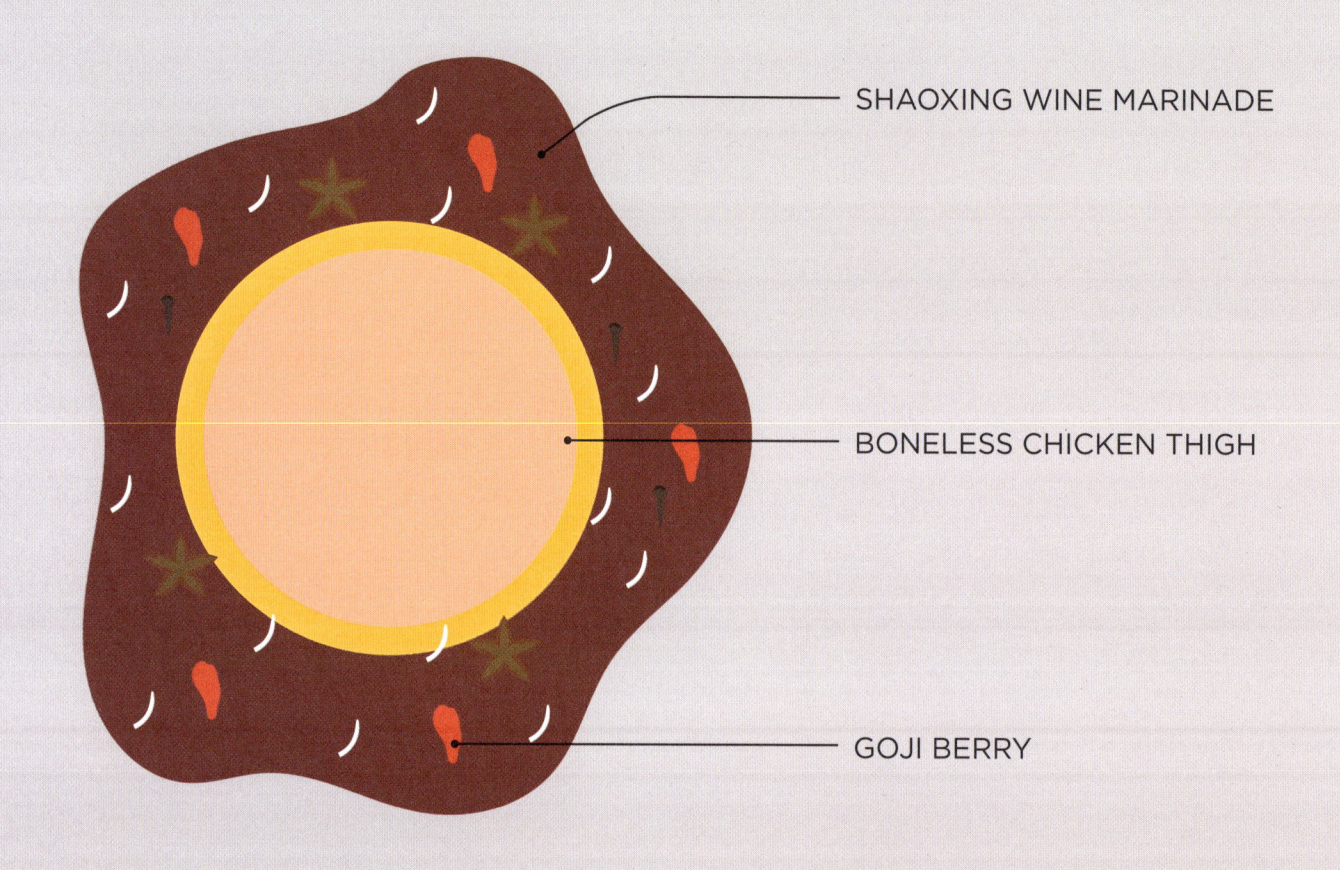

———— SHAOXING WINE MARINADE

———— BONELESS CHICKEN THIGH

———— GOJI BERRY

WHAT IS IT?
A boneless chicken thigh, marinated, then rolled into a bundle and cooked in a broth to which Shaoxing wine is added.

COMPLETION TIME
Preparation time: 1 hour
Resting time: 48 hours
Cooking time: 45 minutes
Storage: The entire bundle can be refrigerated for up to 3 days in its marinade.

SERVING
This dish is served cold as a starter. It is particularly popular during the humid summer months in the Jiangnan region where it originates (Shanghai, Hangzhou, Suzhou, and the surrounding area). Traditionally, the chicken is cooked whole and then cut into pieces, with the bones.

Learning

SHAOXING RICE WINE
Fermented glutinous rice wine. Choose the Pagoda brand (blue label).

GINGER
A rhizome native to southern Asia.

GOJI BERRY
Considered a superfood with antioxidant properties. It has a mild, slightly sweet flavor, with notes of cranberry and cherry.

STAR ANISE
It has an aniseed flavor, with hints of licorice. Aids digestion. Often used in stews. It is one of the ingredients in five-spice powder.

SERVES 4

2 large free-range chicken thighs
½ teaspoon salt

BROTH
1 small onion
- 1 ounce / 30 g fresh ginger
6 cups / 1.5 L water
- 1 star anise pod
2 cloves
1 teaspoon salt

Freshly ground black pepper
- 1 tablespoon plus 1 teaspoon / 20 ml Shaoxing wine

MARINADE
1 cup / 240 ml reduced broth (see step 5)
¾ cup / 180 ml Shaoxing wine
1½ tablespoons organic cane sugar
2 tablespoons soy sauce
- 2 tablespoons goji berries

1 scallion

Making

ZUÌ JĪ

1 One to two days before, debone the chicken thighs (page 34) and set the bones aside. Make the broth: Cut the onion in half and cut the ginger into strips. In a medium saucepan, bring the onion, ginger, water, star anise pod, cloves, salt, and thigh bones to a low boil. Skim off any impurities from the surface. Reduce the heat, and cook at a gentle simmer while preparing the remainder of the ingredients.

2 Place the deboned chicken thighs on a separate cutting board, skin side down. Make incisions in the meat without cutting through it. Season with the salt and some pepper. Sprinkle the wine over the thighs and set aside to marinate for 15 minutes.

3 Roll up the thighs tightly, starting at the narrowest part, into a cylindrical bundle and secure them with kitchen twine.

4 Place the bundle into the simmering broth. Add a little water, if necessary, to cover them. Bring to a boil and cook for 5 minutes. Turn off the heat, cover, and let cool for 40 minutes. The chicken will finish cooking gently in the residual heat, making the meat much more tender.

5 Make the marinade: In a small saucepan over medium heat, add 2 cups / 480 ml of cooking broth from the pot with the thigh bundles and cook to reduce by half (you should have about 1 cup / 240 ml). Add the wine, sugar, and soy sauce and cook for 2 to 3 minutes. Taste, and adjust with salt, if necessary. Transfer the chicken to a medium-size airtight container. Add the marinade to cover the chicken. Add the goji berries. Let cool, then refrigerate for 24 to 48 hours.

6 When the chicken is marinated, cut the scallion into three sections. Cut each section into strips. Set them aside in a bowl of ice water. Drain the chicken, remove the twine, and cut the thighs into slices of about ¼ inch / 4 to 5 mm. Transfer the slices to a deep serving dish. Add the marinade over them and top with the drained scallion.

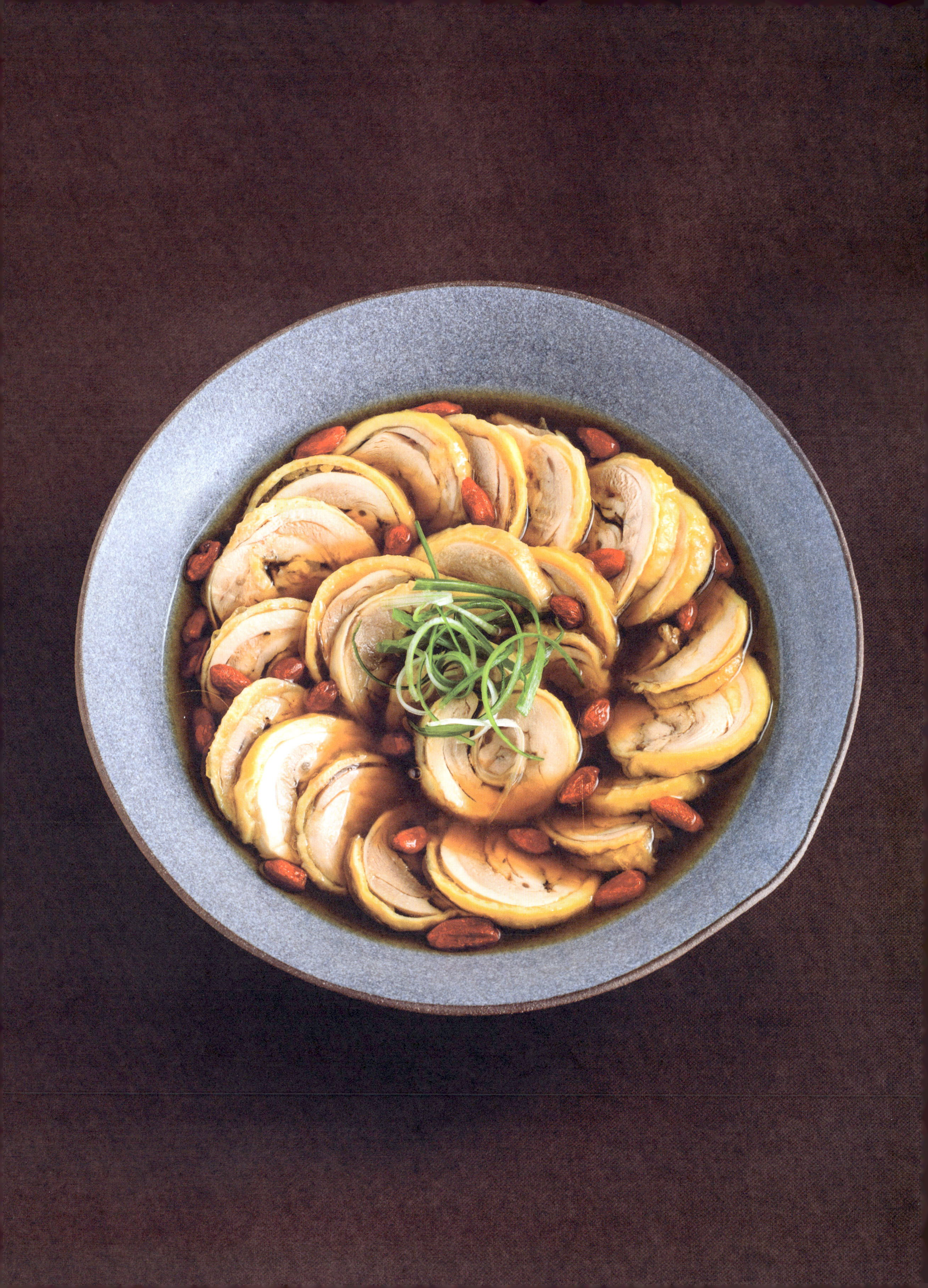

Understanding

GŌNG BĂO JĪ DĪNG
KUNG PAO CHICKEN

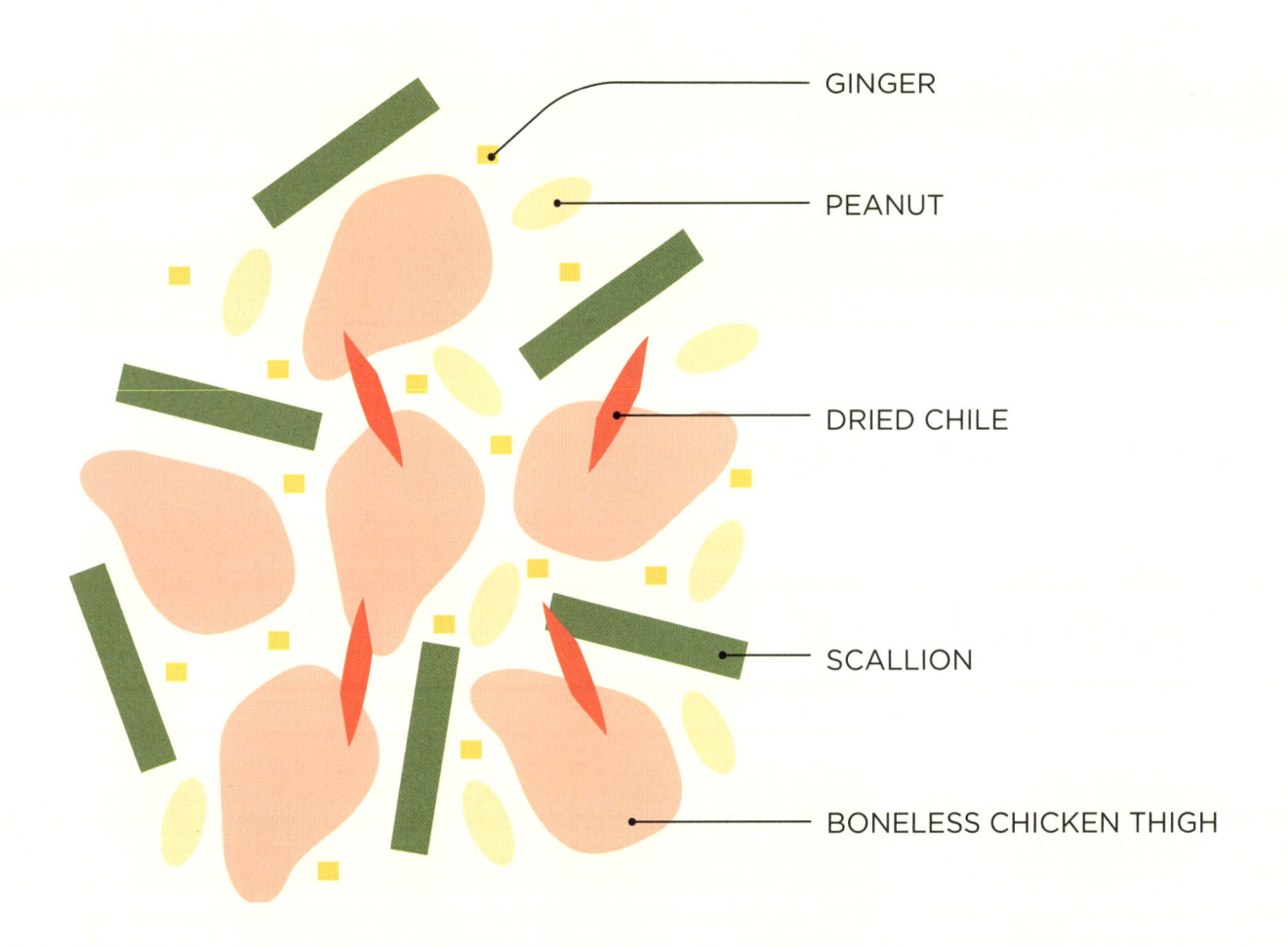

- GINGER
- PEANUT
- DRIED CHILE
- SCALLION
- BONELESS CHICKEN THIGH

WHAT IS IT?

A stir-fried chicken dish with dried chile peppers, Szechuan pepper, and peanuts. Its balance between spicy, salty, sweet, and tangy makes it a popular dish.

ORIGIN

This dish is attributed to Ding Baozhen (Qing Dynasty 1644–1911), a high-ranking official who had the title of *gongbao* ("palace guardian"). The story says that his cook, influenced by his official travel across China, created this dish.

COMPLETION TIME

Preparation time: 35 minutes
Resting time: 3 hours
Cooking time: 15 minutes
Storage: It can be refrigerated for up to 2 days, but the peanuts will soften

SKILLS TO MASTER

Boning a chicken thigh (page 34)
Cutting into julienne (page 281)

SERVES 4 TO 6

1 pound 2 ounces / 500 g free-range chicken thighs, deboned (page 34)

MARINADE

1 heaping tablespoon cornstarch
1 tablespoon Shaoxing wine
1 tablespoon soy sauce
½ teaspoon salt

SAUCE

1 tablespoon soy sauce
1 teaspoon dark soy sauce
2 tablespoons Chinkiang black rice vinegar
1 tablespoon organic cane sugar
¼ cup / 60 ml Basic Broth (page 38) or water

Learning

1 teaspoon Szechuan pepper
4 cloves garlic
¾ ounce / 20 g fresh ginger
12 dried chile peppers
5 scallions
¼ cup / 60 ml peanut oil
½ cup / 80 g shelled and peeled raw peanuts

1 Cut the chicken thighs into even, bite-size pieces and set aside in a large bowl. Make the marinade: Combine the cornstarch, wine, and soy sauce. Add the salt. Pour the marinade over the chicken. Stir to combine, and refrigerate for at least 3 hours.

2 Make the sauce: Combine the soy sauces, vinegar, sugar, and broth.

3 Crush the Szechuan pepper using a mortar and pestle. Set aside. Chop or press the garlic. Cut the ginger into thin julienne (page 281) and then into small cubes. Cut the chile peppers in half or in thirds using scissors, and remove the seeds. Cut the scallions into ⅓- to ⅔-inch / 1 to 1.5 cm sections. Separate the white and green sections.

4 In a wok over medium heat, heat the oil and brown the peanuts for 2 to 3 minutes, stirring constantly. Remove from the heat.

5 In the same oil, sauté the garlic and chile. When the garlic begins to brown, add the Szechuan pepper and ginger. Stir, add the chicken, and cook for 4 to 5 minutes, or until browned. Add the scallion whites and the sauce. Cook for several minutes; the sauce should thicken to a coating consistency. Check the chicken for doneness and add a little water, if necessary. Turn off the heat, add the peanuts and scallion greens. Stir to combine. Serve with rice (page 12).

Understanding
SĀN BĒI JĪ
THREE-CUP CHICKEN

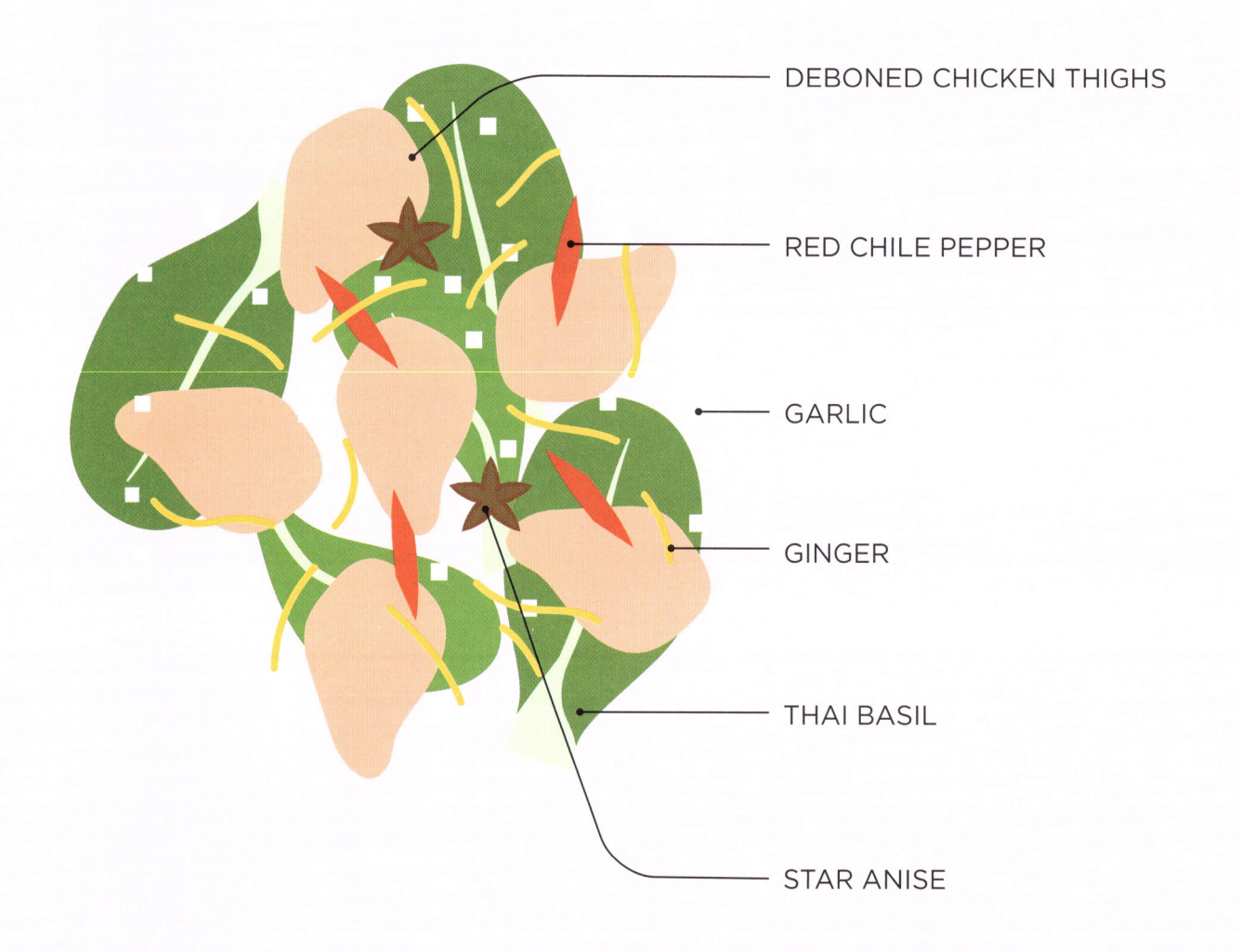

- DEBONED CHICKEN THIGHS
- RED CHILE PEPPER
- GARLIC
- GINGER
- THAI BASIL
- STAR ANISE

WHAT IS IT?
A chicken dish simmered in a sweet and sour sauce made with soy sauce, rice wine, and sesame oil.

ORIGIN
It is native to the province of Jiangxi, southwest of Shanghai. It was adopted and popularized in Taiwan where it became a staple of Taiwanese cuisine. The dish dates to the Song Dynasty (960–1279). A Chinese general, Wen Tianxiang, a prisoner of the Mongols, is said to have sympathized with his captors. On the day of his execution, they cooked him a dish of chicken with the only three ingredients they had available: lard, wine, and soy sauce. The recipe has, of course, evolved over time. The contents of the three cups (measured as ¾ cup / 180 ml each) have been adjusted. The lard was replaced with sesame oil, and the addition of sugar and vinegar balances the flavors.

COMPLETION TIME
Preparation time: 20 minutes
Cooking time: 45 minutes
Storage: 2 to 3 days in the refrigerator

SPECIAL EQUIPMENT
Wok

SKILL TO MASTER
Cutting into julienne (page 281)

VARIATIONS
You can also remove the skin from the chicken. In this case, double the amount of oil used for cooking.

Learning

SERVES 6

6 free-range chicken thighs, deboned (page 34)

1¾ ounces / 50 g fresh ginger

8 cloves garlic

4 red chile peppers (or to taste)

2 tablespoons neutral-flavor oil of your choice (sunflower, peanut)

2 star anise pods

3 packed tablespoons / 40 g brown sugar

⅔ cup / 150 ml rice wine (kwangtung mijiu) or Shaoxing wine

⅓ cup / 80 ml soy sauce

3 tablespoons / 45 ml white rice vinegar

2 tablespoons sesame oil

Freshly ground black pepper

1 large bunch of Thai basil

1 Cut each chicken thigh into six large bite-size pieces (not too small).

2 Peel and cut the ginger into julienne (page 281). Slice the garlic. Halve the chile peppers lengthwise and remove the seeds.

3 In a wok or large Dutch oven, heat the oil. When the oil is hot, add the chicken pieces skin side down and brown them on each side (about 10 to 12 minutes). Remove, and drain the grease from the wok.

4 Add the garlic, ginger, star anise pods, and brown sugar. Sauté for 2 to 3 minutes without adding fat.

5 Stir, deglaze with the wine, then bring to a boil. Add the chicken pieces back to the wok. Add 3 tablespoons / 45 ml water, the soy sauce, vinegar, sesame oil, and chile peppers. Season with pepper, cover, and cook for about 30 minutes over medium heat, stirring occasionally. At the end of cooking time, the sauce should be reduced and thickened. Off the heat, add the basil leaves. Stir. Serve with white rice (page 12).

Understanding

CHAR SIU
LACQUERED PORK

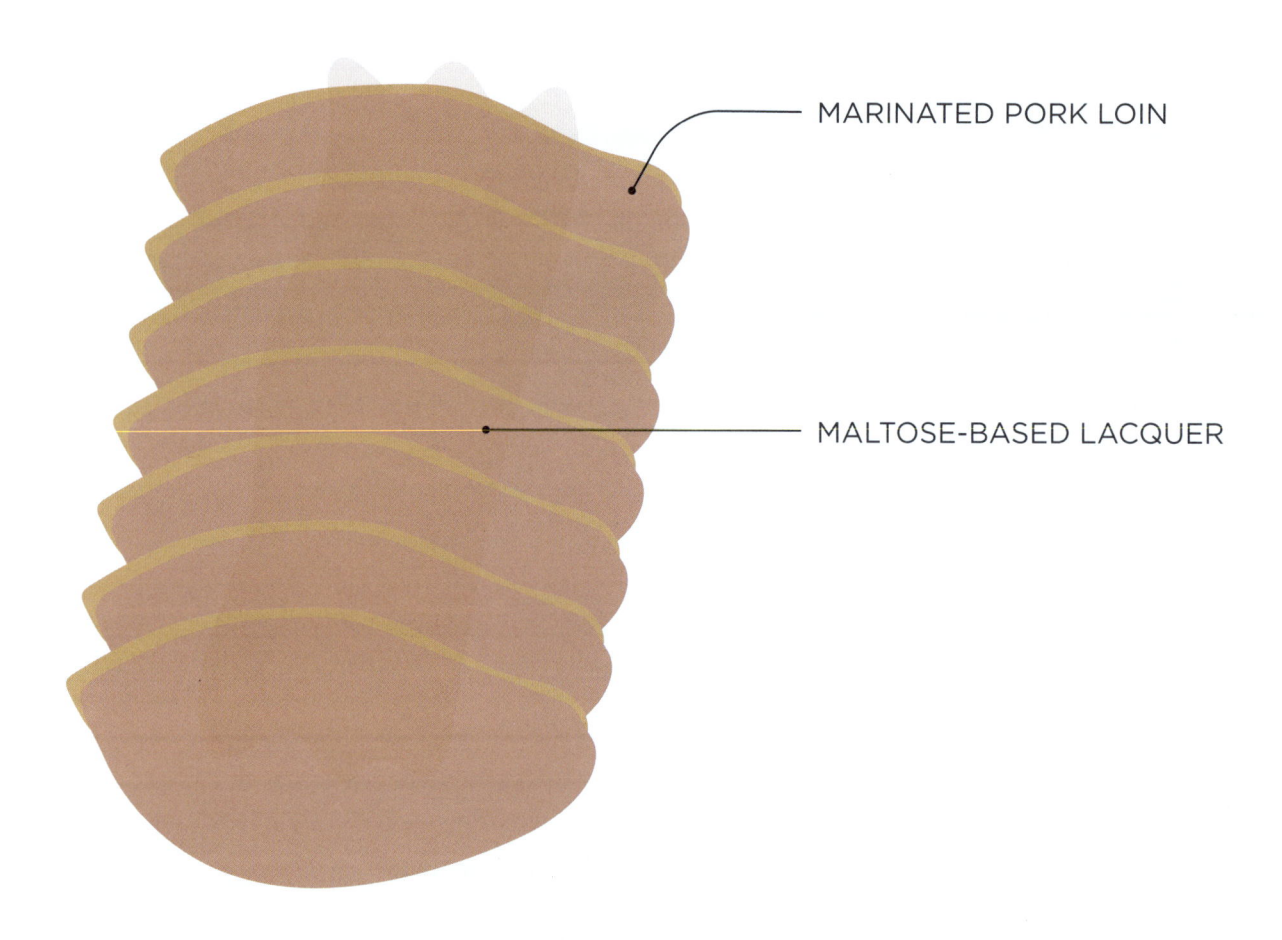

— MARINATED PORK LOIN

— MALTOSE-BASED LACQUER

WHAT IS IT?
Pieces of pork loin marinated in a mixture of sauces, honey, spices, and sometimes alcohol, roasted in the oven and brushed with a lacquer glaze.

ORIGIN
This is a great classic of Cantonese rotisserie. Recognizable by its red color and sweet and savory taste. Char siu literally means "fork roasted" and refers to the traditional method of cooking where pork was threaded onto forks before being roasted over an open fire.

COMPLETION TIME
Preparation time: 10 minutes
Resting time: Overnight
Cooking time: 40 minutes
Storage: Once cooked, it can be refrigerated for 3 to 4 days. Reheat, covered with foil, in a preheated oven at 300°F / 150°C for 15 to 20 minutes. Add a little marinade to the bottom of the dish to prevent the meat from drying out.

SERVING
It is most often served with rice or noodles, but it is also used as a filling for baos (char siu bao), rice pancakes, or banh mi.

USEFUL TIPS
If the meat does not caramelize sufficiently, finish by roasting for 5 minutes on each side at 475°F / 250°C. Bring the remaining marinade to a boil for 2 to 3 minutes. Let cool before storing in a jar to use for char siu baos (page 72).

SERVES 4 TO 6

MARINADE
1 ounce / 30 g fresh ginger
5 cloves garlic
3 tablespoons / 45 ml hoisin sauce
Scant ¼ cup / 75 g acacia honey

Learning

3 tablespoons / 45 ml soy sauce

1½ teaspoons fermented red soybean paste

2½ packed tablespoons / 35 g brown sugar

2 tablespoons mei kuei lu chiew (sorghum liquor)

1 teaspoon five-spice powder

½ heaping teaspoon salt

½ teaspoon freshly ground black pepper

1 tablespoon beetroot powder (optional)

2¼ pounds / 1 kg pork loin

1 level teaspoon baking soda

GLAZE

3½ ounces / 100 g maltose

1 Make the marinade: Finely chop the ginger and crush the garlic cloves (page 281). In a saucepan, combine the ginger, garlic, hoisin sauce, honey, soy sauce, soybean paste, brown sugar, mei kuei lu chiew, five-spice powder, salt, pepper, and beetroot powder, if using. Bring to a low boil for 2 minutes. Mix well. Let cool.

2 Cut the pork into 4 or 5 pieces.

3 Arrange the pork in a large dish. Combine the baking soda into the cooled marinade and pour it over the meat. Cover with plastic wrap and refrigerate for at least 12 hours.

4 Preheat the oven to 400°F / 200°C. Heat the maltose until liquefied. Mix with a scant ½ cup / 100 ml of the marinade. Arrange the pork on a rack over a large baking sheet filled with a little water. Brush the meat with the maltose mixture. Bake for 20 minutes, brushing regularly with the glaze. Flip the pieces and continue cooking for 20 minutes, brushing frequently. As soon as the pork ends start to caramelize, remove the pork. Set aside for 10 minutes, then slice.

Understanding

SIU YUK
CRISPY PORK

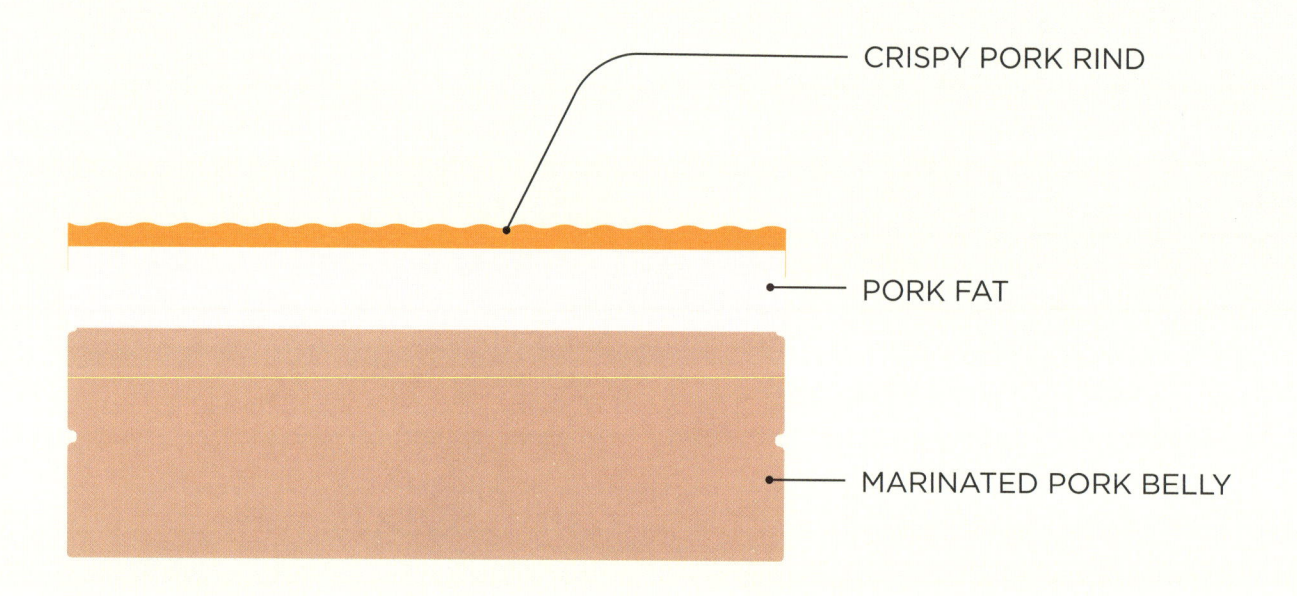

--- CRISPY PORK RIND

--- PORK FAT

--- MARINATED PORK BELLY

WHAT IS IT?
A piece of pork belly with pierced and marinated meat. The moisture is extracted from the rind by pricking and salting it. The pork belly is then slowly cooked in its own fat and grilled until the rind becomes crispy.

ORIGIN
This is a flagship dish of the Cantonese rotisserie.

COMPLETION TIME
Preparation time: 30 minutes
Resting time: 48 hours
Cooking time: 2 hours
Storage: Enjoy it for as long as the rind is crisp.

SPECIAL EQUIPMENT
Basting brush

SERVING
The pork belly is cut into cubes, served as-is with rice, or sometimes accompanied with mustard and hoisin sauce.

USEFUL TIP
To become crisp, the rind must be as dry as possible. It should look like leather and not show any traces of moisture.

Learning

MEI KUEI LU CHIEW (SORGHUM LIQUOR)

A rose-infused sorghum liquor. It is ideal as a marinade for rotisseries and with duck.

FIVE-SPICE POWDER

A powdered mix containing coriander seeds, fennel, anise, cinnamon, black or Szechuan pepper, and cloves.

SERVES 4 TO 6

3 pounds 5 ounces / 1.5 kg pork belly, with the rind and without too much fat

MARINADE

- 2 tablespoons mei kuei lu chiew (sorghum liquor)

  2 teaspoons organic cane sugar

  ½ teaspoon salt

- ½ teaspoon five-spice powder

  1 large pinch of white pepper

  Salt

  1 large tablespoon neutral-flavor oil of your choice (sunflower, peanut)

Making

SIU YUK

1 If necessary, even out the thickness of the pork belly by removing some of the meat from the thickest parts. The piece should lie flat so that the rind cooks evenly. Wipe the rind dry with paper towels. Using a sharp skewer or the tip of a sharp knife, pierce the rind, taking care not to go all the way to the meat. Make rows of holes every ⅛ inch / 4 mm. This will allow the moisture to rise to the surface.

2 Two days before, make the marinade: Combine the mei kuei lu chiew, sugar, salt, five-spice powder, and pepper. Make incisions in the meat lengthwise every ¾ to 1 inch / 2 to 2.5 cm. Using a basting brush, brush the marinade over the meat and in the gaps, taking care not to get any on the rind.

3 Turn the meat over and wipe off the rind, if necessary. Transfer to a baking dish. Cover with a layer of salt, and refrigerate for 24 hours, uncovered, to dry.

4 The next day, scrape excess salt from the rind and wipe it with paper towels to remove all the moisture. Set aside for another 24 hours to dry.

5 The next day, preheat the oven to 300°F / 150°C. Salt the rind, add the oil, and massage the pork to distribute the salt. Place the pork rind side up on a roasting pan and roast for 1½ hours.

6 Remove the roasting pan from the oven. Increase the temperature to 425°F / 220°C. Place the pork on a rack. Protect the exposed edges of the meat using pieces of foil. Pour a little water into a roasting pan to prevent the fat from burning. Move the oven rack up a level and bake for about 30 minutes. Monitor the browning. The rind should puff and become crispy. Rotate the pan, if necessary, to help it roast evenly.

7 Let cool for 15 to 20 minutes. Turn the meat over and carve it, following the incisions. Cut the slices into cubes. Serve with rice (page 12), noodles, in a gua bao (page 242), or in a sandwich.

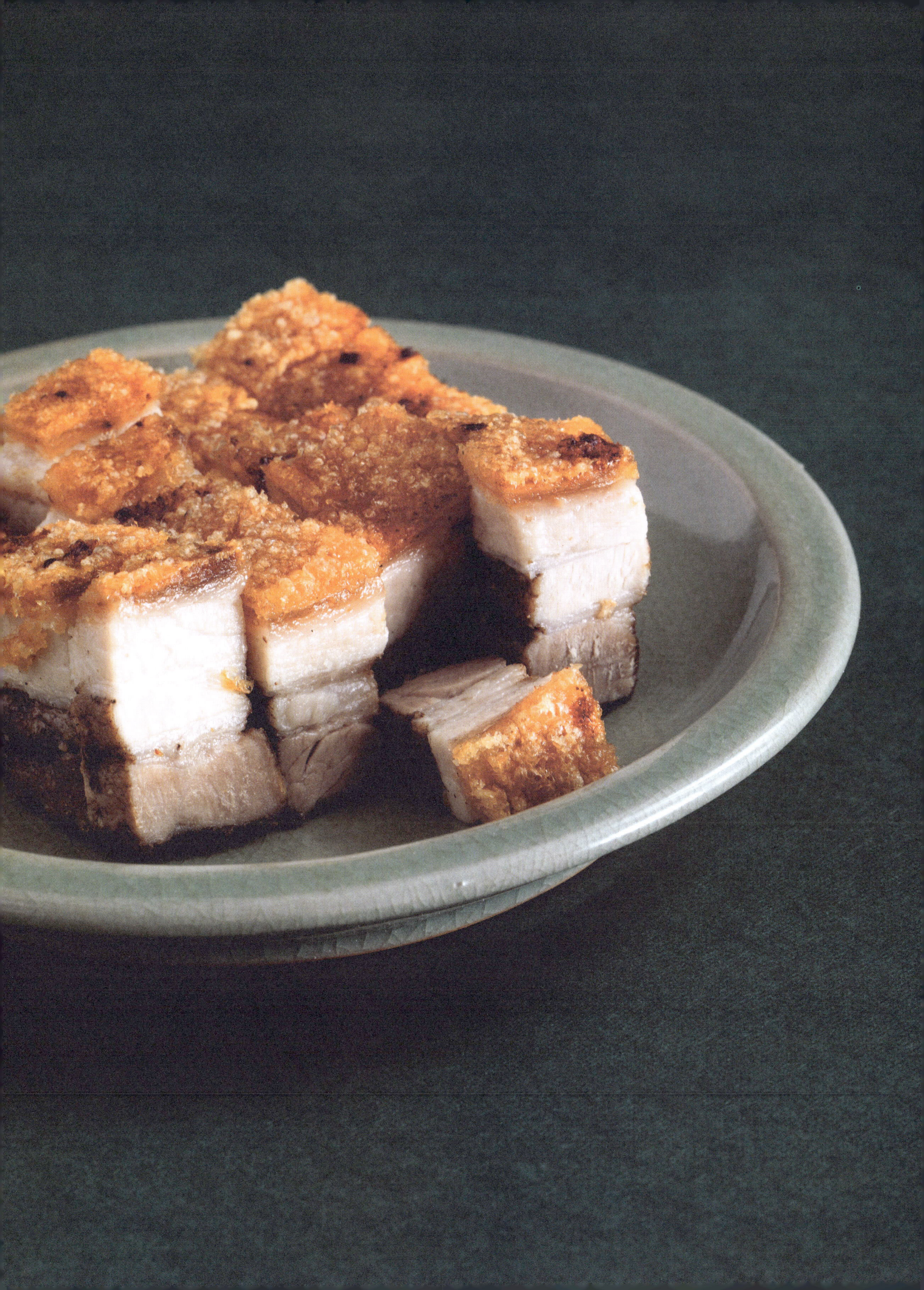

Understanding

DŌNG PŌ RÒU
DONG PO PORK

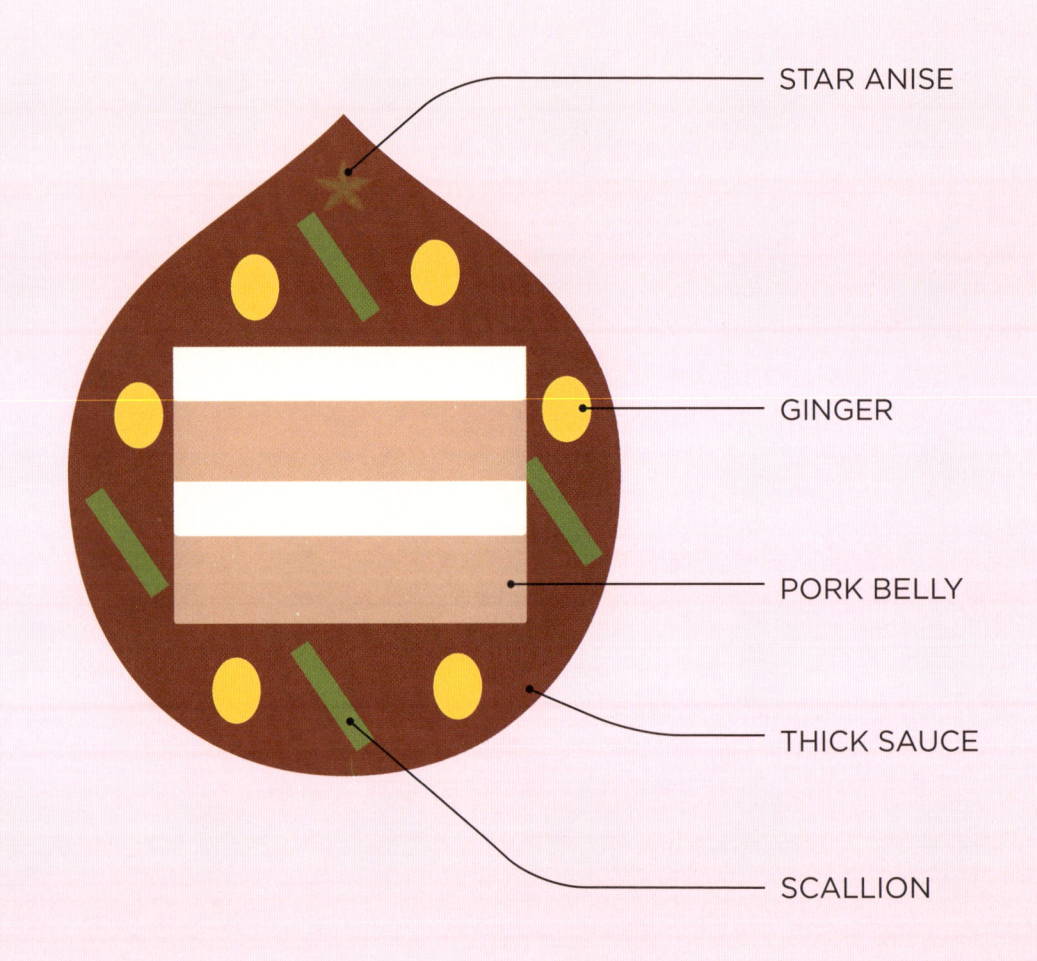

- STAR ANISE
- GINGER
- PORK BELLY
- THICK SAUCE
- SCALLION

WHAT IS IT?
Pieces of pork belly braised in a sauce made from Shaoxing wine, soy sauce, sugar, and ginger, then gently steamed to finish.

ORIGIN
This is one of the most famous dishes in Hangzhou cuisine (Zhejiang province in eastern China). The dish takes its name from Su Dongpo (1037–1101), a famous poet, writer, calligrapher, pharmacist, statesman, gourmet, and talented cook. Legend has it that the dish was created when Su Dongpo completely forgot about his pork cooking on the fire while playing a game of chess with a friend.

COMPLETION TIME
Preparation time: 20 minutes
Cooking time: 3½ hours
Storage: Dong po pork can be refrigerated for 4 to 5 days. Reheat over low heat, covered, for about 20 minutes. Add a little water, if needed.

SPECIAL EQUIPMENT
Medium-size pot
Steamer

SKILL TO MASTER
Cutting into julienne (page 281)

Learning

SHAOXING RICE WINE
Fermented glutinous rice wine. Choose the Pagoda brand (blue label).

SOY SAUCE
Choose bottles that state "natural fermentation."

DARK SOY SAUCE
Less salty than classic soy sauce and thicker and slightly sweet. It is mainly used to lend more color and flavor to dishes.

ROCK SUGAR
Yellow candy sugar. Adds shine to the dish. It has a delicate flavor and is less sweet than sugar.

SERVES 4 TO 6

2 pounds / 900 g pork belly with the rind
4 large cloves garlic
1½ ounces / 45 g fresh ginger
1 bunch of scallions (7 stems)
2 star anise pods
- 3 ounces / 80 g rock sugar
- 2 cups / 480 ml Shaoxing wine
- ⅓ cup / 80 ml soy sauce
- 2 tablespoons dark soy sauce

2 tablespoons plus 2 teaspoons / 20 g cornstarch

Making

DŌNG PŌ RÒU

1 Fill a saucepan or large wok with water. Add the pork and bring to a boil. Reduce the heat and blanch for 5 minutes to remove all the impurities.

2 Drain the pork and rinse it under cold water. Let cool, trim off excess fat, and cut it into uniform cubes about 2⅓ inches / 6 cm.

3 Crush the garlic cloves (page 281). Rinse the ginger and cut it into strips. Cut the scallions into 2-inch / 5 cm pieces. Slice four of the sections into julienne strips (page 281). Set the strips aside in a bowl of cold water.

4 Arrange the scallion sections in the bottom of a pot. Add the star anise pods. Distribute the garlic, ginger, and rock sugar over the bottom of the pot. Add the pork cubes, rind side down.

5 Add the wine and soy sauces. The meat must be submerged. Bring to a boil. Reduce the heat, cover, and simmer gently for 1½ hours. Carefully flip the pieces of pork over. Continue cooking for 30 minutes, covered, at a simmer. The pork can be served as-is, or continue with the recipe.

6 Transfer the pork to a deep dish. Add the cooking sauce. Place the dish in a steamer and continue steaming for 1½ hours. Monitor the water level of the steamer. Arrange the pork in a serving dish. Strain the sauce into a small saucepan over medium heat and reduce to 1⅔ cups / 400 ml. Dissolve the cornstarch in 2½ tablespoons / 40 ml water. Add the mixture a little at a time to the saucepan while stirring. As soon as the sauce thickens and has a coating consistency, turn off the heat. Coat the pork and garnish it with the drained julienned scallions. Serve with rice (page 12) and blanched greens. The sauce will be enough to season the vegetables.

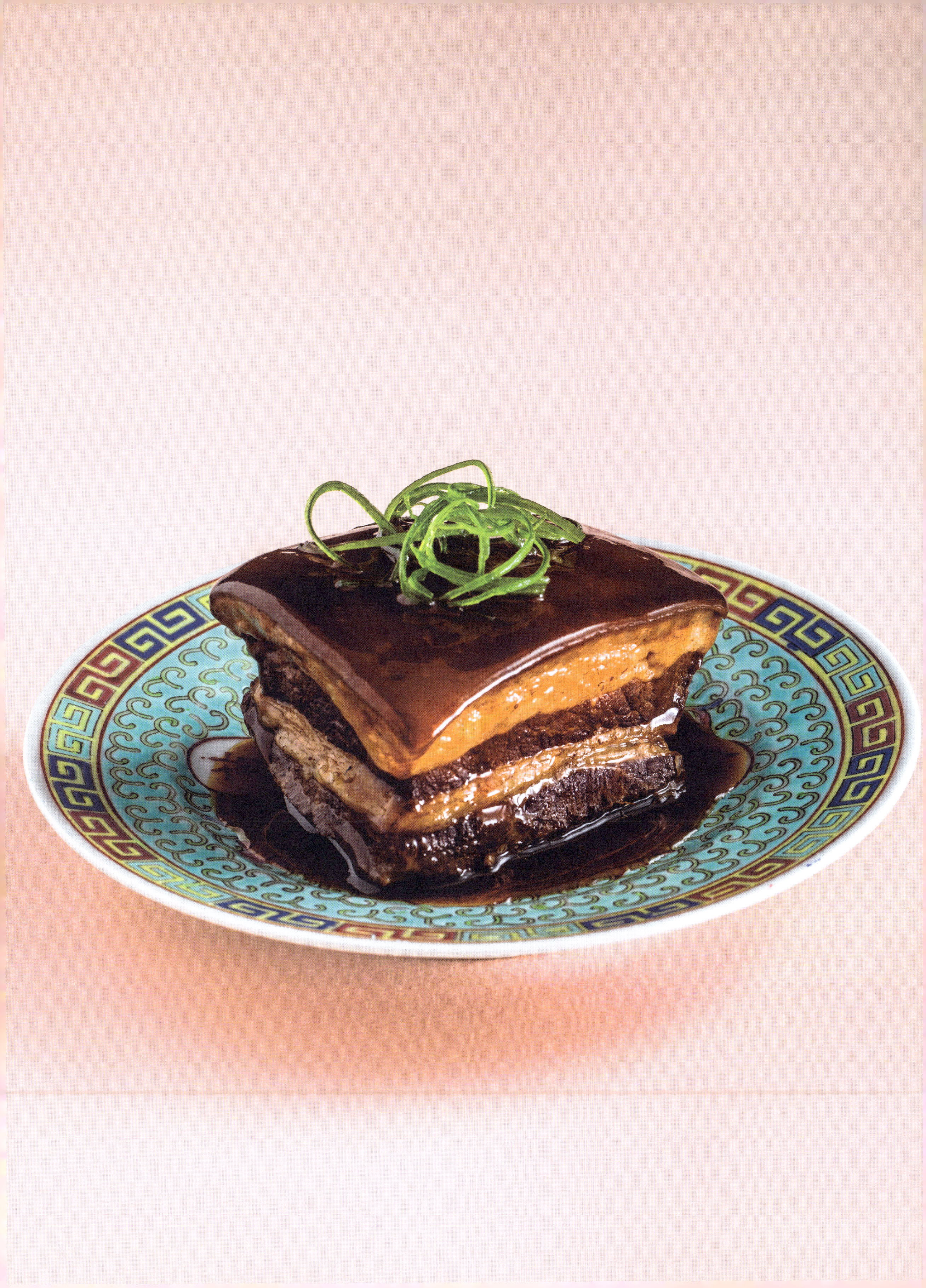

Understanding

GŪLǓ RÒU
SWEET AND SOUR PORK

- GREEN CHILE PEPPER
- PINEAPPLE
- BREADED PORK TENDERLOIN
- RED BELL PEPPER
- SAUCE

WHAT IS IT?
Fried breaded pork pieces, coated in a sweet and sour sauce with pineapple and bell pepper.

ORIGIN
This is probably the most widespread and popular Cantonese dish in the world. Waves of migration from the Cantonese diaspora allowed Chinese restaurants to expand around the world, especially in the United States during the nineteenth century. This boom has largely contributed to the spread of this dish, which has become a quintessential classic. The dish is called gūlǔ ròu in Cantonese or "meat gūlǔ," but gūlǔ has no meaning. It is believed to be a phonetic transcription of the word "good." Western merchants exclaimed "Good! good!" after tasting the dish.

COMPLETION TIME
Preparation time: 45 minutes
Cooking time: 20 minutes
Storage: The dish is best when freshly made.

SPECIAL EQUIPMENT
Wok

VARIATIONS
Pork can be substituted with the same amount of deboned chicken (page 34) or large shrimp.

Learning

SHAOXING RICE WINE
Fermented glutinous rice wine. Choose the Pagoda brand (blue label).

WHITE RICE VINEGAR
Vinegar made from glutinous rice, with 4.6 percent acidity. Choose the Narcissus brand.

SOY SAUCE
Choose bottles that state "natural fermentation."

SERVES 4

1 pound 2 ounces / 500 g pork tenderloin
2 tablespoons soy sauce
- 3 tablespoons / 45 ml Shaoxing rice wine (optional)
Salt and freshly ground black pepper

SAUCE

½ pineapple
4 cloves garlic
1 ounce / 30 g fresh ginger
1 onion
1 small red bell pepper
1 long green chile pepper (optional)
¼ cup plus 2 tablespoons / 50 g cornstarch
¾ cup / 100 g all-purpose or bread flour
1 large / 50 g egg
Oil, for frying
2 star anise pods
½ packed cup / 115 g brown sugar
- 3 tablespoons / 45 ml soy sauce
- Scant ½ cup / 100 ml rice vinegar

Making

GŪLŬ RÒU

1 Cut the tenderloin into slices of about ¼ inch / 5 mm. Place them in a container with the soy sauce and wine. Season lightly with salt and pepper, stir to combine, and refrigerate while you prepare the remaining ingredients.

2 Make the sauce: Slice the pineapple, then cut it into even small pieces. Chop the garlic. Peel the ginger and cut it into very small cubes. Cut the onion and bell pepper into cubes. Chop the chile, if using. Set aside.

3 Heat a large amount of oil in a deep skillet. In a small bowl, combine the cornstarch and flour (set aside 1 tablespoon of the flour for finishing). Add the egg to the pork mixture and combine. Roll each pork piece in the flour mixture.

4 When the oil is hot, immerse the pork pieces for 2 to 3 minutes, just until whitened. Transfer the meat to a strainer to drain. Set aside the pan of hot oil.

5 In a wok, heat 2 tablespoons of oil. Brown the garlic and ginger. Add the onion, bell pepper, and star anise pods. Fry for 1 minute, then add the brown sugar, soy sauce, and vinegar. Bring to a boil.

6 Combine the reserved 1 tablespoon of flour with a little water. Add this to the sauce and stir until thickened. Remove from heat.

7 Reheat the pan of oil and, when hot, add the meat to fry again. The pieces will brown quickly. Set aside on paper towels to drain.

8 Reheat the sauce, add the pineapple, chile, and pork. Stir briskly to coat the pieces with the sauce. Serve immediately with white rice (page 12).

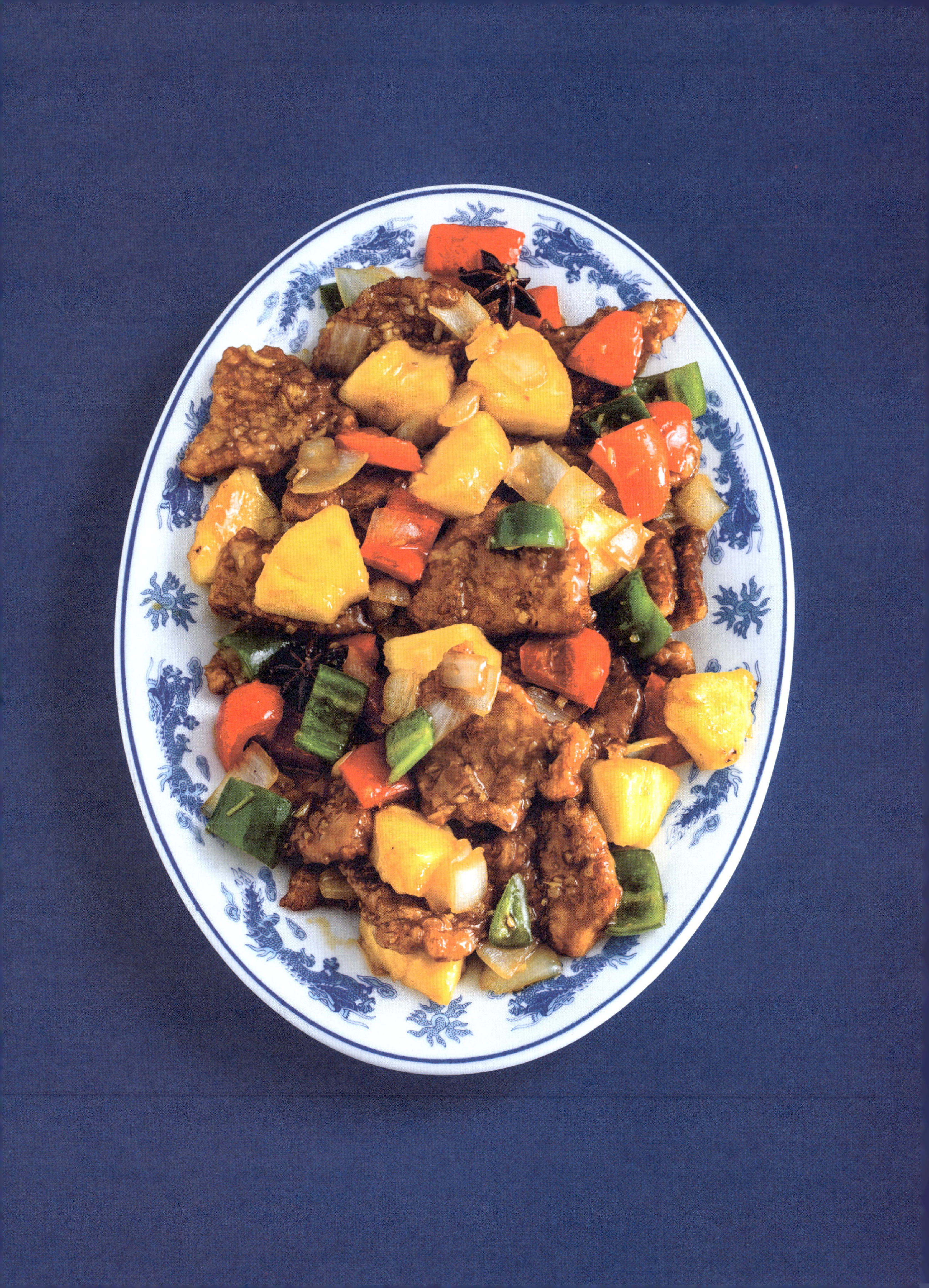

Understanding

CHĬ ZHĪ NIÚRÒU
STIR-FRIED BEEF WITH BLACK SOYBEANS

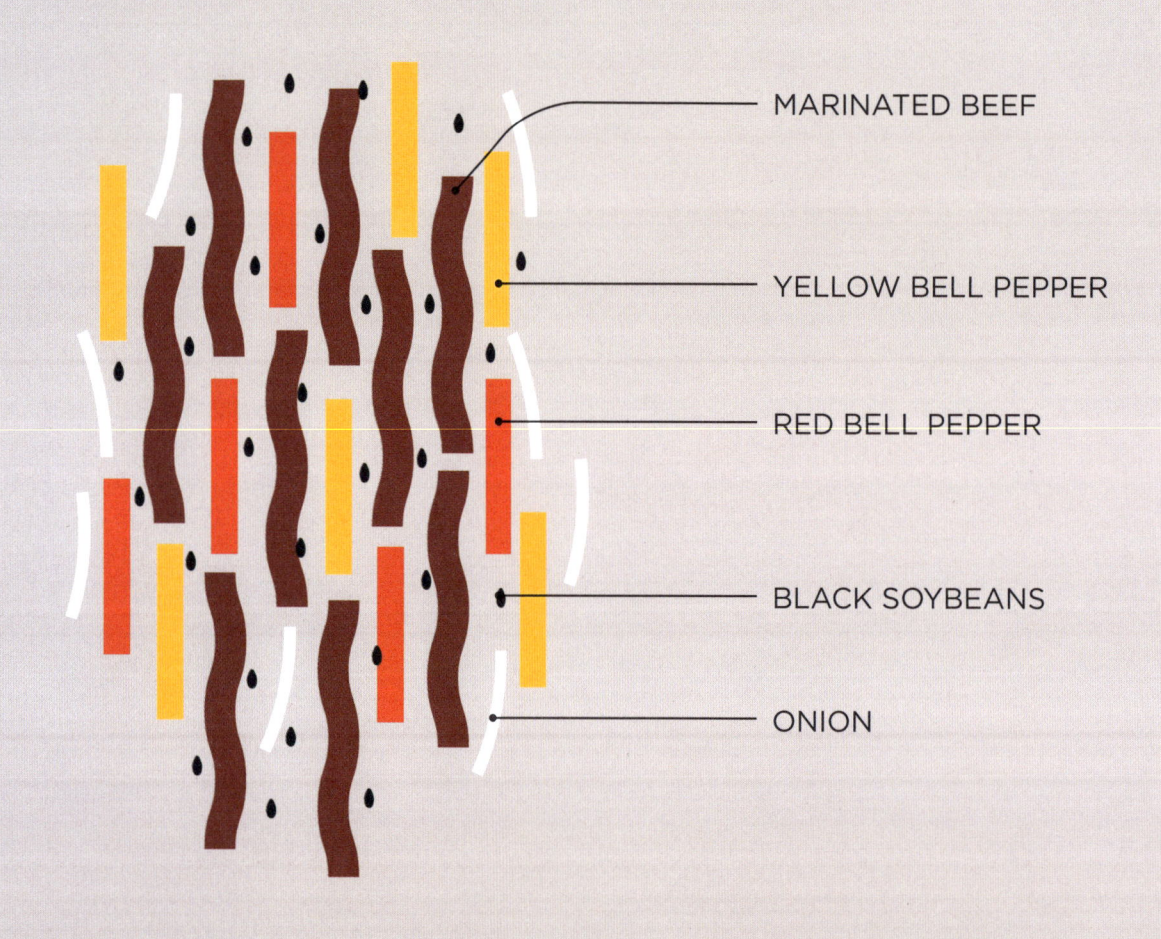

- MARINATED BEEF
- YELLOW BELL PEPPER
- RED BELL PEPPER
- BLACK SOYBEANS
- ONION

WHAT IS IT?
Beef strips marinated, then sautéed with fermented black soybeans and bell pepper. This dish is of Cantonese origin.

COMPLETION TIME
Preparation time: 20 minutes
Resting time: 2 hours
Cooking time: 12 minutes
Storage: 2 days

SPECIAL EQUIPMENT
Wok

INGREDIENT INFO
Fermented black soybeans (dòuchī) are one of the oldest condiments in Chinese gastronomy, their use dating to more than two thousand years ago. They are an integral part of Cantonese cuisine (used in steamed pork ribs, fried rice, etc.). They should be rinsed before use to remove excess salt.

SERVES 4
1 pound 2 ounces / 500 g beef (top round, skirt, etc.)

MARINADE
½ level teaspoon baking soda
2 tablespoons Shaoxing wine
1 heaping tablespoon oyster sauce
1 tablespoon soy sauce
1 teaspoon organic cane sugar
1 tablespoon cornstarch
1 tablespoon neutral-flavor oil of your choice (sunflower, peanut)
½ teaspoon cracked black peppercorns

Learning

1 ounce / 30 g fermented black soybeans

4 large cloves garlic

¾ ounce / 20 g fresh ginger

1 onion

½ red bell pepper

½ yellow bell pepper

4 tablespoons / 60 ml neutral-flavor oil of your choice (sunflower, peanut)

1 heaping teaspoon organic cane sugar

Scant ½ cup / 100 ml Basic Broth (page 38) or water

1 Cut the beef into strips of about ¹⁄₁₀ to ⅛ inch / 2 to 3 mm. Make the marinade: Combine the baking soda, wine, oyster sauce, soy sauce, sugar, cornstarch, oil, and the peppercorns. Add the meat and stir to coat. Set aside at room temperature for at least 30 minutes, or for 2 hours in the refrigerator.

2 Roughly chop the soybeans and garlic. Cut the ginger into strips and then into small cubes. Slice the onion and cut the bell peppers into strips.

3 Heat 1 tablespoon of the oil in a wok or skillet. When the oil is hot, add the marinated meat and spread it out in the pan. Let caramelize for about 2 minutes before stirring. Stir, and continue browning the other side. Remove the meat from the pan.

4 In the same pan, heat the remaining 3 tablespoons / 45 ml of the oil. Sauté the garlic for 1 minute, then add the ginger, soybeans, and sugar. Cook for 2 to 3 minutes. Add the onion and peppers. Sauté for 3 to 4 minutes. The vegetables should remain slightly crunchy.

5 Return the meat to the pan over high heat. Add the broth and cook for 1 minute to bind the ingredients. Serve hot with rice (page 12).

Understanding

YÁNGRÒU BĀO
BRAISED LAMB CASSEROLE

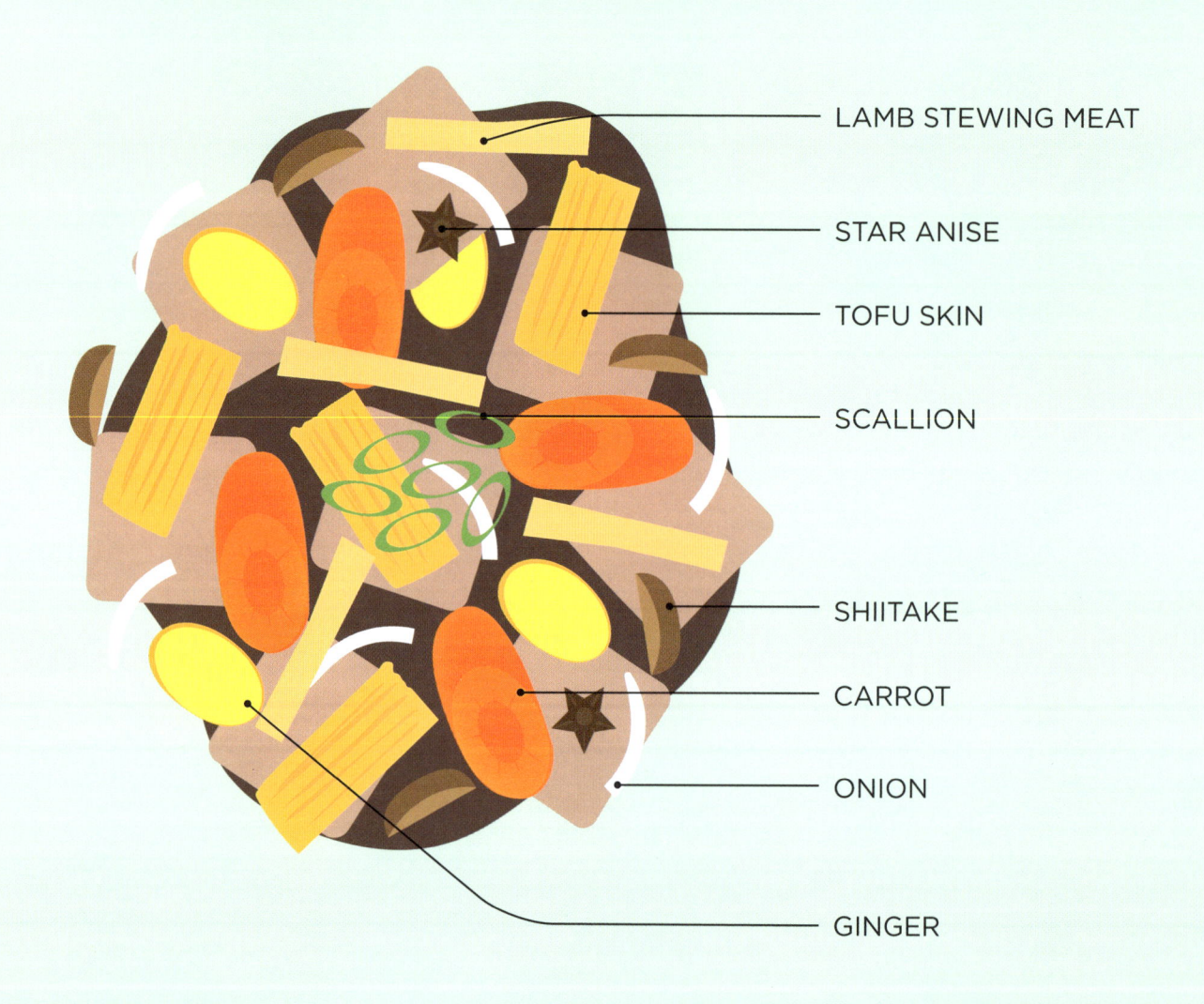

- LAMB STEWING MEAT
- STAR ANISE
- TOFU SKIN
- SCALLION
- SHIITAKE
- CARROT
- ONION
- GINGER

WHAT IS IT?
Lamb simmered in a sauce made from spices and fermented soy.

COMPLETION TIME
Preparation time: 50 minutes
Resting time: 3 hours
Cooking time: 1 hour 20 minutes
Storage: The stew can be refrigerated for 5 days. Reheat over low heat, covered, for about 20 minutes. Add a little water, if needed.

SPECIAL EQUIPMENT
Cast-iron Dutch oven

SKILLS TO MASTER
Rehydrating mushrooms (page 280)
Rehydrating tofu skins (page 280)
Blanching bamboo shoots (page 281)

SERVING
This dish is commonly made with pork belly, which is fattier. This dish is served at family meals or parties during the winter. Lamb is considered a "hot" food according to traditional Chinese medicine. It is believed to warm the body and improve blood circulation.

USEFUL TIP
Blanching bamboo removes its pungent odor.

Learning

TOFU SKINS
The dried skin of soymilk.

BAMBOO SHOOTS
Canned bamboo shoots. Boil them in water before using them to remove the pungent smell.

ROCK SUGAR
Yellow candy sugar. Adds shine to the dish. It has a delicate flavor and is less sweet than sugar.

CHU HOU PASTE
A paste made from fermented soybean paste, sesame, garlic, ginger, and spices.

FERMENTED RED TOFU CUBES
A traditional Chinese condiment. It has a powerful and salty taste.

SERVES 4 TO 6

10 dried shiitake mushrooms
- 3 ounces / 80 g tofu skins
- 14 ounces / 400 g canned bamboo shoots

14 ounces / 400 g carrots (about 4 to 5)
4 scallions
1 onion
¾ ounce / 20 g fresh ginger
6 cloves garlic
2¼ pounds / 1 kg stewing lamb pieces (shoulder or collar)
¼ cup / 60 ml neutral-flavor oil
2 star anise pods
1 heaping tablespoon all-purpose flour
Scant ½ cup / 100 ml Shaoxing wine
- ¾ ounce / 20 g rock sugar

⅛ ounce / 5 g dried orange peel, or 1 strip fresh orange peel
- 3½ tablespoons / 70 g chu hou paste

1 tablespoon dark soy sauce
2 tablespoons oyster sauce
- 1 ounce / 30 g fermented red tofu cubes

Salt and freshly ground black pepper

Making

YÁNGRÒU BĀO

1 Rehydrate shiitake mushrooms and tofu skins (page 280). Blanch the bamboo shoots (page 281). Peel the carrots and cut them on the diagonal about 1¾ to 2 inches / 4 to 5 cm thick. Remove the rough ends from the shiitake mushrooms. Cut the mushrooms in half, if necessary, for any that are large. Cut the tofu skins into pieces about 2 inches / 5 cm. Chop the scallions. Chop the onion, cut the ginger into strips, and crush the garlic (page 281).

2 Preheat the oven to 350°F / 180°C. Cut the meat into pieces, if necessary. Season with salt. In a Dutch oven, heat the oil. Brown the lamb pieces. Transfer the contents of the pot to a bowl.

3 In the same Dutch oven, add the onion, ginger, garlic, and star anise pods. Cook for 5 minutes, or until the vegetables are softened. Add the flour and stir to combine.

4 Place the lamb pieces back in the pot and add the wine to deglaze the pot. Add the rock sugar, orange peel, chu hou paste, soy sauce, oyster sauce, and tofu cubes. Add just enough water to cover the contents. Bring to a boil and skim off any impurities, if necessary.

5 Bake for 30 minutes with the lid on. Skim off any impurities from the surface using a spoon. Add the carrots and shiitake mushrooms and stir gently to combine. Place back in the oven and continue baking for 30 minutes.

6 Add the tofu skins and bamboo, stir gently, and bake for an additional 20 minutes. When ready to serve, add the chopped scallions. Serve with rice.

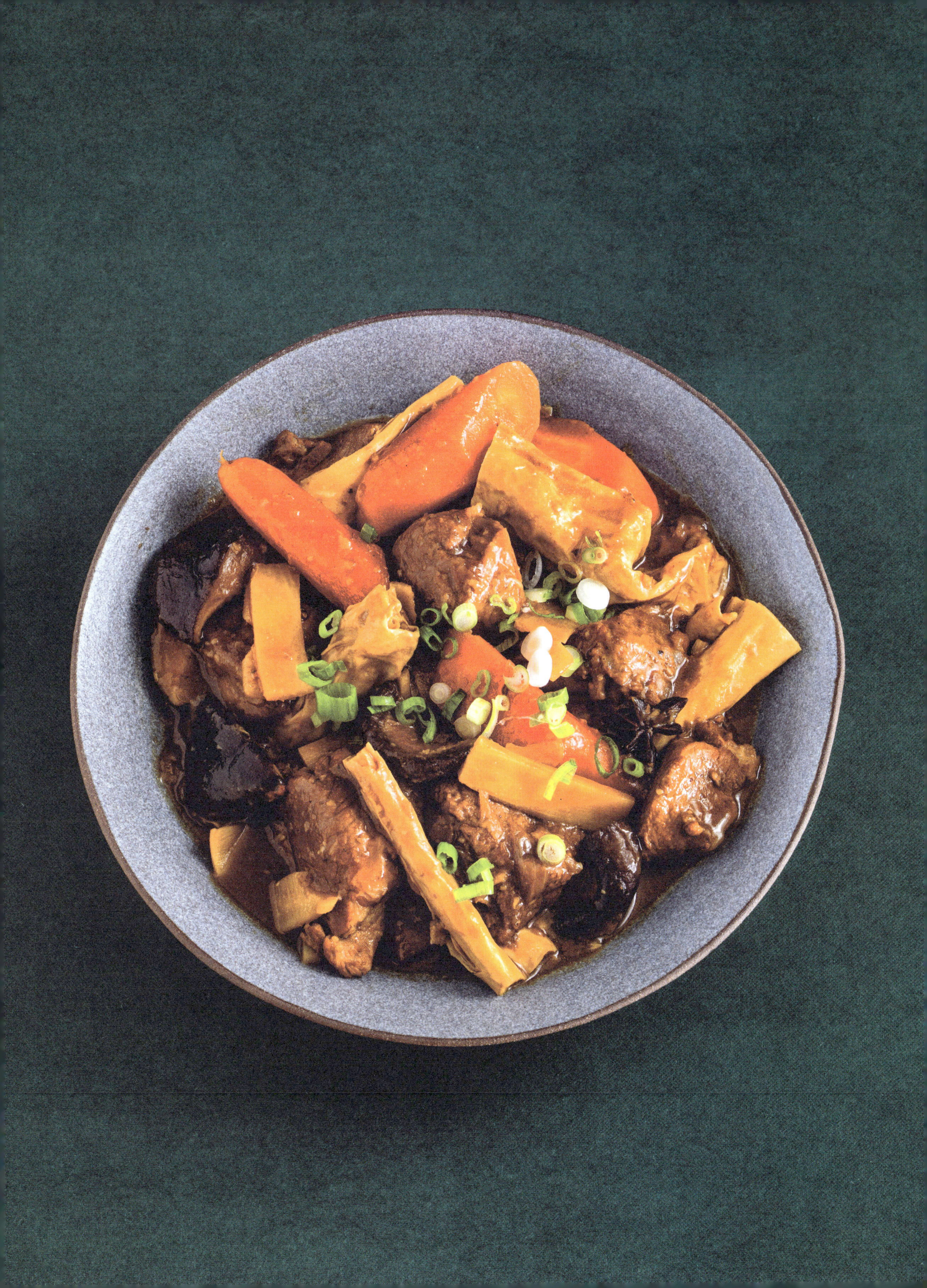

Understanding

JIĀNG CŌNG YÚ
STEAMED TURBOT WITH GINGER AND SCALLION SAUCE

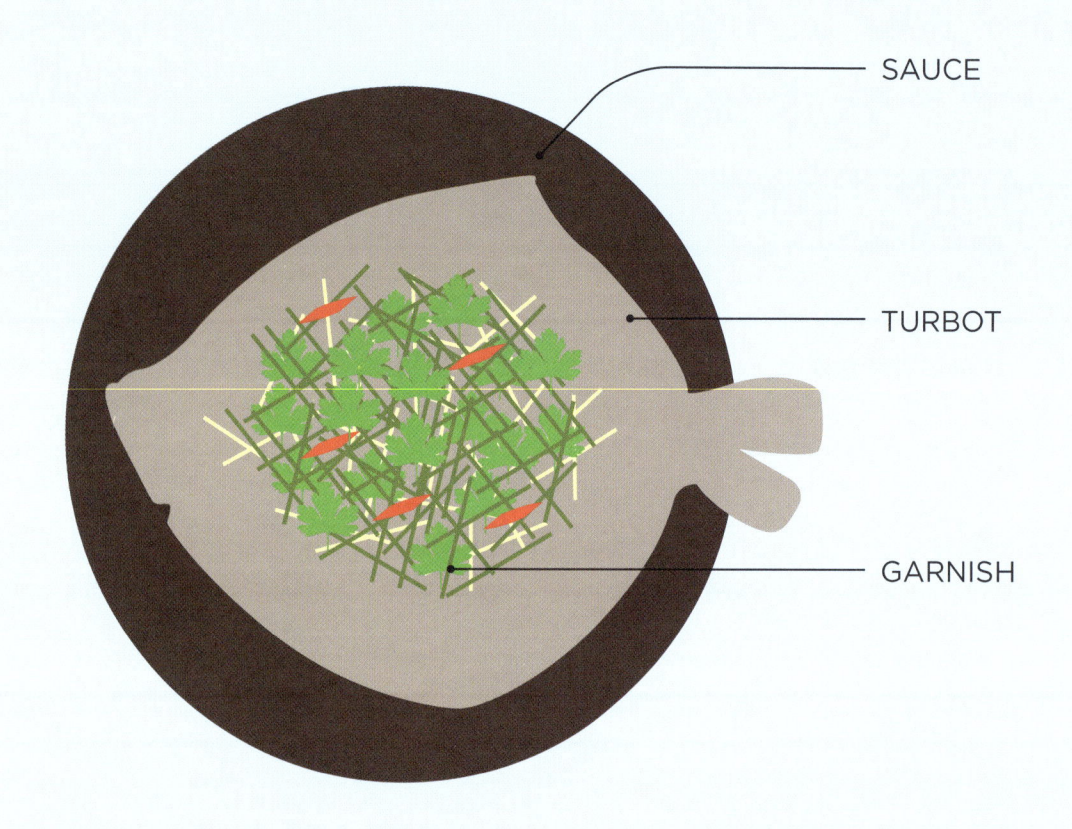

- SAUCE
- TURBOT
- GARNISH

WHAT IS IT?
A turbot cooked at a low temperature in the oven (250°F / 120°C), then topped with a sauce made from hot oil and oyster sauce. Serve it with a generous amount of ginger and julienned scallions.

ORIGIN
Whole fish is an important symbolic delicacy of Chinese gastronomy. The head and tail must be intact to symbolize integrity and completeness. Because it sounds similar to the word "surplus" in Mandarin, whole fish is considered a sign of abundance and success.

COMPLETION TIME
Preparation time: 20 minutes
Cooking time: 40 minutes
Storage: 1 or 2 days

SKILL TO MASTER
Cutting into julienne (page 281)

SERVING
The fish in this recipe is usually steamed. This requires proper equipment and limits the number of servings. Cooking gently in the oven is a good alternative, as this preserves the tenderness of the fish by avoiding overcooking it.

USEFUL TIP
After 30 minutes, make a light incision in the meat at the spine. The meat should be slightly pearly but should easily peel off the bone. Continue cooking if necessary.

VARIATIONS
Replace the turbot with sea bass, sea bream, or snapper (of the same weight).

Learning

SERVES 6

3 scallions

1¾ ounces / 50 g fresh ginger

4 small red chile peppers (optional)

6 sprigs of cilantro

1 drained, cleaned turbot (about 3 pounds 5 ounces / 1.5 kg)

Scant ½ cup / 100 ml Shaoxing wine

SAUCE

⅓ cup / 80 ml neutral-flavor oil of your choice (sunflower, peanut)

¼ cup / 60 ml soy sauce

¼ cup / 60 ml oyster sauce

1 Cut the scallions into sections and then into julienne (page 281). Soak them in a bowl of ice water. Thinly slice the ginger, then cut it into julienne. Cut the chile peppers in half, if using, and remove the seeds. Remove the leaves from the cilantro and reserve the stems.

2 Preheat the oven to 250°F / 120°C. Place the cilantro stems in a large baking dish. Place the turbot on top. Drizzle with the Shaoxing wine and bake for 40 minutes.

3 After 35 minutes of cooking, add the ginger and chile on top of the fish.

4 Make the sauce: Heat the oil in a small saucepan. When hot, turn off the heat and add the soy sauce and oyster sauce. Stir to combine. Pour the sauce over the fish.

5 Add the julienned scallions and the cilantro leaves. Serve with rice (page 12).

Understanding

SHUĬ ZHŬ YÚ
SZECHUAN POACHED FISH

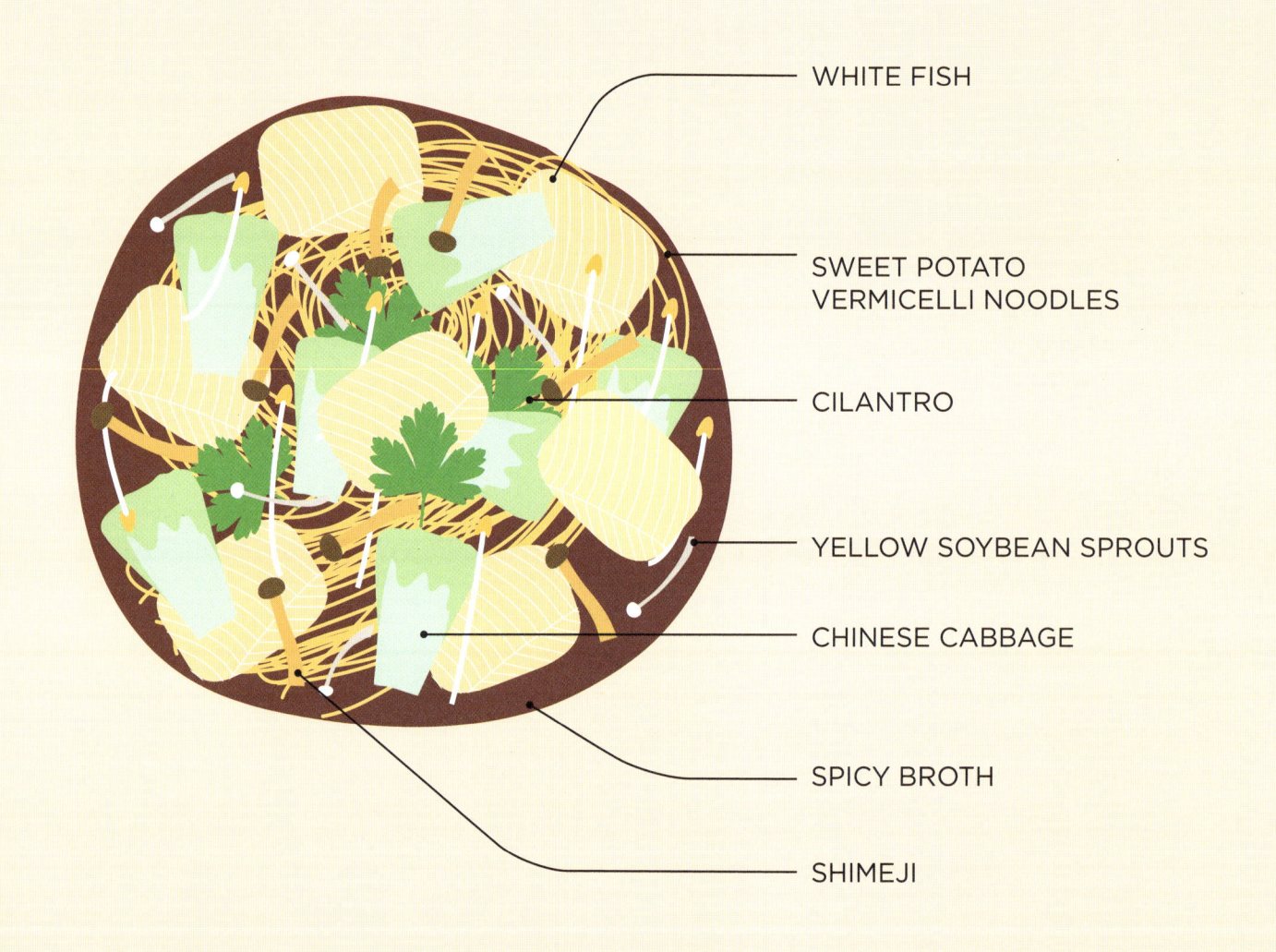

- WHITE FISH
- SWEET POTATO VERMICELLI NOODLES
- CILANTRO
- YELLOW SOYBEAN SPROUTS
- CHINESE CABBAGE
- SPICY BROTH
- SHIMEJI

WHAT IS IT?
Fish poached in a seasoned, fragrant, spicy, and numbing broth.

ORIGIN
This is a famous dish of Szechuan cuisine. Its name in Chinese means "fish cooked in water," which suggests a bland and healthy dish.

COMPLETION TIME
Preparation time: 1½ hours
Resting time: 20 minutes
Cooking time: 40 minutes

SERVING
When ready to serve, boiling oil is poured in to release all the aromas. Each guest is then served the fish and vegetables. The oily broth serves only as an aromatic sauce, but this version allows you to drink the broth, and the amount of spices is based on personal preference.

USEFUL TIP
For this recipe, green Szechuan pepper is used. This is the same berry as the red Szechuan pepper, but it is picked before maturity. Because it is fresher with citrus notes, the green berry goes particularly well with fish but use the one you prefer.

VARIATIONS
For a less spicy version, remove the dried chile peppers and reduce the dòubànjiàng to 1½ tablespoons.

Learning

DÒUBÀNJIÀNG

A spicy and savory Szechuan paste made from fermented beans and chile peppers.

SWEET POTATO VERMICELLI NOODLES

They must be soaked before use. After cooking, they become translucent, elastic, and slightly rubbery. They have a neutral taste, perfect for soaking up sauces and broths.

GREEN SZECHUAN PEPPER

This is the same berry as the red one, but it is picked before maturity. It has more lemony notes and a great deal of freshness.

YELLOW BEAN SPROUTS

Not to be confused with mung bean sprouts. They have thicker, sturdier stems. They remain firm and crunchy after cooking.

SZECHUAN LONG DRIED CHILE PEPPERS

Dried chile from China of medium size and intensity.

SHIMEJI

A small Asian mushroom with a nutty taste. It can be white or brown. It is often sold in plastic trays.

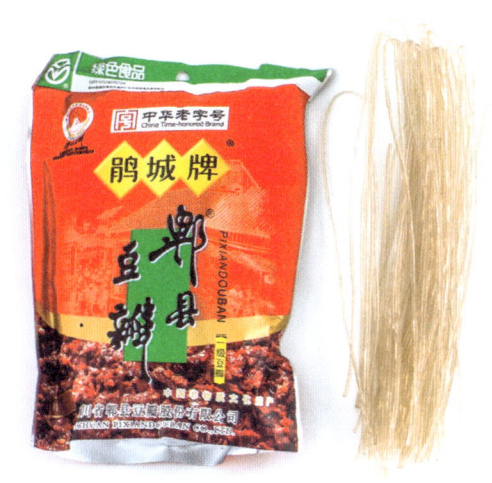

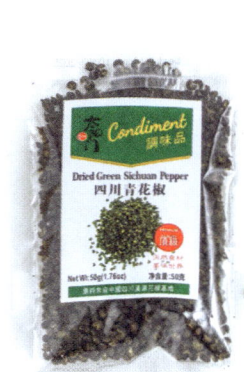

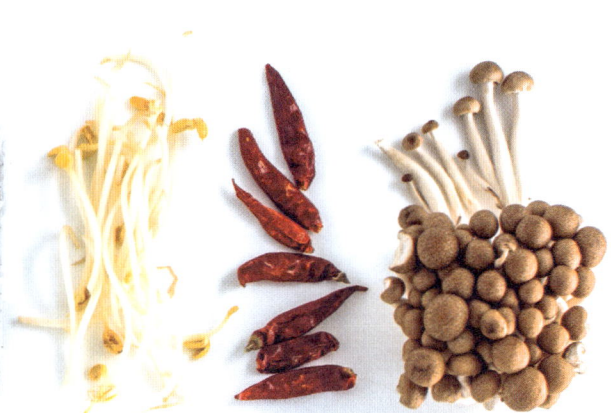

SERVES 4 TO 6

1 pound 2 ounces / 500 g sea bass or sea bream filets (with head and bones)

1 level teaspoon salt

1 teaspoon sugar

2 tablespoons Shaoxing wine

1 large / 30 g egg white

2 tablespoons cornstarch

1 tablespoon neutral-flavor oil of your choice (sunflower, peanut)

BROTH

Fish heads and bones (from the filets)

3 shallots

Celery leaves (from the stalks)

1 teaspoon salt

½ teaspoon organic cane sugar

3 stalks celery

5¼ ounces / 150 g Chinese cabbage

½ bunch of cilantro

- 6 to 15 Szechuan long dried chile peppers

1 ounce / 30 g fresh ginger

5 cloves garlic

⅓ cup / 80 ml neutral-flavor oil of your choice (sunflower, peanut)

- 2 tablespoons green (or red) Szechuan pepper
- 1 to 2½ tablespoons / 20 to 50 g dòubànjiàng

2 level tablespoons organic cane sugar

¼ cup / 60 ml soy sauce

- 7 ounces / 200 g yellow bean sprouts or mung bean sprouts
- 3½ ounces / 100 g shimeji mushrooms
- 3½ ounces / 100 g sweet potato vermicelli noodles, rehydrated (optional)

Making

SHUĬ ZHŬ YÚ

1   Remove the bones and skins from the fish filets. Slice the fish at a slight angle.

2   Combine the fish with the salt, sugar wine, and egg white. Massage to coat the fish in the egg, then add the cornstarch. Add the 1 tablespoon oil to help loosen the pieces. Refrigerate for 20 minutes.

3   Make the broth: In a pot, add the fish heads and bones. Finely chop the shallots and celery leaves and add them to the pot. Add the salt, cane sugar, and 6 cups / 1.5 L water and bring to a simmer over low heat for 20 minutes. Strain, and reserve the broth.

4   Cut the celery into sticks about 1½ inches / 4 cm long and evenly chop the cabbage. Chop the cilantro. Cut the Szechuan chile peppers into sections and remove the seeds. Grate the ginger. Press the garlic. Heat the oil in a saucepan or large wok. Sauté the garlic, ginger, chile peppers, and Szechuan pepper. As soon as the peppers start to brown, add the dòubànjiàng.

5   Add the broth. Add the 2 tablespoons of cane sugar and the soy sauce. Bring to a simmer and cook for 5 to 10 minutes. Skim off any impurities from the surface, if necessary. Increase the heat and blanch the celery, cabbage, bean sprouts, and mushrooms in the broth separately, lowering them into the broth in a strainer. Blanch the celery for 2 minutes and the cabbage, bean sprouts, and mushrooms for 1 minute. Cook the vermicelli, if using, in the broth for 3 minutes. Arrange all the ingredients in an earthenware pot or serving dish.

6   Add the fish to the broth. Turn off the heat, and let cook for 1 minute in the residual heat. Taste the broth, adjust the seasoning, if necessary (adding salt, sugar, or soy sauce). Carefully arrange the ingredients in the earthenware pot. Add the hot broth on top (strained or not, depending on your preference), and top with the cilantro.

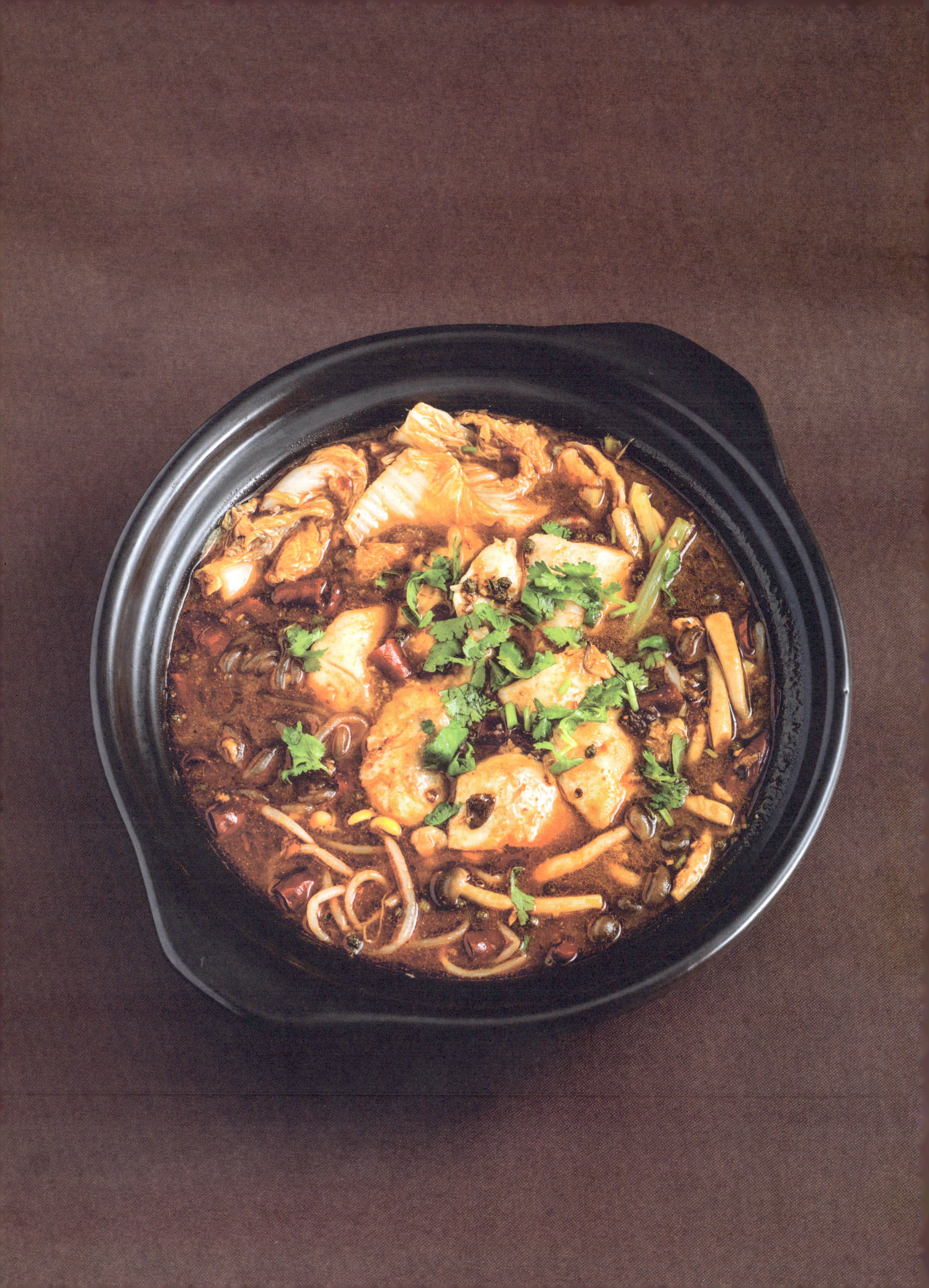

Understanding
YÚ SHĒNG
PROSPERITY SALAD

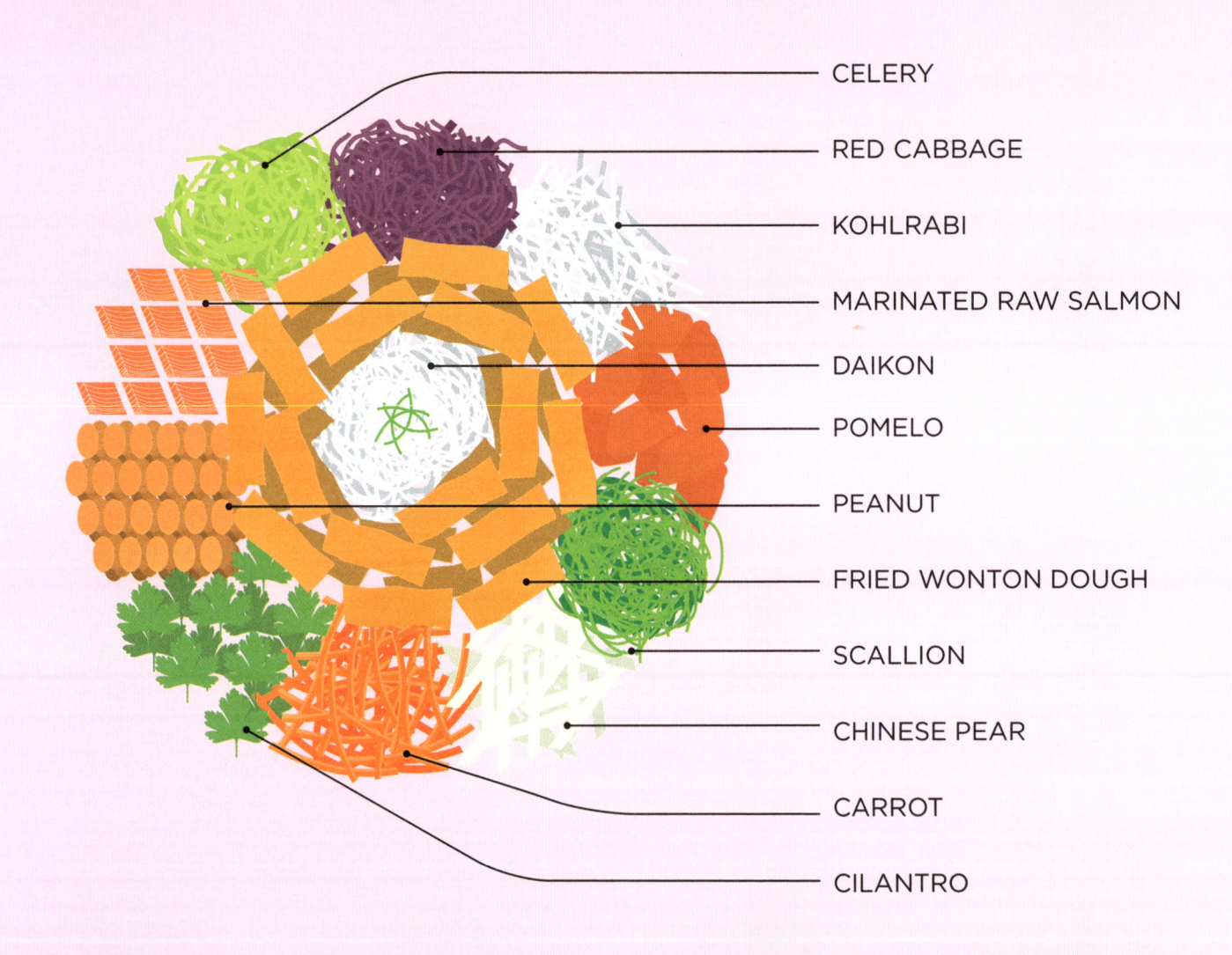

- CELERY
- RED CABBAGE
- KOHLRABI
- MARINATED RAW SALMON
- DAIKON
- POMELO
- PEANUT
- FRIED WONTON DOUGH
- SCALLION
- CHINESE PEAR
- CARROT
- CILANTRO

WHAT IS IT?
A salad made of twelve ingredients with a plum dressing.

ORIGIN
This is a dish enjoyed during the Chinese New Year in Singapore, Malaysia, and other parts of southeast Asia. It is also called *lo hei*, which means "to mix happily." The salad should have twelve ingredients arranged in a circle, and each ingredient or color symbolizes a virtue, such as prosperity, health, wealth, kindness, or good luck.

COMPLETION TIME
Preparation time: 2 hours
Resting time: 6 hours
Cooking time: 20 minutes

SKILL TO MASTER
Cutting into julienne (page 281)

SERVING
Guests should be gathered around the salad with their chopsticks to vigorously mix all the ingredients, proclaiming their wishes for the new year. The higher you raise the chopsticks to stir, the better the new year will be.

Learning

CHINESE PEAR
An Asian fruit with a flavor between an apple and a pear.

DAIKON
A juicy and mildly sweet white radish.

HOISIN SAUCE
A Chinese barbecue sauce. It is brown, thick, and salty-sweet.

FIVE-SPICE POWDER
A powdered mix containing coriander seeds, fennel, anise, cinnamon, black or Szechuan pepper, and cloves.

WONTON WRAPPERS
Squares of wheat-flour dough, used to make dumplings.

SERVES 6

MARINATED SALMON
5 tablespoons / 60 g coarse salt
3 tablespoons / 40 g sugar of your choice
- 2¼ teaspoons five-spice powder
1 pound 5 ounces / 600 g skinless salmon

SAUCE
14 ounces / 400 g red plums (fresh or frozen)
¼ cup plus 2 teaspoons / 60 g organic cane sugar
¼ cup / 60 ml cider vinegar
Juice of 2 oranges (⅔ cup / 150 ml)
3 cloves garlic, pressed
1 tablespoon grated ginger
1 stick cinnamon
1 star anise pod
1 teaspoon salt
1 bunch of cilantro stems
- 1 or 2 tablespoons hoisin sauce
3 tablespoons / 45 ml olive oil
Juice of 1 lemon

- 1¾ ounces / 50 g wonton wrappers
2 cups / 480 ml oil, for frying
- 12 ounces / 350 g daikon radish
7 ounces / 200 g celery (3 stalks)
1 bunch of scallions
5¼ ounces / 150 g red cabbage
10½ ounces / 300 g carrots
7 ounces / 200 g kohlrabi
- 2 Chinese pears (12 ounces / 350 g)
2 pomelo, or ½ Chinese grapefruit
1 bunch of cilantro
1 cup / 150 g salted roasted peanuts
3½ tablespoons / 25 g toasted sesame seeds

Making

YÚ SHĒNG

1 Prepare the salmon: Combine the salt, sugar, and five-spice powder. Coat the salmon with the mixture. Refrigerate for 6 hours.

2 Make the sauce: Cut the plums in half and remove their pits. Combine the plums, sugar, vinegar, orange juice, garlic, ginger, cinnamon stick, star anise pod, salt, and cilantro stems (tie the stems together with string). Cook for 20 minutes over low heat. Remove the cinnamon sticks, star anise pod, and cilantro bundle. Combine the sauce with hoisin sauce, olive oil, and lemon juice. Taste, and adjust the seasoning, if necessary.

3 Cut the wonton wrappers into large strips. In a saucepan, heat the oil and fry the strips until golden brown. Set aside on paper towels to drain.

4 Shave the daikon with a vegetable peeler (page 279). Cut very thin slices of celery, preferably using a mandoline, then cut the slices into long thin strips. Cut the scallions into fine julienne. Set aside each ingredient in separate bowls of ice water.

5 Slice the red cabbage as finely as possible, preferably using a mandoline. Shave the carrots with a vegetable peeler. Shave the kohlrabi and pears. Cut the pomelo into quarters. Remove the skin from each quarter. Remove the leaves from the cilantro.

6 Rinse the salmon and pat it dry. Cut it into thin slices or small cubes.

7 Drain all the vegetables that were soaked in ice water. Neatly arrange all the ingredients in a large dish. Add the sauce just before serving. Sprinkle with the peanuts and sesame seeds and garnish the center with some scallions.

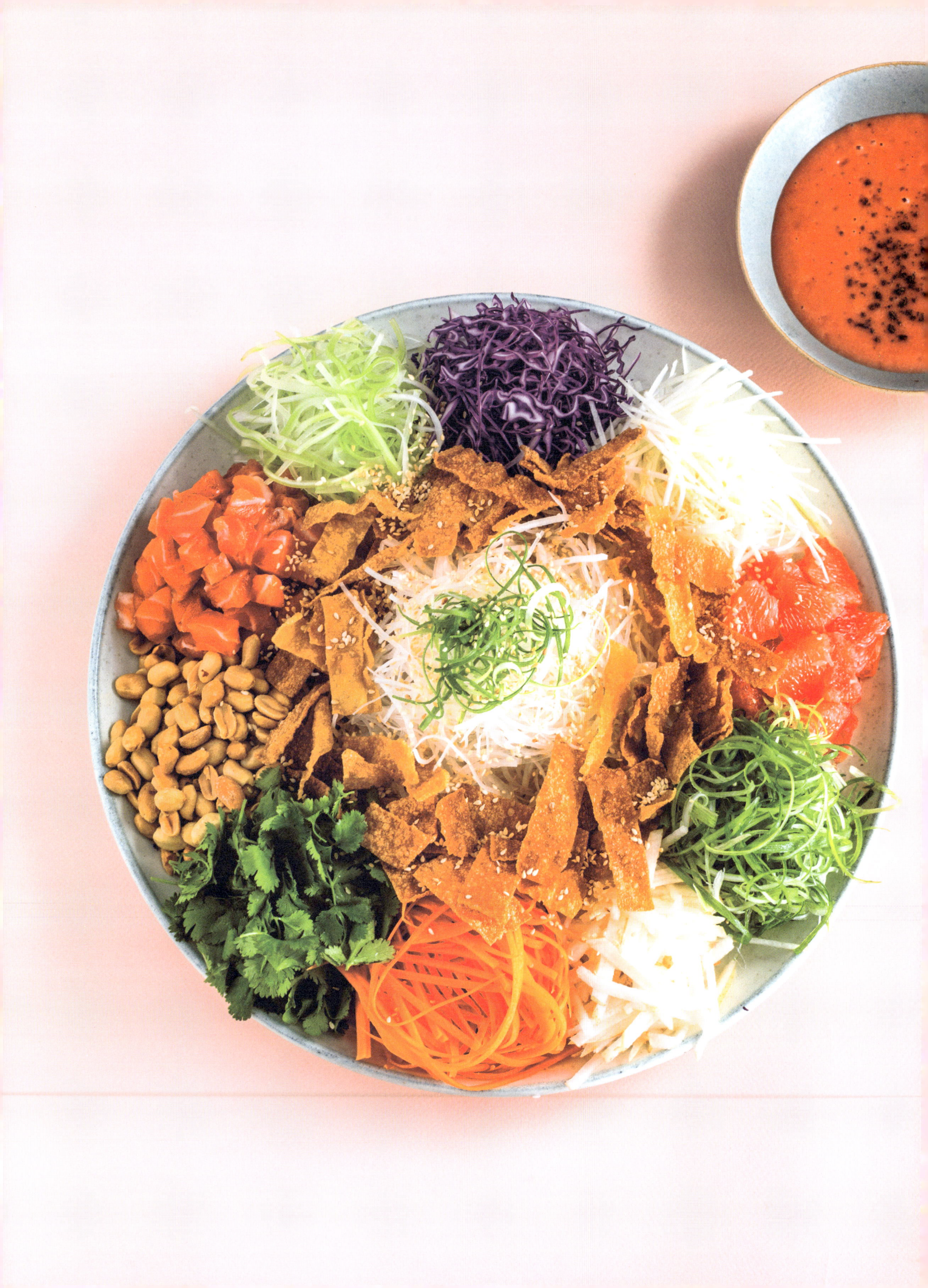

Understanding

SŌNGSHŬ YÚ
SWEET AND SOUR FISH

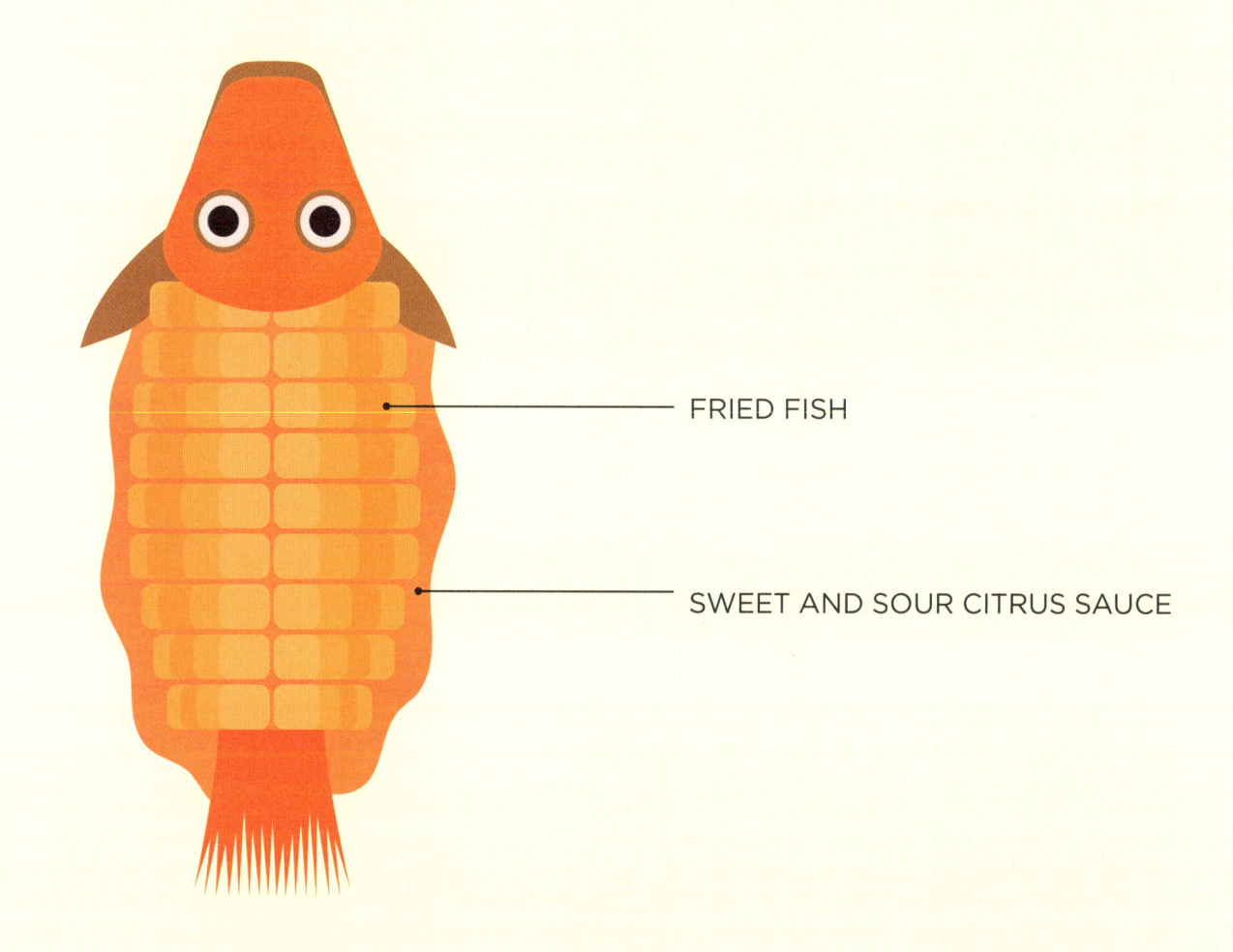

— FRIED FISH

— SWEET AND SOUR CITRUS SAUCE

WHAT IS IT?

A fish, cut crisscross, coated with starch and egg. It is then fried and served with a sweet and sour sauce.

ORIGIN

In the original recipe, a mandarin fish or a Chinese perch is used. The dish's name in Chinese means "squirrelfish" because the golden color and the way the fish is cut give the appearance of a tail of a squirrel. The dish originated in Suzhou in the eastern province of Jiangsu, China. On a private tour in Suzhou, the hungry Qianlong Emperor (1711–1799) ordered the chef of a local restaurant to cook him a fish that he saw being served. For such a distinguished guest, the chef improvised the dish into a spectacular recipe. The emperor was delighted and, since that time, the dish has become a tourist culinary attraction.

COMPLETION TIME

Preparation time: 40 minutes
Cooking time: 40 minutes

SPECIAL EQUIPMENT

Fish filet knife

SKILL TO MASTER

Cutting into julienne (page 281)

SERVING

Serve with rice.

Learning

ROCKFISH
This fish has a fine and delicate meat, similar to sea bream.

SOY SAUCE
Choose bottles that state "natural fermentation."

SERVES 4 TO 6

SWEET AND SOUR CITRUS SAUCE

1 red onion
1 ounce / 30 g fresh ginger
½ bunch of cilantro
1 dried chile of your choice
1½ cups / 350 ml freshly squeezed orange juice
Zest of 1 organic orange
Zest of 1 organic lemon
Scant ½ cup / 100 ml lemon juice
¼ cup plus 2 tablespoons packed / 80 g brown sugar
- 1 tablespoon soy sauce
½ teaspoon salt

- 1 rockfish or sea bass, 3 pounds 5 ounces / 1.5 kg with head and tail (the filets can be removed by the fishmonger, if desired)
¾ cup / 100 g cornstarch
1 large / 50 g egg
Salt
6 cups / 1.5 L oil, for frying
1 scallion (optional)

Making

SŌNGSHŬ YÚ

1 Make the sweet and sour citrus sauce: Slice the red onion, cut the ginger into strips, and cut the cilantro sprigs into thirds. Remove the seeds from the chile. Place the onion, ginger, cilantro, and chile in a saucepan with the orange juice and zests. Bring to a boil, then reduce the heat. Cook until reduced to about ½ cup / 120 ml.

2 Strain. Return the strained juice to the pot. Add the lemon juice, brown sugar, soy sauce, and salt. Bring to a boil. Taste, and adjust the salt, if necessary. Set aside.

3 Cut off the head of the fish and remove the fins at the gills.

4 Remove the filets. Remove the bones and fatty parts of the belly that do not contain meat.

5 Using a fish knife, make slits every ¼ inch / 5 mm by tilting the blade at an angle, but leave the meat attached to the skin along the entire length of the fish. Proceed in the same way lengthwise, making the slits slightly wider apart, to obtain a crisscross grid pattern. Repeat in the same way with the second filet.

6 Place the cornstarch in a large dish. Beat the egg with salt and pour it over the fish filets. Massage the egg into the slits. Lightly coat the filets with the cornstarch, ensuring each cut section is coated.

7 In a wok, heat the oil to 350°F / 180°C. Lightly pat the filets to remove excess cornstarch and set the cornstarch aside. Hold a filet at each end, skin up, to arch it upward. Dip the lowered curved center portion in the hot oil.

8 When the center starts to crisp, gently let go of the filet to lower it into the oil and cook until browned. Remove the filet using a slotted spoon. Set aside on paper towels to drain. Repeat with the second filet.

9 Fry the head and tail. Arrange the fish to look reconstructed, with the head and tail in place, neatly in a serving dish. Place 2 teaspoons of the cornstarch in a bowl and dilute it with a little water. Reheat the sauce, add the diluted cornstarch, and stir until the sauce thickens. Coat the fish and decorate with the julienned (page 281) scallion, if desired.

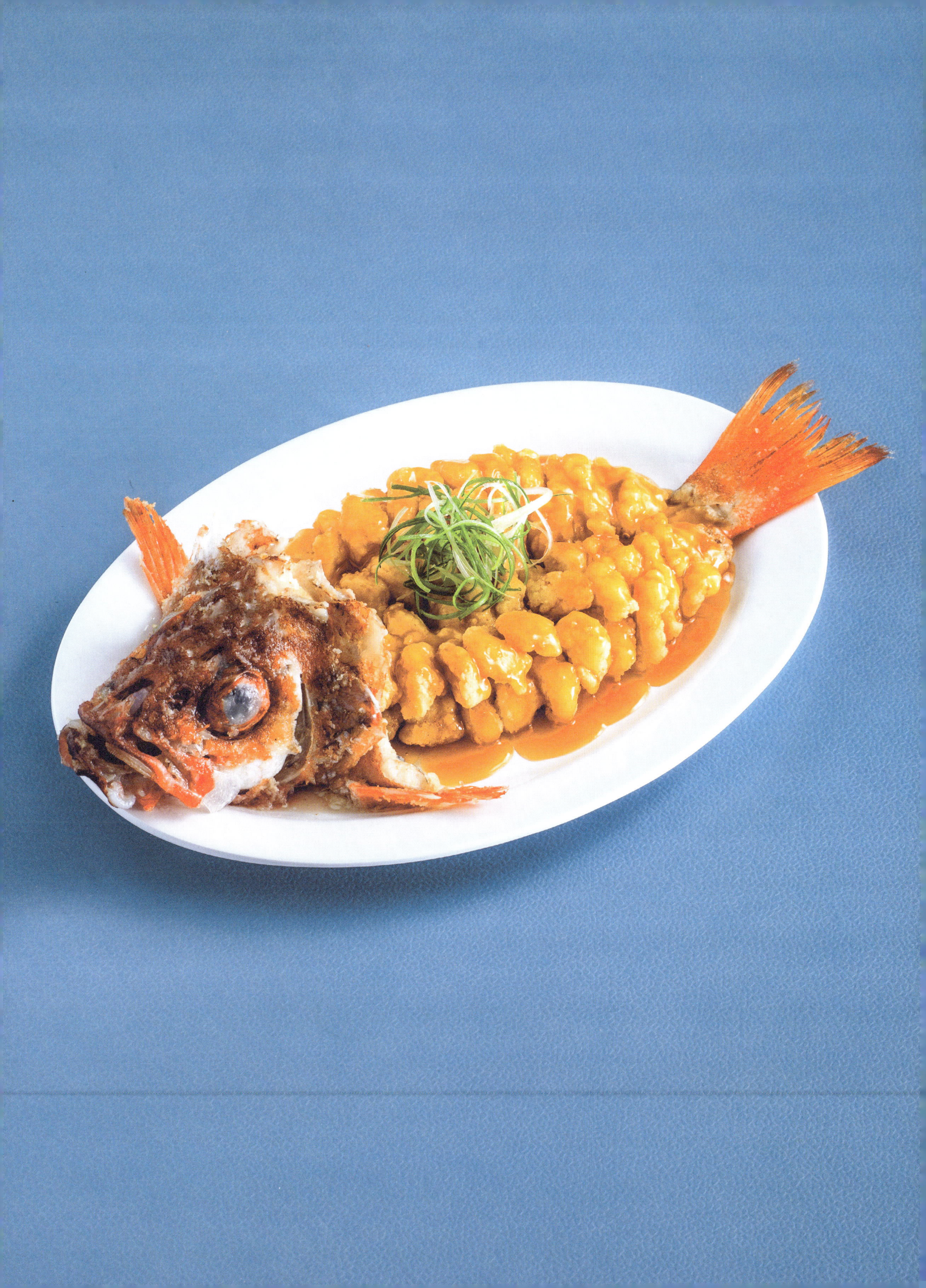

Understanding

JIĀOYÁN XIĀ
SALT AND PEPPER SHRIMP

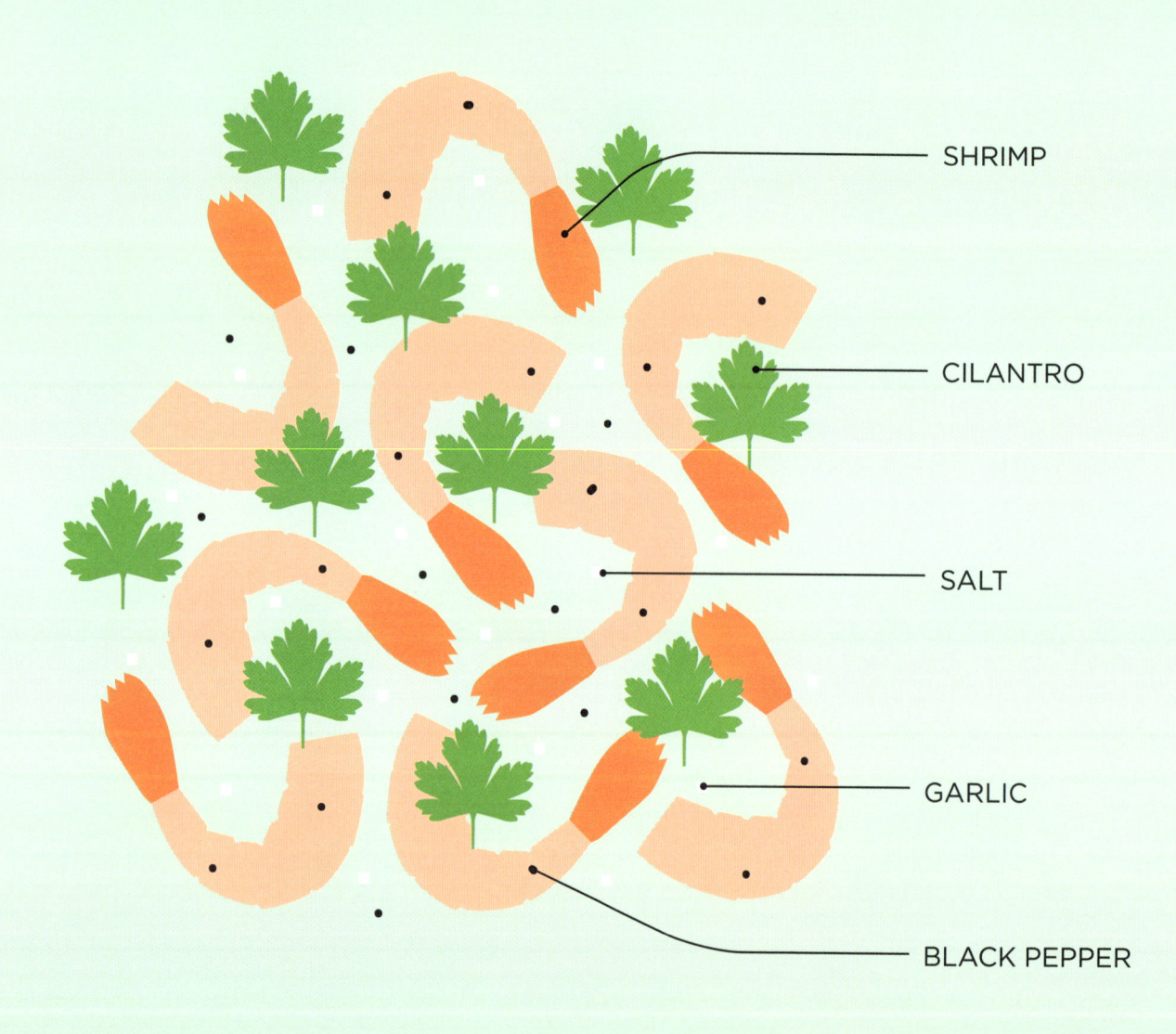

- SHRIMP
- CILANTRO
- SALT
- GARLIC
- BLACK PEPPER

WHAT IS IT?
Shrimp marinated in garlic, salt, pepper, and cilantro, then sautéed.

ORIGIN
This is a great classic of Cantonese cuisine, simple and satisfying.

COMPLETION TIME
Preparation time: 15 minutes
Cooking time: 4 minutes
Storage: 1 or 2 days

SKILL TO MASTER
Preparing shrimp (page 36)

VARIATIONS
Add 1 or 2 finely chopped chile peppers for a spicy version. Replace the shrimp with 10½ ounces / 300 g cuttlefish cut into strips, or 10½ ounces / 300 g firm tofu cut into cubes.

Learning

SERVES 2 TO 4

10½ ounces / 300 g thawed raw shrimp (preferable size 16/20)

4 large cloves garlic

½ bunch of cilantro

1 teaspoon black peppercorns

½ teaspoon salt

1½ teaspoons cornstarch

¼ cup / 60 ml vegetable oil

1 Prepare the shrimp using the method on page 36 and peel them. Press the garlic. Roughly chop the cilantro. Crush the peppercorns using a mortar and pestle.

2 Combine the shrimp, garlic, peppercorns, and salt. Add the cornstarch and stir to combine.

3 In a wok or skillet over very high heat, heat the oil. Add the shrimp and cook, stirring frequently, for 3 to 4 minutes.

4 Sprinkle with cilantro and stir to combine. Serve with rice (page 12).

Understanding

STEAMED PRAWNS, VERMICELLI NOODLES, AND FRIED GARLIC

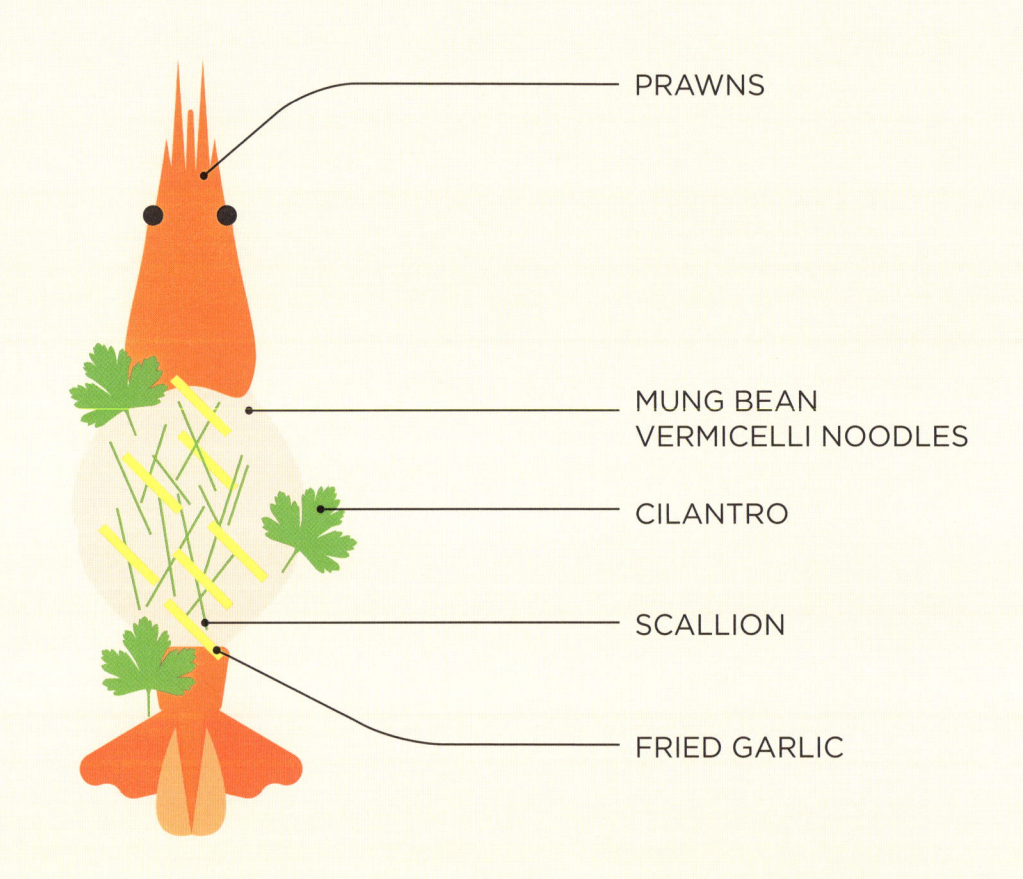

- PRAWNS
- MUNG BEAN VERMICELLI NOODLES
- CILANTRO
- SCALLION
- FRIED GARLIC

WHAT IS IT?
Marinated and steamed prawns or jumbo shrimp on a bed of mung bean vermicelli noodles.

ORIGIN
The dish is of Cantonese origin.

COMPLETION TIME
Preparation time: 35 minutes
Resting time: 30 minutes
Cooking time: 10 minutes

SKILL TO MASTER
Cutting into julienne (page 281)

SERVING
Garlic is usually sprinkled raw on the shrimp before steaming it. This version is browned for extra texture. The oil used to cook it can be added to the vermicelli noodles for more flavor.

Learning

OYSTER SAUCE
Choose the Megachef or Lee Kum Kee (Premium) brands.

SOY SAUCE
Choose bottles that state "natural fermentation."

MUNG BEAN VERMICELLI NOODLES
They must be soaked before use. They become transparent after cooking.

SERVES 4

MARINATED PRAWNS
4 prawns, size 8/12
- 1 tablespoon soy sauce
- 1 tablespoon oyster sauce
½ teaspoon organic cane sugar
Freshly ground black pepper

VERMICELLI NOODLES
- 5¼ ounces / 150 g mung bean vermicelli noodles
¾ ounce / 20 g fresh ginger
2 scallions
6 sprigs of cilantro
1 tablespoon soy sauce
2 tablespoons oyster sauce
Freshly ground black pepper
1 cup / 240 ml Basic Broth, hot (page 38)

GARLIC OIL
4 large cloves garlic
3 tablespoons / 45 ml neutral-flavor oil of your choice (sunflower, peanut)

Making

STEAMED PRAWNS, VERMICELLI NOODLES, AND FRIED GARLIC

1 Marinate the prawns: Shell the prawns, keeping the heads and tails attached. Cut open the backs and remove the black vein that runs down the center.

2 Combine the soy sauce, oyster sauce, and sugar. Season with pepper. Add the prawns and stir to coat. Set aside at room temperature for at least 30 minutes.

3 Prepare the vermicelli: Rehydrate the vermicelli noodles in a container of cold water for about 30 minutes. Cut the ginger into julienne (page 281). Thinly slice one of the scallions. Cut the remaining scallion widthwise into sections and then into julienne. Place the julienne strips in a bowl of cold water. Remove the leaves from the cilantro and finely chop the stems.

4 Make the garlic oil: Chop the garlic. In a small saucepan, heat the oil and add the garlic. Fry until golden brown. Strain over a small bowl. Set the fried garlic aside in a separate small bowl.

5 Drain the vermicelli. Cut them with scissors in half or in thirds. Season with some of the garlic oil, the soy sauce, oyster sauce, ginger, cilantro stems, chopped scallion, and pepper. Stir to combine and pour into a dish and add the hot broth.

6 Place the prawns on top of the vermicelli. Pour the vermicelli marinade over the dish. Add the remaining oil.

7 Bring the water in a steamer to a boil. Cook the prawns for 8 to 10 minutes. When cooked, place the fried garlic on each prawn. Sprinkle with cilantro leaves and the julienned scallion, drained.

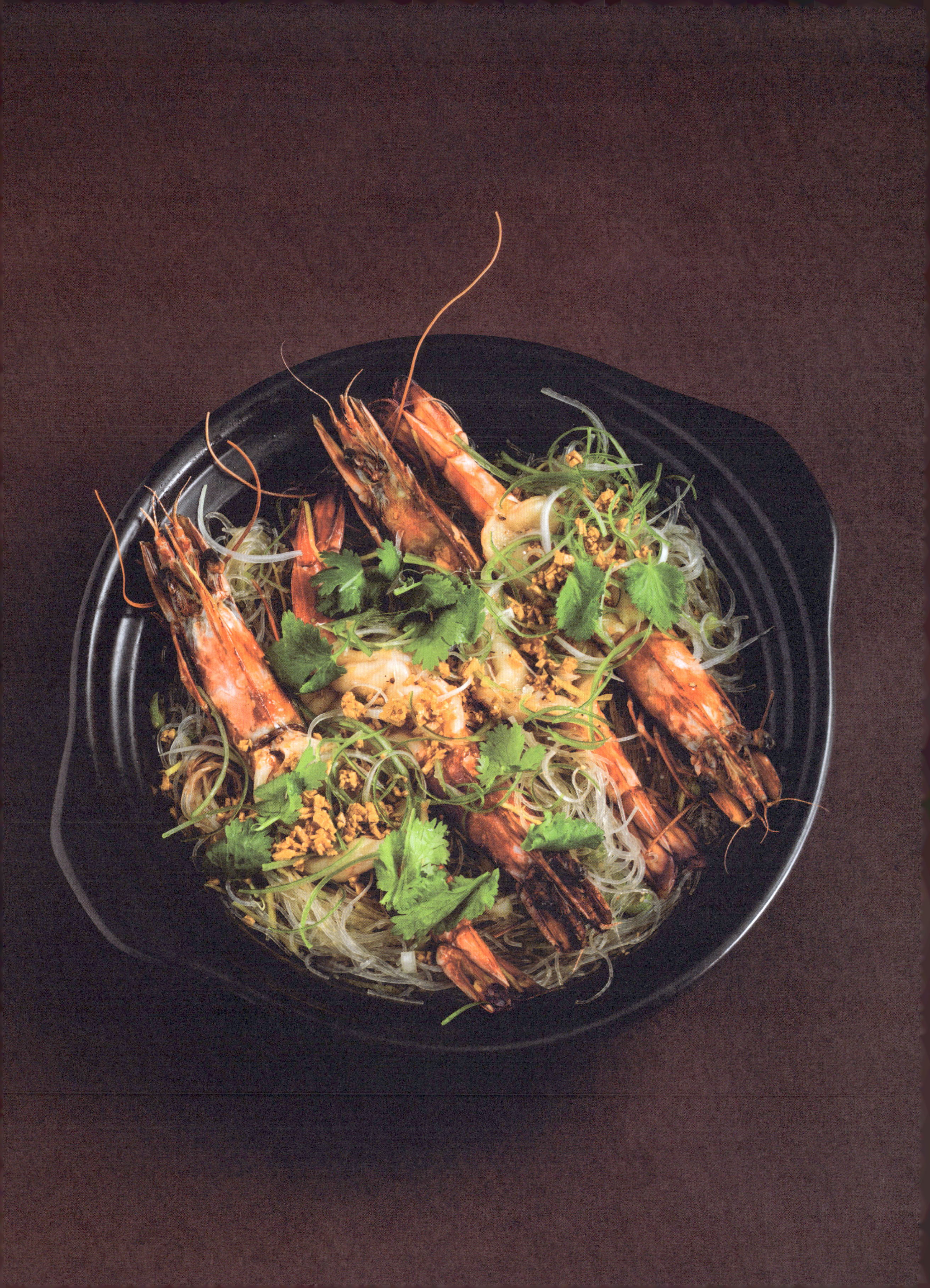

Understanding

CHǍO LÓNGXIĀ
SAUTÉED LANGOUSTINE

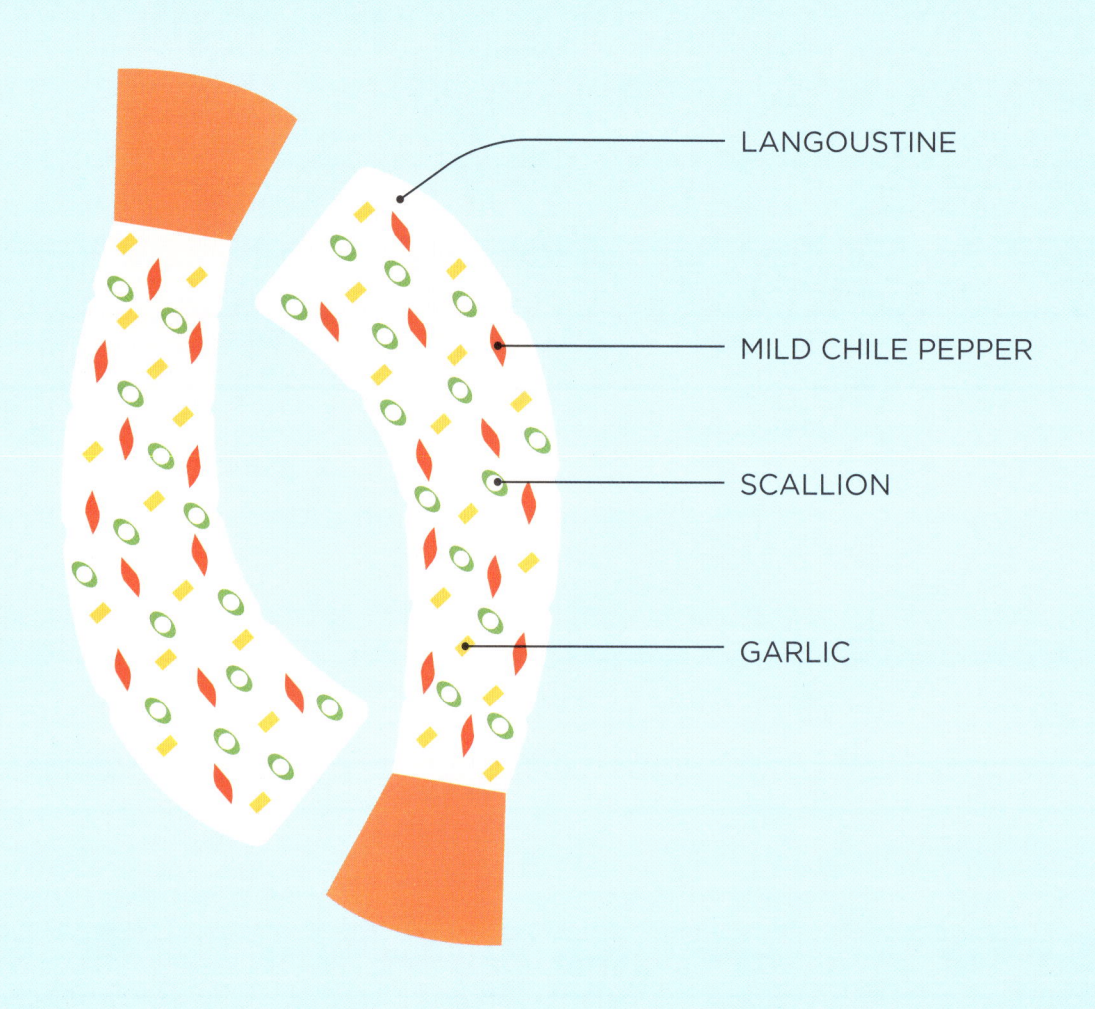

- LANGOUSTINE
- MILD CHILE PEPPER
- SCALLION
- GARLIC

WHAT IS IT?
Langoustine tails coated in cornstarch, fried briefly, then sautéed with aromatics.

COMPLETION TIME
Preparation time: 30 minutes
Cooking time: 8 minutes

VARIATIONS
You can add 1 tablespoon chopped ginger and sauté it with the garlic.

Learning

SERVES 2 TO 4

AROMATIC GARNISH

5 large cloves garlic

5 scallions

1 mild red chile pepper, or ¼ red bell pepper

2 langoustines or lobster tails (just over 1 pound / 480 g total)

SEASONING

1 level teaspoon salt

½ teaspoon organic cane sugar

1 level teaspoon ground black pepper

¼ cup plus 2 tablespoons / 50 g cornstarch

2½ cups / 600 ml oil, for frying

2 tablespoons Shaoxing wine

1 Prepare the garnish: Chop the garlic and scallions. Cut the chile peppers in half, remove the seeds, and cut into small cubes.

2 Using scissors, remove the small legs from the langoustines, then cut the langoustines lengthwise in half.

3 Make the seasoning: Combine the salt, sugar, and pepper. Season the lobster meat with the mixture and set aside; save some of the seasoning for finishing. Place the cornstarch in a shallow dish and dredge the langoustines in it.

4 Heat the oil to 450°F / 230°C. Fry the langoustines for 2 minutes. Set aside on paper towels to drain.

5 In a wok, heat 2 tablespoons of the oil that was used for frying.

6 Brown the garlic. Add the chile peppers and the scallions. Stir, and add the langoustine tails. Deglaze with the wine, and cook for an additional 2 to 3 minutes while stirring. Add the remaining seasoning.

163

Understanding
MÁPÓ DÒUFU
MAPO TOFU

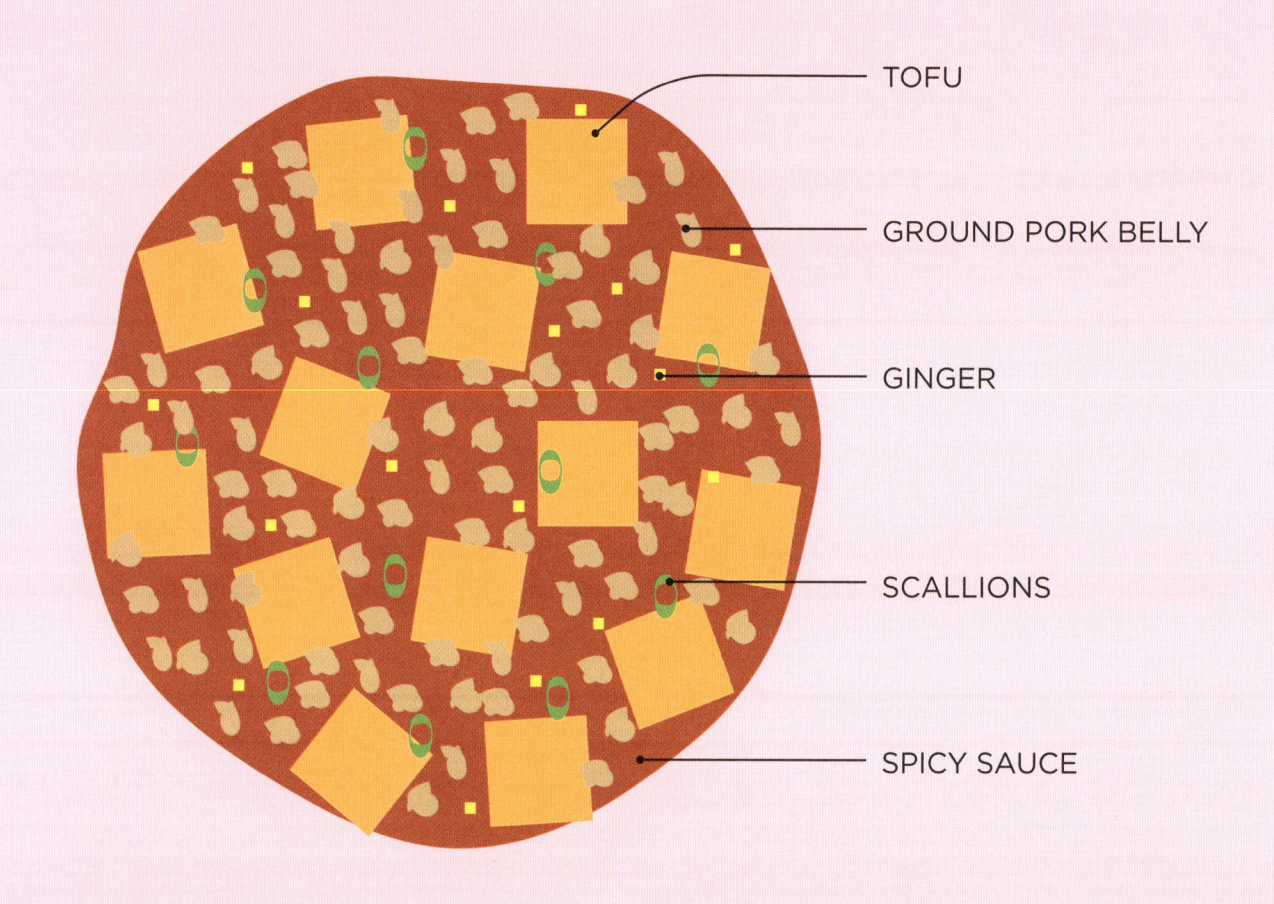

- TOFU
- GROUND PORK BELLY
- GINGER
- SCALLIONS
- SPICY SAUCE

WHAT IS IT?
Tofu cubes simmered in a spicy meat sauce.

ORIGIN
This dish is ranked among the ten most popular dishes in China. It is the most famous dish from Sichuan. The sauce combines spicy, salty, and the famous characteristic mala ("numbness"). Mápó means "old lady with a marked face." Mrs. Chen, whose face was scarred by smallpox, is said to have invented this dish at the end of the nineteenth century in the family's tofu restaurant, located north of Chengdu. The dish was intended for local workers and traveling workers looking for a nutritious and inexpensive meal.

COMPLETION TIME
Preparation time: 30 minutes
Cooking time: 12 to 15 minutes
Storage: The dish can be refrigerated for 3 days. Reheat over low heat, covered, for 10 minutes.

SPECIAL EQUIPMENT
Wok

SKILL TO MASTER
Cutting into julienne (page 281)

VARIATIONS
For a vegan version, replace the pork with 9 ounces / 250 g diced mushrooms of your choice (white button, shiitake, oyster, black, etc.). Fry them in the wok according to how the meat is prepared. The mushrooms must be golden brown before deglazing with the wine.

Learning

TRADITIONAL FIRM TOFU
The term "traditional" corresponds to firm tofu. Those from Asian specialty stores have a little softer consistency than those found in organic stores or supermarkets.

SHAOXING RICE WINE
Fermented glutinous rice wine. Choose the Pagoda brand (blue label).

DÒUBÀNJIÀNG
A spicy and savory Szechuan paste made from fermented beans and chile peppers.

SZECHUAN LONG DRIED CHILE PEPPERS
Dried chile from China of medium size and intensity.

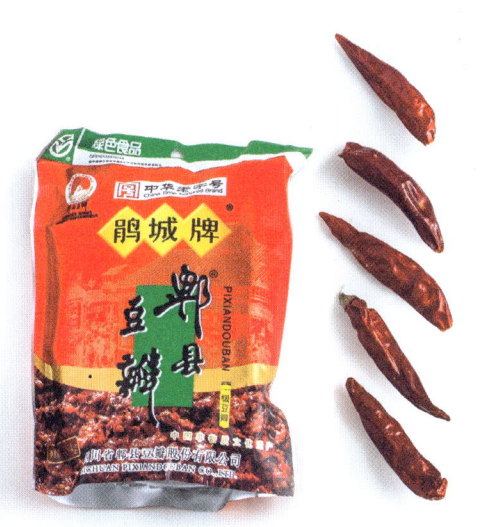

SERVES 4 TO 6

- 1 pound 2 ounces / 500 g firm tofu
- ¾ ounce / 20 g fresh ginger
- 4 cloves garlic
- 6 long dried Szechuan long dried chile peppers
- 1 heaping tablespoon Szechuan pepper
- ¼ cup / 60 ml neutral-flavor oil of your choice (sunflower, peanut)
- 9 ounces / 250 g finely chopped pork belly
- 3 tablespoons / 45 ml Shaoxing wine
- 1 tablespoon soy sauce
- 1 teaspoon five-spice powder
- 1 teaspoon organic cane sugar
- 2 tablespoons dòubànjiàng
- 1 cup / 240 ml unsalted broth or water
- 1½ tablespoons cornstarch
- 3 scallions

Making

MÁPÓ DÒUFU

1 Cut the tofu into ¾-inch / 2 cm cubes. Thinly slice the scallions and set them aside. Cut the ginger into julienne (page 281), then dice them. Press or chop the garlic. Using scissors, cut the chile peppers into pieces and remove the seeds. Crush the Szechuan pepper in a mortar.

2 In a wok or skillet, heat the oil over medium heat. Fry the chile peppers and Szechuan pepper for 1 to 2 minutes while stirring.

3 Add the garlic and ginger, and cook for an additional 1 to 2 minutes. Add the pork. Stir to loosen the pieces. When the meat begins to brown, deglaze the pan with the wine.

4 Add the soy sauce, five-spice powder, sugar, and dòubànjiàng. Cook for 2 minutes. Add the broth, then the tofu cubes.

5 Bring to a low boil. Taste, and adjust the seasoning, if necessary (with sugar and / or soy sauce). Dilute the cornstarch in 3 tablespoons / 45 ml water. Add the mixture to the wok and stir gently. Add the scallions just before serving. Serve with rice.

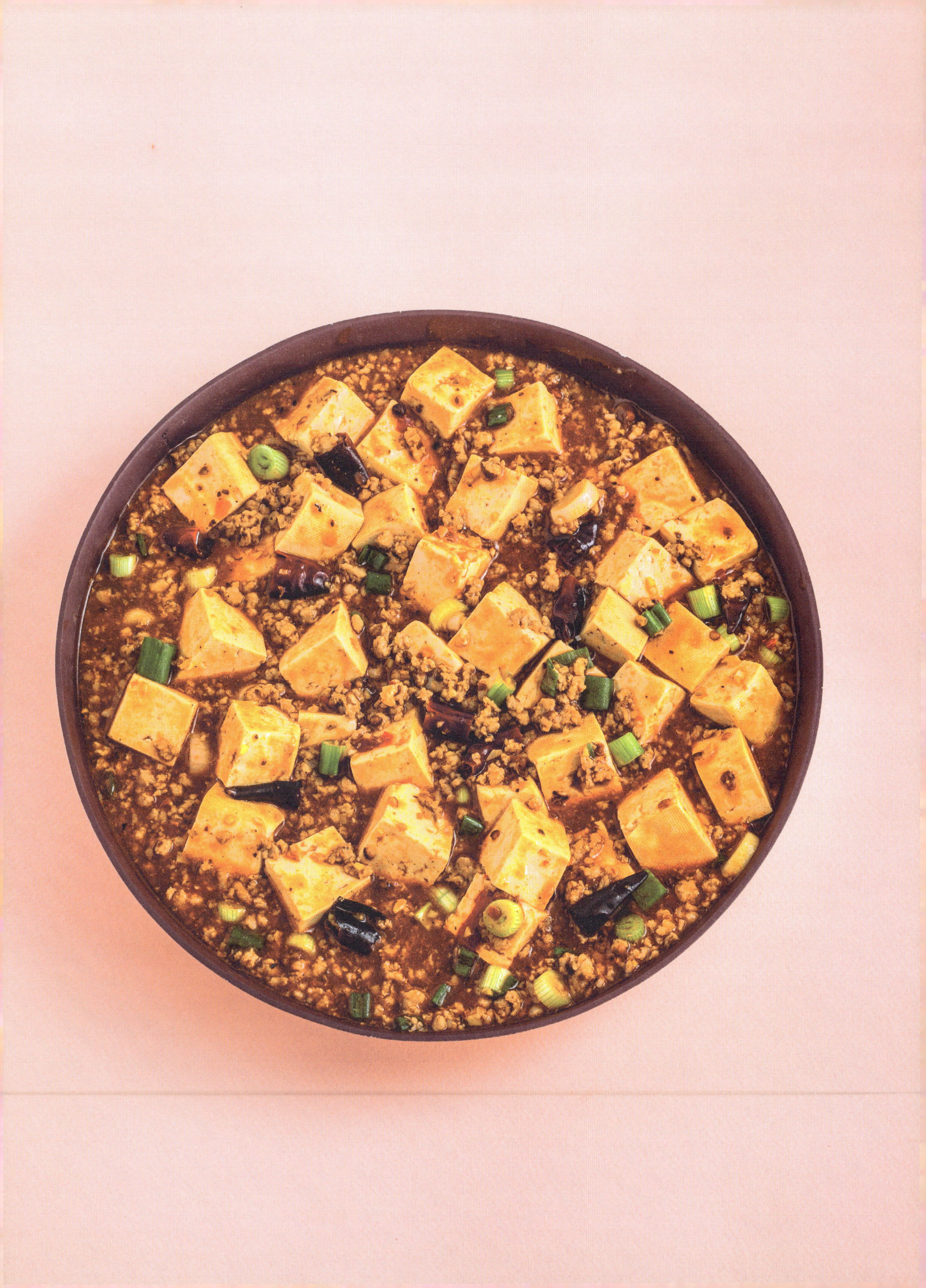

Understanding

JIĀNG CHǍO DOUFU
STIR-FRIED TOFU WITH GINGER

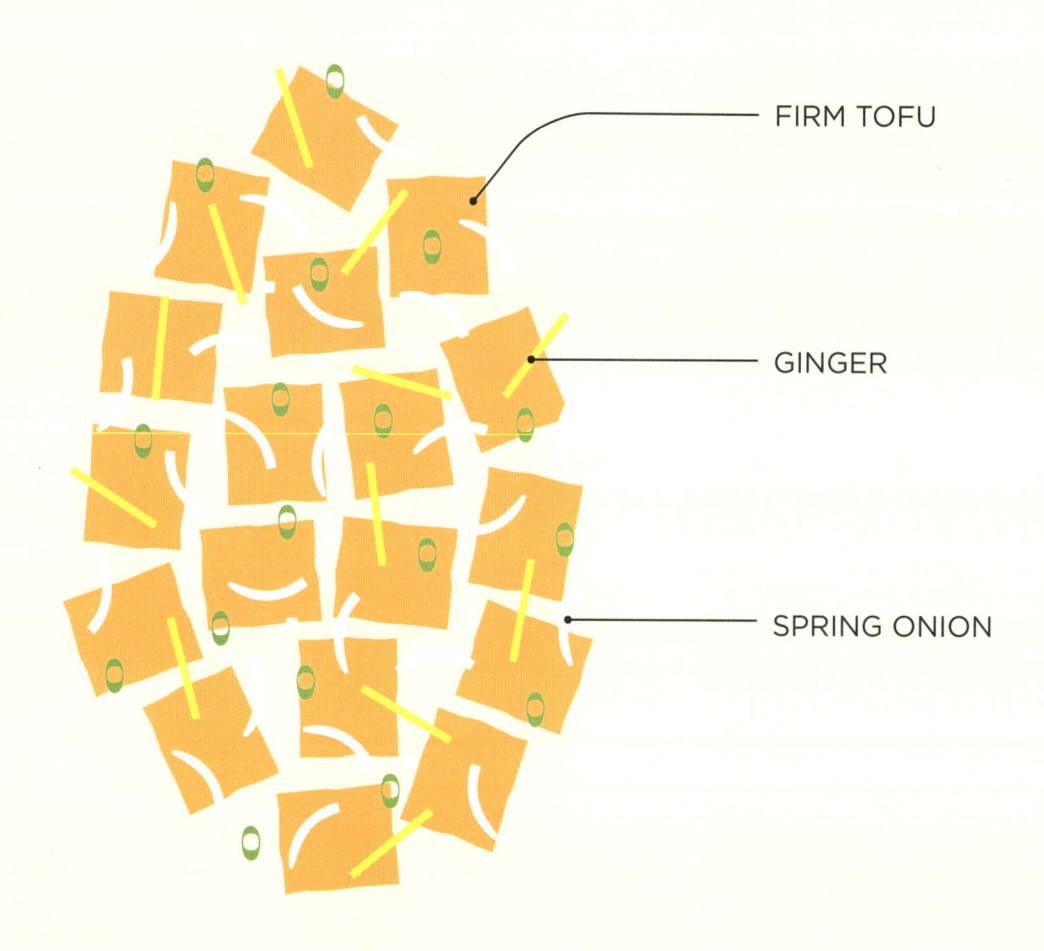

- FIRM TOFU
- GINGER
- SPRING ONION

WHAT IS IT?
Pieces of tofu coated in cornstarch, browned in oil, then sautéed with fresh onion and julienned ginger.

COMPLETION TIME
Preparation time: 15 minutes
Cooking time: 10 minutes
Storage: 2 days in the refrigerator

SKILL TO MASTER
Cutting into julienne (page 281)

VARIATIONS
Replace the oyster sauce with more mushroom sauce for a vegan version.

Learning

SERVES 4

4 spring onions

4 cloves garlic

1¾ ounces / 50 g fresh ginger

1 pound 2 ounces / 500 g traditional firm tofu

½ cup / 60 g cornstarch

¼ cup plus 1 tablespoon / 75 ml neutral-flavor oil of your choice (sunflower, peanut), plus more, as needed

2 tablespoons oyster sauce

2 to 3 tablespoons / 30 to 45 ml soy sauce

1 teaspoon cracked black peppercorns

1 Chop the white and green portions of the spring onions and separate them. Set the green portion aside in a bowl for serving. Chop the garlic. Cut the ginger into julienne (page 281).

2 Pat the tofu dry and cut it into squares. Place the cornstarch in a shallow dish, add the tofu pieces, and stir using your fingers to coat them.

3 In a skillet, heat the oil. Brown the tofu for 2 to 3 minutes on each side. Remove the tofu from the pan and set aside.

4 In the same pan, brown the garlic and ginger. Add a little more oil, if needed. Add the white portion of the spring onions and cook for 1 minute. Add the tofu, oyster sauce, soy sauce, and peppercorns. Cook for 5 minutes. Off the heat, sprinkle the onion greens over the top. Serve with white rice.

Understanding

HÁOYÓU JIÈ LÁN
GAI LAN IN OYSTER SAUCE

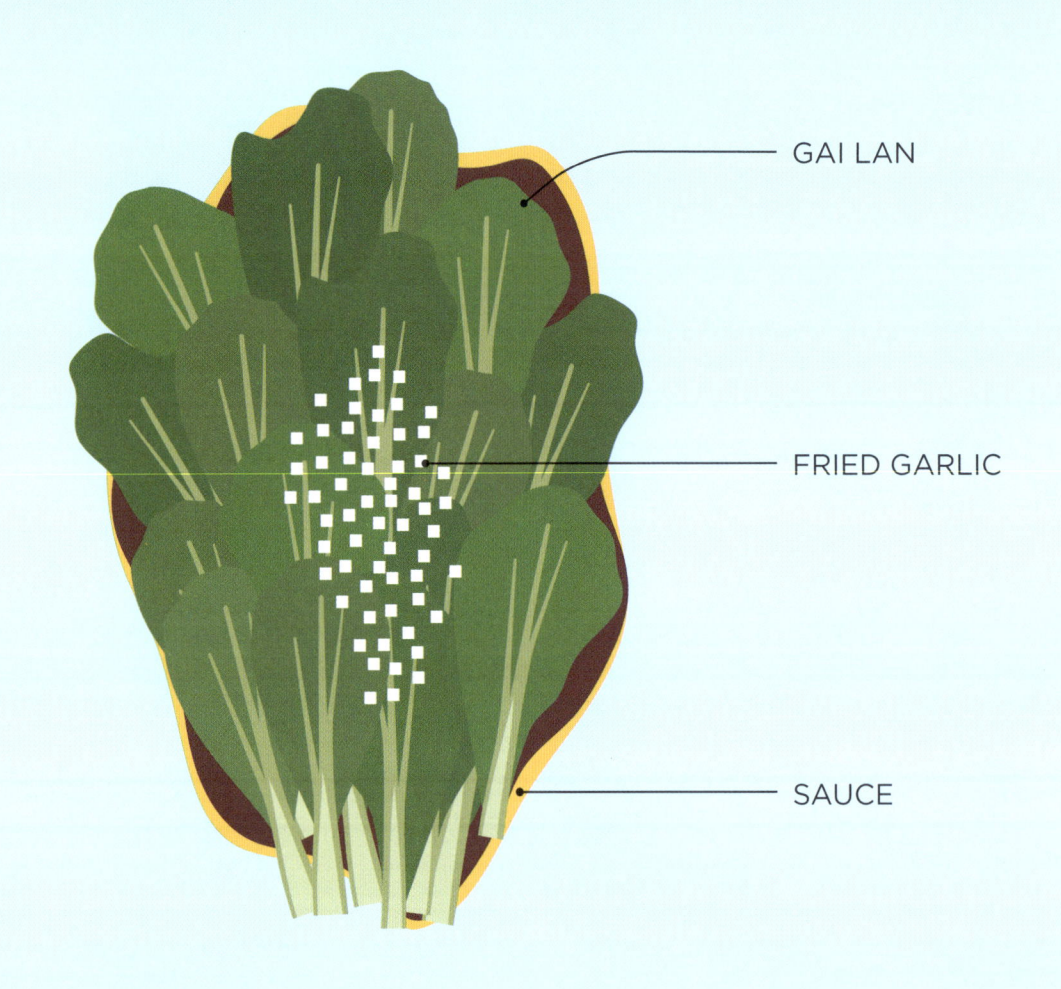

— GAI LAN

— FRIED GARLIC

— SAUCE

WHAT IS IT?
Gai lan cooked in water, topped with oyster sauce and sprinkled with fried garlic.

ORIGIN
Gai lan is a variety of cabbage that is similar to broccoli. It is sometimes called Chinese broccoli. It has large, flat, dark-green leaves with a thick, very crunchy stem. It is a very popular vegetable in Asia, and the oyster sauce recipe is a classic of Cantonese cuisine. The dish was once a luxury dish reserved for banquets due to the expensive price of oyster sauce. It has now become a daily accompaniment. The addition of fried garlic is optional, but it provides extra flavor and texture.

COMPLETION TIME
Preparation time: 15 minutes
Cooking time: 12 minutes
Storage: 2 to 3 days

CHALLENGE
Not overcooking the gai lan. It should remain slightly crunchy.

USEFUL TIP
There is a vegetarian version of oyster sauce made from mushrooms.

VARIATIONS
You can replace the gai lan with broccoli, bok choy, or string beans.

Learning

SERVES 4

1 pound 2 ounces / 500 g gai lan (Chinese broccoli)
5 cloves garlic
Salt
3 tablespoons / 45 ml peanut oil
2 tablespoons oyster sauce

1 Wash the gai lan. Cut off the tips of the gai lan stems and remove any damaged or yellowed leaves. If the stems are too thick, cut them lengthwise in half to make cooking them easier. Chop the garlic.

2 In a small saucepan over medium heat, heat the oil. Add the garlic, stir occasionally, and cook until the garlic is lightly browned. Turn off the heat and let cool; the garlic will continue to cook in the oil while it is still hot. When the garlic is golden brown, remove it and set it aside. Leave the fragrant oil in the pan.

3 Bring a large pot of salted water to a boil. Immerse the gai lan for 3 to 4 minutes. It should remain slightly crunchy. Drain, and arrange on a serving platter.

4 Meanwhile, heat the reserved oil. When hot, turn off the heat, and add the oyster sauce. Stir briskly to combine.

5 Pour over the vegetables and sprinkle with fried garlic. Serve with rice.

|71|

Understanding

LUÓHÀN ZHĀI
BUDDHA'S DELIGHT

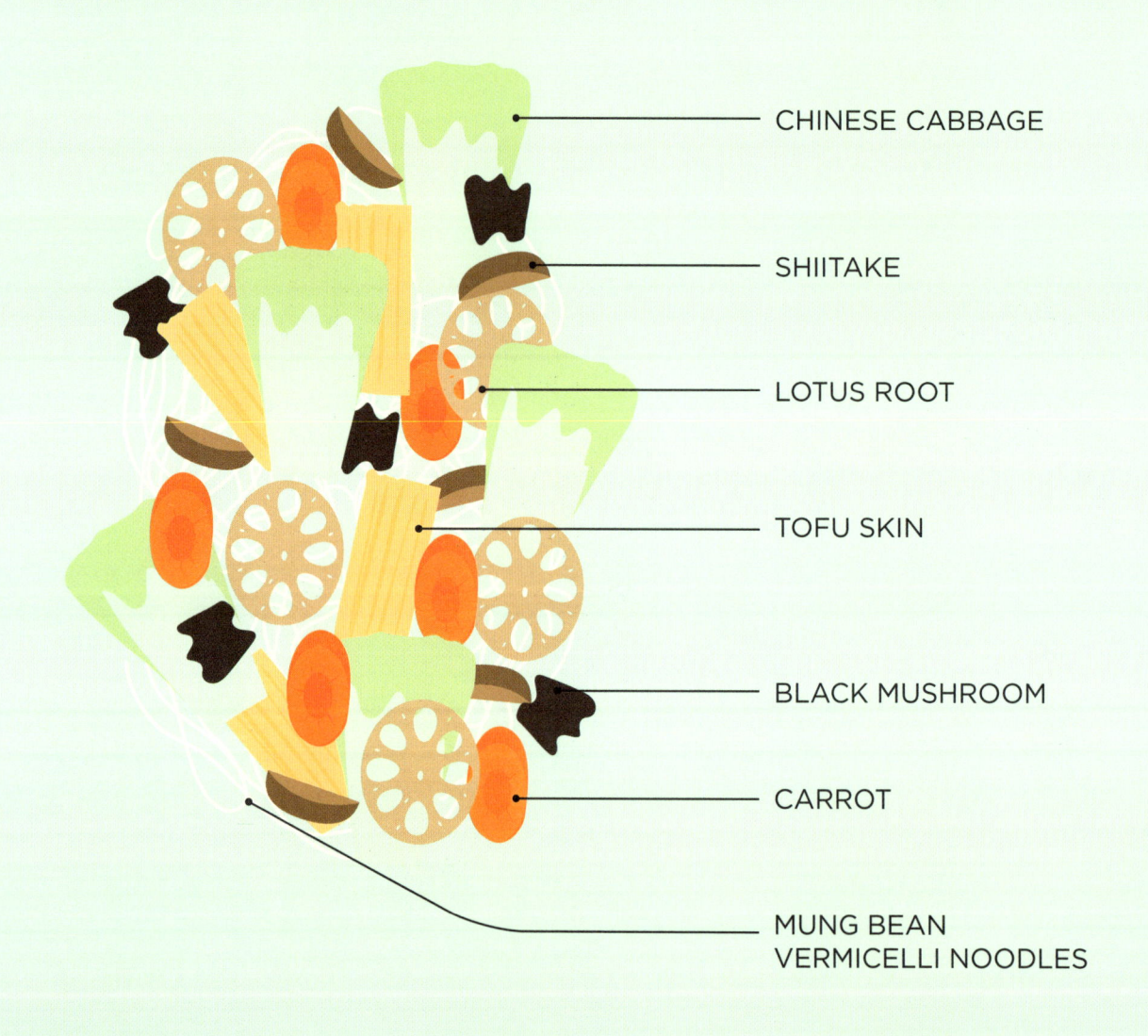

- CHINESE CABBAGE
- SHIITAKE
- LOTUS ROOT
- TOFU SKIN
- BLACK MUSHROOM
- CARROT
- MUNG BEAN VERMICELLI NOODLES

WHAT IS IT?
A vegetarian dish in which the vegetables are cooked in a liquid.

ORIGIN
Originating in Buddhist cuisine, the name means "dish of the arhats," the first disciples of Buddha who reached the last rung of wisdom and enlightenment. Legend has it that eighteen arhats dispersed to give alms. Each of them came back with a small quantity of different ingredients, which they combined to make a communal dish. According to legend, therefore, the dish contains eighteen ingredients that you can, of course, adapt to suit your tastes.

COMPLETION TIME
Preparation time: 40 minutes
Resting time: Overnight
Cooking time: 10 minutes
Storage: 2 days

SKILLS TO MASTER
Rehydrating mushrooms
Rehydrating tofu skins
Cutting into julienne

USEFUL TIP
Sliced frozen lotus roots can also be used.

VARIATIONS
You can use many kinds of tofu or vegetable proteins (seitan, tempeh, etc.) and many kinds of mushrooms, seaweed, or cabbage, as well as lotus seeds, water chestnuts, peanuts, snow peas, mung bean sprouts, or green vegetables.

Learning

CHINESE CABBAGE
This is a tender and mild cabbage. It is eaten cooked in Chinese cuisine but is also very suitable raw in salads.

TOFU SKINS
A film that forms when soymilk is boiled. It is collected and dried into sheets.

MUNG BEAN VERMICELLI NOODLES
They must be soaked before use. They become transparent after cooking.

FERMENTED WHITE TOFU CUBES
A traditional Chinese condiment. Milder than the red variety. Similar to miso.

LOTUS ROOT
Found vacuum-packed in the refrigerated section. The skin must be peeled before cutting it into slices. It has a mild and fresh flavor. It is crunchy when sautéed and becomes tender when boiled.

SERVES 4 TO 6

10 to 12 dried shiitake mushrooms
½ ounce / 15 g dried black mushrooms
- 3⅛ ounces / 90 g dried tofu skins
- 3½ ounces / 100 g mung bean vermicelli noodles
5 cloves garlic
1½ ounces / 45 g fresh ginger
2 carrots
- 5¼ ounces / 150 g fresh lotus root
- 1 pound / 450 g Chinese cabbage
3 tablespoons / 45 ml neutral-flavor oil of your choice (sunflower, peanut)

VEGETARIAN SAUCE

- 3½ ounces / 100 g fermented white tofu
1 heaping teaspoon organic cane sugar
3 tablespoons / 45 ml soy sauce

OYSTER SAUCE

3 tablespoons / 45 ml oyster sauce or vegetarian sauce
¼ cup / 60 ml soy sauce

Making

LUÓHÀN ZHĀI

1   The day before, rehydrate the shiitake mushrooms and the black mushrooms separately. Rehydrate the tofu skins.

2   The next day, rehydrate the vermicelli by soaking it for 30 minutes in a container of cold water.

3   Drain the mushrooms; reserve the water from the shiitake mushrooms. Cut the tofu skins into sections of about 2⅓ inches / 6 cm. Chop or press the garlic. Cut the ginger into fine julienne. Slice the shiitake mushrooms, and roughly chop the black mushrooms. Slice the carrots at a slight angle. Peel the lotus root and cut it into about ⅛-inch-thick / 3 mm slices. Cut the cabbage into even pieces. Combine the ingredients for either the vegetarian sauce or oyster sauce. For the vegetarian sauce, mash the tofu using a spoon before adding the remaining ingredients.

4   In a large wok or skillet, heat the oil and sauté the shiitake, garlic, and ginger. When the garlic is golden, add the carrots, black mushrooms, cabbage, lotus root, and tofu skins. Add the sauce and just over ¾ cup of the reserved shiitake soaking water.

5   Cover and cook for 4 minutes.

6   Stir. Add the drained vermicelli, cover, and continue cooking for 3 to 5 minutes. Stir, and taste to check for doneness. Season as necessary. You can add 1 tablespoon of sesame oil when serving. Serve with rice.

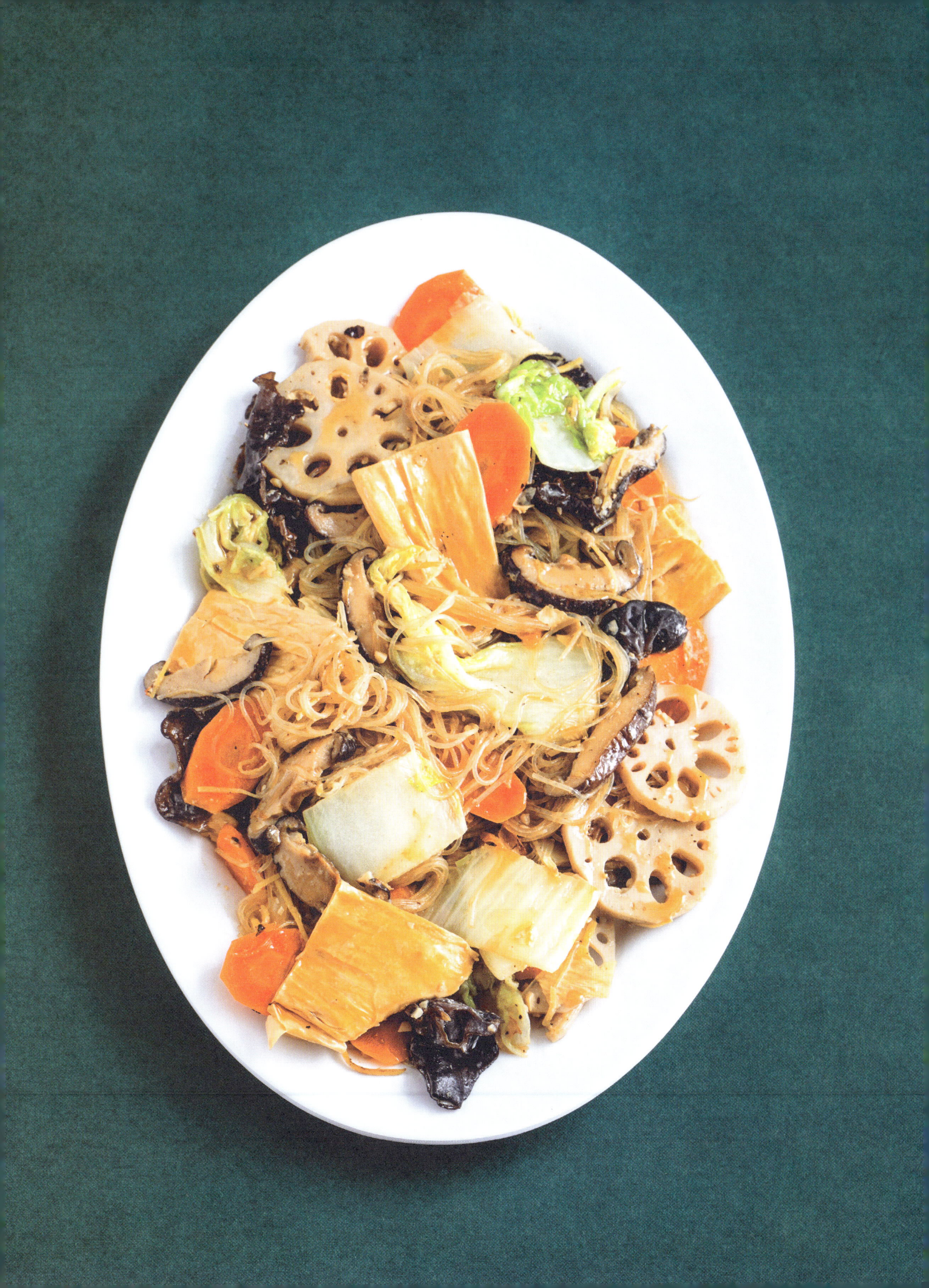

Understanding

PĀI HUÁNGGUĀ
PRESSED CUCUMBER SALAD

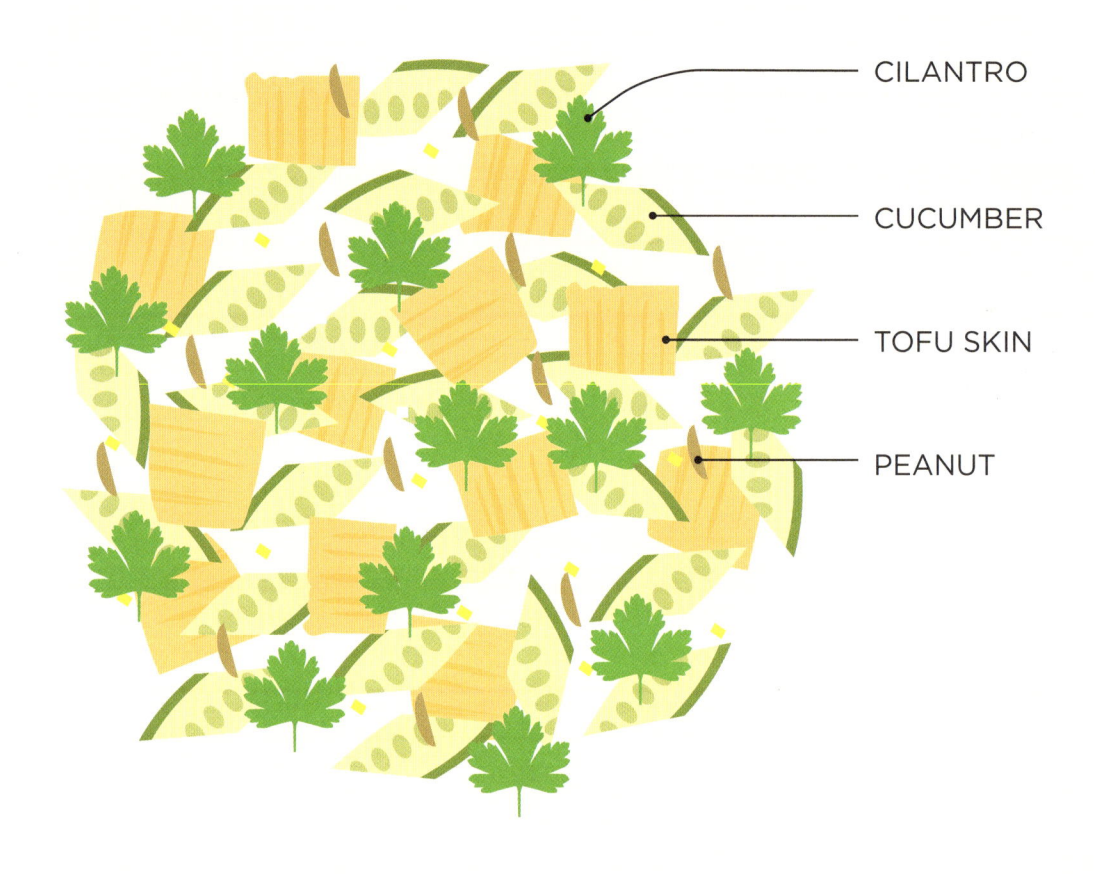

- CILANTRO
- CUCUMBER
- TOFU SKIN
- PEANUT

WHAT IS IT?
A cucumber salad in which the cucumber has been flattened using a cleaver or rolling pin.

COMPLETION TIME
Preparation time: 20 minutes
Resting time: 3 hours 20 minutes
Cooking time: 1 minute

SKILL TO MASTER
Rehydrating tofu skins (page 280).

NOTE
Flattening the cucumber randomly breaks the fibers of the vegetable, allowing the dressing added to the dish to penetrate better.

USEFUL TIP
You can use a commercial chile oil (such as Lao Gan Ma brand).

SERVES 4
1½ ounces / 40 g tofu skins

DRESSING
1 large clove garlic
½ ounce / 15 g fresh ginger
2 tablespoons organic cane sugar
2 tablespoons white rice vinegar
1 tablespoon plus 1 teaspoon / 20 ml Chinkiang black rice vinegar
3 tablespoons / 45 ml soy sauce

Learning

2 cucumbers
(about 1 pound 11 ounces / 750 g)
1 teaspoon salt
1 teaspoon organic cane sugar
½ bunch of cilantro
1 tablespoon Chile Oil (page 44)
1 tablespoon sesame oil
1 tablespoon toasted sesame seeds
⅓ cup / 60 g roasted salted peanuts

1 Rehydrate the tofu skins (page 280). Make the dressing: Press the garlic, and cut the ginger into strips and then into small cubes. In a small saucepan, combine the sugar, vinegars, and soy sauce. Bring to a boil and let cook for 20 seconds. Turn off the heat, and add the garlic and ginger. Set aside to cool.

2 When the tofu skin is rehydrated and no longer has any tough sections, cut it into even pieces. Bring a pot of water to a boil and blanch the tofu skins for 1 to 2 minutes. Drain, and let cool.

3 Wash the cucumbers. Using a vegetable peeler, alternate removing a strip of cucumber skin with a strip that remains. Place the cucumbers on a cutting board and, using a rolling pin, press them lengthwise to flatten them, turning them a quarter turn each time. Once the cucumber is flattened, remove the seeds and cut into bite-size sticks (about 1⅓ inch / 3.5 cm long and ⅓ inch / 8 mm wide).

4 Season the cucumbers with the salt and sugar. Transfer them to a strainer and place the strainer on a plate in the refrigerator for about 20 minutes to drain.

5 Chop the cilantro with its stems. Transfer the dressing to a bowl. Add the chile and sesame oils. Add the cucumber and tofu skins. Add the sesame seeds, peanuts, and chopped cilantro. Stir to combine. Serve.

Understanding

HÓNGSHĀO QIÉZI
BRAISED EGGPLANT

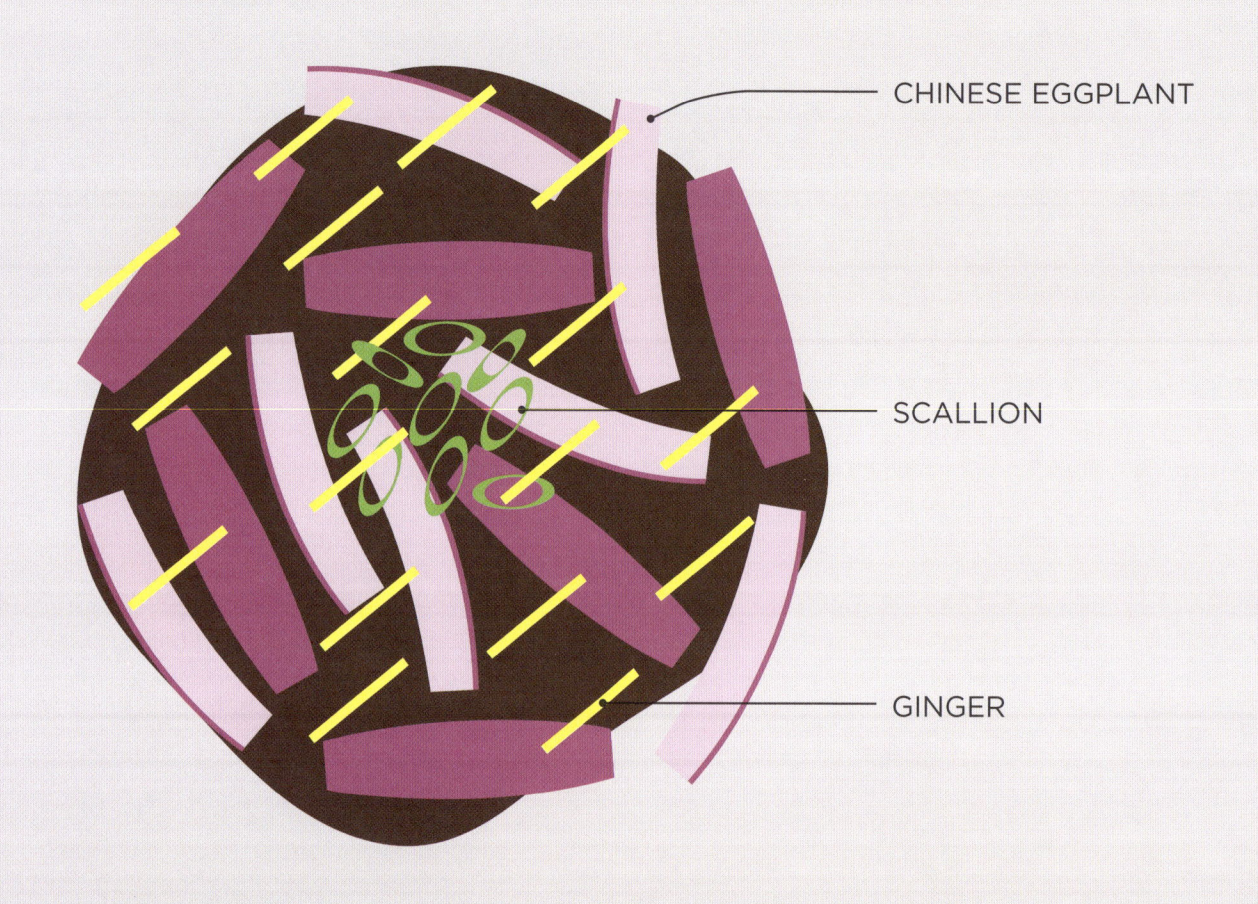

- CHINESE EGGPLANT
- SCALLION
- GINGER

WHAT IS IT?
Eggplant slices coated in cornstarch, browned in oil, and cooked in a sauce of garlic and ginger.

COMPLETION TIME
Preparation time: 20 minutes
Resting time: 30 minutes
Cooking time: 10 minutes
Storage: 2 days

SKILL TO MASTER
Cutting into julienne (page 281)

VARIATIONS
You can replace long Chinese eggplants with classic eggplants. You can also cut the eggplant into pieces or medium rounds.

SERVES 2 TO 4
12 ounces / 350 g Chinese long eggplant (about 2)
1 tablespoon coarse salt
3 large cloves garlic
¾ ounce / 20 g fresh ginger
1 scallion

Learning

SAUCE

2 tablespoons soy sauce

1 teaspoon dark soy sauce

1 teaspoon organic cane sugar

⅔ cup / 150 ml Basic Broth (page 38) or water

Freshly ground black pepper

¼ cup plus 1 tablespoon / 40 g cornstarch

5 tablespoons / 75 ml neutral oil

1 Cut the eggplants lengthwise in half, then into sections of about 2 inches / 5 cm. Place them in a bowl of water, add the salt, and set aside for about 30 minutes to allow them to release their water.

2 Chop the garlic, and cut the ginger into fine julienne (page 281). Slice the scallion. Make the sauce: Combine the soy sauces, sugar, and broth. Season with pepper, and set aside.

3 Drain the eggplants and pat them dry using a clean kitchen towel. Add the cornstarch to a small bowl. Dredge the eggplants in the cornstarch. Remove excess cornstarch by placing the eggplant in a strainer and gently shaking it.

4 In a wok or skillet, heat 4 tablespoons / 60 ml of the oil. Brown the eggplant skin side up for about 3 to 4 minutes.

5 Remove the eggplants. Sauté the garlic and ginger in the remaining oil. Once they are golden brown, add the sauce and then the eggplant. Stir to combine. Cook until the sauce has thickened slightly. Serve garnished with scallions.

Understanding

SHŎU SĪ BĀO CÀI
CABBAGE STIR-FRY IN VINEGAR

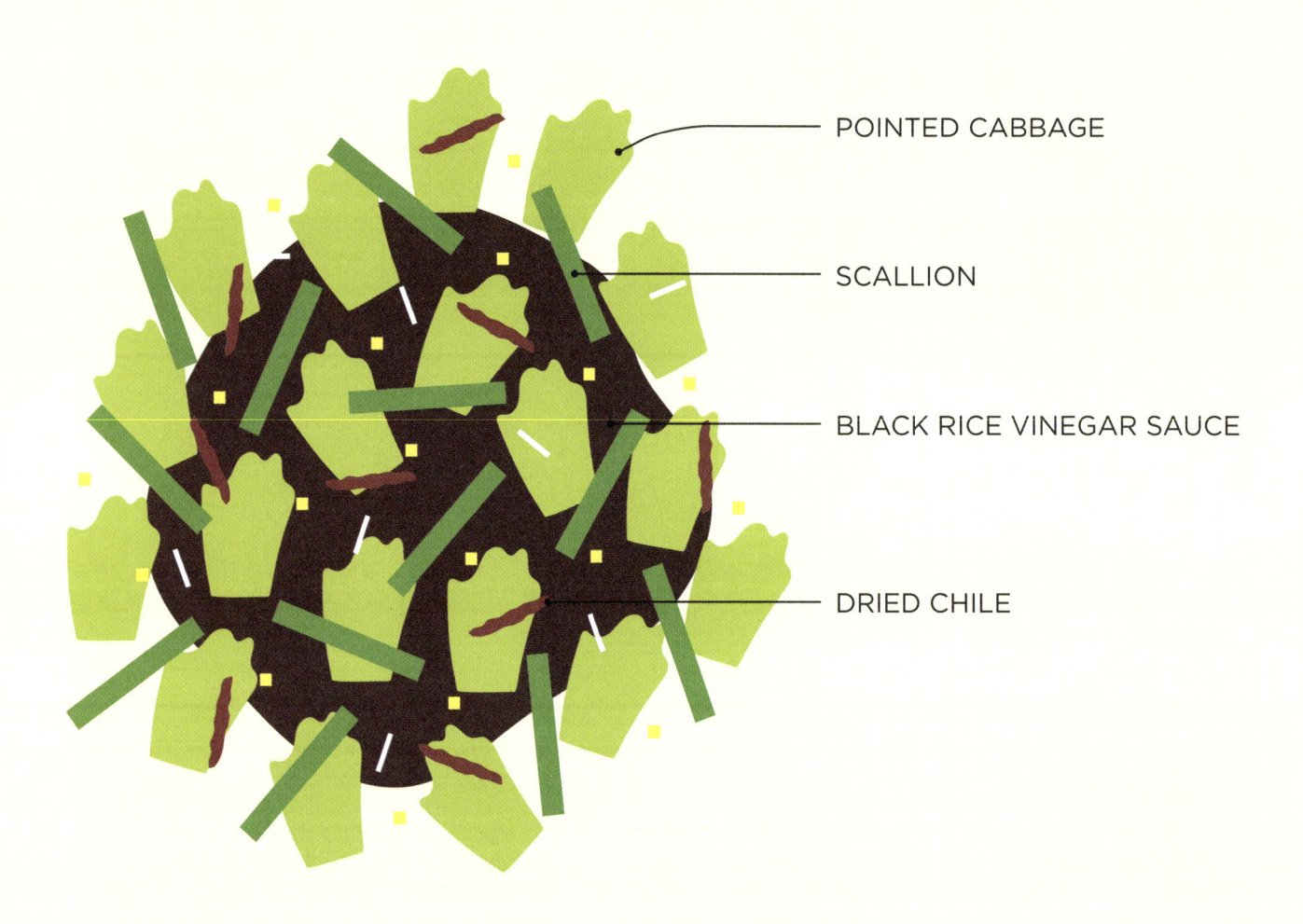

- POINTED CABBAGE
- SCALLION
- BLACK RICE VINEGAR SAUCE
- DRIED CHILE

WHAT IS IT?
Cabbage sautéed in black rice vinegar and chile pepper.

ORIGIN
The name literally means "hand-torn cabbage." This is an easy and quick dish, popular in southern regions, historically linked to farmers who used cabbages grown in their own fields. It combines three local ingredients: cabbage, black rice vinegar, and chile pepper. The hand-torn leaves soak up the sauce better.

COMPLETION TIME
Preparation time: 15 minutes
Cooking time: 5 minutes
Storage: 3 to 4 days

SPECIAL EQUIPMENT
Wok

USEFUL TIP
It is best to use a cabbage with tender leaves.

Learning

SERVES 4

1 pound 5 ounces / 600 g pointed cabbage or other white cabbage
5 large cloves garlic
⅛ ounce / 5 g fresh ginger
2 scallions
5 dried chile peppers

SAUCE

3 tablespoons / 45 ml soy sauce
3 tablespoons / 45 ml Chinkiang black rice vinegar
½ teaspoon salt
1 heaping teaspoon organic cane sugar

3 tablespoons / 45 ml neutral oil
1 teaspoon Szechuan pepper

1   Remove the leaves from the cabbage. Tear the leaves coarsely by hand. Finely chop the tougher parts of the stems.

2   Chop the garlic and grate the ginger. Cut the scallions into sections of about 1½ inches / 4 cm. Separate the white sections from the green sections. Halve the chile peppers and remove the seeds.

3   Make the sauce: Combine the soy sauce, vinegar, salt, and sugar.

4   In a large wok or skillet over medium heat, heat the oil. Sauté the Szechuan pepper with the chile peppers for 30 seconds. Add the garlic and ginger and cook for 10 seconds.

5   Stir, increase the heat to maximum, and add the cabbage and the white sections of the scallions. Cook for 1 to 2 minutes, or until the cabbage leaves have wilted. Add the sauce. Stir to combine, and continue cooking for another 2 to 3 minutes. Taste. The cabbage should be slightly crunchy. Continue cooking to taste and adjust the seasoning, if necessary. Add the scallion greens. Stir to combine.

Understanding

DÌSĀNXIĀN
THREE TREASURES FROM THE EARTH

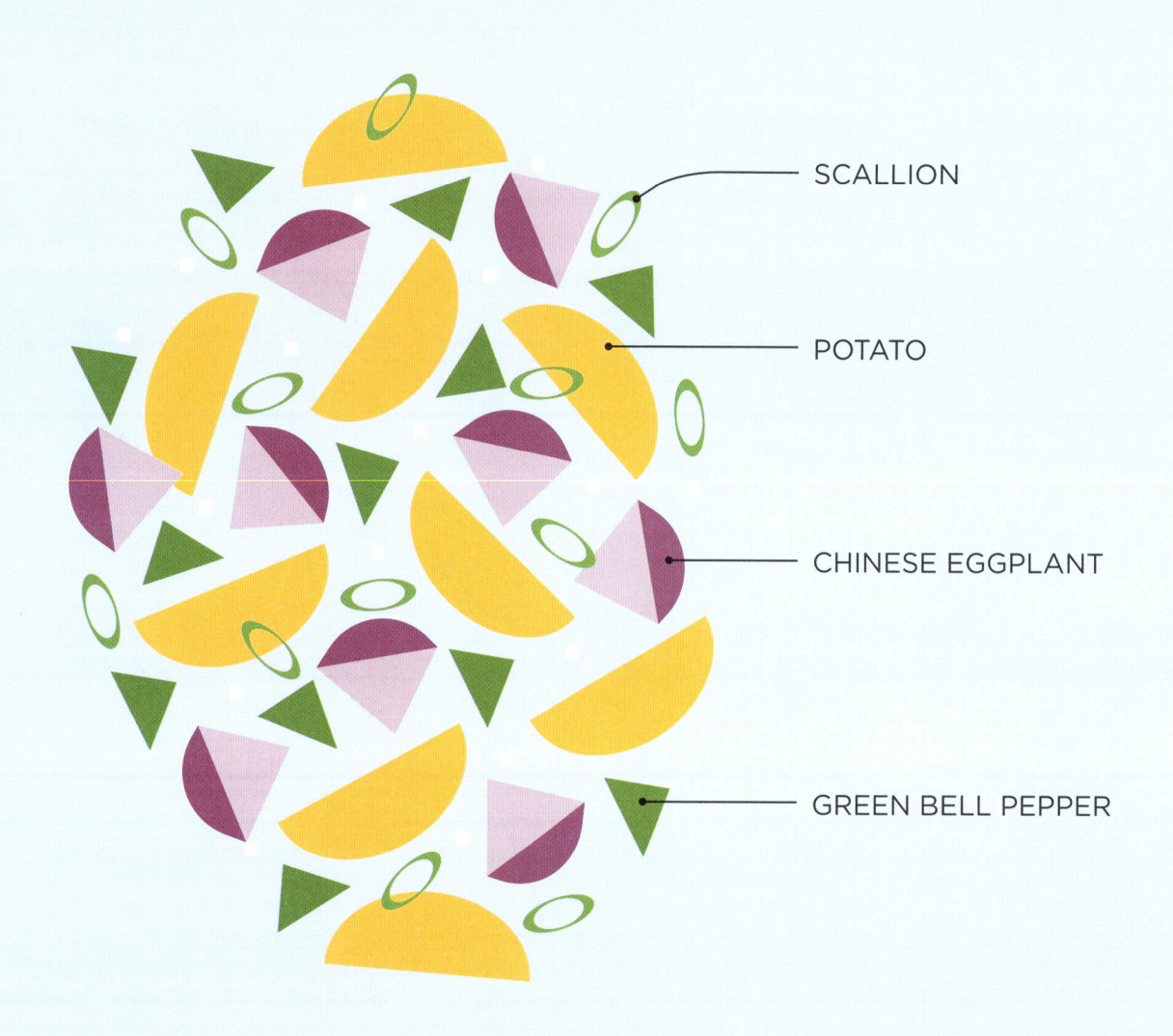

- SCALLION
- POTATO
- CHINESE EGGPLANT
- GREEN BELL PEPPER

WHAT IS IT?
Eggplant, potatoes, and bell peppers steamed then sautéed and coated in sauce.

ORIGIN
This is a dish from Dongbei (northeastern China). The area is known for its rustic and copious cuisine adapted to cold climates.

COMPLETION TIME
Preparation time: 30 minutes
Cooking time: 20 minutes

SPECIAL EQUIPMENT
2 steamer baskets
Steamer

NOTE
Traditionally, the vegetables are chopped and then fried before being sautéed. This version replaces frying with steaming. The pre-steaming allows the vegetables to absorb less oil, making the dish more digestible.

USEFUL TIPS
If the steamer baskets can be stacked, cook the vegetables at the same time and remove the eggplants 2 minutes before the potatoes.

Learning

CHINESE LONG EGGPLANT
A dense-fleshed eggplant with few seeds. It has a mild flavor without bitterness. It should not be peeled.

SOY SAUCE
Choose bottles that state "natural fermentation."

OYSTER SAUCE
Choose the Megachef or Lee Kum Kee (Premium) brands.

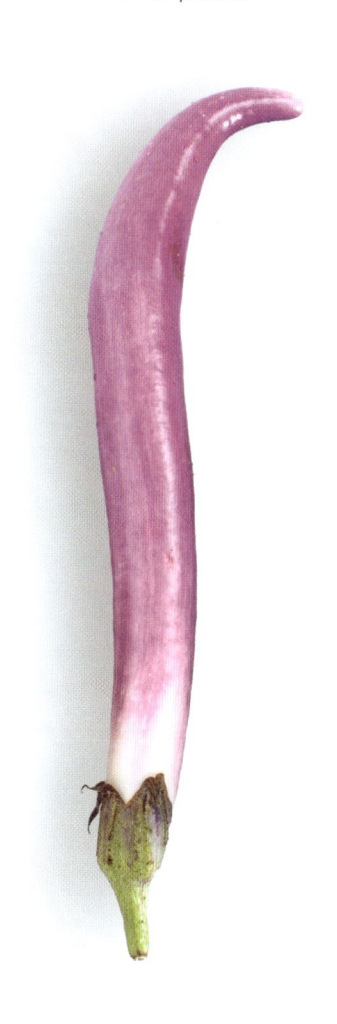

SERVES 2 TO 3

- 9 ounces / 250 g firm potatoes (2 medium)
- 12 ounces / 350 g Chinese long eggplants (about 2)
- 1 small (5¼ ounces / 150 g) green bell pepper
- 3 large cloves garlic
- 2 scallions

SAUCE

- 1 tablespoon soy sauce
- 1 tablespoon oyster sauce
- 1 teaspoon organic cane sugar
- ½ teaspoon salt
- Scant ½ cup / 100 ml Basic Broth (pages 38 and 40) or water
- Freshly ground black pepper

¼ cup plus 1 tablespoon / 75 ml neutral-flavor oil of your choice (sunflower, peanut)

3 tablespoons / 25 g cornstarch

Making

DÌSĀNXIĀN

1 Cut the end of a potato into a bevel by turning a quarter turn and cutting on the diagonal. Repeat these steps, always turning a quarter turn, to obtain angled pieces of about 1 inch / 3 cm. Cut the eggplants in the same way. Cut the bell pepper into quarters and then into angled pieces (about ¾ inch / 2 cm).

2 Cook the potatoes and the eggplants in two separate steamer baskets, 6 to 7 minutes for the potatoes, and 4 minutes for the eggplants. Let cool on two separate plates.

3 Chop the garlic. Slice the scallions. Make the sauce: Combine the soy sauce, oyster sauce, sugar, salt, and broth. Season with pepper.

4 In a nonstick skillet, heat the oil. Sprinkle the potatoes with half the cornstarch and toss to coat well. Over medium heat, brown the potatoes on each side for about 6 minutes. Set aside. Coat the eggplants with the remaining cornstarch and brown them in the same pan for about 5 minutes, without adding oil. Set aside. Sauté the bell pepper in the remaining oil for 1 minute.

5 Add the garlic. When the garlic is golden, add the sauce. As soon the mixture comes to a boil, add the vegetables and scallions. Toss gently to coat the vegetables with the sauce. Serve with rice (page 12).

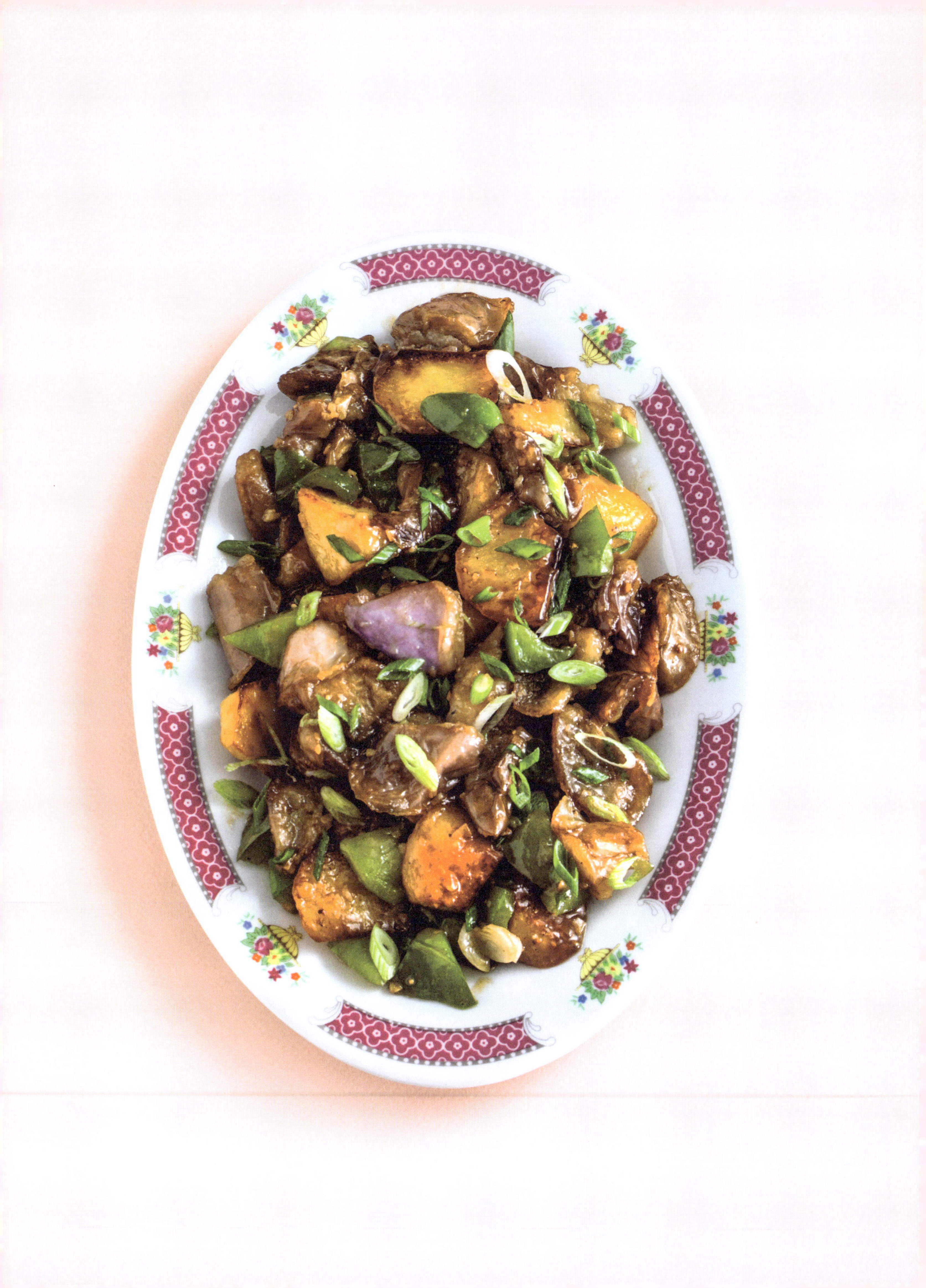

Understanding

SUĀN LÀ TĀNG
HOT AND SOUR SOUP

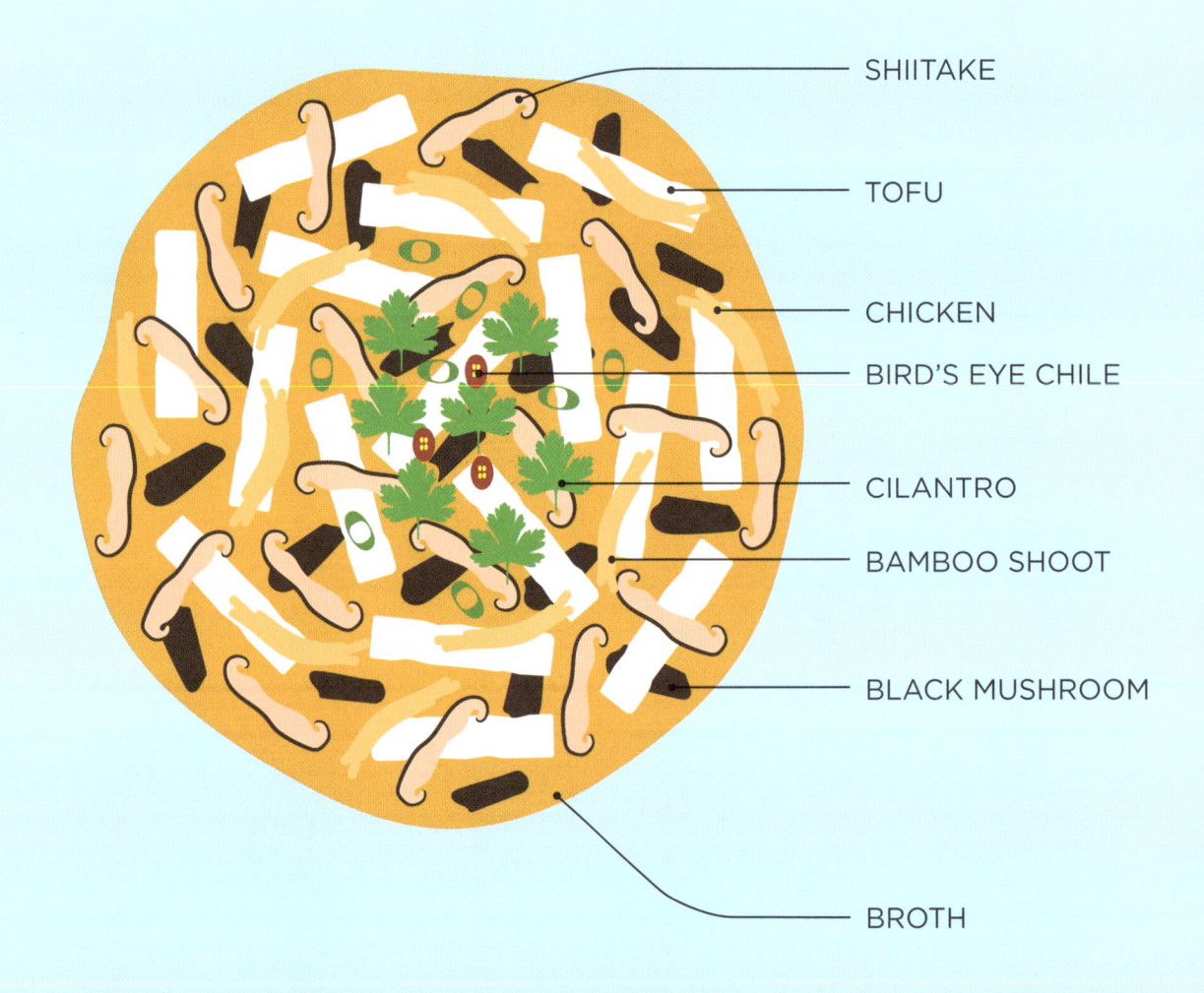

- SHIITAKE
- TOFU
- CHICKEN
- BIRD'S EYE CHILE
- CILANTRO
- BAMBOO SHOOT
- BLACK MUSHROOM
- BROTH

WHAT IS IT?
A soup made with chicken broth, bamboo shoots, tofu, mushrooms, and beaten eggs added in a thin stream, then thickened with cornstarch.

ORIGIN
Referred to as Peking soup in most restaurants, this soup is Szechuan in origin. Its distinction is in its seasoning, a balance between saltiness, acidity, and spiciness, which is very characteristic of Szechuan cuisine. It is said to have health benefits of clearing the sinuses and warming the body in cold weather.

COMPLETION TIME
Preparation time: 40 minutes
Cooking time: 1 hour 15 minutes
Storage: The soup can be kept for 4 to 5 days in the refrigerator. Reheat for 10 minutes over low heat. It will be necessary to add more cornstarch diluted in water, as it will have lost its velvetiness.

SKILL TO MASTER
Rehydrating mushrooms (page 280)

SERVING
Everyone can adjust their flavoring by adding more of the crushed chiles and rice vinegar.

USEFUL TIP
Blanching bamboo shoots removes their pungent smell.

Learning

DRIED SHIITAKE
Depending on their size, rehydrate them for at least 2 hours before use. They are more concentrated and have a more umami taste than fresh ones.

CHINKIANG BLACK RICE VINEGAR
It has a mild acidity, almost sweet and smoky, with hints of malt.

DRIED BLACK MUSHROOMS
Rehydrate them 20 to 30 minutes before use. They have a crunchy, slightly gelatinous texture. Their taste is subtle rather than neutral. They absorb the flavors of other ingredients and provide a textural contrast.

TRADITIONAL FIRM TOFU
The term "traditional" corresponds to firm tofu. Those from Asian specialty stores have a little softer consistency than those found in organic stores or supermarkets.

BAMBOO SHOOTS
Canned bamboo shoots. Boil them in water before using them to remove the pungent smell.

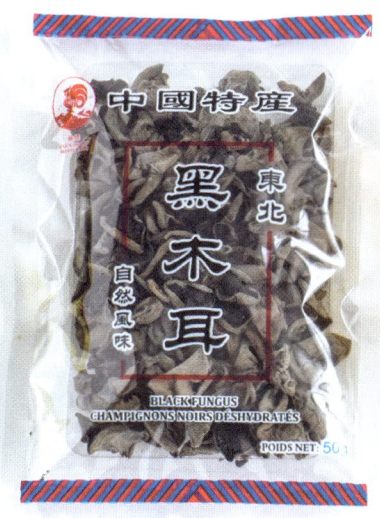

SERVES 6

- ¾ ounce / 20 g dried shiitake mushrooms (6 to 8 small)
- ½ ounce / 15 g dried black mushrooms

BROTH
1 onion
1 carrot
2 stalks celery
1¾ ounces / 50 g fresh ginger
1 red chile pepper
Cilantro stems
3 cloves garlic

2 free-range chicken thighs
¼ cup / 60 ml soy sauce
1 heaping teaspoon organic cane sugar
Salt

- 5¼ ounces / 150 g canned bamboo shoots

3 to 4 long red or bird's eye chile peppers
6 scallions

- 7 ounces / 200 g firm tofu

Scant ½ cup / 100 ml Shaoxing wine (optional)
4 tablespoons / 45 g potato starch
2 large / 100 g eggs
Freshly ground black pepper

- 4 to 6 tablespoons / 60 to 90 ml black rice vinegar of your choice, such as Chinkiang or Yongchun Laogu

¼ cup / 60 ml soy sauce
½ bunch of cilantro

Making

SUĀN LÀ TĀNG

1 Rehydrate the shiitake mushrooms and black mushrooms (page 280) in separate bowls for 2 hours (during the time it takes to prepare the entire dish). Make the broth: Wash and peel the onion, carrot, and celery. Cut the ginger into strips, remove the seeds from the chile pepper (or keep them for more spiciness), and cut the carrot and onion in pieces. Remove the leaves from the cilantro and reserve the stems. Crush the garlic cloves (page 281).

2 In a large Dutch oven, combine the chicken thighs, soy sauce, sugar, onion, carrot, celery, cilantro stems, garlic, and chile pepper. Add 1 teaspoon of salt. Add 2½ quarts / 2.5 L water and bring to a boil. Skim off any impurities from the surface. Reduce the heat to low and cook for 1 hour.

3 Blanch the bamboo shoots for 1 minute in boiling water (page 281). Drain.

4 Depending on your preference, crush the desired quantity of chile peppers with a little salt using a mortar and pestle, or blend it. Chop the scallions. Cut the tofu into small, even rectangles or cubes. Drain the mushrooms and chop them.

5 When the chicken begins to pull away from the bone, strain the broth. Remove the skin from the chicken and shred the meat.

6 Return the chicken to the pot along with the broth. Add the wine, if using, bamboo shoots, and shiitake mushrooms. Bring to a low boil for 5 minutes. Add the black mushrooms and tofu and continue cooking for 5 minutes. Add a little water to the potato starch. Whisk the eggs with a little salt. Pour the diluted cornstarch into the soup while stirring. As soon as the soup thickens, add the eggs in a stream while stirring constantly. Turn off the heat. Season generously with pepper. Add the vinegar and soy sauce. Taste, and adjust the seasoning, if necessary. Serve hot with the scallions, chopped cilantro, and crushed chiles.

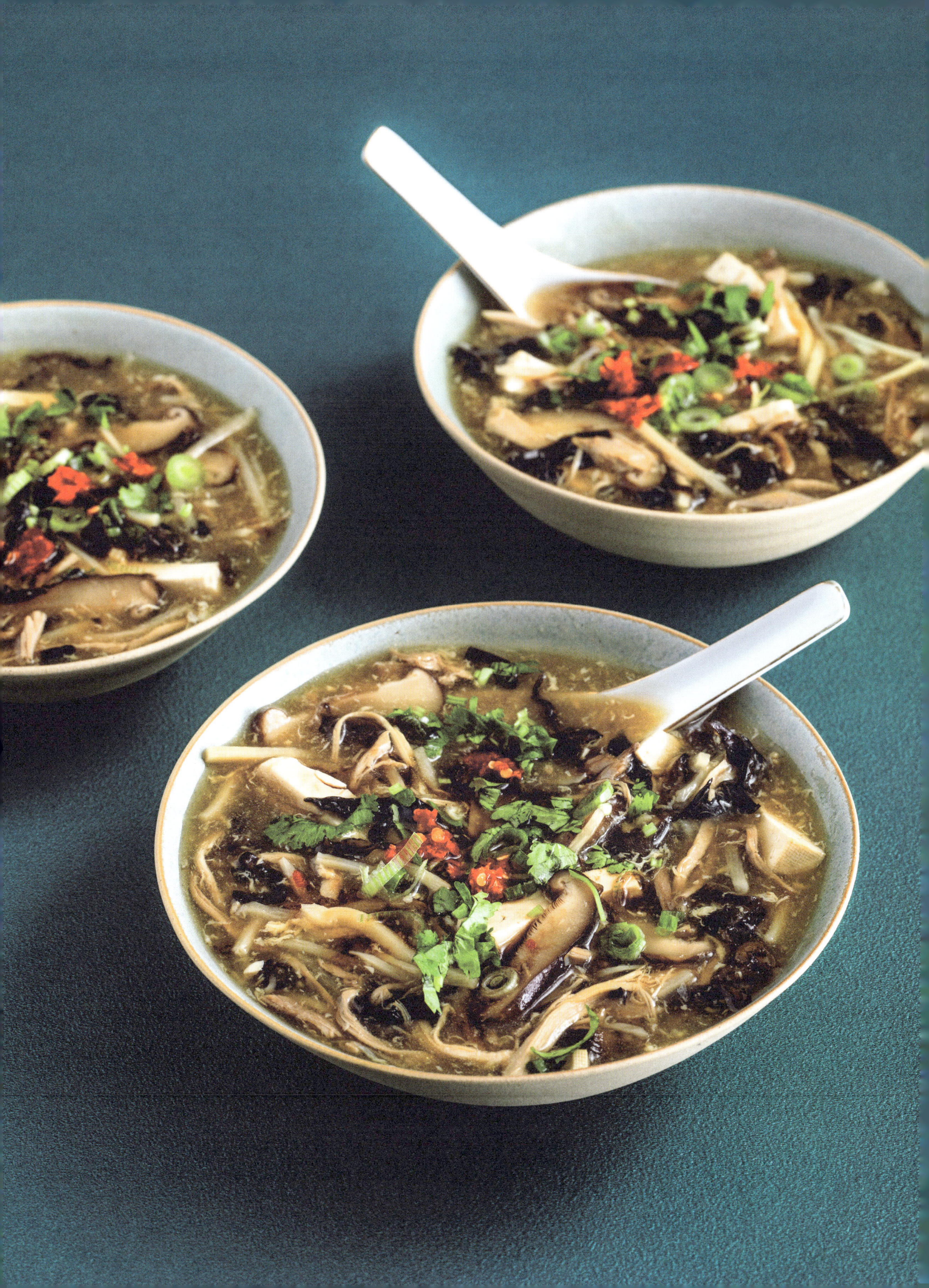

Understanding

CHŪN BǏNG
SPRING PANCAKE

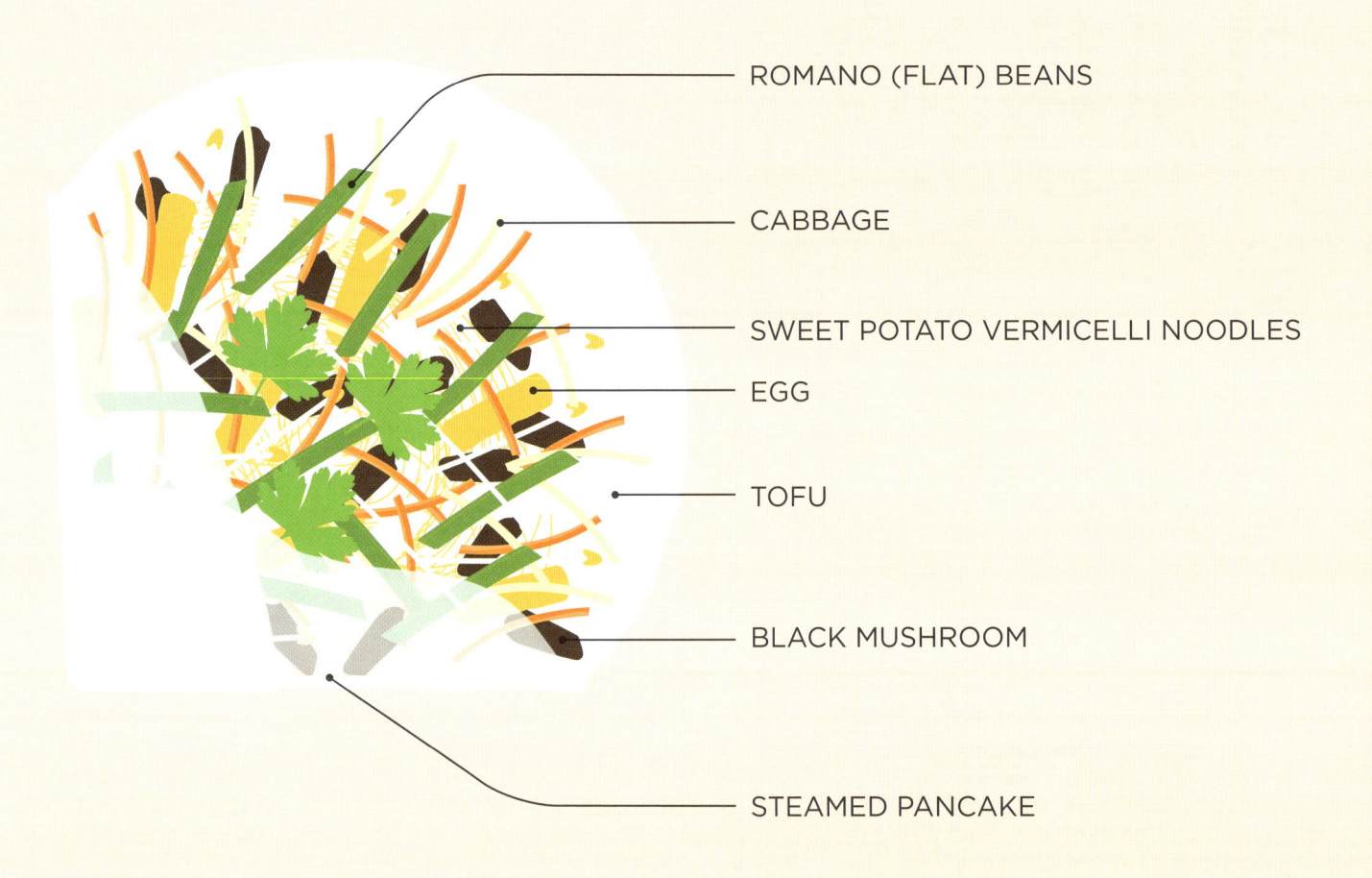

- ROMANO (FLAT) BEANS
- CABBAGE
- SWEET POTATO VERMICELLI NOODLES
- EGG
- TOFU
- BLACK MUSHROOM
- STEAMED PANCAKE

WHAT IS IT?

A pancake made of wheat flour, steamed and topped with stir-fried vegetables, slices of meat, and eggs.

ORIGIN

Originating in northern China (in particular Beijing and neighboring provinces), these pancakes are traditionally prepared during the Lichun festival, which celebrates the arrival of spring in regions where the winter is particularly harsh.

COMPLETION TIME

Preparation time: 1 hour
Cooking time: 15 minutes
Storage: The pancakes can be prepared up to 3 to 4 days in advance. Reheat them for 5 minutes by steaming. Separate them one by one when they are hot by peeling them, then wrap them in plastic wrap and set them aside in a cool place.

SKILL TO MASTER

Cutting into julienne (page 281)

Learning

SWEET POTATO VERMICELLI NOODLES

They must be soaked before use. After cooking, they become translucent, elastic, and slightly rubbery. They have a neutral taste, perfect for soaking up sauces and broths.

HOISIN SAUCE

A Chinese barbecue sauce. It is brown, thick, and salty-sweet.

TRADITIONAL FIRM TOFU

The term "traditional" corresponds to firm tofu. Those from Asian specialty stores have a little softer consistency than those found in organic stores or supermarkets.

YELLOW BEAN SPROUTS

Not to be confused with mung bean sprouts. They have thicker, sturdier stems. They remain firm and crunchy after cooking.

DRIED BLACK MUSHROOMS

Rehydrate them 20 to 30 minutes before use. They have a crunchy, slightly gelatinous texture. Their taste is subtle rather than neutral. They absorb the flavors of other ingredients and provide a textural contrast.

SERVES 4

- 3½ ounces / 100 g sweet potato vermicelli noodles
- ⅛ ounce / 5 g dried black mushrooms
- 4 cloves garlic
- 5¼ ounces / 150 g spring cabbage
- 7 ounces / 200 g tofu of your choice
- 3½ ounces / 100 g carrot
- 3½ ounces / 100 g Romano beans
- 3½ ounces / 100 g yellow bean sprouts or mung bean sprouts
- 4 scallions
- 3 tablespoons / 45 ml neutral-flavor oil of your choice (sunflower, peanut)
- 3 tablespoons / 45 ml oyster sauce
- 3 tablespoons / 45 ml soy sauce
- 1 teaspoon organic cane sugar
- Freshly ground black pepper

EGGS

6 large / 350 g eggs
1 tablespoon soy sauce
1 pinch of organic cane sugar
Freshly ground black pepper
2 tablespoons neutral-flavor oil of your choice (sunflower, peanut)

16 Steamed Wheat-Flour Pancakes (page 32)
- Hoisin sauce
Chile Oil (page 44)
4 scallions
½ bunch of cilantro

|91

Making

CHŪN BĬNG

1 Rehydrate the sweet potato vermicelli noodles according to the packet instructions and the black mushrooms (page 281). Chop or press the garlic.

2 Slice the cabbage, and cut the tofu into strips or cubes. When the mushrooms are rehydrated, slice them. Cut the carrot into sections, then into 1/10-inch / 2 mm strips, then into julienne strips (page 281). Cut the beans into thirds, then cut each portion into julienne. Cut the scallions into sections and then into julienne.

3 Bring a saucepan of water to a boil. Cook the vermicelli for 30 seconds, then drain and rinse with cold water.

4 Heat the 3 tablespoons / 45 ml of neutral-flavor oil in a wok. Add the garlic, and cook until lightly browned. Add the carrot and mushrooms. Cook for 2 minutes, then add the vermicelli and the cabbage, beans, sprouts, scallions, and tofu. Add the oyster sauce, 3 tablespoons / 45 ml of soy sauce, and the sugar. Season with pepper. Stir, and cook for 5 minutes. Taste, and adjust the seasoning, if necessary. Set aside.

5 Prepare the eggs: Lightly beat the eggs with the soy sauce and sugar. Season with pepper. In a wok or skillet, heat the 2 tablespoons of oil and add the eggs. As soon as the eggs begin to firm up, scramble them, and cook for just 1 minute. Set aside.

6 Heat the pancakes for 5 minutes by steaming them. Arrange the vegetables, eggs, hoisin sauce, chile oil, scallions, and finely chopped cilantro in small bowls and arrange them on the table. Each person will roll up their selected ingredients in a pancake, adding a little sauce and garnish. To fold them: Fold the bottom edge of the pancake up over the ingredients, then fold in the two sides and roll them up like a spring roll.

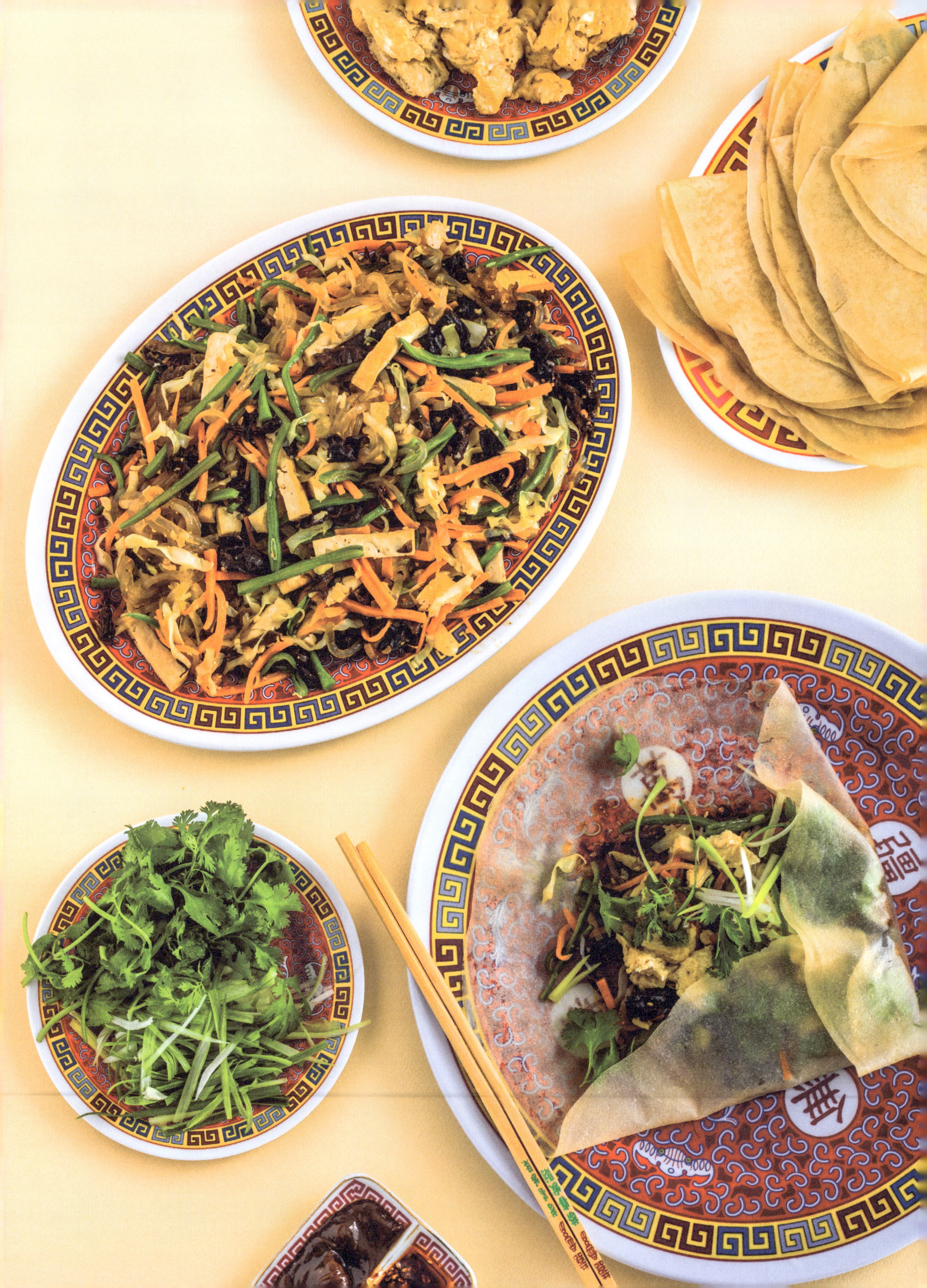

Understanding

HĂIXIĀN CHĂOMIAN
SEAFOOD NOODLES

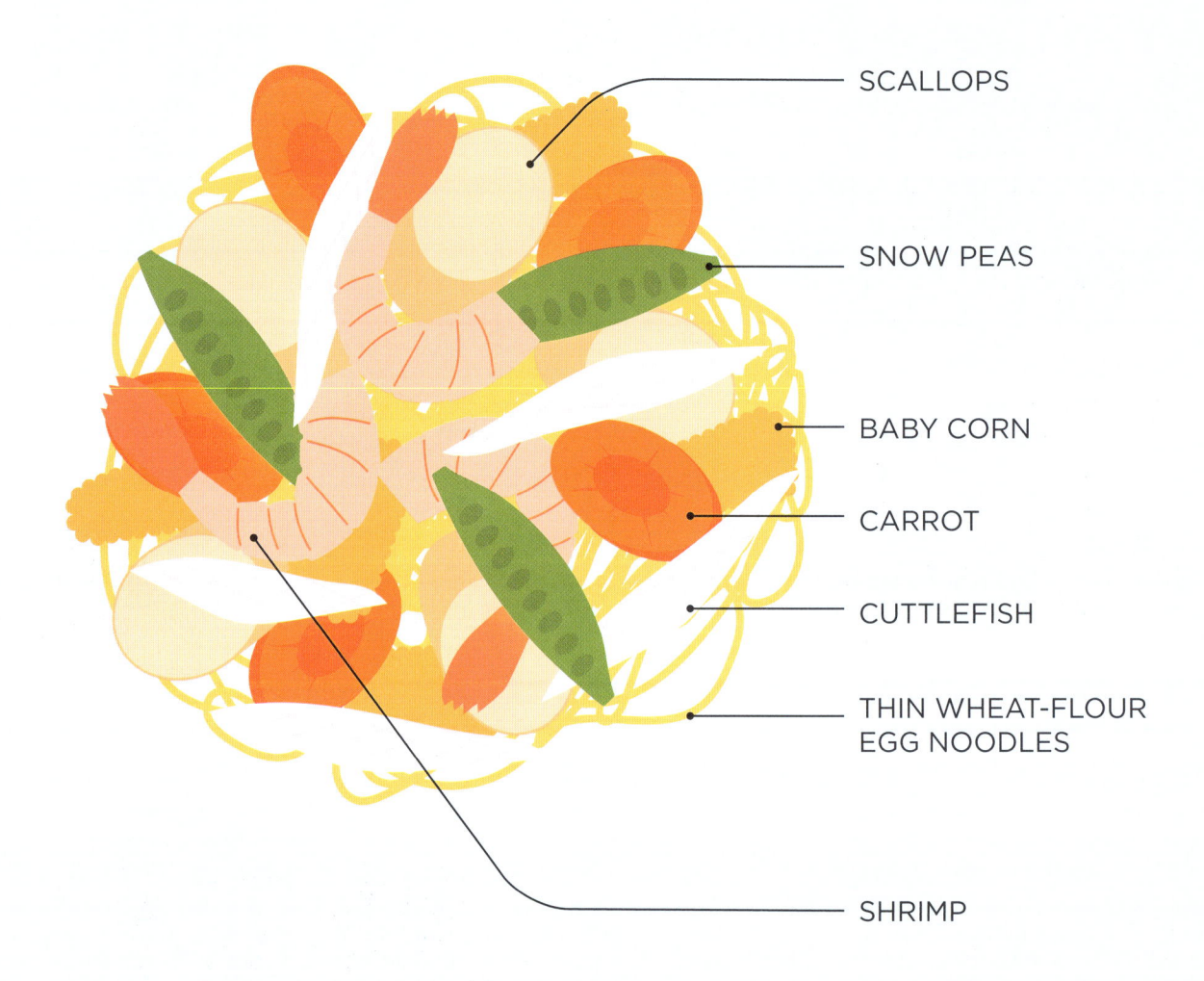

- SCALLOPS
- SNOW PEAS
- BABY CORN
- CARROT
- CUTTLEFISH
- THIN WHEAT-FLOUR EGG NOODLES
- SHRIMP

WHAT IS IT?
A crispy noodle dish topped with a seafood and vegetable sauce.

ORIGIN
This is an iconic dish from Hong Kong. In restaurants, noodles are fried in an oil bath. This version makes a less fatty dish, but above all noodles that have both crispy and soft textures.

COMPLETION TIME
Preparation time: 35 minutes
Resting time: 20 minutes
Cooking time: 12 minutes
Storage: 2 days, but the noodles will lose their crisp texture.

VARIATIONS
You can replace the seafood with 14 ounces / 400 g white meat of your choice. Add salt to the marinade.

Learning

KWANTUNG MIJIU
Fermented glutinous rice wine, similar to sake.

OYSTER SAUCE
Choose the Megachef or Lee Kum Kee (Premium) brands.

SOY SAUCE
Choose bottles that state "natural fermentation."

THIN WHEAT-FLOUR EGG NOODLES
Available in the refrigerated section of Asian grocery stores. If using dried, choose the thinnest ones possible.

BABY CORN
Immature ears of corn picked at the very beginning of the season. They come from Asia and are sold fresh in trays in Asian grocery stores.

SERVES 4 TO 6

- 14 ounces / 400 g Egg Noodles (page 26) or store-bought egg noodles

MARINATED SEAFOOD

8 peeled shrimp

5 ounces / 200 g cuttlefish (use the mantle)

6 scallops

- 3 tablespoons / 45 ml kwangtung mijiu
- 1 tablespoon oyster sauce

Freshly ground black pepper

1 carrot
- 8 baby corn

2 ounces / 60 g snow peas

4 cloves garlic

⅓ ounce / 10 g fresh ginger (optional)

Neutral-flavor oil of your choice (sunflower, peanut)

1⅔ cups / 400 ml Basic Broth (pages 38 and 40) or water

- 1 tablespoon soy sauce
- 2 tablespoons oyster sauce

1 level teaspoon organic cane sugar

4 tablespoons / 30 g cornstarch

Freshly ground black pepper

195

Making

HĂIXIĀN CHĂOMIÀN

1 Prepare the egg noodles (page 26). Prepare the shrimp (page 36). Score the outside of the cuttlefish in a crisscross pattern, making an incision about every ⅛ inch / 4 mm. Cut the cuttlefish into rectangles of about 2 by 1 inch / 5 by 3 cm.

2 Marinate the seafood: Combine the shrimp, cuttlefish, scallops, kwangtung mijiu, and oyster sauce. Season with pepper. Stir to combine, and refrigerate for 20 minutes to marinate.

3 Slice the carrot at a slight angle. Cut the baby corn into two angled sections. Cut off the ends of the snow peas. Chop the garlic, and slice the ginger, if using, into thin strips and then into small cubes.

4 Bring a pot of water to a boil. Add the noodles and cook for 10 seconds. Drain, and rinse briefly with cold water. Drain again, and carefully pat dry using a clean kitchen towel. Set aside.

5 In a wok or nonstick skillet over medium heat, heat ¼ cup / 60 ml of oil. Add half the noodles, spreading them out evenly in the bottom of the pan. Shape them into a kind of a nest. Cook for 2 to 3 minutes, watching them carefully. The underside should be golden and crisp. Turn the noodle nest over, similar to turning over a pancake. Cook the other side in the same way. Add a little oil, if needed. Transfer the noodle nest to paper towels, then transfer them to a serving platter. Repeat with the remaining noodles.

6 In a saucepan or nonstick skillet over medium heat, heat ¼ cup / 60 ml of oil. Brown the garlic, then add the ginger and carrot. Cook for 1 minute, then add the broth, soy sauce, oyster sauce, and sugar. Bring to a boil.

7 Combine the cornstarch with 3 tablespoons / 45 ml water. Add the shrimp, snow peas, and corn to the skillet. Cook for 1 minute. Add the cuttlefish and scallops and cook for 1 minute. Add the diluted cornstarch mixture and stir until the sauce thickens and develops a coating consistency. Season with pepper. Taste, and adjust the seasoning, if necessary. Pour the sauce over the noodles, arranging the elements harmoniously together.

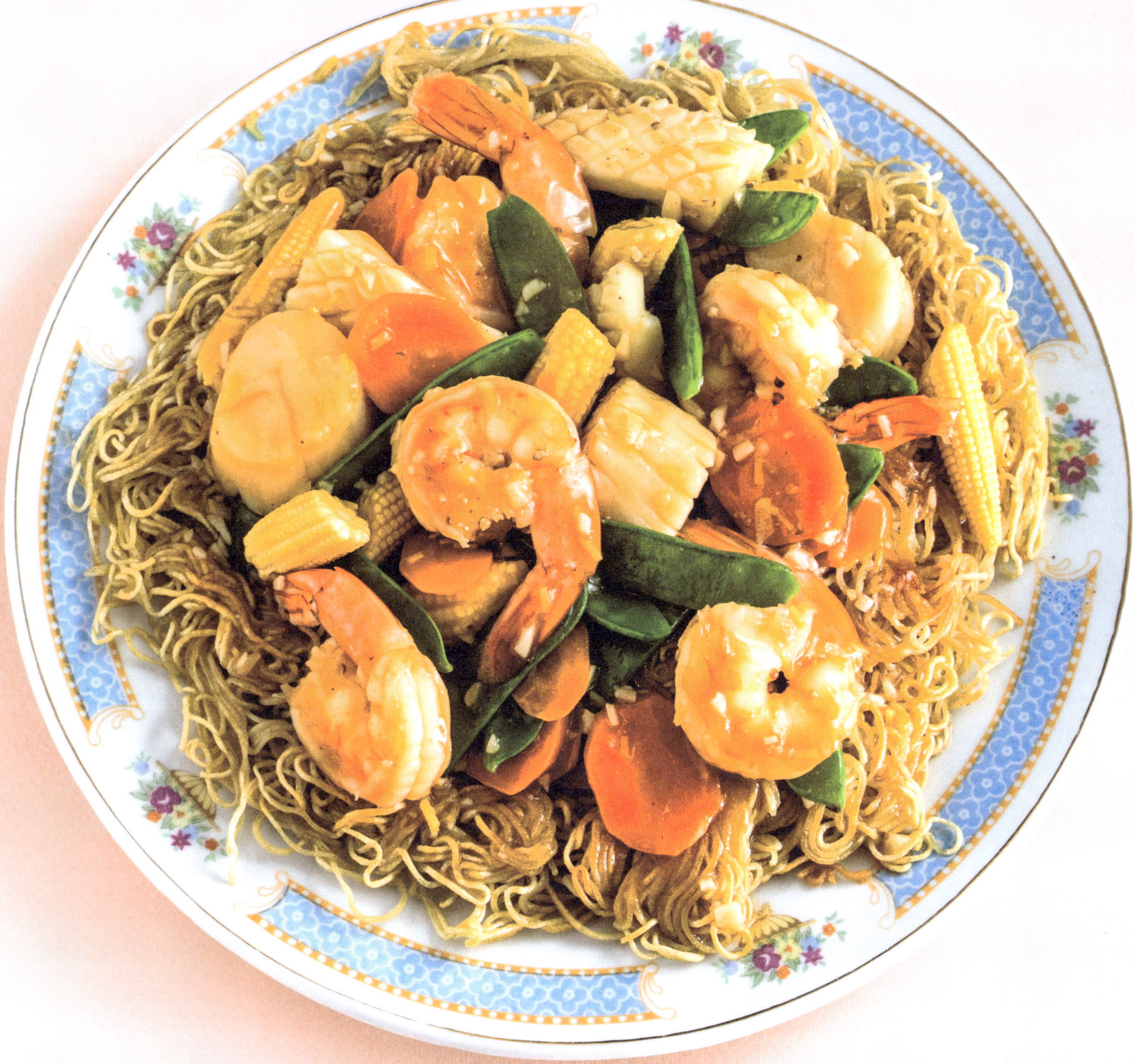

Understanding

SÙCÀI CHĂOMIÀN
STIR-FRIED NOODLES WITH VEGETABLES

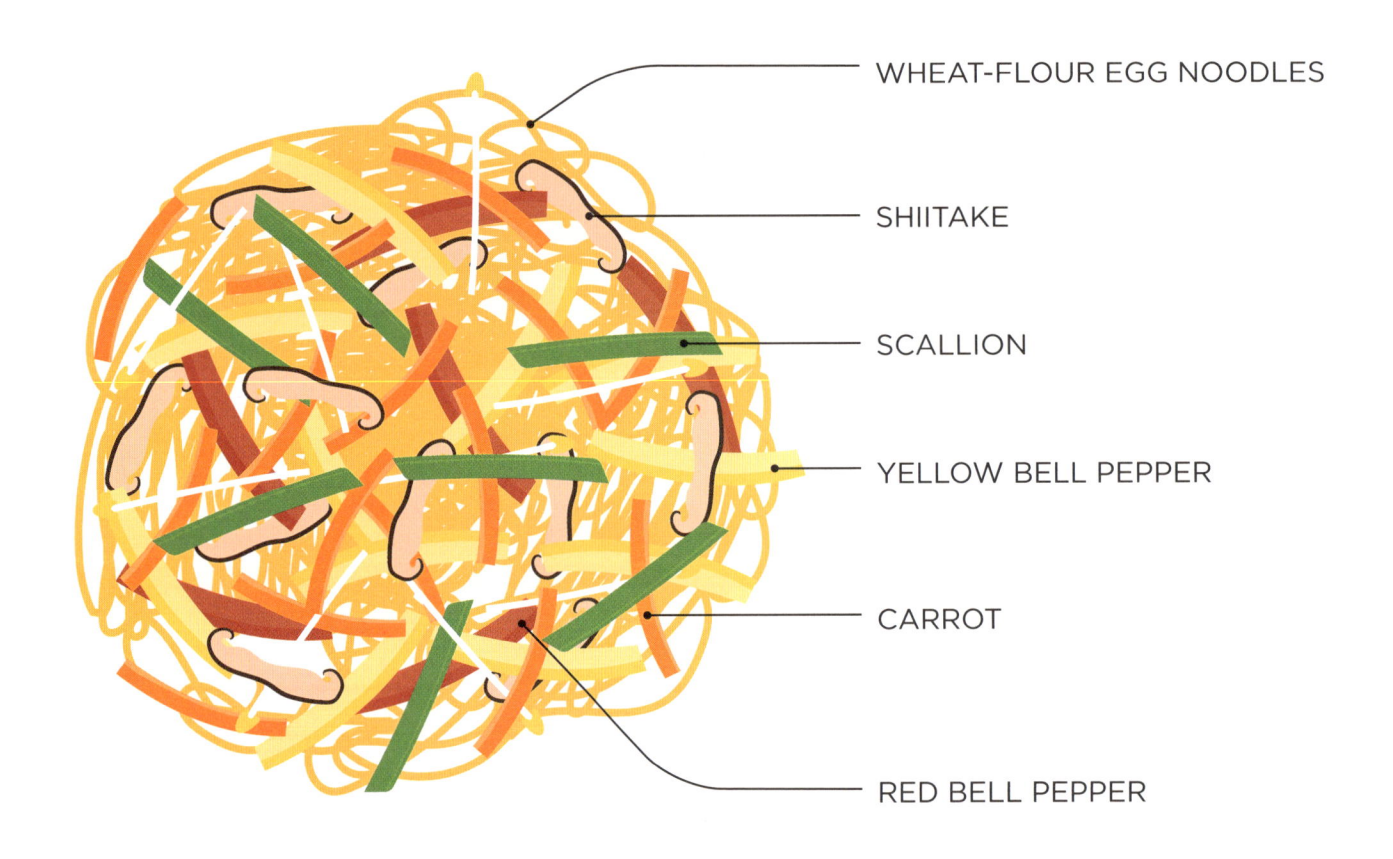

- WHEAT-FLOUR EGG NOODLES
- SHIITAKE
- SCALLION
- YELLOW BELL PEPPER
- CARROT
- RED BELL PEPPER

WHAT IS IT?

A family-style dish of homemade egg noodles, stir-fried with vegetables.

COMPLETION TIME

Preparation time: 35 minutes
Cooking time: 12 minutes
Storage: 4 to 5 days. Reheat for 4 to 5 minutes in a pan.

SKILL TO MASTER
Rehydrating mushrooms (page 280)

VARIATIONS
You can replace shiitake mushrooms with button mushrooms.
You can use 10½ ounces / 300 g store-bought dried egg noodles. Cook them in boiling water for 1 minute.

SERVES 4 TO 6

10 dried shiitake mushrooms
4 spring onions
4 cloves garlic
1 ounce / 30 g fresh ginger
10½ ounces / 300 g carrots (about 3 carrots)
5 scallions
1 small bell pepper (red and/or yellow)

Learning

SAUCE

¼ cup / 60 ml soy sauce

1 tablespoon dark soy sauce

2 or 3 tablespoons / 30 to 45 ml oyster sauce or vegetarian sauce

1 heaping teaspoon organic cane sugar

Freshly ground black pepper

1 pound / 450 g Egg Noodles (page 26) or store-bought egg noodles

¼ cup plus 1 tablespoon / 75 ml neutral-flavor oil of your choice (sunflower, peanut)

7 ounces / 200 g mung bean sprouts

1 Rehydrate the mushrooms (page 280). Finely chop the onions. Chop or press the garlic. Chop the ginger. Cut the carrots and scallions into 2-inch / 5 cm sections. Slice the carrot sections into about ⅒- to ⅛-inch / 2 to 3 mm strips, then cut the slices into thin sticks. Cut the bell pepper into strips. Slice the shiitake mushrooms once they are rehydrated.

2 Make the sauce: In a bowl, combine the soy sauces, oyster sauce, and sugar. Season with pepper.

3 Bring a pot of water to a boil. Cook the noodles for 1 minute. Drain, and rinse briefly under cold water. Drain again, and place them on a kitchen towel. Pat them to remove as much moisture as possible.

4 Add the oil to the wok. Cook the shiitake mushrooms for 1 minute, then add the garlic and ginger. When the garlic is golden brown, add the carrots and onions.

5 Cook for 3 minutes. Add the bell pepper and noodles. Add the sauce. Increase the heat to very high. Cook for 2 minutes, stirring regularly with chopsticks and a spatula.

6 Add the scallions and mung bean sprouts. Stir, and turn off the heat. Taste, and adjust the seasoning, if necessary. Serve immediately.

Understanding

YÓU PŌ CHĚ MIÀN
BIANG BIANG NOODLES WITH SPICY OIL

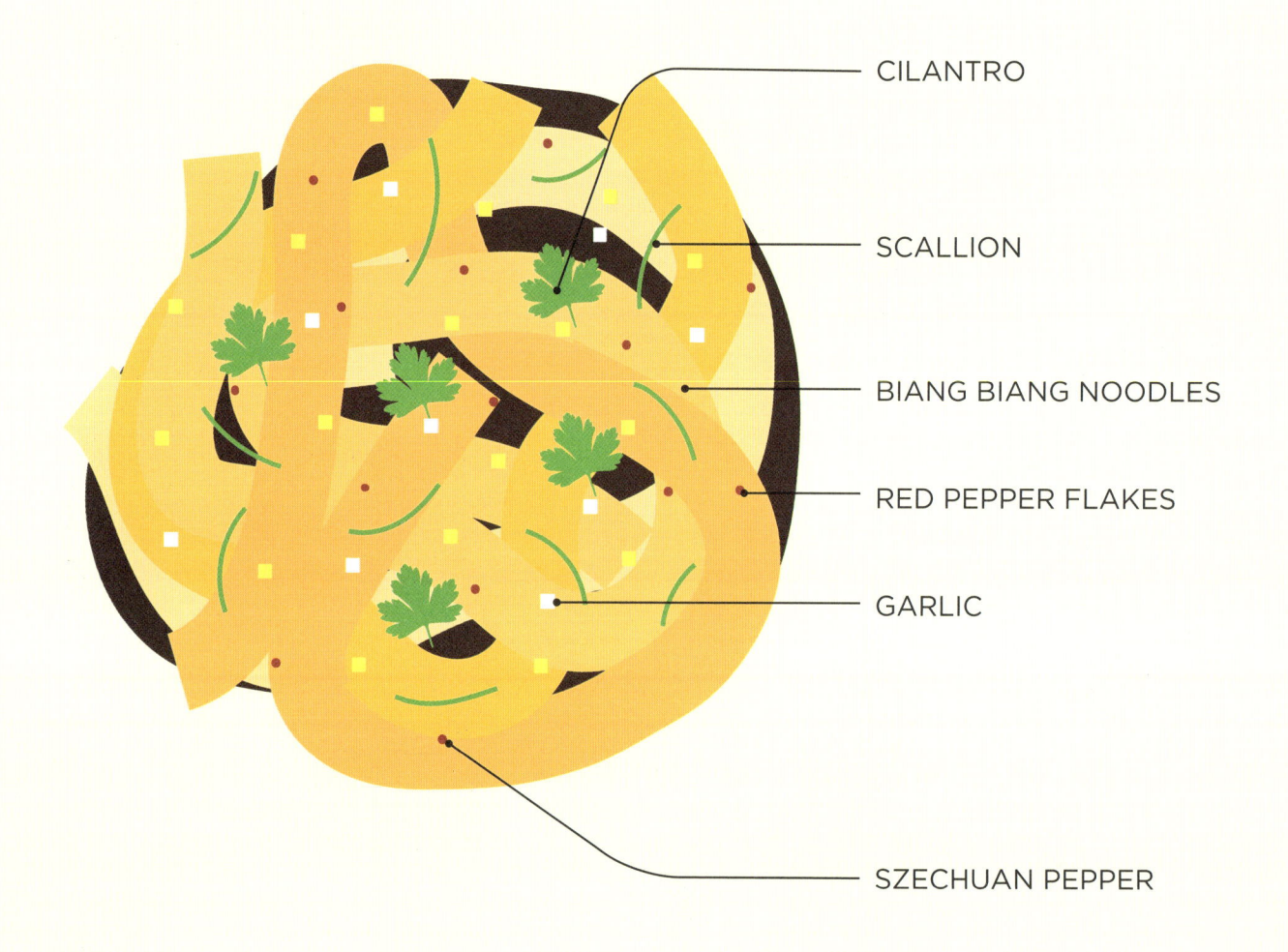

- CILANTRO
- SCALLION
- BIANG BIANG NOODLES
- RED PEPPER FLAKES
- GARLIC
- SZECHUAN PEPPER

WHAT IS IT?
Biang biang noodles seasoned with vinegar, soy sauce, and sugar, to which garlic, chile pepper, and Szechuan pepper are added.

ORIGIN
The name in Chinese literally means "stretched noodles drizzled with oil."

COMPLETION TIME
Preparation time: 40 minutes
Resting time: Overnight
Cooking time: 3 minutes

SERVING
When ready to serve, hot oil is poured over the dish. This is a common Chinese technique, called "blooming." It allows you to exhale and extract as many flavors as possible. The oil then diffuses all the aromas and binds the elements together, creating an enveloping and fragrant sauce.

USEFUL TIP
To stretch the noodles, work in batches, or stretch all of them at once and place the noodles on a clean kitchen towel or baking sheet without overlapping them.

Learning

SERVES 4

1 pound 5 ounces / 600 g Biang Biang Noodles (page 28)

4 cloves garlic

1 tablespoon Szechuan pepper

3 scallions

⅓ bunch of cilantro

4 teaspoons organic cane sugar

¼ cup / 60 ml Chinkiang black rice vinegar

½ cup / 120 ml soy sauce

½ cup / 120 ml neutral-flavor oil of your choice (sunflower, peanut)

4 teaspoons toasted sesame seeds

4 teaspoons red pepper flakes

Salt

1 The day before, prepare the biang biang noodle dough (page 28). The next day, finely chop or press the garlic. Crush the Szechuan pepper. Chop the scallions and cilantro.

2 Stir together the sugar, vinegar, and soy sauce. Divide the mixture among four large bowls. Add a pinch of salt to each bowl and stir to combine.

3 Take the dough pieces out 30 minutes prior to cooking them. Bring a large pot of water to a boil. Meanwhile, add the oil to a small saucepan over medium heat. Stretch the noodles (page 30). Add the noodles to the boiling water, stir using chopsticks, and cook for about 3 minutes. They should be slightly al dente.

4 Drain, and divide the noodles among the bowls. Evenly divide the garlic, sesame seeds, red pepper flakes, and Szechuan pepper on top.

5 Pour the hot oil over the toppings. Add the cilantro and scallions. Stir well to combine.

Understanding

YÁNGRÒU MIÀN
BIANG BIANG NOODLES WITH LAMB

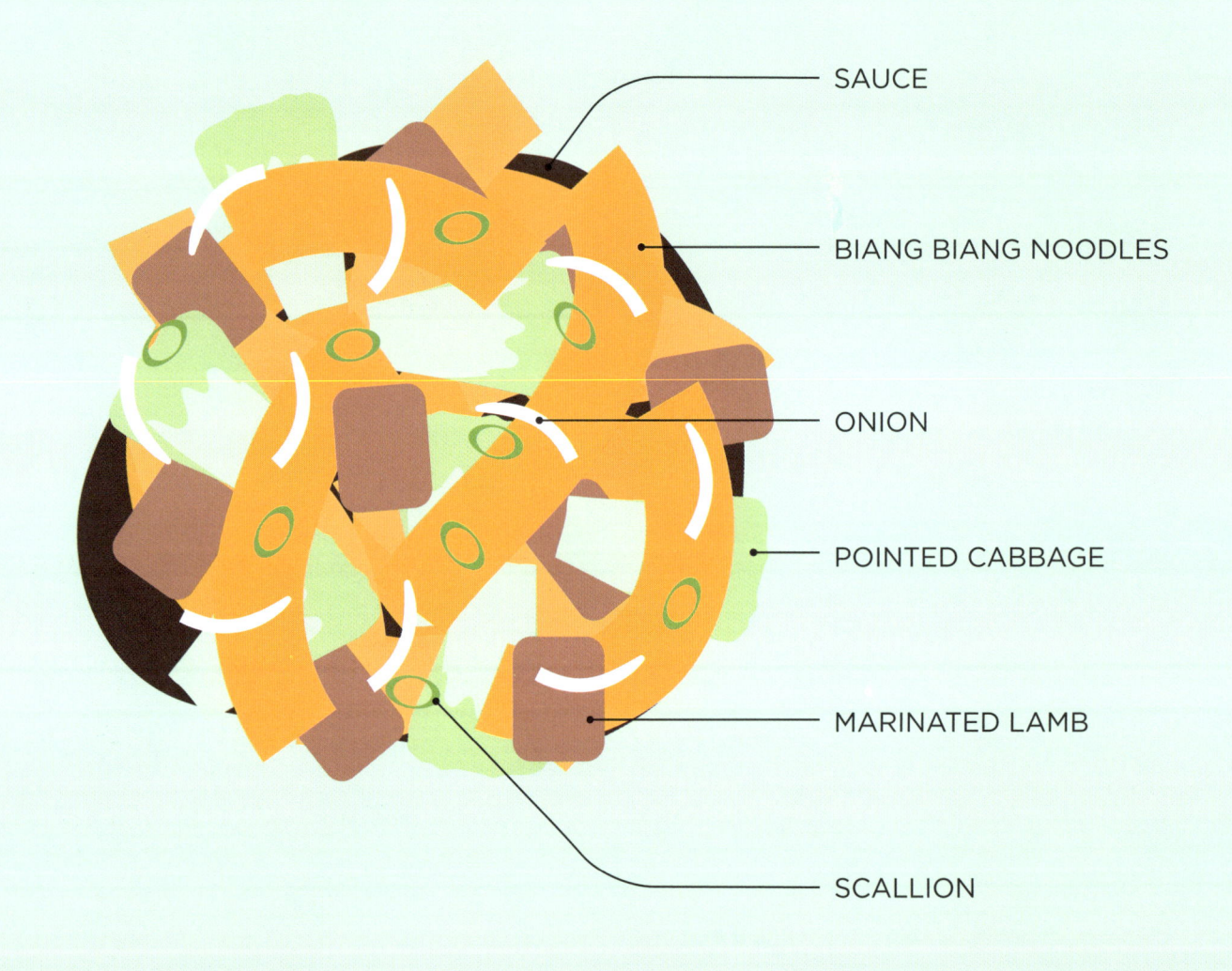

- SAUCE
- BIANG BIANG NOODLES
- ONION
- POINTED CABBAGE
- MARINATED LAMB
- SCALLION

WHAT IS IT?
Biang biang noodles stir-fried with lamb, cabbage, and spices.

COMPLETION TIME
Preparation time: 45 minutes
Resting time: Overnight + 1 hour
Cooking time: 10 minutes

SPECIAL EQUIPMENT
Wok

USEFUL TIP
Rinsing the noodles briefly in cold water will remove excess starch and make them less sticky when sautéed.

Learning

SHAOXING RICE WINE
Fermented glutinous rice wine. Choose the Pagoda brand (blue label).

BIANG BIANG NOODLES
Stretched wheat-flour noodles.

CHINKIANG BLACK RICE VINEGAR
It has a mild acidity, almost sweet and smoky, with hints of malt.

HOMEMADE CHILE OIL
Oil mixed with chile pepper and spices.

SERVES 4

- 1 pound 5 ounces / 600 g Biang Biang Noodles (page 28)

MARINATED LAMB

10½ ounces / 300 g lamb (shoulder, saddle, filet)
2 tablespoons soy sauce
- 2 tablespoons Shaoxing wine
1 teaspoon ground cumin
1 teaspoon organic cane sugar
½ level teaspoon baking soda
1 tablespoon cornstarch

SPICE MIX

1½ tablespoons cumin seeds
1 tablespoon coriander seeds
1 tablespoon Szechuan pepper
1 teaspoon white peppercorns

1 onion
6 cloves garlic
¾ ounce / 20 g fresh ginger
2 scallions
12 ounces / 350 g pointed cabbage (purchase a tender one)

SAUCE

3 tablespoons / 45 ml soy sauce
- 2½ tablespoons / 40 ml Chinkiang black rice vinegar
1 level tablespoon sugar of your choice
⅔ cup / 150 ml Basic Broth (page 38) or cooking water from the noodles
- Chile Oil (page 44)

5 tablespoons / 75 ml vegetable oil

203

Making

YÁNGRÒU MIÀN

1 The day before, make the biang biang noodle dough (page 28). Make the marinated lamb: The next day, slice the lamb into slices about 1/10-inch / 2 mm thick. Combine the soy sauce, wine, cumin, sugar, baking soda, and cornstarch with the lamb. Refrigerate for at least 1 hour. Make the spice mix: In a dry skillet over low heat, toast the cumin and coriander seeds for 12 minutes. Crush them to a fine powder with the Szechuan pepper and peppercorns using a mortar and pestle. Set aside.

2 Chop the onion and garlic, grate the ginger, and finely chop the scallions. Tear the cabbage leaves by hand, and finely chop the tougher sections.

3 Make the sauce: Combine the soy sauce, vinegar, sugar, broth, and chile oil (adjusted to taste).

4 Remove the noodle dough 30 minutes in advance to come to room temperature. In a wok or skillet, heat 2 tablespoons of the vegetable oil. When the oil is hot, add the marinated meat and cook until browned, about 2 minutes, over very high heat. Set aside. Add the remaining vegetable oil. Brown the garlic for 1 minute over medium heat. Add the ginger and spice mix and stir to combine. Add the onion and cook for 2 to 3 minutes, just until translucent. Turn off the heat.

5 Bring a large pot of water to a boil. For this recipe, do not pull the pasta too thin (page 30). Add the noodles and cabbage to the boiling water and cook for about 3 minutes. Drain, and rinse under cold water.

6 While the noodles are cooking, heat the wok over high heat. Add the meat back to the pan and add the sauce. Bring to a boil. Add the noodles and cabbage, and toss to combine, cooking for 1 to 2 minutes to coat them with the sauce. Taste, and adjust the seasoning, if necessary. Sprinkle with the scallions and serve immediately.

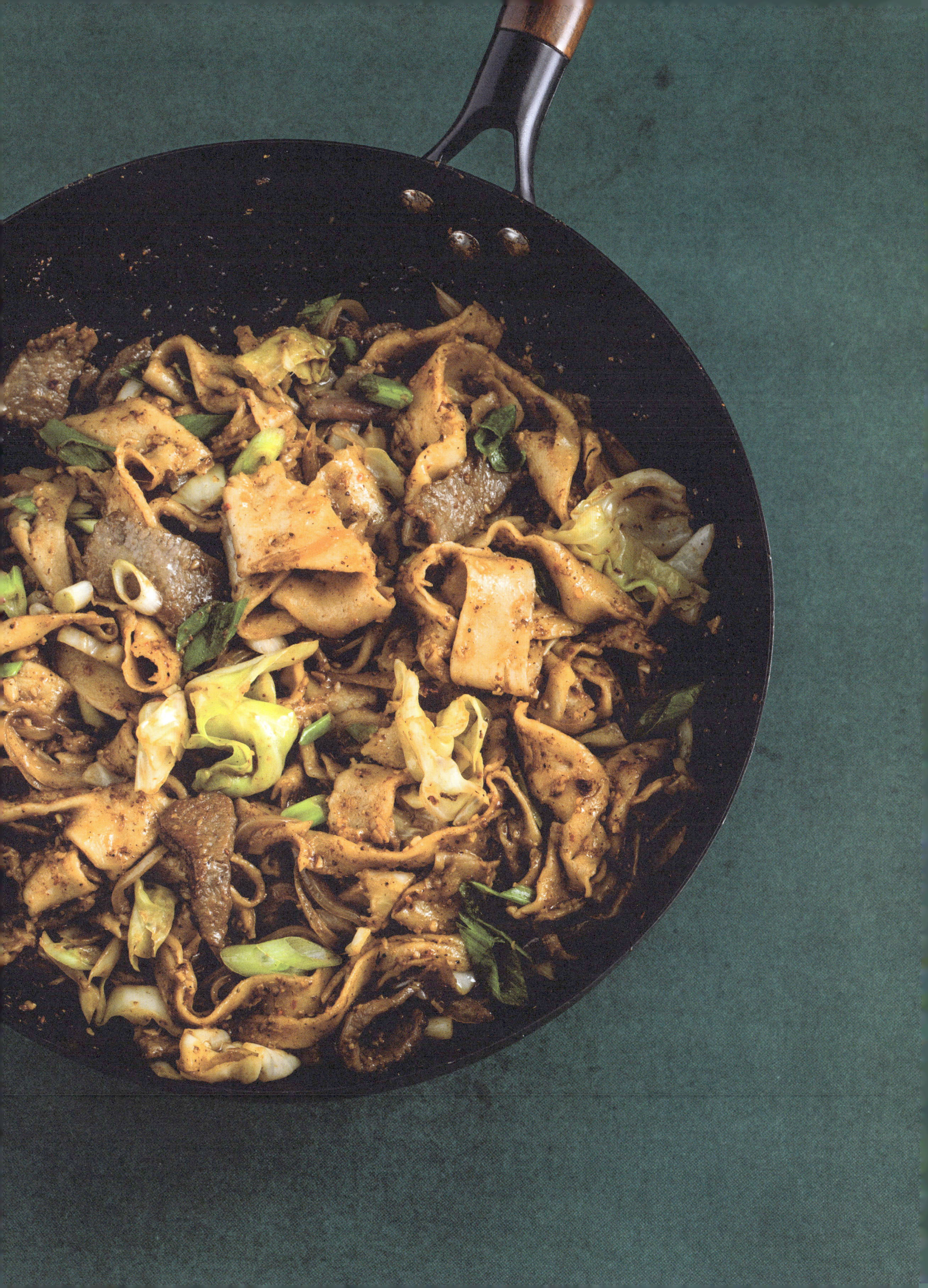

Understanding

NIÚRÒU MIÀN
BEEF NOODLE SOUP

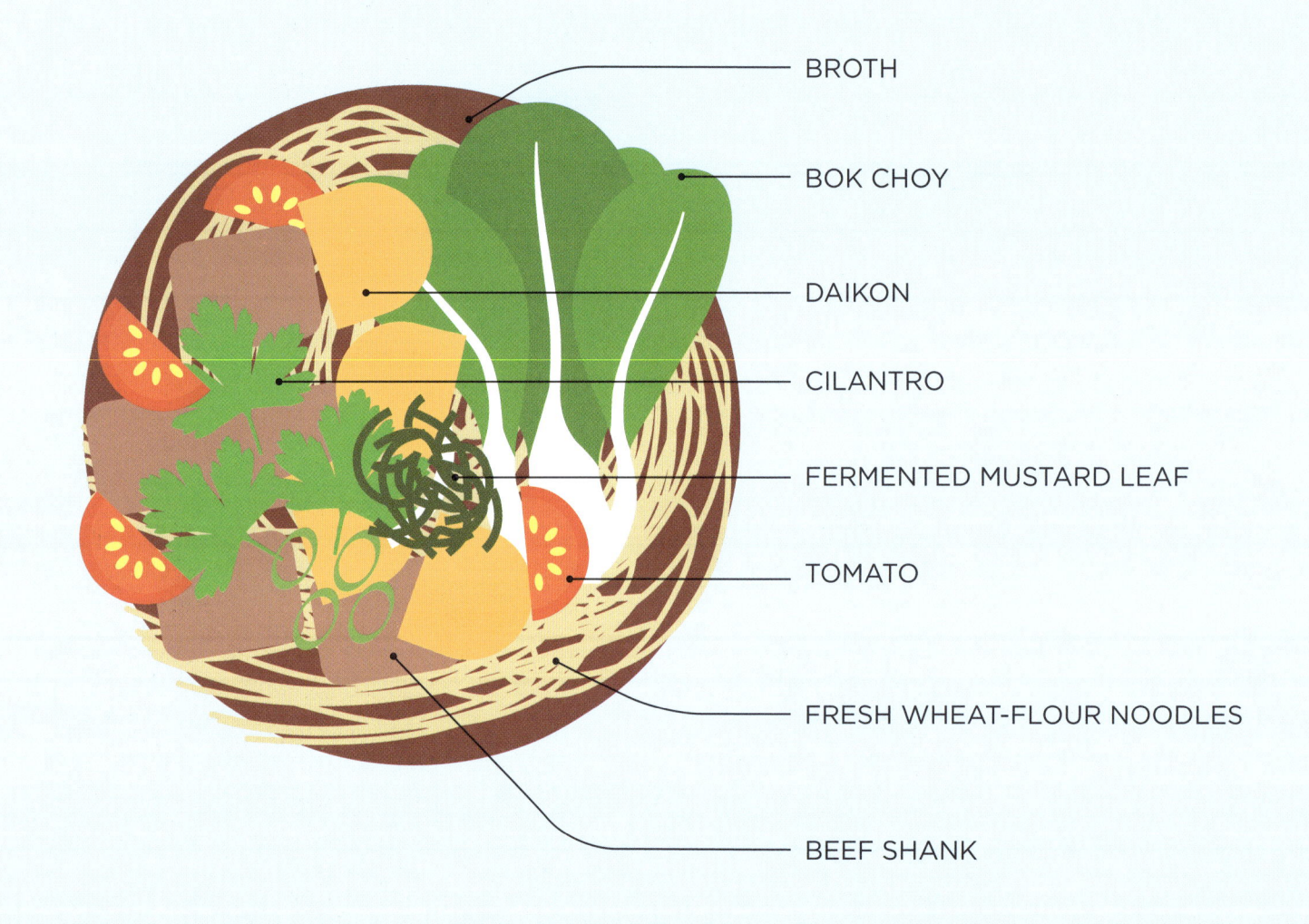

- BROTH
- BOK CHOY
- DAIKON
- CILANTRO
- FERMENTED MUSTARD LEAF
- TOMATO
- FRESH WHEAT-FLOUR NOODLES
- BEEF SHANK

WHAT IS IT?
Wheat noodles and braised beef in a spicy soup.

COMPLETION TIME
Preparation time: 45 minutes
Cooking time: 2½ to 3 hours
Storage: The broth can be kept for 3 days.

SPECIAL EQUIPMENT
Dutch oven
Cheesecloth

USEFUL TIP
If the broth becomes too strong, add a little water to dilute it.

Learning

FRESH WHEAT-FLOUR NOODLES
Egg-free wheat-flour noodles sold in the refrigerated section. Choose any kind and size according to your taste.

FERMENTED MUSTARD GREENS
The fermented bulb or greens of the mustard plant. Sold vacuum-packed. Regardless of the type, they lend a tangy and crunchy note as a condiment for this dish.

ROCK SUGAR
Yellow candy sugar. Adds shine to the dish. It has a delicate flavor and is less sweet than sugar.

DÒUBÀNJIÀNG
A spicy and savory Szechuan paste made from fermented beans and chile peppers.

RED SZECHUAN PEPPER
A variety of berry (not pepper) with a powerful flavor and aroma with notes of flowers and citrus. It has a numbing effect.

SERVES 6

1 pound 10 ounces / 1.2 kg beef shank or flat iron
2 onions
9 ounces / 250 g tomatoes
8 cloves garlic
12 ounces / 350 g daikon radish
2 ounces / 60 g fresh ginger
1 small leek
6 leaves bok choy
1 bunch of cilantro

SPICE MIX

- 2 tablespoons Szechuan pepper
1 tablespoon cumin seeds
1 tablespoon coriander seeds
1 tablespoon fennel seeds (optional)

5 tablespoons / 75 ml neutral-flavor oil of your choice (sunflower, peanut)
Salt
3 tablespoons / 50 g tomato paste
- 3 to 5 tablespoons / 60 to 100 g dòubànjiàng
- 2½ ounces / 70 g rock sugar, or 3 tablespoons / 50 g organic cane sugar
1¼ cups / 300 ml Shaoxing wine

Scant ½ cup / 100 ml soy sauce
3 tablespoons / 45 ml dark soy sauce
1 stick cinnamon
4 star anise pods
4 bay leaves
1 teaspoon cracked black peppercorns
1 teaspoon five-spice powder
- 1¾ pounds / 800 g fresh wheat-flour noodles
- 2 ounces / 60 g fermented mustard greens (sui mi ya cai; page 283, optional)

Making

NIÚRÒU MIÀN

1   Cut the beef shank into even pieces ⅓- to ⅔-inch-thick / 1 to 1.5 cm.

2   Cut the onions and tomatoes into quarters. Crush the garlic (page 281). Cut the daikon into thick rounds. Cut the ginger into strips and the leek into sections. Cut the bok choy into two to four wedges. Chop the cilantro. Make the spice mix: Combine the Szechuan pepper, cumin seeds, coriander seeds, and fennel seeds, if using, and place them in a cheesecloth or tea ball.

3   In a large Dutch oven, heat 2½ tablespoons / 40 ml of the oil. Season the meat pieces with salt and add them to the pot. Brown on each side. Cook in two batches, if necessary. Remove and set aside.

4   Add the onions, garlic, ginger, and leeks to the pot. Scrape to loosen the browned bits from the bottom of the pot. Cook for about 5 minutes. Add the tomato paste, dòubànjiàng, and sugar. Stir, then deglaze the pot with the wine. Let reduce until almost all of the juices have evaporated.

5   Add the tomatoes, soy sauces, cinnamon stick, star anise pods, bay leaves, peppercorns, and five-spice powder. Add the meat back to the pot, then add about 3 quarts / 3 L water. Add the spice packet. Bring to a boil, and skim off any impurities from the surface. Reduce the heat and simmer for 2½ to 3 hours, depending on the piece of meat chosen. Add the daikon 1 hour before the end of the cooking time.

The meat should be tender. If not, continue cooking as needed. Taste the broth, and adjust the seasoning, if necessary. Remove the spice packet and bay leaves.

6   Bring a large pot of water to a boil. Cook the noodles according to your taste. Add the bok choy 2 minutes before the end of the cooking time. Drain, and divide the ingredients among serving bowls. Add pieces of beef, and top with hot broth. Serve with the cilantro and fermented mustard greens, if desired.

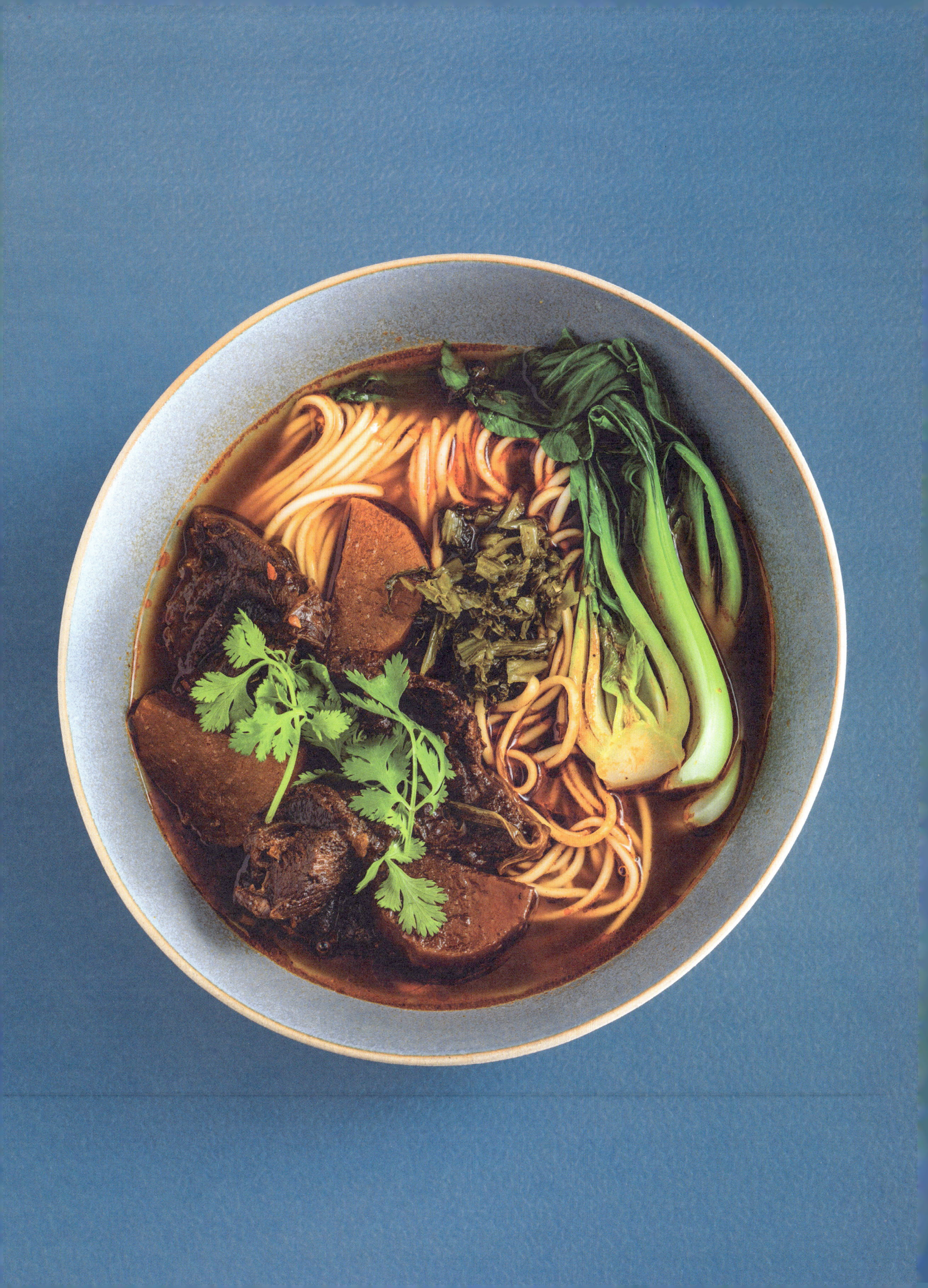

Understanding
ZHÁJIÀNG MIÀN

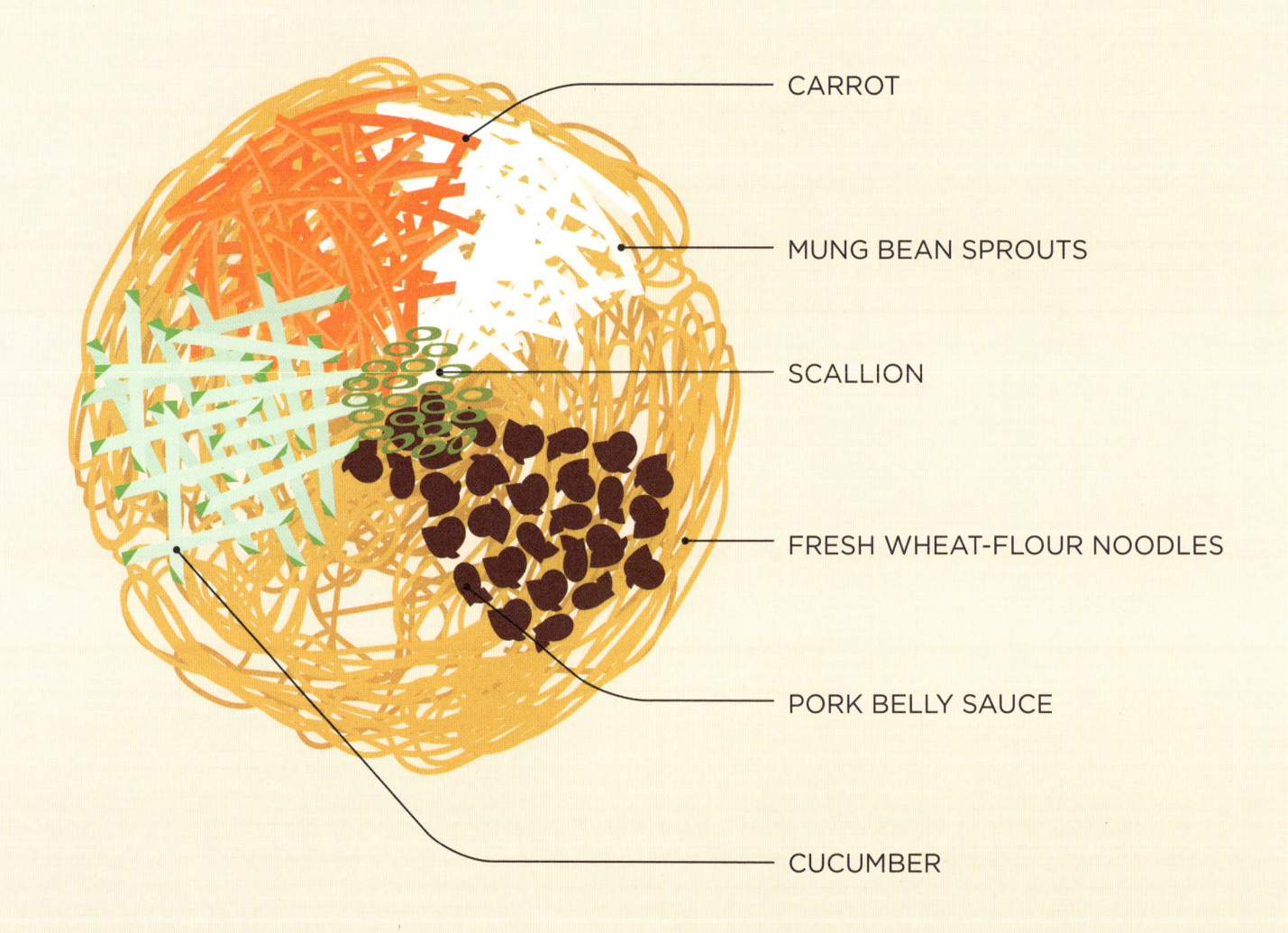

- CARROT
- MUNG BEAN SPROUTS
- SCALLION
- FRESH WHEAT-FLOUR NOODLES
- PORK BELLY SAUCE
- CUCUMBER

WHAT IS IT?
Large noodles, covered with a salty-sweet brown pork sauce and garnished with raw vegetables. It could be described as a Chinese Bolognese.

ORIGIN
The dish originates from northern China (the Shandong province) and is especially popular in Beijing during the summer months. Zhájiàng miàn is the origin of Korean jajangmyeon.

COMPLETION TIME
Preparation time: 40 minutes
Cooking time: 25 minutes
Storage: The sauce will keep for up to 3 days.

SKILL TO MASTER
Cutting into julienne (page 281)

VARIATIONS
You can use ground pork in the mixture but choose a fatty piece of meat (such as the belly) to prevent the sauce from being too dry.

Learning

FRESH WHEAT-FLOUR NOODLES
Egg-free wheat-flour noodles sold in the refrigerated section. Choose any kind of large noodles for the recipe.

SHAOXING RICE WINE
Fermented glutinous rice wine. Choose the Pagoda brand (blue label).

TIAN MIAN JIANG OR SWEET BEAN PASTE
A paste made of wheat flour and sometimes soy, fermented. It is essential for zhájiàng miàn sauce. It is often sold in small vacuum packs.

YELLOW BEAN SAUCE
A fermented yellow bean sauce (soy). It is a thick, light brown sauce with visible bits of fermented beans. The taste is mainly salty and umami. It is used to sauté vegetables, as a meat marinade, or to make sauces.

SERVES 4

ZHAJIANG SAUCE
14 ounces / 400 g fatty pork belly
1 large onion
4 cloves garlic
¾ ounce / 20 g fresh ginger
- ⅔ cup / 150 ml Shaoxing wine
- 3½ tablespoons / 70 g tián miàn jiàng
- 1 tablespoon yellow bean sauce (optional)
1½ tablespoons sugar of your choice
1 tablespoon neutral-flavor oil of your choice (sunflower, peanut)
2 bay leaves
2 star anise pods
⅔ cup / 150 ml water

GARNISH
2 scallions
½ cucumber
1 carrot

7 ounces / 200 g mung bean sprouts
- 1 pound 5 ounces / 600 g fresh wheat-flour noodles

Making

ZHÁJIÀNG MIÀN

1 Cut the pork belly into small cubes and then roughly chop it with a cleaver or large chef's knife.

2 Chop the onion. Press the garlic. Cut the ginger into strips, then into small cubes. Slice the scallions. Chop or grate the cucumber. Julienne the carrot (page 281).

3 Combine the Shaoxing wine, tián miàn jiàng, yellow bean sauce, if using, and sugar. In a wok, heat the oil and brown the pork.

4 When the meat is browned, add the garlic, ginger, and onion. Cook for 2 to 3 minutes.

5 Add the tián miàn jiàng mixture, bay leaves, star anise pods, and the water. Reduce the heat and simmer for 15 to 20 minutes. The sauce should be reduced and thickened to a coating consistency. Set aside.

6 Bring a pot of water to a boil. Blanch the mung bean sprouts for 10 seconds in a strainer; drain. Cook the noodles according to the instructions on the package. Drain, rinse under cold water, and drain again.

7 Divide the ingredients among bowls. Add the sauce (remove the star anise pods and bay leaves) and toppings to each bowl: cucumber, carrot, scallions, and mung bean sprouts. Guests should stir the ingredients together in their bowls to enjoy.

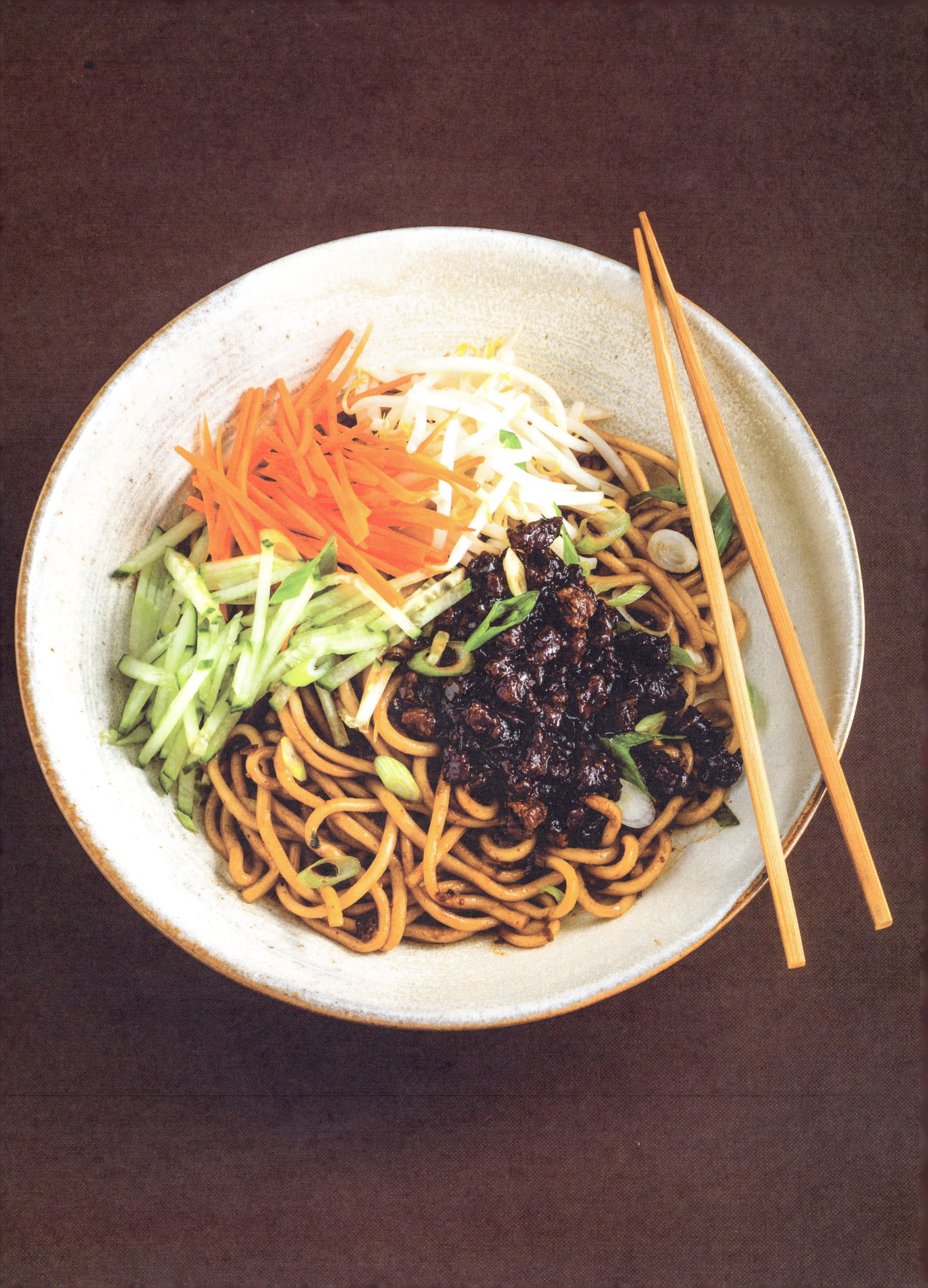

Understanding

DÀNDÀN MIÀN
DAN DAN NOODLES

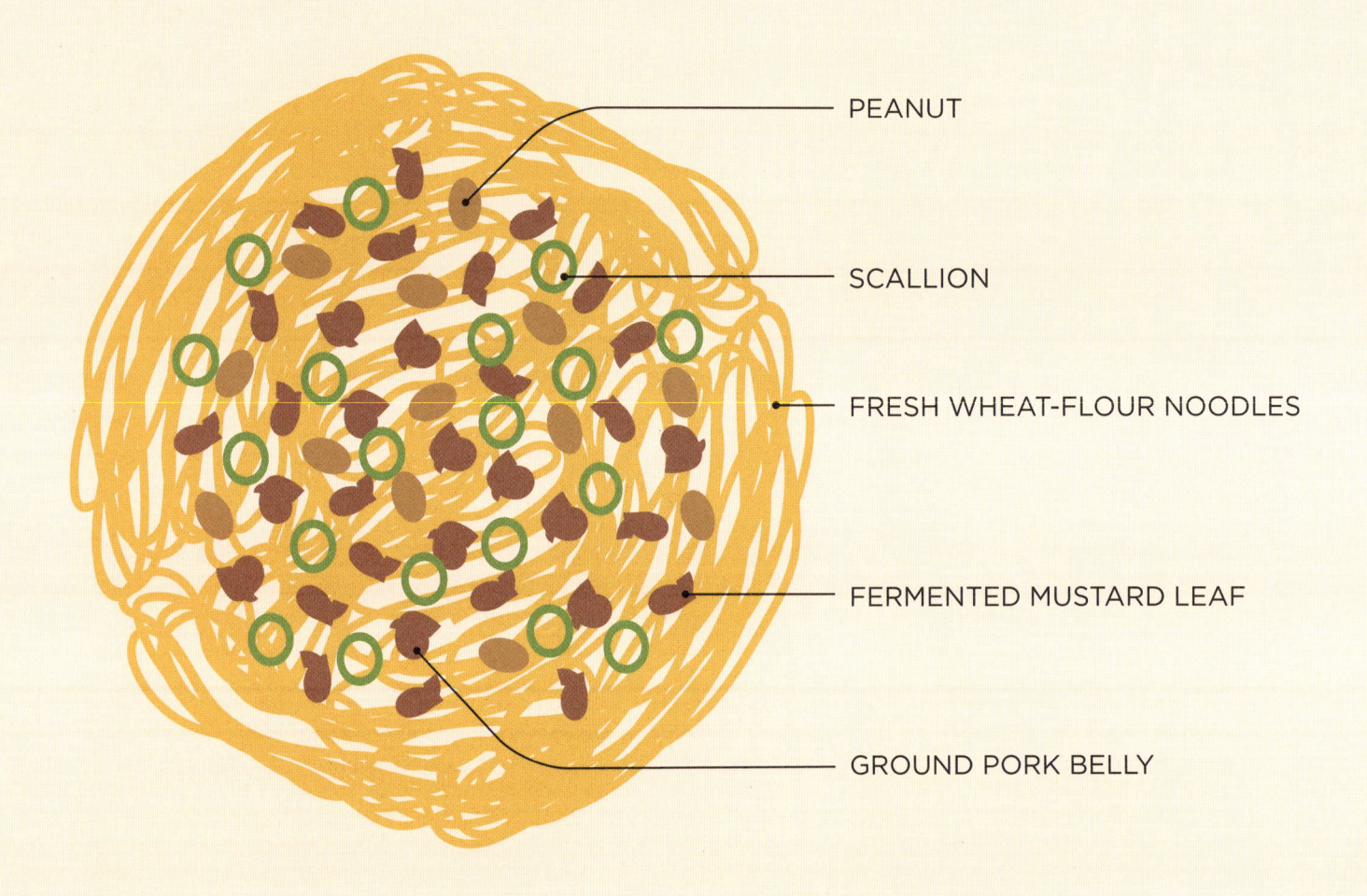

- PEANUT
- SCALLION
- FRESH WHEAT-FLOUR NOODLES
- FERMENTED MUSTARD LEAF
- GROUND PORK BELLY

WHAT IS IT?
Noodles seasoned with toasted sesame sauce and topped with ground pork sautéed with fermented mustard greens.

ORIGIN
This is a famous specialty of Szechuan cuisine. The word "dan dan" comes from street vendors who carried baskets hanging from a stick. Dan dan means "to carry a burden." It could be translated as "peddler's noodles."

COMPLETION TIME
Preparation time: 30 minutes
Cooking time: 15 minutes
Storage: 2 to 3 days in the refrigerator for the meat, 2 weeks in the refrigerator for the sesame sauce.

VARIATIONS
You can add vegetables to cook at the same time as the noodles (bok choy, cabbage, gai lan, etc.).

SERVES 4
2 ounces / 60 g fermented mustard greens (sui mi ya cai; page 283)
1 ounce / 30 g fresh ginger
3 cloves garlic
½ cup / 80 g salted roasted peanuts
3 scallions

SAUCE
¼ cup / 80 g toasted sesame sauce (page 283)
2 teaspoons organic cane sugar
3 tablespoons / 45 ml Chinkiang black rice vinegar or white rice vinegar

Learning

3 tablespoons / 45 ml soy sauce

2 tablespoons neutral-flavor oil of your choice (sunflower, peanut)

14 ounces / 400 g finely chopped pork belly or finely chopped fatty beef

1 heaping teaspoon ground Szechuan pepper

Scant ½ cup / 100 ml Shaoxing wine

2 teaspoons organic cane sugar

2 tablespoons soy sauce

1 pound 5 ounces / 600 g fresh wheat-flour noodles

Chile Oil (page 44)

Freshly ground black pepper

1 Rinse the mustard greens and drain them. Grate the ginger, press the garlic, and crush the peanuts. Slice the scallions.

2 Make the sauce: Dilute the sesame sauce with 2 tablespoons hot water. Add the sugar, vinegar, and soy sauce.

3 In a skillet or wok, heat the oil. Add the ginger, garlic, pork, and Szechuan pepper. Stir to loosen the pieces. Add the wine, sugar, soy sauce, and mustard greens.

4 Cook the noodles according to the packet instructions to al dente. Drain, then divide them among bowls.

5 Season the noodles with the sesame sauce. Divide the meat among the bowls. Sprinkle with the peanuts and scallions. Add chile oil, to taste. Season with pepper. Guests should stir the ingredients together in their bowls to enjoy.

Understanding

JIĂNDĀO MIÀN
SCISSOR-CUT NOODLES

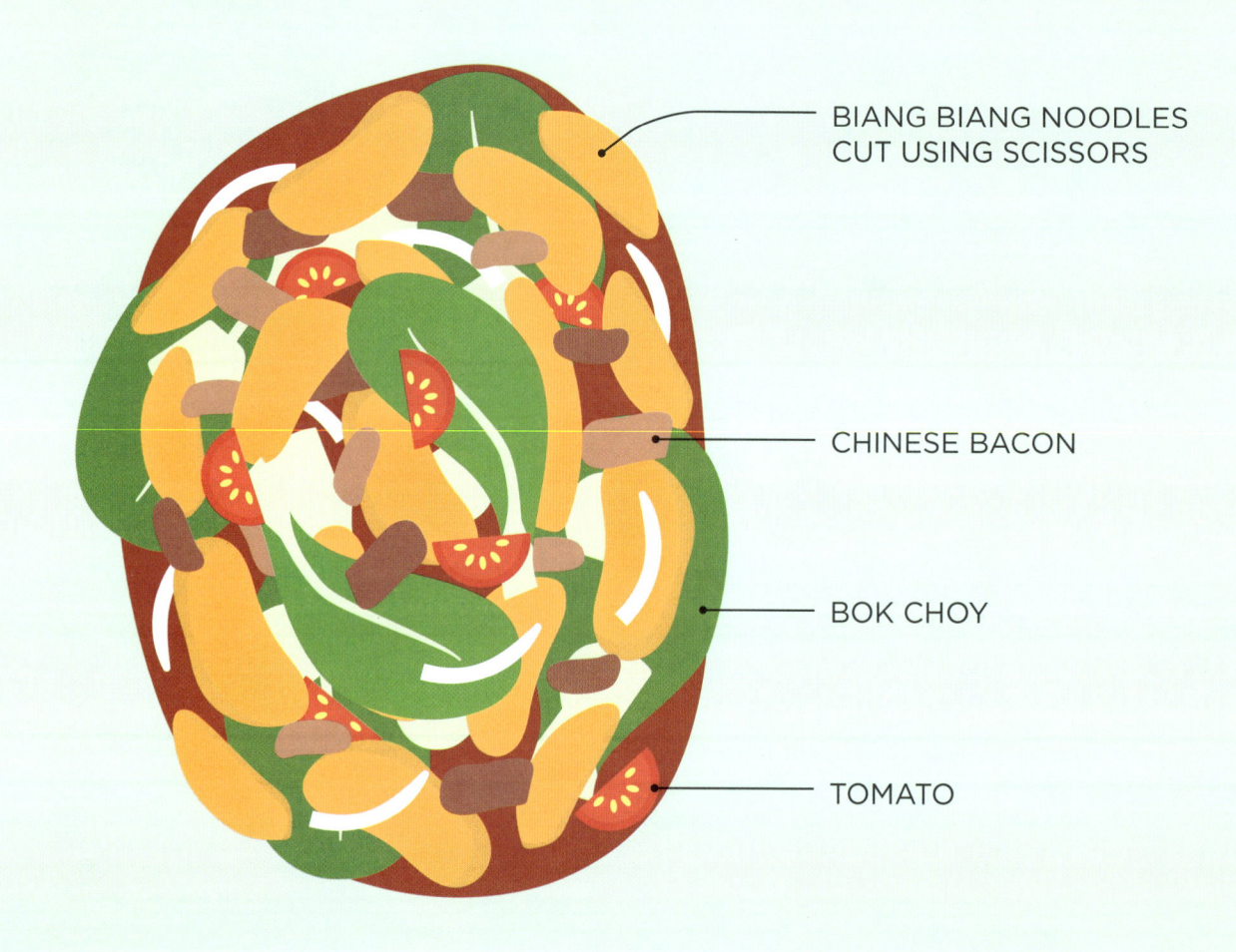

- BIANG BIANG NOODLES CUT USING SCISSORS
- CHINESE BACON
- BOK CHOY
- TOMATO

WHAT IS IT?
Noodle dough cut using scissors into small pieces, boiled in water and sautéed with bacon, bok choy, and chile oil.

COMPLETION TIME
Preparation time: 40 minutes
Cooking time: 12 minutes

CHALLENGE
The pasta swells when cooked. Take this into account and cook to your preferred level of thickness.

USEFUL TIPS
Because this dough is not stretched, up to 1 percent of kansui can be added to the weight of the flour (page 43). Traditionally, the dough is cut directly over the pot of boiling water to prevent it from sticking together. Here, the dough rests in the refrigerator so that it will stick less and allow you to cook all the strips at the same time for even cooking.

VARIATION
Make a veggie version: Replace the bacon with 4 large / 200 g eggs beaten with 1 tablespoon of soy sauce. Cook the eggs in the oil by scrambling them. Once cooked, remove them from the pan. Continue with the recipe and return the eggs to the pasta when the bok choy is added.

Learning

BIANG BIANG NOODLES
Wheat-flour dough, not stretched here but instead cut with scissors.

CHINESE BACON
Pork belly marinated in spices and soy sauce and cut into strips. It is sold vacuum-packed in the refrigerated section.

BOK CHOY OR PAK CHOY OR SHANGHAI CABBAGE
A tender variety of Chinese cabbage. It has a crunchy texture and quick cooking time.

SOY SAUCE
Choose bottles that state "natural fermentation."

SERVES 2 TO 4

- Biang Biang Noodle Dough, made with 2⅓ cups / 300 g all-purpose flour (page 28)
- 1 onion
- 4 cloves garlic
- 3½ ounces / 100 g spiced Chinese bacon or classic smoked slab bacon
- 9 ounces / 250 g tomatoes
- 9 ounces / 250 g bok choy
- 3 tablespoons / 45 ml neutral-flavor oil of your choice (sunflower, peanut)
- Chile Oil (page 44)
- ¼ cup / 60 ml soy sauce
- 1 level tablespoon sugar

Making

JIĂNDĀO MIÀN

1 Make the noodle dough (page 28). Once the second kneading is completed, roll it into a sausage shape and divide it into three portions. Coat the dough portions in a little oil, wrap them in plastic wrap, and refrigerate for 1 hour. Meanwhile, finely chop the onion. Press the garlic. Cut the bacon into even slices and the tomatoes into quarters. Remove the leaves from the bok choy, cut the base into cubes, and keep the leaves whole. Set the bok choy pieces aside separately.

2 Bring a pot of water to a boil. Lightly grease a pair of scissors with oil. Cut the dough portions into small strips on top of a sheet of parchment paper. Avoid overlapping them too much.

3 Add the noodles to the boiling water and cook for 2 minutes. Drain, rinse briefly under cold water, and drain again.

4 In a wok or skillet, heat the oil. Fry the bacon until golden brown. Add the garlic, onion, and your preferred amount of chile oil. Cook until the onion is softened. Add the tomatoes, the white portion of the bok choy, the noodles, soy sauce, sugar, and a small ladleful of the noodle cooking water. Stir to combine. Cook for 3 to 4 minutes. Add the bok choy greens. Taste, add more chile oil, if desired, and adjust the seasoning, if necessary.

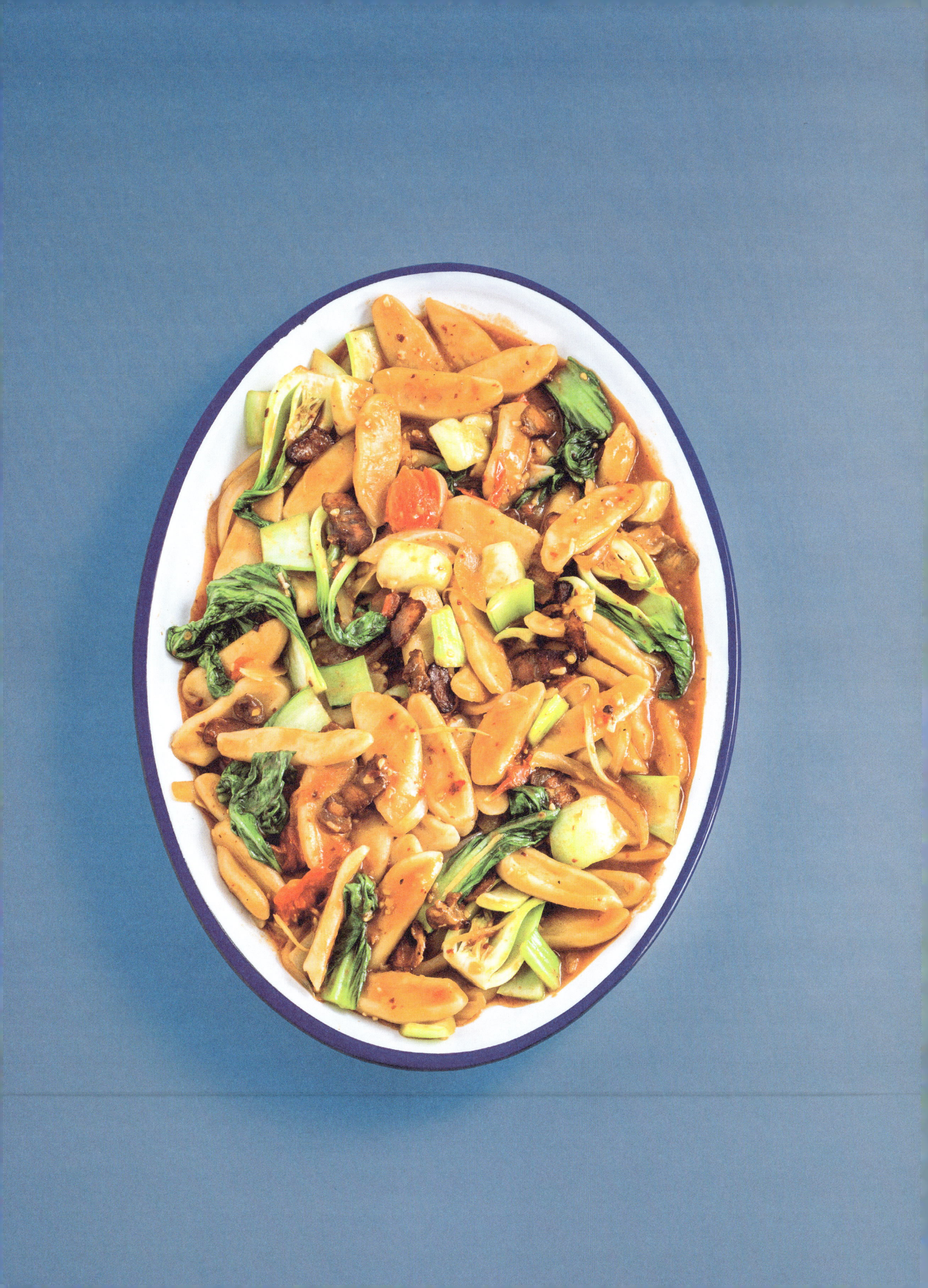

Understanding

GON CHOW NGAU HO
STIR-FRIED BEEF NOODLES

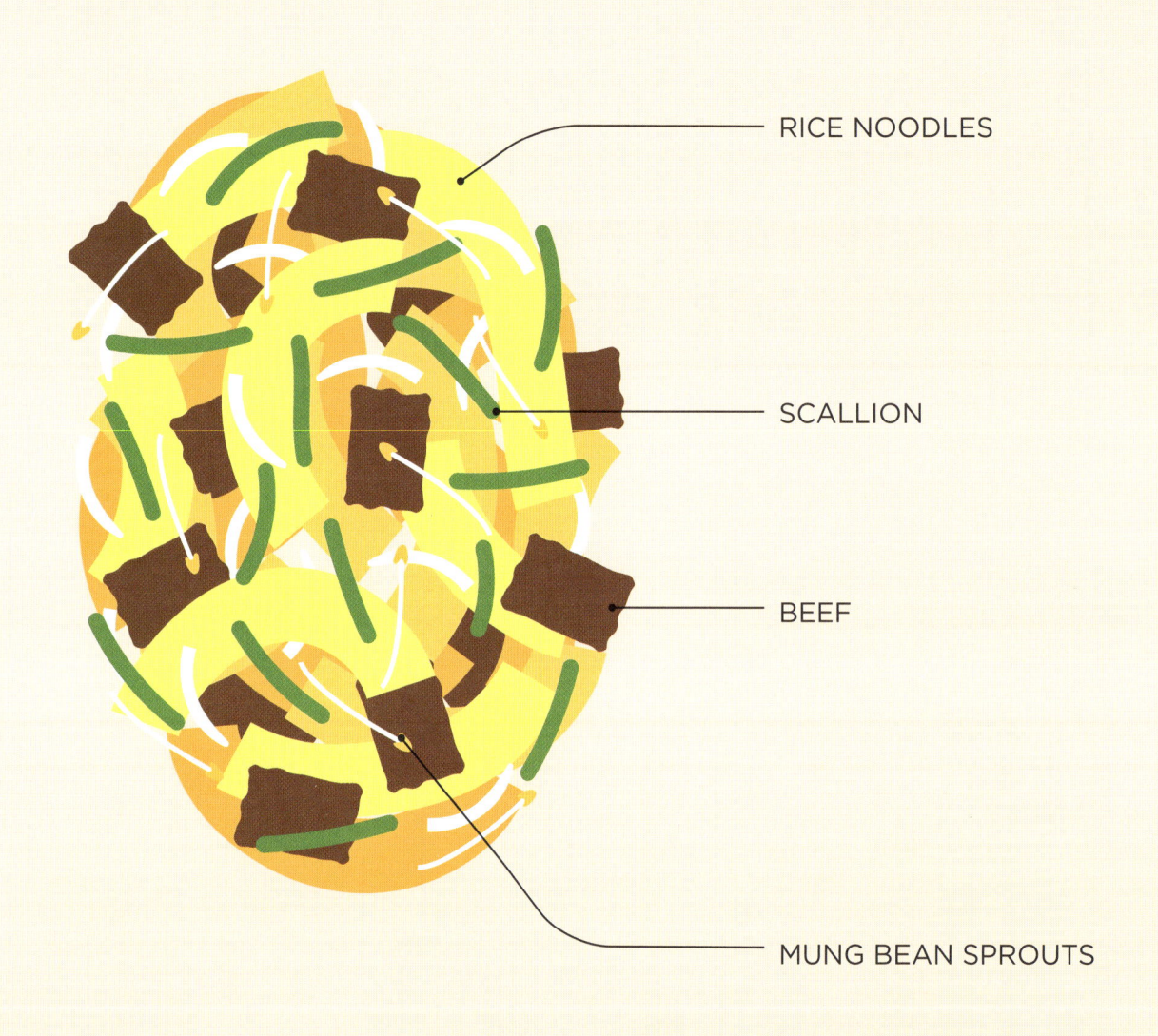

—— RICE NOODLES

—— SCALLION

—— BEEF

—— MUNG BEAN SPROUTS

WHAT IS IT?
Stir-fried rice noodles with marinated strips of beef.

ORIGIN
In Chinese, it is stipulated that the noodles are to be sautéed dry (implying without sauce: *gon chow*, or *gàn chaǒ*). This is a Cantonese comfort food.

COMPLETION TIME
Preparation time: 40 minutes
Resting time: 30 minutes
Cooking time: 10 minutes

Learning

KWANGTUNG MIJIU
Alcohol made from fermented glutinous rice. Similar to sake.

DARK SOY SAUCE
Less salty than classic soy sauce and thicker and slightly sweet. It is mainly used to lend more color and flavor to dishes.

RICE NOODLES
Sheets of dough made from rice flour and tapioca starch, steamed, then layered and cut into strips to obtain noodles.

OYSTER SAUCE
Choose the Megachef or Lee Kum Kee (Premium) brands.

SOY SAUCE
Choose bottles that state "natural fermentation."

MUNG BEAN SPROUTS
Not to be confused with bean sprouts. Eaten raw or just blanched.

SERVES 2 TO 4

MEAT
9 ounces / 250 g beef (top round, skirt, etc.)
½ level teaspoon baking soda
1 tablespoon oyster sauce
1 tablespoon soy sauce
1 tablespoon dark soy sauce
- 1 tablespoon rice wine (kwangtung mijiu)
1 teaspoon sugar
1 tablespoon cornstarch
Freshly ground black pepper

Neutral-flavor oil of your choice (sunflower, peanut)

½ onion
2 scallions
- 1 pound 2 ounces / 500 g Rice Noodles (page 22), cooked

SAUCE
- 2 tablespoons soy sauce
- 1 tablespoon dark soy sauce
- 2 tablespoons oyster sauce
1 teaspoon sugar

- 3½ ounces / 100 g mung bean sprout

Making

GON CHOW NGAU HO

1 Cut the beef into thin strips of about 1/10 inch / 1.5 to 2 mm. Combine the meat with the baking soda, oyster sauce, soy sauces, wine, sugar, and cornstarch. Season generously with pepper. Refrigerate for at least 30 minutes. Add 1 tablespoon of oil, then stir to coat and loosen the beef strips.

2 Slice the onion. Cut the scallions into sections of about 1½ inches / 4 cm, separating the white from the green portion. Loosen the rice noodles.

3 Make the sauce: Combine the soy sauces, oyster sauce, and sugar. Add the noodles and stir to coat.

4 In a wok or skillet, heat 3 tablespoons / 45 ml of oil. When the oil is hot, add the meat. Stir and cook for 1 minute. Place a strainer over a bowl and scrape the meat and the pan contents into the strainer to collect the oil.

5 In the same wok, heat 1 tablespoon of oil and sauté the onion and the white portion of the scallions for 20 seconds.

6 Add the noodles with the sauce. Add the oil that was collected from cooking the beef.

7 Cook over high heat for 3 minutes, stirring from time to time. The noodles should be seared. Add the green portion of the scallions. Add the mung bean sprouts. Combine by shaking the wok, and cook for 10 seconds. Add the beef. Stir to combine, and continue cooking for 1 minute. Serve hot.

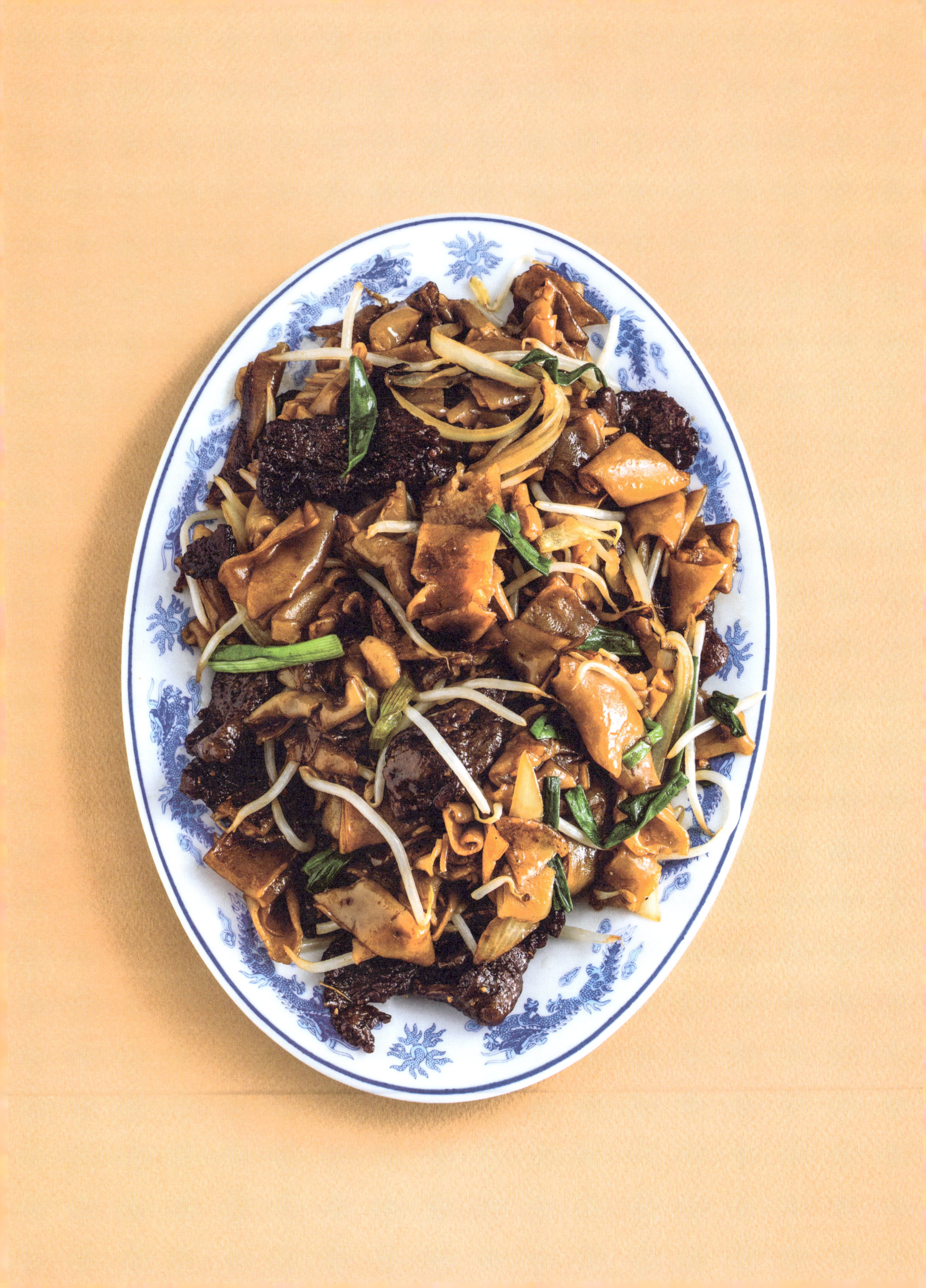

Understanding

YÁNGZHŌU CHǍOFÀN
YANGZHOU STIR-FRIED RICE

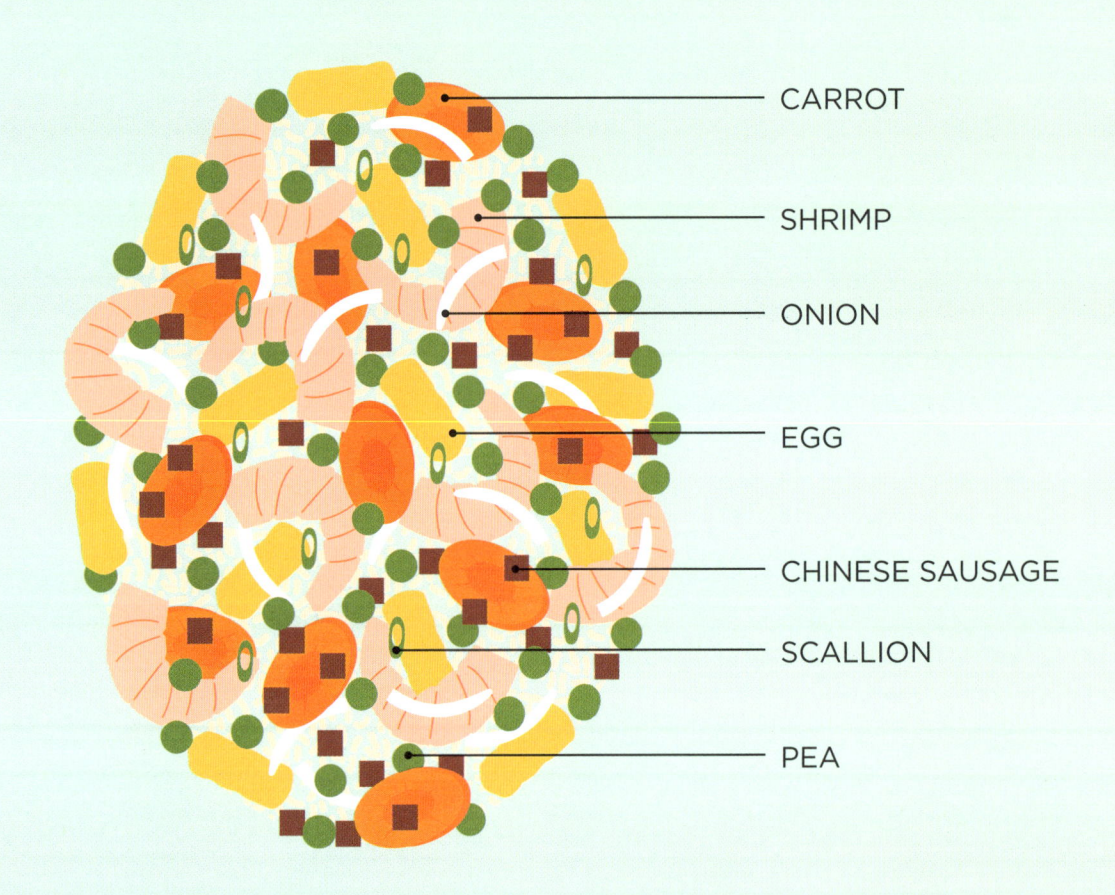

- CARROT
- SHRIMP
- ONION
- EGG
- CHINESE SAUSAGE
- SCALLION
- PEA

WHAT IS IT?
Sautéed leftover cooked rice, garnished with grilled vegetables and cooked egg.

ORIGIN
The dish originates in Yangzhou in the province of Jiangsu in eastern China. Yangzhou stir-fried rice is considered the "king of stir-fried rice" in China. There is a charter published by the Yangzhou Quality and Technical Supervision Bureau that lists a strict list of ingredients that must be adhered to. This version is an interpretation and does not include certain ingredients, such as dried scallops, Jinhua ham, sea cucumber, bamboo, chicken thighs, or shiitake mushrooms.

COMPLETION TIME
Preparation time: 30 minutes
Cooking time: 12 minutes
Storage: 2 to 3 days. Reheat in a pan over medium heat.

SKILL TO MASTER
Preparing shrimp (page 36)

Learning

CHINESE SAUSAGE (LAP CHEONG)

Dried pork sausage with mei kuei lu chiew (sorghum liquor) and spices. It has a salty-sweet taste.

OYSTER SAUCE

Choose the Megachef or Lee Kum Kee (Premium) brands.

SOY SAUCE

Choose bottles that state "natural fermentation."

SERVES ABOUT 4 TO 6

SHRIMP

10½ ounces / 300 g raw shrimp, size 30/40
1 tablespoon sesame oil
- 1 tablespoon soy sauce

1 onion (about 3½ ounces / 100 g)
3 scallions
1 carrot (about 4¼ ounces / 120 g)
- 2 Chinese sausages (lap cheong; about 4¼ ounces / 120 g)
3 large / 150 g eggs
3½ cups / 700 g cooked leftover rice, or about 2 cups / 350 g uncooked (page 12)
- 2 tablespoons soy sauce
- 2 tablespoons oyster sauce
1 teaspoon organic cane sugar
Freshly ground black pepper
5 tablespoons / 75 ml neutral-flavor oil of your choice (sunflower, peanut)
¾ cup / 120 g frozen peas

225

Making

YÁNGZHŌU CHǍOFÀN

1 Prepare the shrimp (page 36) and peel them. Combine them with the sesame oil and soy sauce. Set aside in the refrigerator.

2 Chop the onion and slice the scallions. Dice the carrot and cut the sausages into cubes. Lightly beat the eggs using a fork.

3 Combine the rice with the soy sauce, oyster sauce, and sugar. Season with pepper.

4 In a wok or skillet, heat 1 tablespoon of the oil. Add the eggs. As soon as they start to firm up, stir them. Set aside.

5 Add 1 tablespoon of the oil to the wok and cook the shrimp over high heat for 30 seconds while stirring. Set aside. Add the remaining oil and sauté the sausage for 1 to 2 minutes. Add the onion and carrot, and cook for 2 minutes. Add the rice. Stir, then add the frozen peas and cook for an additional 3 to 5 minutes.

6 Add the eggs and shrimp. Cook for 1 to 2 minutes. Turn off the heat, and add the scallions. Stir to combine. Serve hot.

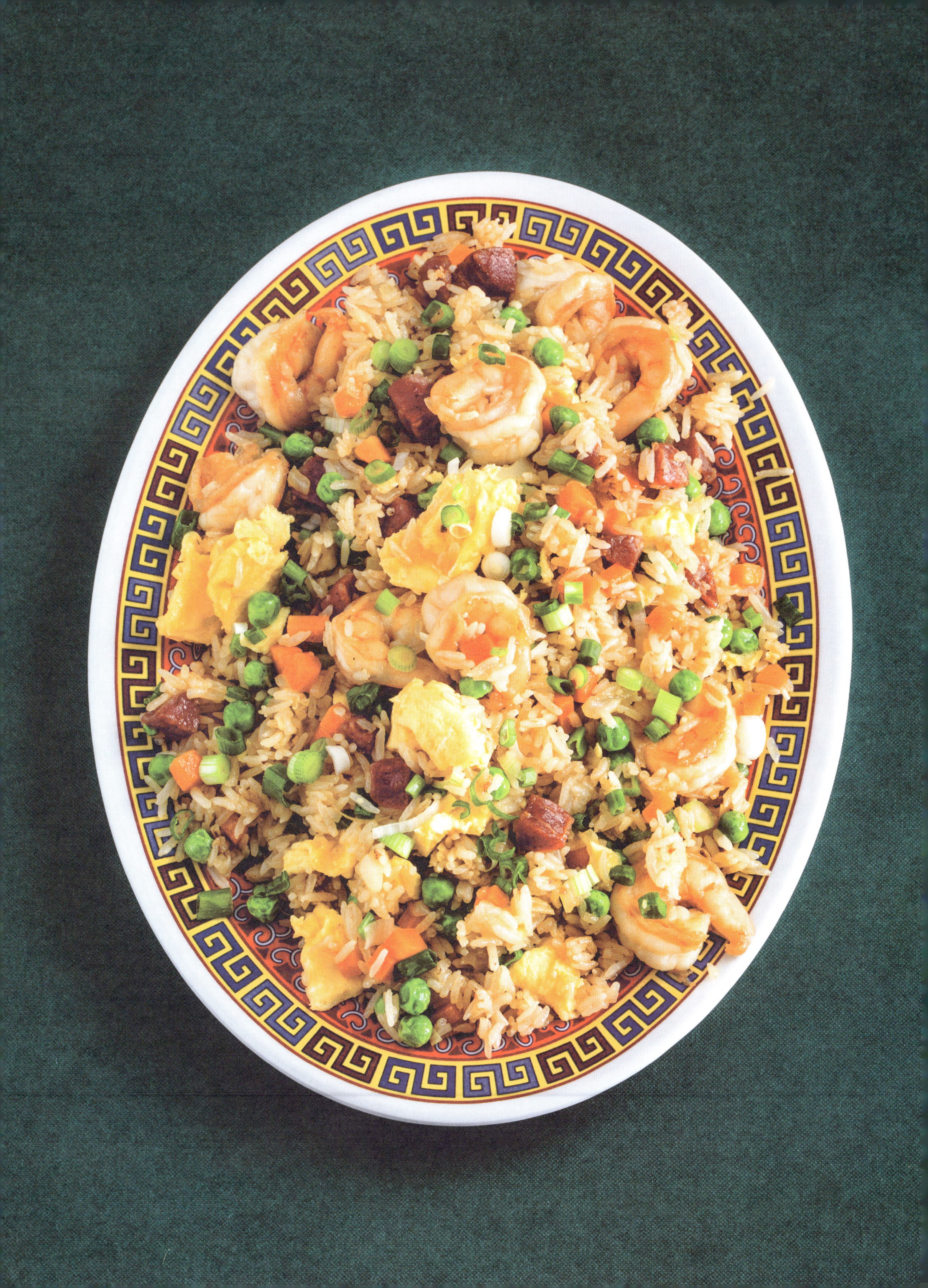

Understanding

BĀO ZAĬ FÀN
CLAY POT RICE

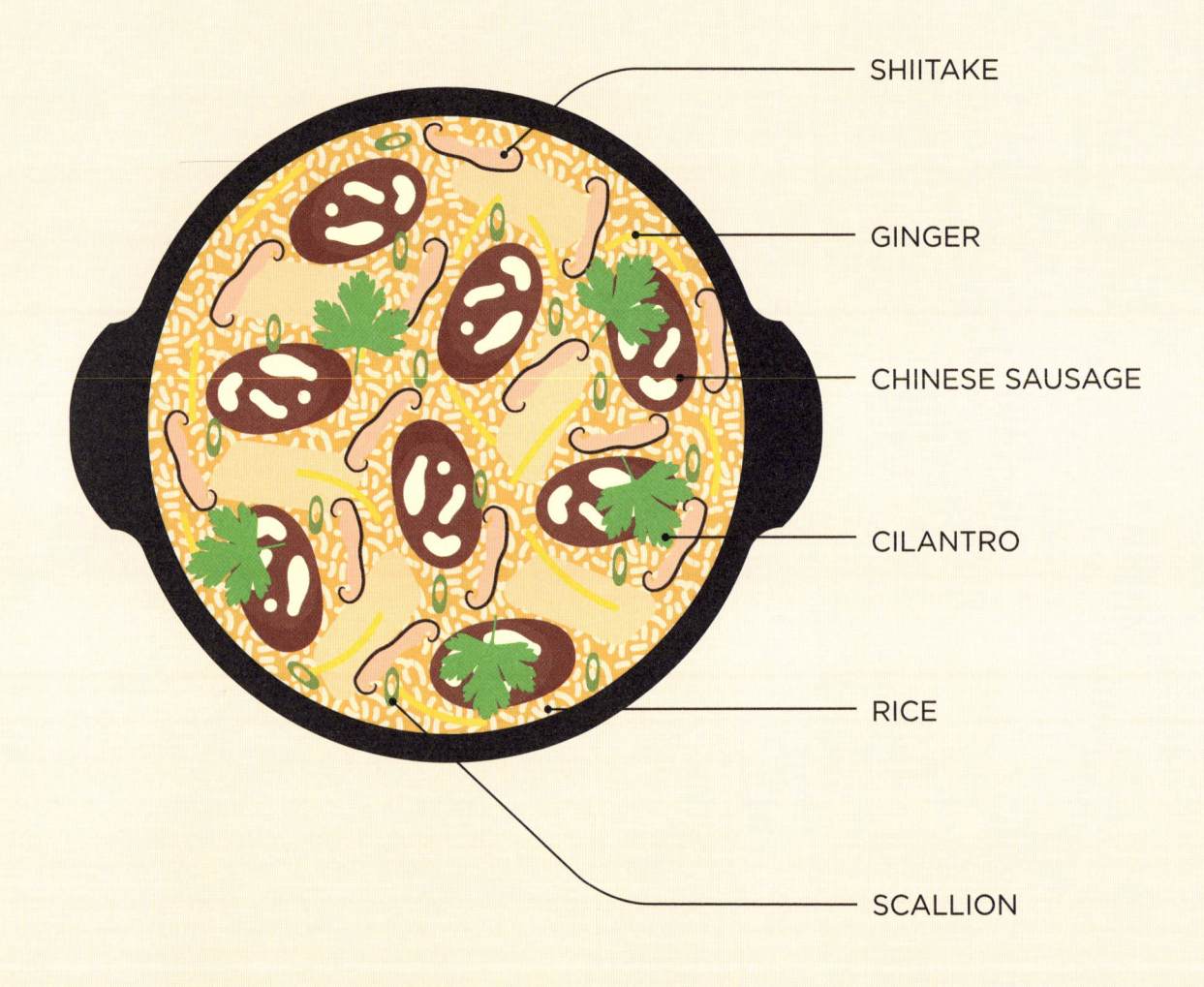

- SHIITAKE
- GINGER
- CHINESE SAUSAGE
- CILANTRO
- RICE
- SCALLION

WHAT IS IT?
Rice cooked with broth and fillings served in an earthenware pot.

ORIGIN
This is a traditional Cantonese dish especially popular in Hong Kong.

COMPLETION TIME
Preparation time: 1 hour
Resting time: 2½ hours
Cooking time: 50 minutes
Storage: 2 to 3 days

SPECIAL EQUIPMENT
Terracotta or cast-iron pot

SKILLS TO MASTER
Boning a chicken thigh (page 34)
Cutting into julienne (page 281)
Rehydrating mushrooms (page 280)

SERVING
Once cooked, season with the sauce. Combine all the ingredients in the pot. Scrape the rice from the bottom, which should be crisp.

CHALLENGE
The crucial point of the recipe is to create a crusted rice layer on the bottom of the pot at the end of the cooking time. To achieve this, oil is poured around the lid and flows little by little down the sides of the pot until it reaches the bottom. The heat is reduced, and the rice crisps.

USEFUL TIPS
Soaking the rice reduces the cooking time. You can also use a cast-iron pot, in which case remove the lid and pour the oil along the sides around the rice. For a complete meal, add green vegetables blanched in salted water.

Learning

SHAOXING RICE WINE
Fermented glutinous rice wine. Choose the Pagoda brand (blue label).

DARK SOY SAUCE
Less salty than classic soy sauce and thicker and slightly sweet. It is mainly used to lend more color and flavor to dishes.

SOY SAUCE
Choose bottles that state "natural fermentation."

DRIED SHIITAKE
Depending on their size, rehydrate them for at least 2 hours before use. They are more concentrated and have a more umami taste than fresh ones.

CHINESE SAUSAGE (LAP CHEONG)
Dried pork sausage with mei kuei lu chiew (sorghum liquor) and spices. It has a salty-sweet taste.

SERVES 4 TO 6

10½ ounces / 300 g free-range chicken thighs, deboned and with skin separated and reserved for another use (about 2 small thighs; page 34)
- 2 Chinese sausages (lap cheong)
- 6 dried shiitake mushrooms (about ¾ ounce / 20 g)

2¾ cups / 500 g rice

SAUCE

½ onion

2 shallots

4 cloves garlic

1 tablespoon neutral-flavor oil of your choice (sunflower, peanut)
- 2 tablespoons Shaoxing wine
- 2½ tablespoons / 40 ml soy sauce
- 2 tablespoons dark soy sauce

2 tablespoons organic cane sugar

Scant ½ cup / 100 ml Basic Broth (page 38)

1 bunch of cilantro

¾ ounce / 20 g fresh ginger

1¾ teaspoons salt

1 level tablespoon baking soda

2 tablespoons Shaoxing wine

1 heaping tablespoon cornstarch

1 tablespoon soy sauce

1 tablespoon oyster sauce

1 tablespoon neutral-flavor oil of your choice (sunflower, peanut)

Freshly ground black pepper

1⅔ cups / 400 ml Basic Broth (page 38)

3 tablespoons / 45 ml neutral-flavor oil of your choice (sunflower, peanut)

3 to 4 scallions

A few sprigs of cilantro

Making

BĀO ZAĬ FÀN

1 Cut the meat of the chicken thighs into even pieces. Slice the sausage on the diagonal. Rehydrate the shiitake mushrooms (page 280). Rinse the rice two times, then soak it in water for 2 hours.

2 Make the sauce: Slice the onion and shallots. Press the garlic. In a wok, heat the 1 tablespoon of oil. Add the chicken skins and cook for about 5 minutes to brown them. Remove the skins, and add the onion, shallots, and garlic. Reduce the heat and cook until softened, about 5 minutes. While cooking, scrape the browned bits from the bottom. Add the 2 tablespoons of wine, the soy sauces, sugar, scant ½ cup / 100 ml of broth, and cilantro. Bring to a boil, reduce the heat, and simmer, partially covered, for 20 minutes. Strain, and set aside.

3 Peel and cut the ginger into julienne (page 281). Once the shiitake mushrooms have been rehydrated, squeeze them with your hands to remove excess water, and finely chop them. Combine the 1¾ teaspoons of salt with the baking soda and 1 cup / 240 ml water. Soak the chicken for 5 minutes in this mixture. Drain, rinse, and drain again. Combine the 2 tablespoons of wine, the cornstarch, soy sauce, oyster sauce, and 1 tablespoon of oil. Season with pepper. Add the chicken, ginger, and shiitake mushrooms. Marinate for at least 30 minutes at room temperature.

4 Drain the rice and add it to the pot. Add the 1⅔ cups / 400 ml of broth. Bring to a boil, covered. After 3 minutes of boiling, arrange the chicken, mushrooms, and sausage slices on top of the rice. Place over low heat and cook for 15 minutes, covered.

5 Pour the 3 tablespoons / 45 ml of oil around the lid. The oil will flow little by little along the side of the pot and will help form a crunchy rice crust. Increase the heat and cook for 4 to 5 minutes, or until you hear crackling sounds.

6 Turn off the heat, set aside for 5 minutes, covered. Add 4 to 5 tablespoons of the sauce. Stir to combine. Taste, and adjust the level of seasoning using the sauce. The rice crust will peel off as it cools. Serve with chopped scallions and cilantro sprinkled on top.

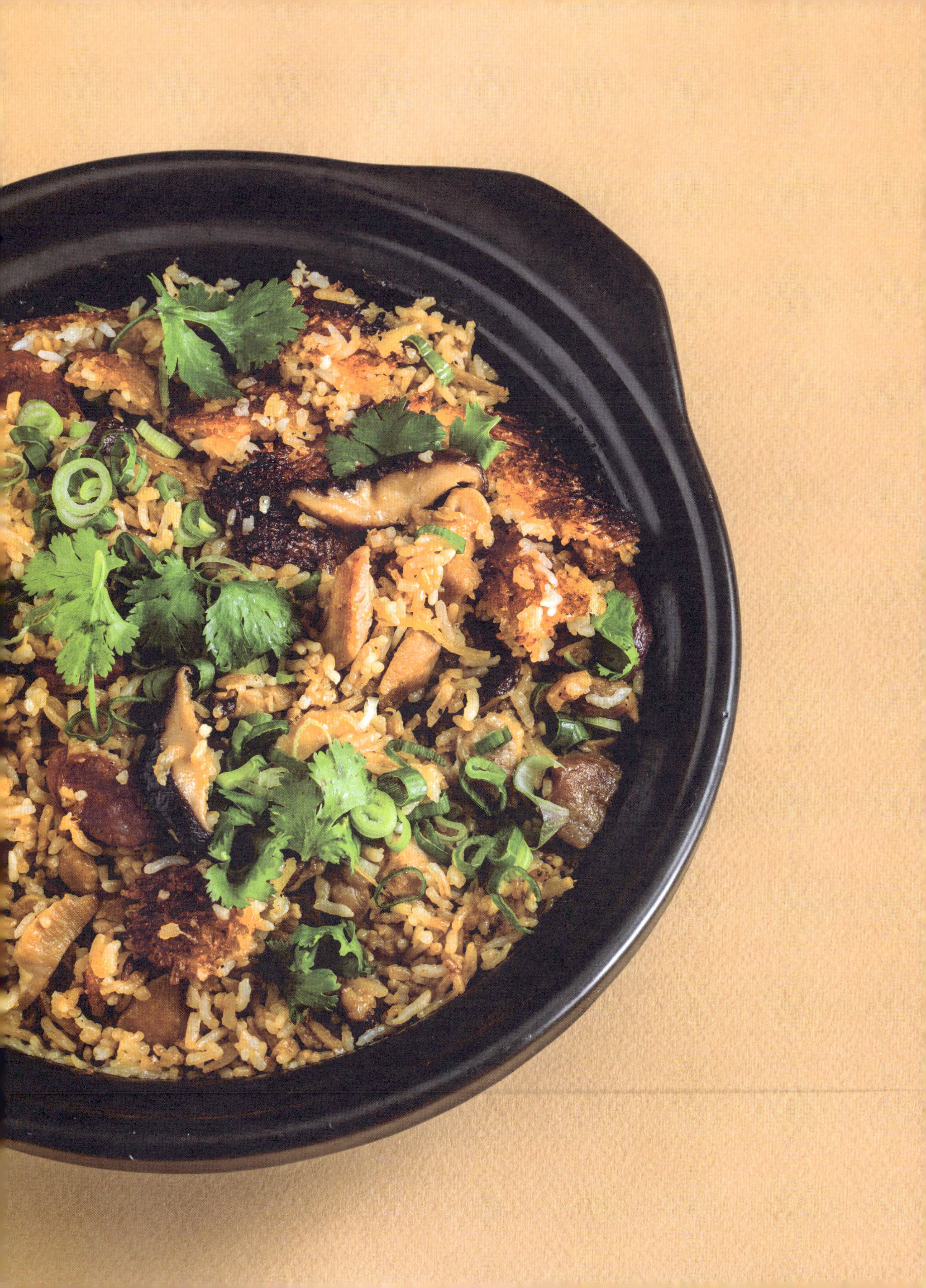

Understanding

PÍDÀN JĪRÒU ZHŌU
CENTURY EGG CHICKEN CONGEE

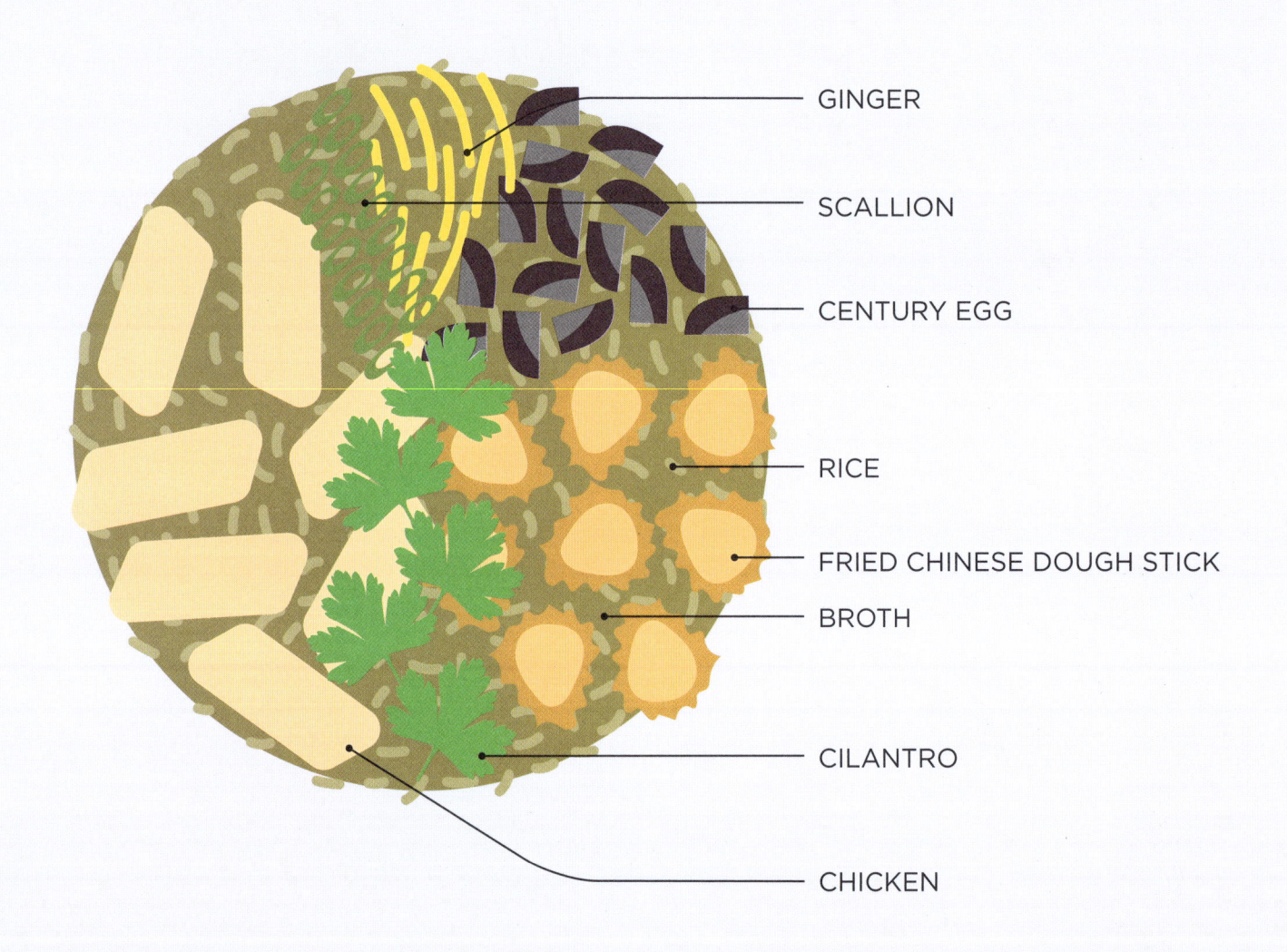

- GINGER
- SCALLION
- CENTURY EGG
- RICE
- FRIED CHINESE DOUGH STICK
- BROTH
- CILANTRO
- CHICKEN

WHAT IS IT?

A rice soup cooked in chicken broth served with fried dough and century eggs.

COMPLETION TIME

Preparation time: 35 minutes
Cooking time: 35 minutes
Storage: 2 to 3 days without the toppings

SKILLS TO MASTER

Boning a chicken thigh (page 34)
Cutting into julienne (page 281)

SERVING

This is the comforting dish eaten for breakfast or requested when sick.

VARIATIONS

Replace the chicken with 10½ ounces / 300 g white fish cut into cubes cooked for 5 minutes. For a veggie version, replace the chicken with chopped vegetables (carrots, mushrooms, celery, Chinese cabbage, etc.) and cook for 10 minutes.

Learning

SERVES 2

BROTH

⅔ cup / 130 g jasmine (Thai) rice
6 cups / 1.5 L Basic Broth of your choice (pages 38 and 40)
½ teaspoon salt
1 tablespoon soy sauce
Freshly ground black pepper

CHICKEN

1 chicken thigh, deboned (page 34)
1 tablespoon soy sauce
½ teaspoon organic cane sugar
Salt and freshly ground black pepper

TOPPINGS

2 Chinese dough sticks, thawed
⅛ ounce / 5 g fresh ginger
1 scallion
6 sprigs of cilantro
2 century eggs (page 282)
Oil, for frying

1 Slice the chicken thigh and marinate it in the soy sauce, sugar, and a pinch of salt and pepper. Set aside at room temperature.

2 Fry the dough sticks according to the instructions on the package. Set aside on paper towels to drain.

3 Rinse the rice two times. In a large saucepan, bring the broth to a boil. Add the rice, reduce the heat, and simmer for 20 minutes. Stir frequently to prevent the rice from sticking to the bottom. Add the chicken and broth seasonings. Continue cooking for 10 minutes. Taste, and adjust the seasoning, if necessary.

4 Cut the ginger into thin julienne (page 281). Chop the scallion and cilantro. Peel the eggs, then rinse them and cut them into cubes. Slice the dough sticks. Serve the congee topped with the eggs, dough sticks, ginger, scallion, and cilantro.

Understanding

ZÒNGZI
STUFFED GLUTINOUS RICE

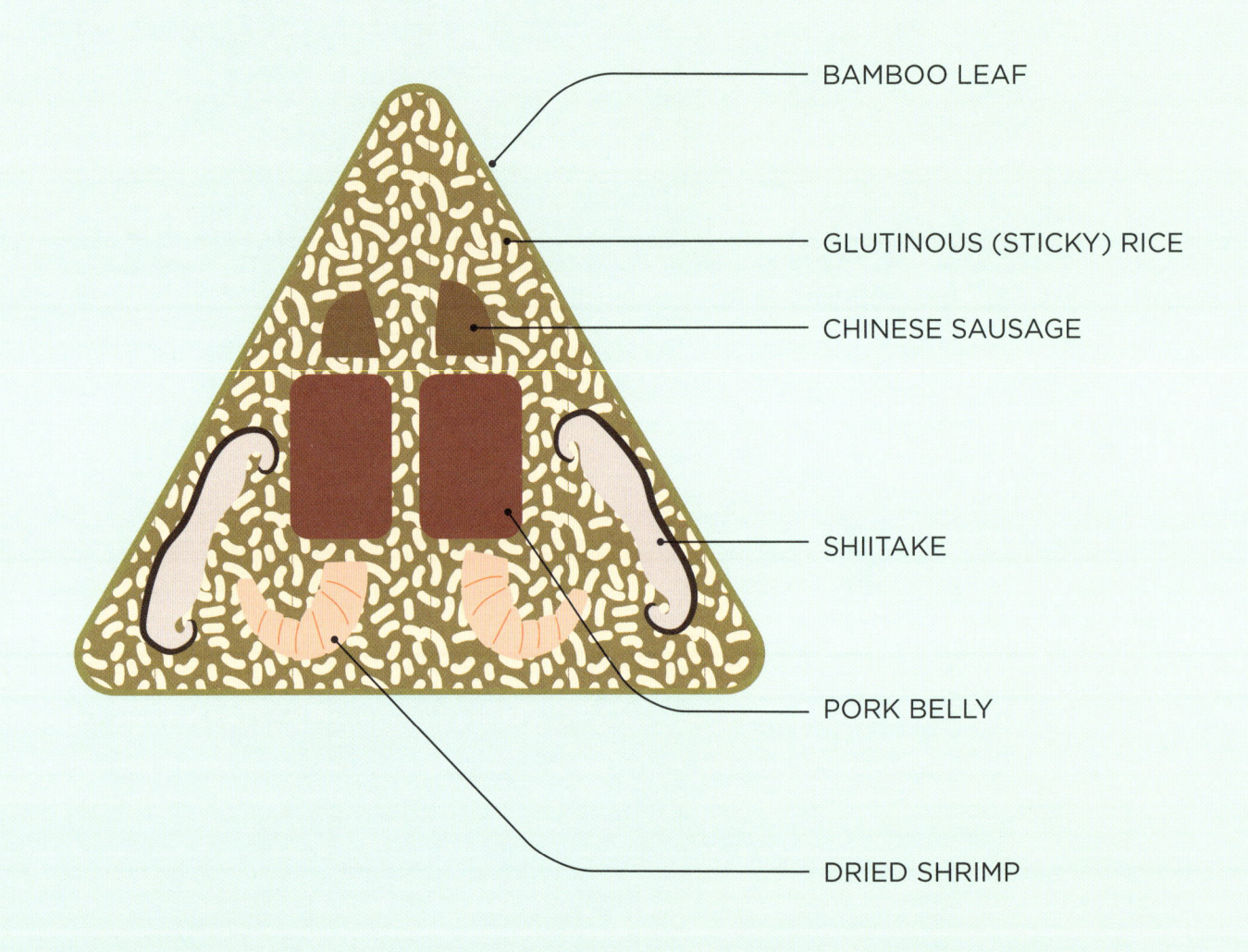

- BAMBOO LEAF
- GLUTINOUS (STICKY) RICE
- CHINESE SAUSAGE
- SHIITAKE
- PORK BELLY
- DRIED SHRIMP

WHAT IS IT?

Glutinous rice filled with pork, shrimp, and shiitake mushrooms, then wrapped and cooked in bamboo leaves.

ORIGIN

Zòngzi are made for the Dragon Boat Festival (the 5th day of the 5th month of the Chinese lunar calendar). The festival commemorates the death of the poet and minister Qu Yuan (Warring States period, 475–221 BC). Qu Yuan was a loyal minister of the Chu state. After being unjustly exiled on charges of treason, he drowned in the Miluo River out of desperation. The inhabitants, who held him in high esteem, rushed into boats to try to save him (the origin of dragon boat races). Unable to save him, they attempted to recover his body. According to legend, they threw rice balls into the river to prevent fish and evil spirits from devouring his body.

COMPLETION TIME

Preparation time: 2½ to 3 hours
Resting time: Overnight
Cooking time: 45 minutes
Storage: 3 to 4 days

SPECIAL EQUIPMENT

Kitchen twine

SKILLS TO MASTER

Rehydrating shrimp (page 280)
Rehydrating shiitake mushrooms (page 280)
Softening bamboo leaves (page 280)

USEFUL TIP

Rice sacks are marked with the year the rice is harvested. If the rice purchased is more than two years old, extend the cooking time by 15 minutes.

Learning

BAMBOO LEAVES
They have natural nonstick properties and are used to wrap foods for cooking. They transmit their fresh, herbaceous scent to foods. They are sold dried and need to be rehydrated before use.

SHAOXING RICE WINE
Fermented glutinous rice wine. Choose the Pagoda brand (blue label).

GLUTINOUS RICE
It should be soaked between 4 hours to overnight, depending on the recipe. Without soaking, the rice will remain firm, even after prolonged cooking.

DRIED SHRIMP
Sold in the refrigerated section. Choose size XL (about ¾ to 1⅛ inches / 2 to 3 cm). Soak them for 30 minutes in lukewarm water before use. They lend an umami taste to dishes.

MAKES ABOUT 12 PIECES
- 3 cups / 500 g glutinous rice
- 1¾ ounces / 50 g dried shrimp
  16 small dried shiitake mushrooms

MARINATED PORK BELLY
14 ounces / 400 g pork belly, with or without the rind
- 2 tablespoons Shaoxing wine
  1 heaping teaspoon five-spice powder
  1 tablespoon soy sauce
  1 tablespoon dark soy sauce
  1 tablespoon oyster sauce
  1 teaspoon organic cane sugar
  ½ teaspoon salt

- 32 bamboo leaves
  2 shallots
  1 onion
  2 Chinese sausages (lap cheong)
  ¼ cup / 60 ml neutral-flavor oil of your choice (sunflower, peanut)
  2 tablespoons soy sauce
  1¾ teaspoons salt
  1¾ teaspoons organic cane sugar
  Freshly ground black pepper

235

Making

ZÒNGZI

1 The day before, soak the rice in a container of cold water. The water level should be about 3 inches / 8 cm above the rice. Rehydrate the shrimp and shiitake mushrooms (page 280). Marinate the pork belly: Cut the pork belly into pieces ⅓-inch / 1 cm thick and about 1½ inches / 4 cm long. Combine the wine, five-spice powder, soy sauces, oyster sauce, sugar, and salt. Add the pork belly to this mixture to marinate.

2 The next day, soak the bamboo leaves in a container of boiling water (page 280). When softened, cut off the base of the stems. Set aside in water.

3 Drain the rice, shiitake mushrooms, and shrimp. Chop the shallots and onion. Cut the shiitake mushrooms in half, if necessary. Slice the sausages. In a wok or skillet, heat the oil. Sauté the shallots and onion for 5 minutes over low heat. Add the drained rice, soy sauce, salt, and sugar. Season with pepper, stir to combine, and set aside.

4 Take two bamboo leaves, overlap them slightly from top to bottom, then fold them in the middle, forming a cone.

5 Fill the bottom of the cone with rice. Add 1 or 2 shiitake mushrooms, 2 shrimp, pieces of pork, and 1 piece of sausage. Cover with rice.

6 Press the top of the rice down using a spoon. Fold in the sides of the leaves, then fold in the top to form a pyramid.

7 Turn the pyramid over onto the palm of your hand. Fold over the piece of leaf that protrudes on one side.

8 Tie together tightly to secure the contents.

9 Bring a pot of water to a boil. Immerse the zòngzi in the boiling water. Boil, covered, for 45 minutes. Monitor the water level and add more water, if necessary. Remove the bundle. Let cool before serving.

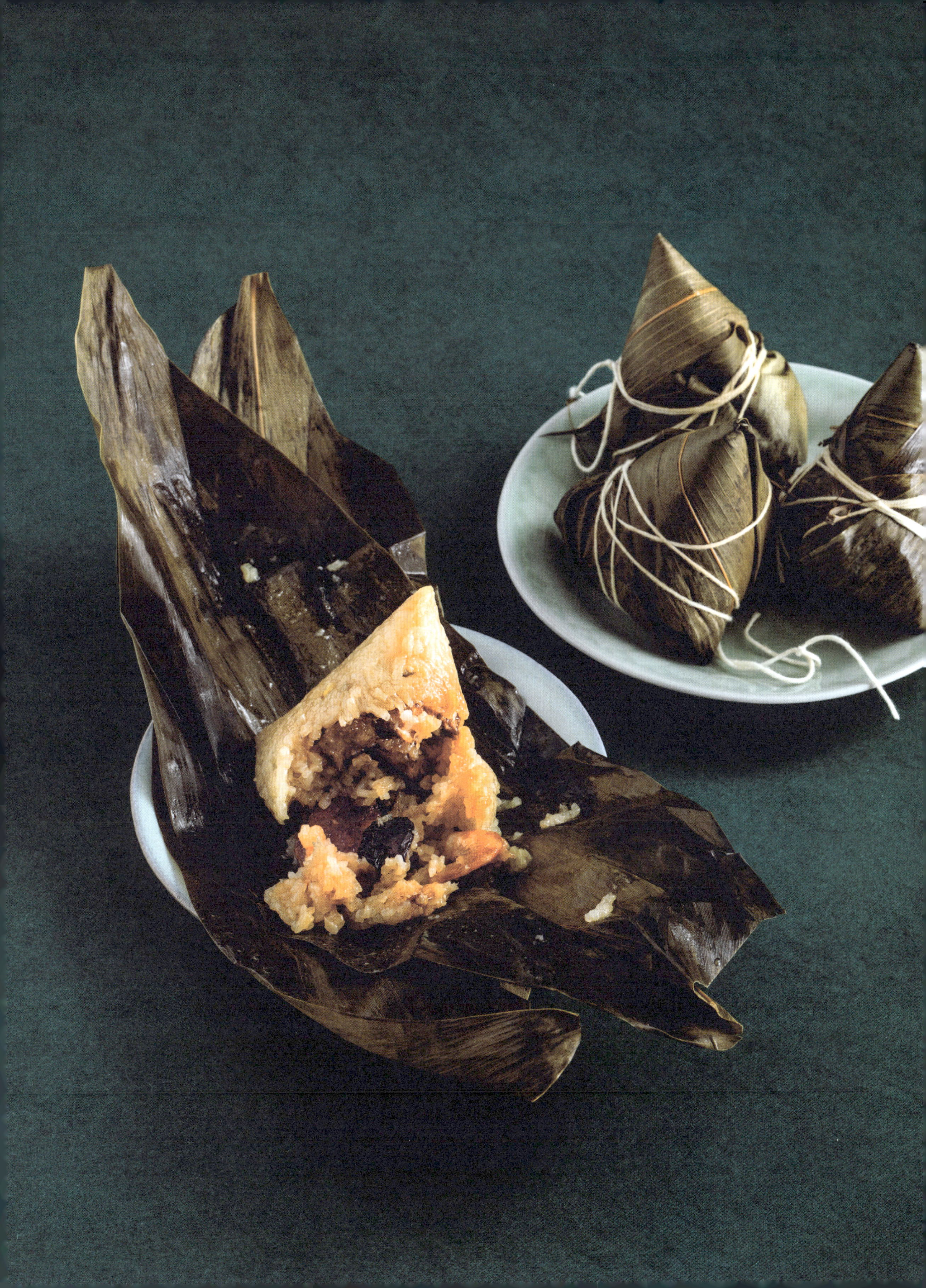

Understanding

XIÁN YÚ CHǍOFÀN
SALTED FISH FRIED RICE

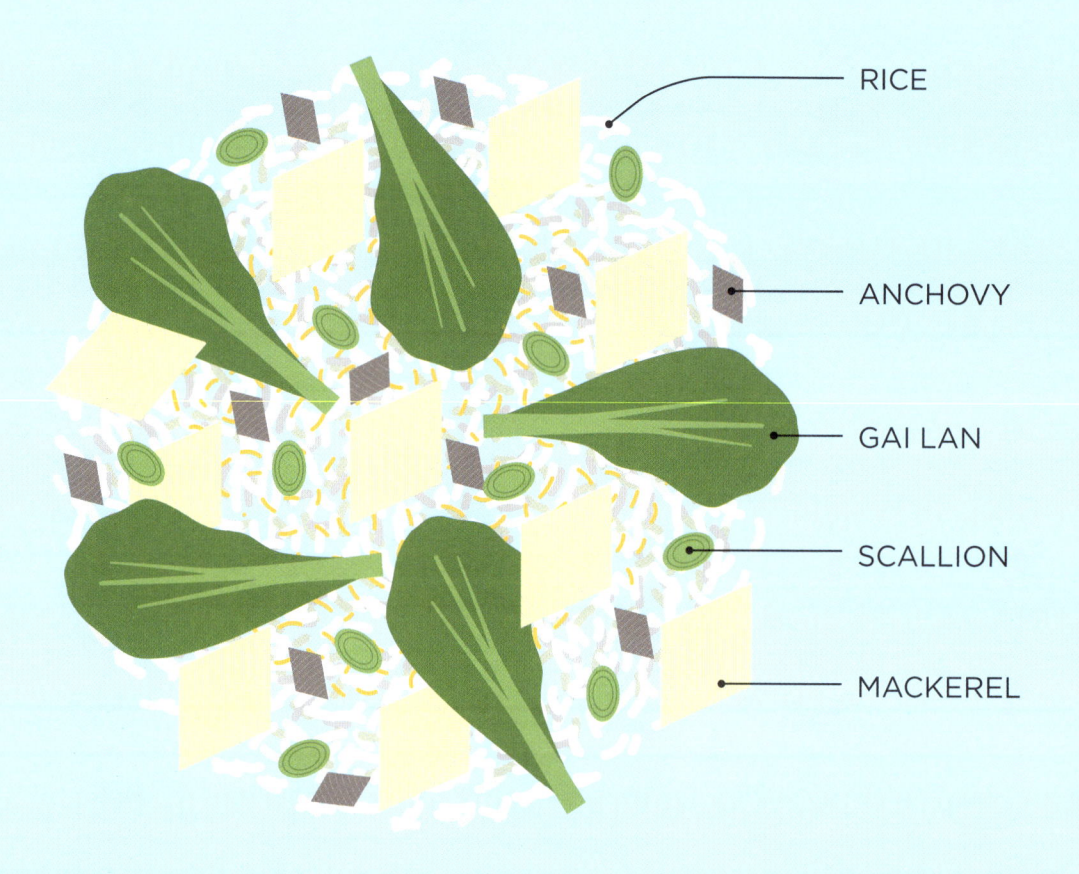

- RICE
- ANCHOVY
- GAI LAN
- SCALLION
- MACKEREL

WHAT IS IT?
Cantonese fried rice in which pieces of salted mackerel are added.

ORIGIN
Traditionally, salted and dried pieces of a type of Chinese cod are used.

COMPLETION TIME
Preparation time: 40 minutes
Resting time: 1½ hours
Cooking time: 15 minutes
Storage: 2 days

SERVING
Add a squeeze of lemon juice and fresh, finely chopped chile pepper just before serving, just like the Chinese who live in Bangkok do.

Learning

SOY SAUCE
Choose bottles that state "natural fermentation."

GAI LAN
Also called Chinese broccoli. The leaves and stems can be eaten.

SERVES 4 TO 6

SALTED MACKEREL

12 ounces / 350 g mackerel filets (about 2 medium mackerel)

3 tablespoons / 35 g coarse salt

FRIED RICE

5 cloves garlic

1 onion

- 14 ounces / 400 g gai lan

  1¼ ounces / 35 g anchovies in oil

  4 cups / 800 g cooked leftover rice, or about 2 cups / 360 to 400 g uncooked (page 12)

- 2 tablespoons soy sauce

  1 heaping teaspoon organic cane sugar

  ⅓ cup / 80 ml neutral-flavor oil of your choice (sunflower, peanut)

  Freshly ground black pepper

Making

XIÁN YÚ CHĂOFÀN

1 Remove the bones from the mackerel filets. Cut the filets into cubes of about ⅓ inch / 1 cm. Combine the mackerel with the salt. Refrigerate for 1½ hours. Rinse, and drain in a strainer. Wipe dry with paper towels, and set aside in the refrigerator.

2 Chop the garlic and onion. Cut the gai lan stems on a slight diagonal and finely chop the leaves. Set aside separately.

3 Chop the anchovies and stir them together with the rice, soy sauce, and sugar. Season with pepper.

4 In a wok or skillet, heat the oil. Fry the garlic until golden. Remove it using a slotted spoon, and set aside.

5 In the same oil, brown the mackerel pieces for 3 to 4 minutes. Remove them using a slotted spoon.

6 In the same oil, cook the onion until softened. Add the gai lan stems and cook for 1 to 2 minutes, then add the leaves. Stir, increase the heat, and add the rice. Cook the rice for about 5 minutes, then add the mackerel. Stir to combine, taste, and adjust the seasoning, if necessary. Off the heat, add the fried garlic.

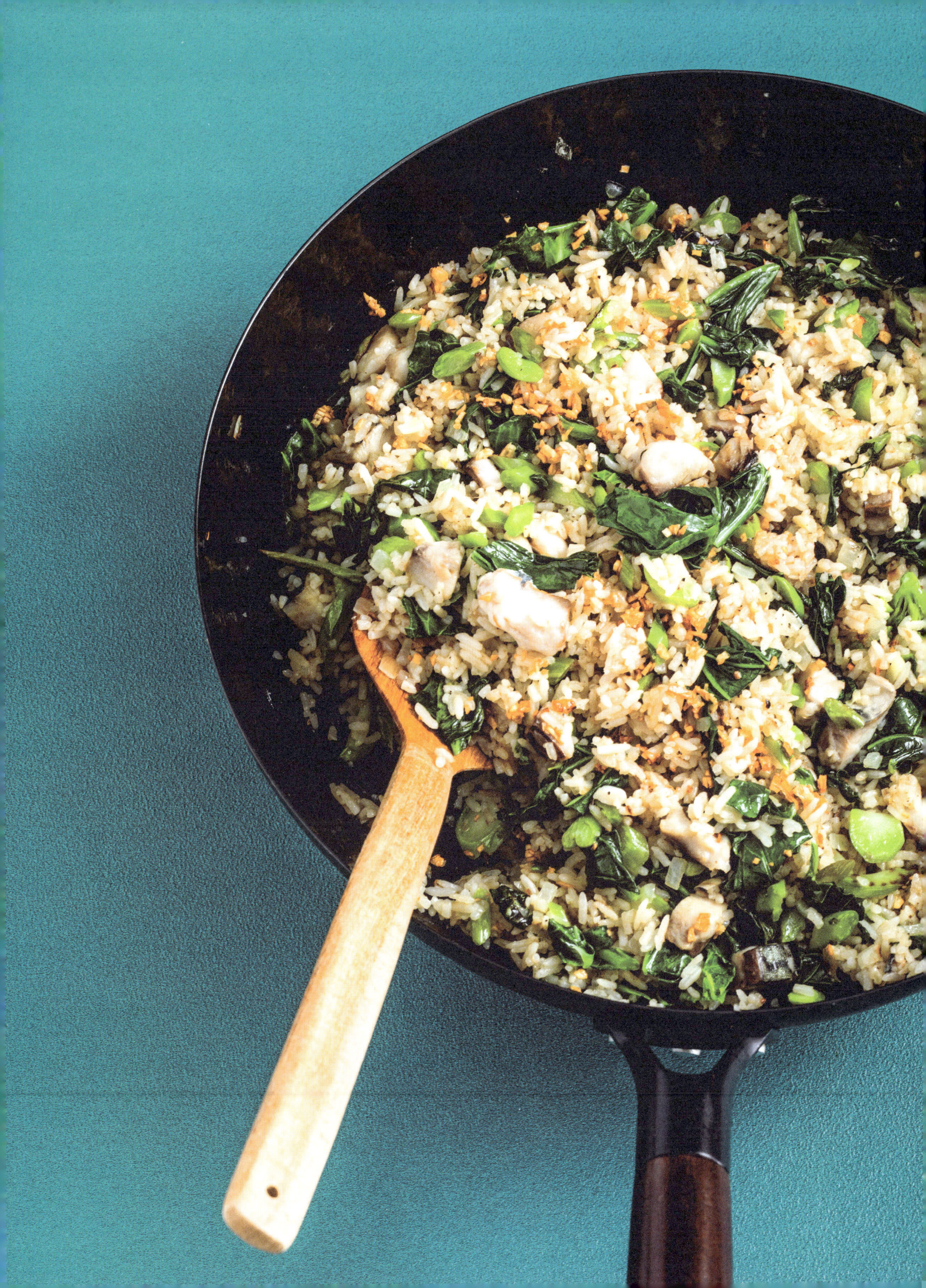

Understanding

GĒ BĀO
DONG PO PORK GUA BAO

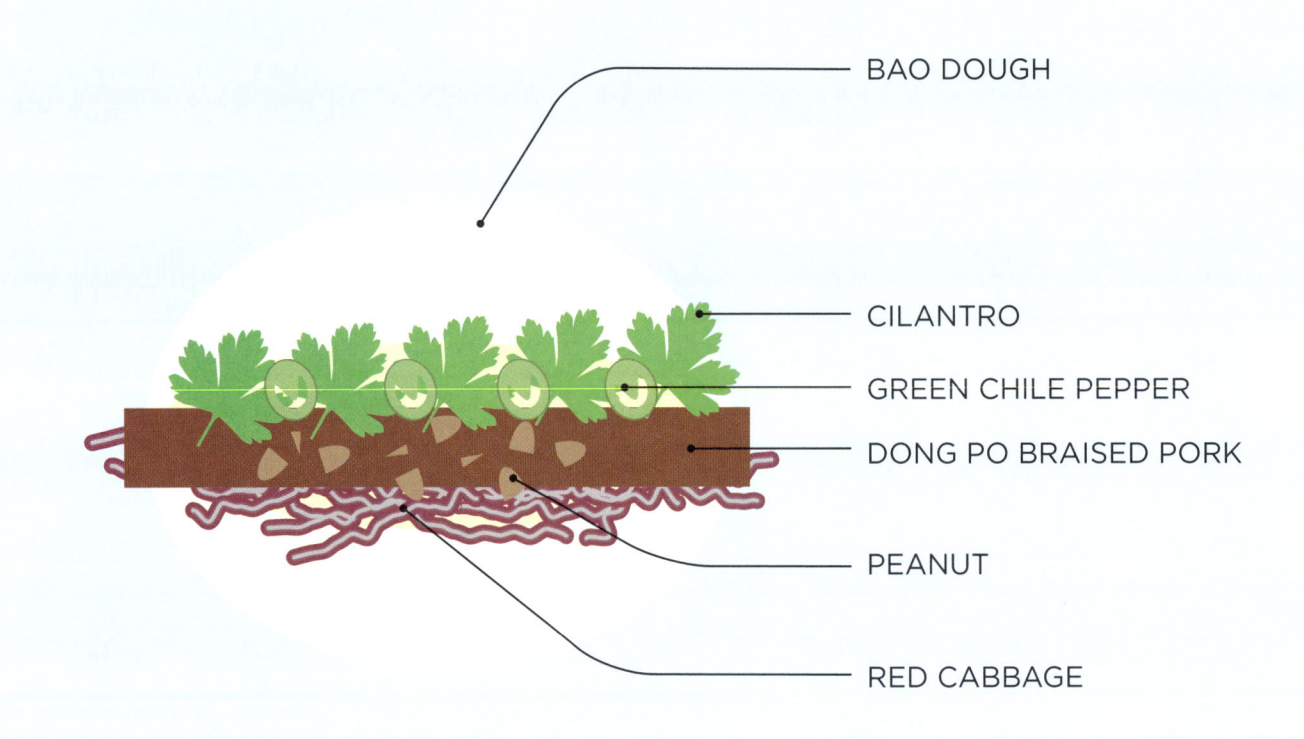

- BAO DOUGH
- CILANTRO
- GREEN CHILE PEPPER
- DONG PO BRAISED PORK
- PEANUT
- RED CABBAGE

WHAT IS IT?
A steamed bun, folded in half like a sandwich, and filled with braised pork, peanuts, and raw vegetables.

ORIGIN
Originating from Fujian, a coastal province in southeastern China, its open crescent shape is said to evoke a full purse, a symbol of wealth and prosperity. It was prepared during the festival of Mazu, the patron deity of sailors and fishermen.

COMPLETION TIME
Preparation time: 1 hour
Resting time: 1 hour 15 minutes
Cooking time: 12 minutes
Storage: You can make the buns up to 4 days in advance and store them in the refrigerator. They can also be frozen. Simply reheat them for 3 to 4 minutes by steaming if they are thawed, or for 8 minutes if they are frozen. The don po pork can also be prepared the day before, or up to 2 days before.

SPECIAL EQUIPMENT
Steamer basket
Steamer
Perforated parchment paper (optional)
Mandoline

VARIATIONS
You can replace the cabbage with carrots and add a few slices of cucumber.

Learning

MAKES 10 GUA BAO

Classic Bao Dough (page 20)
Dong Po Pork (page 128)

PICKLED CABBAGE

10½ ounces / 300 g red cabbage
3 tablespoons / 45 ml white rice vinegar or white vinegar
1 tablespoon organic cane sugar
½ teaspoon salt

2 long green chile peppers
½ bunch of cilantro
⅓ cup / 50 g crushed peanuts

1 Make the bao dough (page 20) and the dong po pork (page 128).

2 Once the bao dough has risen, divide it into ten balls. Lightly dust the work surface with flour, roll out each ball into an oval approximately 3 inches / 8 cm wide and 4⅓ inches / 11 cm long. Grease the dough with a little oil and fold it in half.

3 Place the buns in a steamer basket fitted with perforated parchment paper, if using, or place them on a rectangle of parchment paper. Repeat these steps for the remaining dough pieces, ensuring to space them apart, as they will swell during cooking. Cover with a kitchen towel or lid and let rise for 15 minutes. Bring the water in a steamer to a boil. Steam the buns for 12 minutes.

4 Finely slice the cabbage, preferably using a mandoline. In a dish, combine the cabbage, vinegar, sugar, and salt. Stir well to combine, and set aside in the refrigerator.

5 Chop the chile peppers and remove the leaves from the cilantro stems. Reheat the dong po pork, if needed. Once the pork is hot, cut it into slices of about ¼ inch / 5 mm and coat them with the sauce. Open the gua bao bun and tuck in one slice of meat. Add cabbage, cilantro, and chile slices. Sprinkle the top with peanuts.

Understanding

CŌNG YÓUBǏNG
FRIED SCALLION PANCAKE

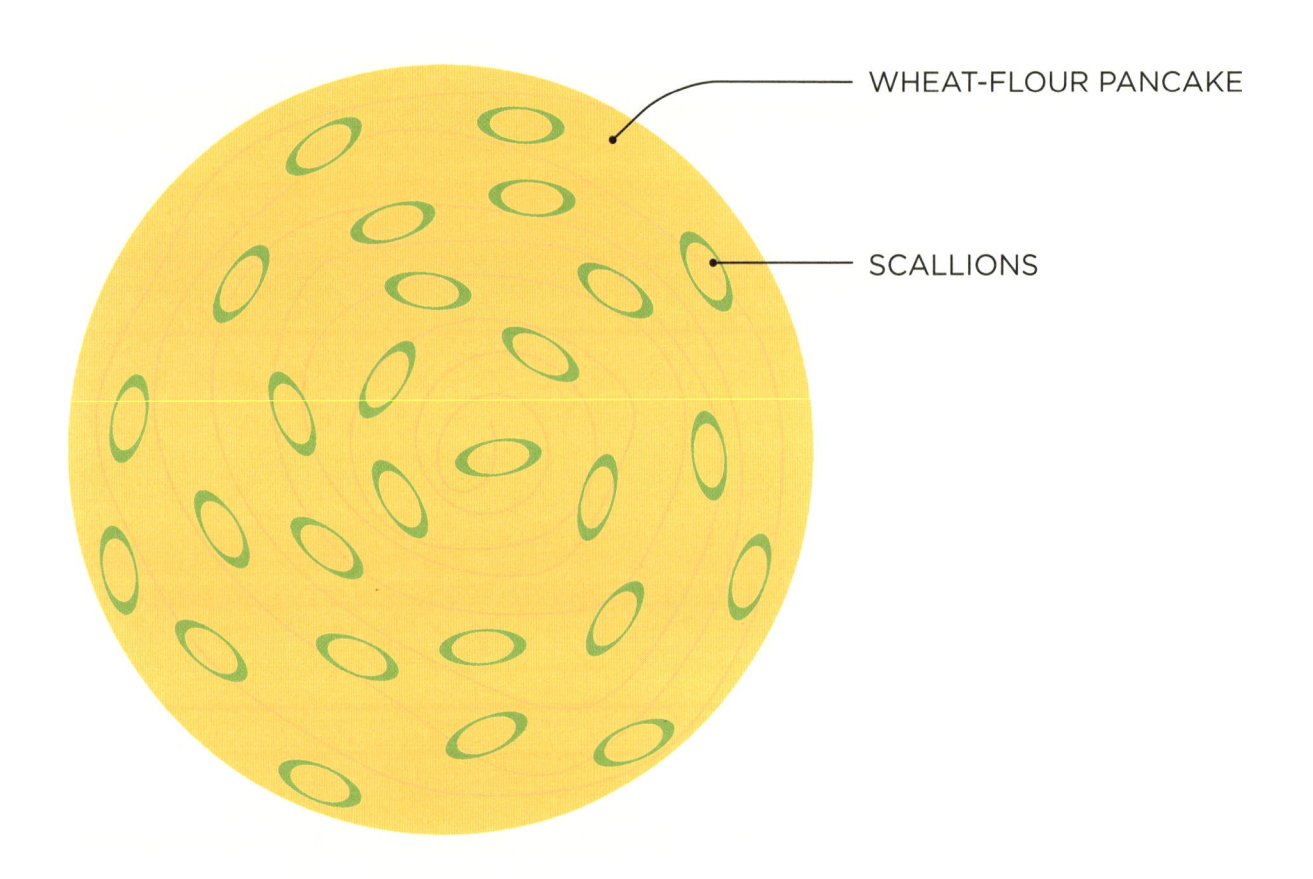

— WHEAT-FLOUR PANCAKE

— SCALLIONS

WHAT IS IT?
A crispy wheat-flour flat cake, filled with chopped scallions.

ORIGIN
Like many wheat-flour specialties, this cake originates from the northern regions.

COMPLETION TIME
Preparation time: 45 minutes
Resting time: 45 minutes
Cooking time: 12 minutes per cake
Storage: Once shaped, they can be frozen between two sheets of parchment paper and wrapped in plastic wrap. Once cooked, they will keep for 2 to 3 days in the refrigerator and can be warmed up in a pan.

SERVING
This crispy cake can be eaten hot for breakfast or as a snack that can be found in markets and street stalls.

USEFUL TIP
When the cake begins to turn golden, you can aerate the layers by separating them using two spatulas.

VARIATIONS
Replace the scallions with chile oil (page 44). You can also add toasted sesame seeds along with the scallions.

Learning

SCALLIONS
Abundant and omnipresent in Chinese cuisine. They have a milder flavor than regular white onion. They can be replaced with spring onion stems. Store wrapped in a damp cloth or paper.

FIVE-SPICE POWDER
A powdered mix containing coriander seeds, fennel, anise, cinnamon, black or Szechuan pepper, and cloves.

MAKES 4 PANCAKES

- 5½ ounces / 160 g scallions

SCALLION OIL
½ onion
- 4¼ ounces / 120 g scallions
  1¼ cups / 300 ml peanut oil

  2 ⅓ cups / 300 g all-purpose or bread flour
  1 level teaspoon salt
- 1 slightly heaping teaspoon five-spice powder (optional)
  Just over ¾ cup / 200 ml water at 122°F / 50°C
  Peanut oil

1 Chop the 5½ ounces / 160 g scallions and the onion. Cut the remaining 4¼ ounces / 120 g scallions into sections. In a small saucepan over medium heat, heat the 1¼ cups / 300 ml of peanut oil. Add the chopped onion and the scallion sections. Reduce the heat and let steep for 10 minutes. Turn off the heat, let cool, then remove the scallions with a slotted spoon.

2 In the bowl of a stand mixer fitted with the dough hook, add the flour, salt, and five-spice powder, if using. Add the water and knead to form a smooth dough. The dough should be soft but not be sticky. Shape the dough into a ball, lightly coat it with oil, and cover with plastic wrap. Set aside for 30 minutes.

3 Weigh the dough and divide it into four equal portions. Shape the portions into balls. Set the balls of dough aside under plastic wrap or a clean kitchen towel. Dust the work surface with flour. Roll out a piece of dough into a large rectangle about 14 by 10 inches / 35 by 25 cm and ⅓ inch / 1 mm thick. Brush the entire surface of the dough with scallion oil. Sprinkle with the chopped scallions. Starting on the long end, roll the dough into a log.

Making

CŌNG YÓUBĬNG

1

2

3

4

5

6

7

4 Stretch the roll slightly, pushing out the air. Roll one end into a spiral until two-thirds of it is rolled up. Roll the other end into a spiral toward the other rolled end.

5 Position the larger spiral end on top of the smaller one. Press lightly to adhere them together. Apply a little oil to the top. Repeat these steps for the other dough pieces. Set them aside under a piece of plastic wrap for 15 minutes.

6 In a skillet over medium, heat 1 tablespoon of oil. Shape the spirals into flat cakes by pressing them down with the palm of your hand. Gradually flatten the dough using your fingertips, increasing the diameter of the cake to about 8 inches / 20 cm.

7 Place each cake in a pan one at a time, and cook for 4 to 5 minutes, covered. Turn the cake over and add a little oil to the pan. Cover, and cook for an additional 5 minutes. Check the browning. Remove the lid and cook for an additional 3 to 4 minutes, turning the cake over frequently and adding a little oil, if necessary. Serve slightly warm.

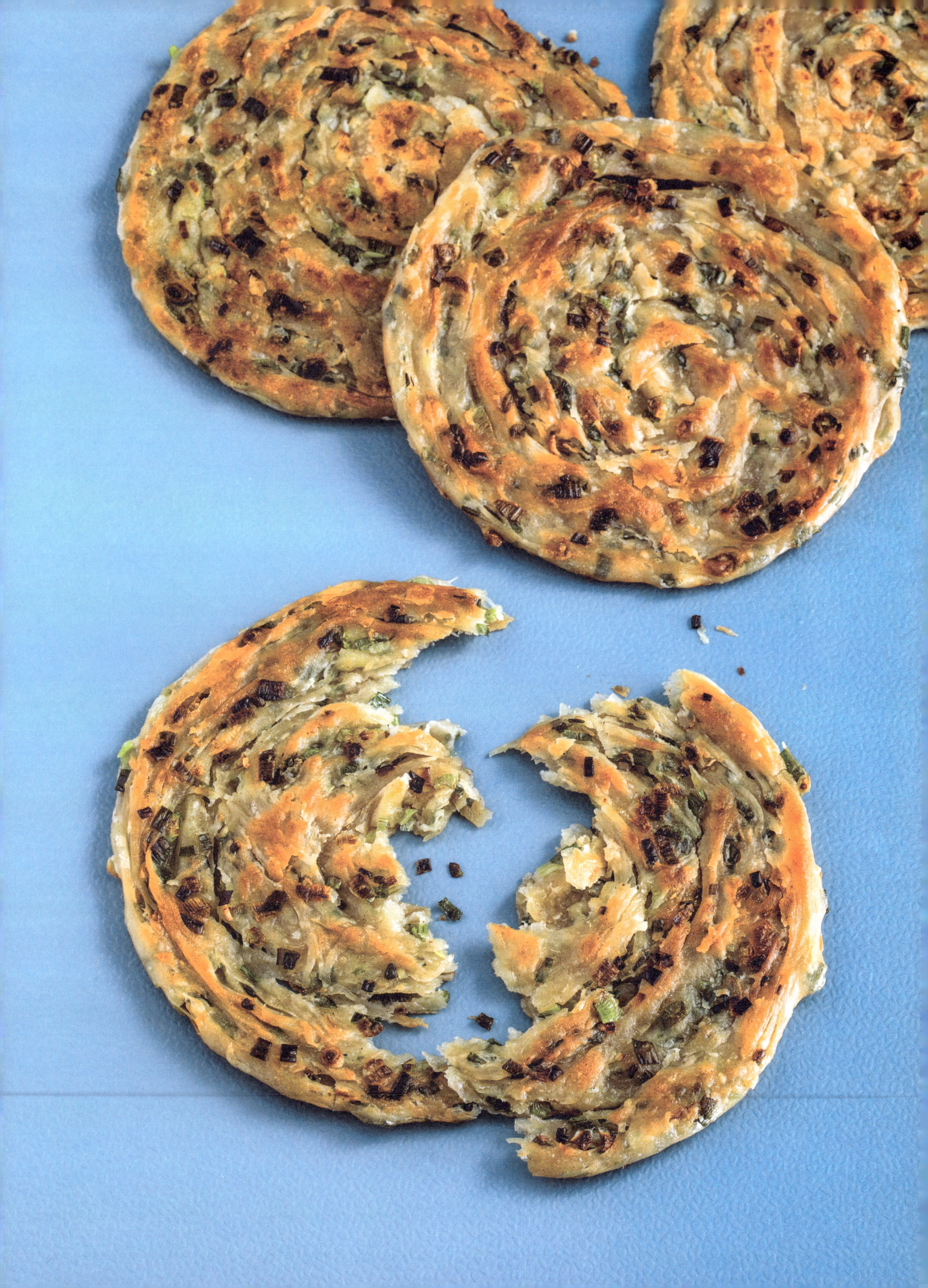

Understanding

YÈ ER BĀ
STUFFED DUMPLINGS WRAPPED IN LEAVES

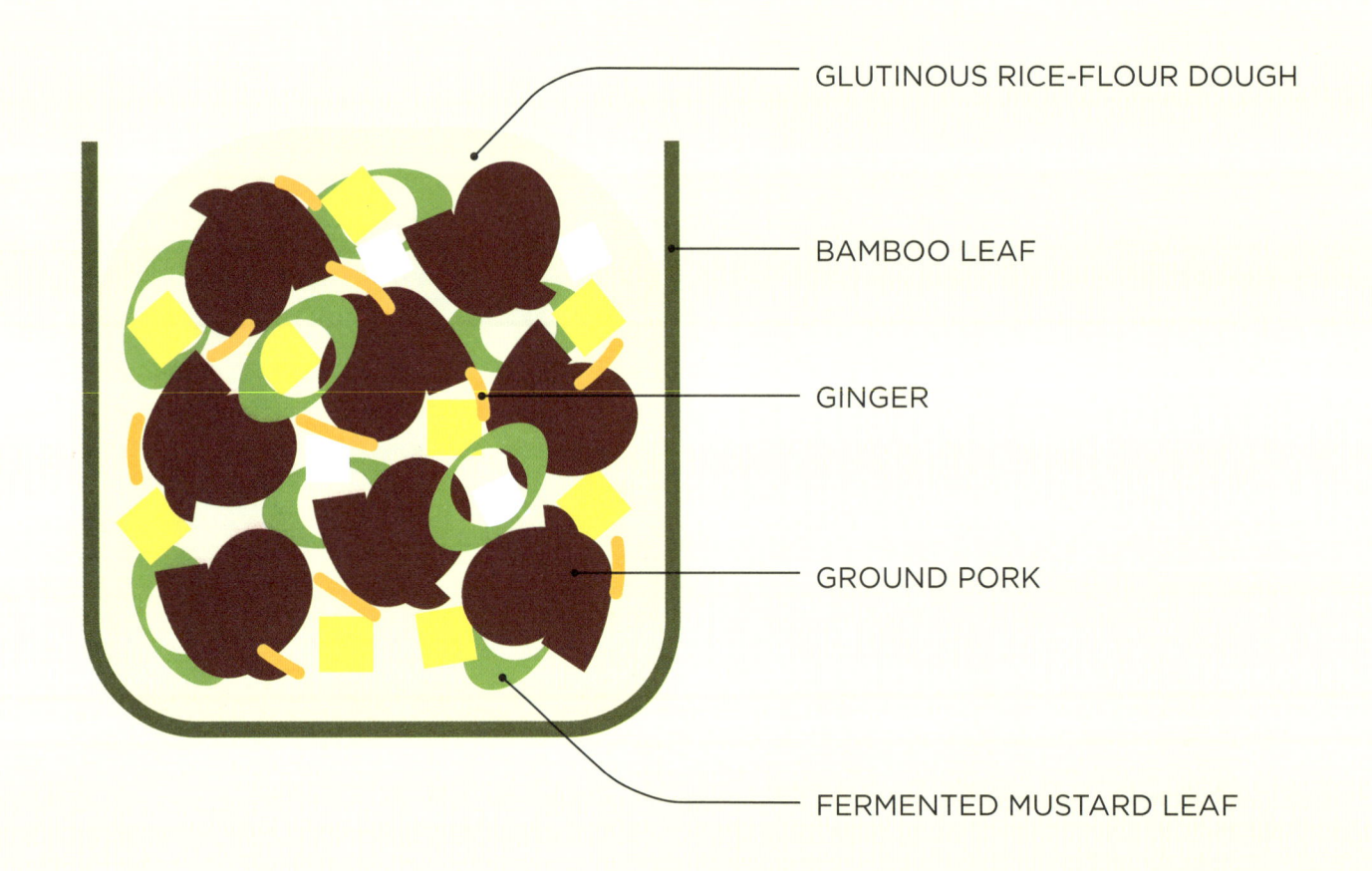

- GLUTINOUS RICE-FLOUR DOUGH
- BAMBOO LEAF
- GINGER
- GROUND PORK
- FERMENTED MUSTARD LEAF

WHAT IS IT?
A snack made from glutinous rice flour, stuffed with pork and fermented vegetables, then steamed.

ORIGIN
This is a Szechuan specialty. Yè means "leaf" and bā is a generic term for cakes made of rice or flour. This dish is associated with the Qingming festival, "Day of Sweeping the Graves," which is held at the beginning of April for families to pay tribute to their ancestors. The leaves used to wrap the dumplings represent the return of spring.

COMPLETION TIME
Preparation time: 1 hour
Resting time: 20 minutes
Cooking time: 8 minutes
Storage: 2 days

SPECIAL EQUIPMENT
Steamer basket
Steamer

SKILL TO MASTER
Softening bamboo leaves (page 280)

USEFUL TIP
The mustard greens can be replaced with any fermented vegetable.

MAKES 10 DUMPLINGS
4 bamboo leaves

FILLING
1¾ ounces / 50 g fermented mustard greens (sui mi ya cai; page 283)
3 large cloves garlic
½ ounce / 15 g fresh ginger
4 to 5 scallions
1 teaspoon Szechuan pepper

Learning

2 tablespoons neutral-flavor oil

7 ounces / 200 g finely chopped pork (belly and loin)

1 teaspoon dark soy sauce

1 tablespoon organic cane sugar

2 tablespoons Shaoxing wine

DOUGH

1¼ cups / 200 g glutinous rice flour

¼ cup plus 1 tablespoon / 50 g rice flour

½ teaspoon salt

2 tablespoons neutral-flavor oil, or ¾ ounce / 20 g lard

Just over ¾ cup / 210 ml water

1 Soak the bamboo leaves for 20 minutes in boiling water to soften them (page 280). Cut them into strips of about 2⅓ inches / 6 cm.

2 Make the filling: Rinse the mustard greens and drain them. Chop the garlic and ginger. Slice the scallions. Crush the Szechuan pepper. In a skillet, heat the oil and sauté the garlic, ginger, and Szechuan pepper for 1 minute. Add the pork, mustard greens, soy sauce, and sugar. Toss to loosen the meat pieces. Add the wine, and cook to reduce. Taste, and season with additional soy sauce, if needed. Add the scallions and stir to combine. Set aside to cool.

3 Make the dough: Combine the flours and salt. Add the oil and water. Mix to a smooth dough. Divide the dough into ten balls ¾ ounce / 24 g each. Set aside under a piece of plastic wrap.

4 Take a piece of dough and flatten it using your thumbs, turning it to form a 2¾-inch / 7 cm disc. Place 1 tablespoon of filling in the center (½ ounce / 15 g). Close the meatball in a half-moon shape and securely seal it in the center, pinching the dough closed. Roll the filled dough gently between your palms to round it out and even out the thickness. It should be a smooth oval shape.

5 Place the dumpling on a piece of bamboo leaf and place it in a steamer basket. Repeat until all the ingredients are used. Bring the water in a steamer to a boil. Cook for 8 minutes. Serve slightly warm.

Understanding

YÁN SŪ JĪ
POPCORN CHICKEN

CHICKEN

SWEET POTATO STARCH BREADING

THAI BASIL

WHAT IS IT?
Marinated chicken pieces, coated in breading, then fried twice and garnished with fried basil leaves and spiced salt.

ORIGIN
Popcorn chicken is a staple of Taiwanese street culture. It has been very popular since the 1970s with the expansion of night markets. It is associated with popcorn because it is sold in paper bags. Its bite size makes it easy to eat, and its breading, which has an irregular appearance, creates a popcorn appearance.

COMPLETION TIME
Preparation time: 1 hour
Resting time: 3 hours minimum
Cooking time: 8 minutes

SKILL TO MASTER
Boning a chicken thigh (page 34)

USEFUL TIP
Chinese sweet potato starch is grainy and may contain large pieces. Although this recipe's appearance relies the look of an irregular breading, it is best to crush any large pieces.

Learning

FIVE-SPICE POWDER

A powdered mix containing coriander seeds, fennel, anise, cinnamon, black or Szechuan pepper, and cloves.

SWEET POTATO STARCH

A starch in the form of granules. It can be purchased in Asian grocery stores.

RED SZECHUAN PEPPER

A variety of berries (not pepper) with a powerful flavor that is very aromatic with notes of flowers and citrus. It has a numbing effect.

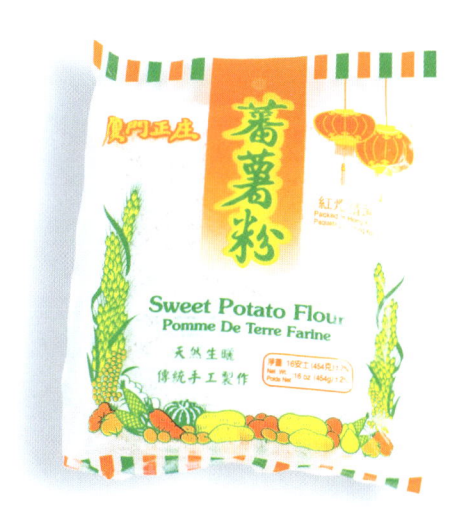

SERVES 3 TO 4

1 pound 2 ounces / 500 g free-range chicken thighs, deboned (page 34)

MARINADE

6 cloves garlic
3 tablespoons / 45 ml Shaoxing wine
3 tablespoons / 45 ml soy sauce
1 slightly heaping teaspoon organic cane sugar
- 1 teaspoon five-spice powder

SPICED SALT

- 1 heaping teaspoon Szechuan pepper
1 teaspoon white pepper
- ½ teaspoon five-spice powder
½ teaspoon chile powder, or to taste
½ teaspoon salt

BATTER

4½ tablespoons / 35 g all-purpose flour
- 1 tablespoon sweet potato starch
½ cup / 120 ml water
½ teaspoon / 2 g baking powder
½ teaspoon organic cane sugar

Oil, for frying
6 sprigs of Thai basil
- ⅔ cup / 120 g sweet potato starch

Making

YÁN SŪ JĪ

1 Cut the chicken thighs into even, bite-size pieces. Press the garlic.

2 Make the marinade: In a large bowl, combine the garlic, wine, soy sauce, sugar, and five-spice powder. Add the chicken pieces and stir to coat. Cover the bowl with plastic wrap, and refrigerate for at least 3 hours, ideally overnight.

3 Make the spiced salt: In a small skillet over medium heat, roast the Szechuan pepper and white pepper for about 5 minutes. Grind with a mortar and pestle or a blender. Combine with the five-spice powder, chile powder, and salt. Set aside.

4 Make the batter. In a bowl, combine the flour, starch, water, baking powder, and sugar. Pour the batter over the chicken and stir to coat.

5 In a deep frying pan, heat about 1 inch / 3 cm of oil to 340°F / 170°C. Thoroughly wash and dry the basil leaves. Immerse them in the hot oil until they turn dark green. Transfer them carefully to paper towels to drain. Set aside.

6 Add the ⅔ cup / 120 g sweet potato starch to a shallow dish. Dredge the chicken pieces in the starch to coat them completely.

7 Fry the chicken pieces for 2 minutes, but without browning them. Set aside to drain.

8 Increase the temperature of the oil to between 350° and 375°F / 180° and 190°C. Fry the chicken pieces a second time until golden brown. Set aside on paper towels to drain. Toss the fried chicken with the spiced salt. Transfer to a dish and add the basil leaves. Serve hot as an appetizer, or with rice (page 12) or as a filling for gua bao (page 242).

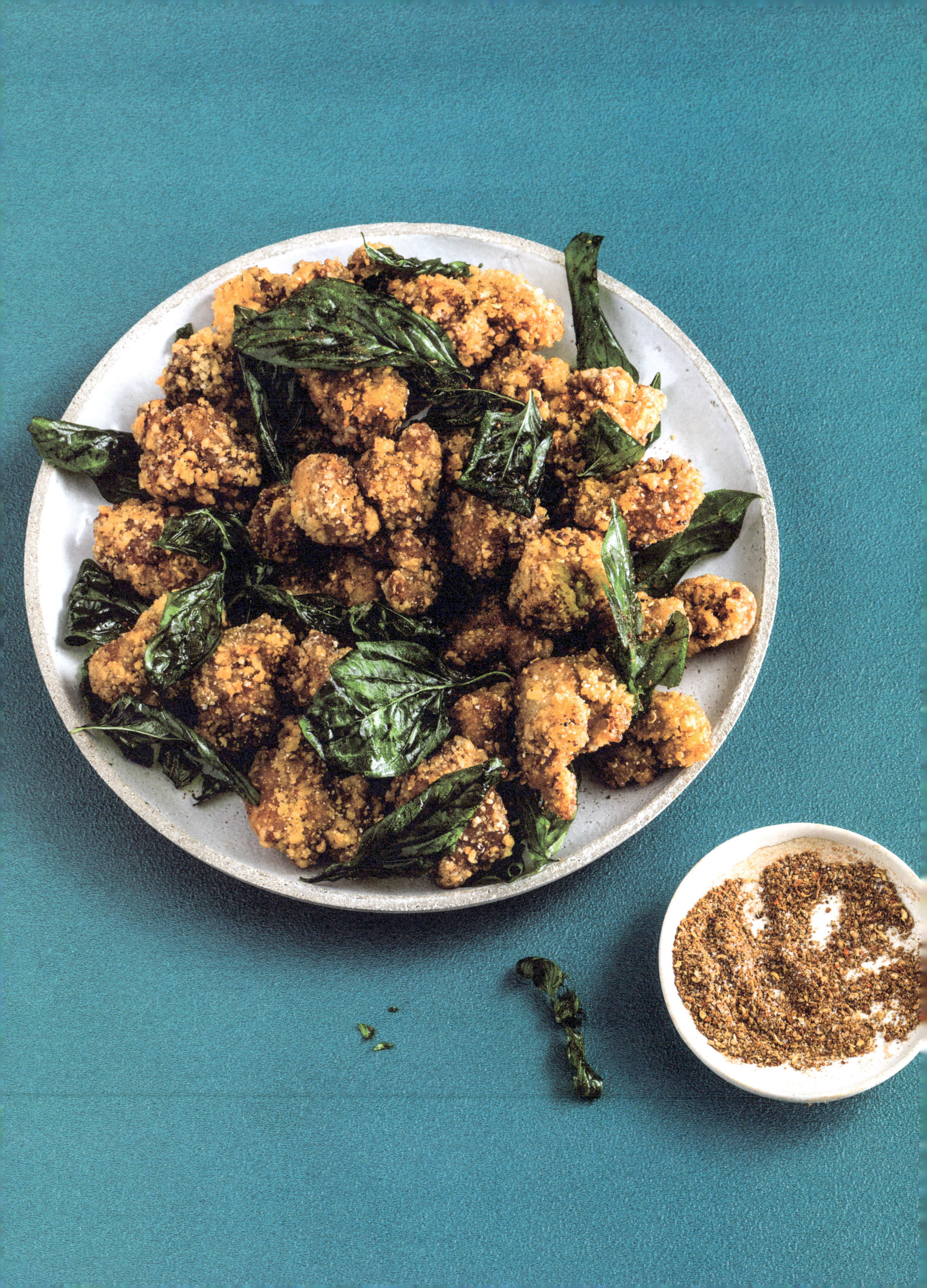

Understanding

MA LAI GO
STEAMED SPONGE CAKE

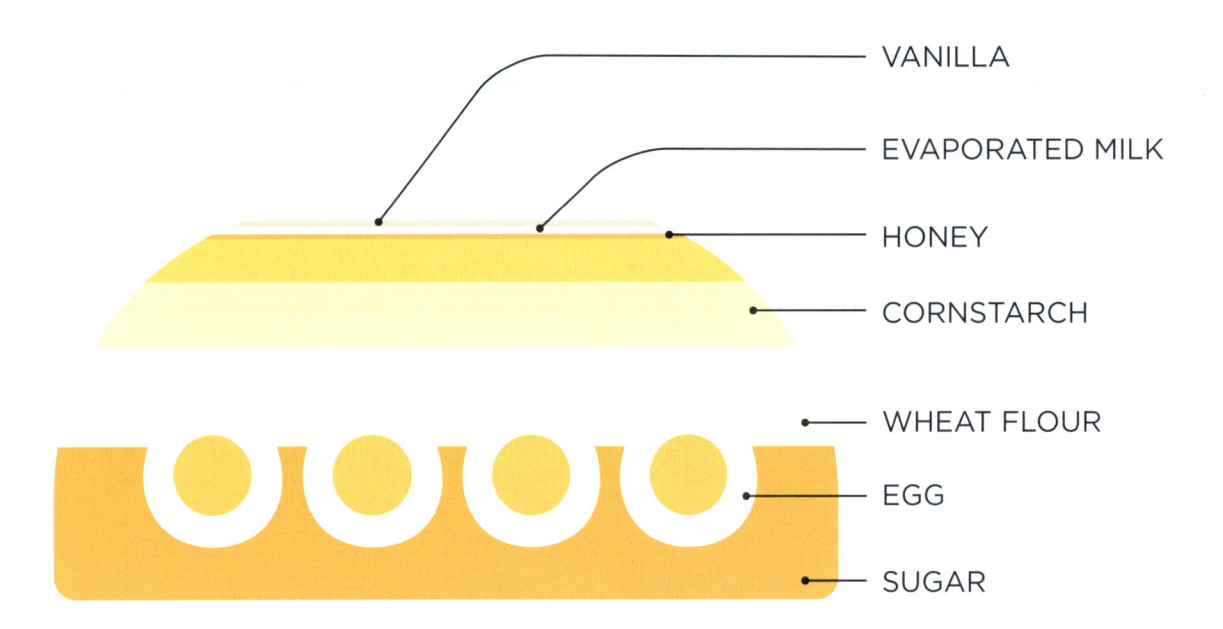

- VANILLA
- EVAPORATED MILK
- HONEY
- CORNSTARCH
- WHEAT FLOUR
- EGG
- SUGAR

WHAT IS IT?
A steamed Cantonese sponge cake.

ORIGIN
This dish bears the intriguing name of "Malay cake" in Chinese. In 1786, the British established the first trading post in the Far East on the Malay Peninsula. They brought with them the custom of afternoon tea and sponge cakes. Not having access to certain ingredients or an oven, the Malays adapted baking the cake by steaming and added coconut milk and pandan leaves. During the British-Malaysian era, many immigrants from the Canton province frequently traveled between Malaysia and mainland China, introducing the Malaysian version of the cake. The Cantonese chefs further adapted the Malay recipe by removing the ingredients they did not have, namely the coconut milk and pandan leaves. Since this time, ma lai go has been a classic of dim sum and tea rooms.

COMPLETION TIME
Preparation time: 20 minutes
Resting time: 2 hours
Cooking time: 35 minutes
Storage: The cake can be kept for several days in a cool place. Reheat the slices for a few seconds in the microwave or steam them to warm them.

SPECIAL EQUIPMENT
8-inch / 20 cm bamboo basket, or standard 8-inch / 20 cm cake pan

USEFUL TIP
The lid should not touch the cake when baking. You can also use a steaming rack placed at the bottom of a large, lidded pot, or a large wok with a domed lid.

Learning

SERVES 6

4 large / 200 g eggs, room temperature

⅔ cup packed / 150 g brown sugar

1 vanilla bean, split and scraped, seeds reserved

1½ tablespoons honey

1 cup / 125 g all-purpose or bread flour

½ cup / 60 g cornstarch or potato starch

3 tablespoons / 45 ml evaporated milk

1 teaspoon / 4 g baking powder

3 tablespoons / 45 ml neutral-flavor oil of your choice (sunflower, peanut)

1 In the bowl of a stand mixer fitted with the whisk beater, beat together the eggs, brown sugar, vanilla bean seeds, and honey for 10 minutes. The mixture should double in size and be thick. Sift together the flour and cornstarch two times. Gently fold the flour mixture into the egg mixture, then fold in the evaporated milk. Cover with plastic wrap and set aside at room temperature for 2 hours.

2 In a small bowl, carefully combine a small portion of the batter with the baking powder and oil.

3 Line an 8-inch / 20 cm bamboo basket or a cake pan with parchment paper. Check that the pan fits into the steamer; the lid should not touch the cake when baking. Wrap the lid with a clean kitchen towel to prevent drops of water from falling onto the cake while it is baking, which could make the top soggy.

4 Scrape the batter into the pan. Tap the pan on the table to remove any air bubbles. Bring the water in the steamer to a boil and place the cake inside. Bake for 30 to 35 minutes.

5 Check the doneness by piercing the center of the cake with a skewer. The skewer should come out clean. Set the cake aside on a rack to cool before unmolding. Serve warm.

Understanding

DAN TAT
EGG TARTS

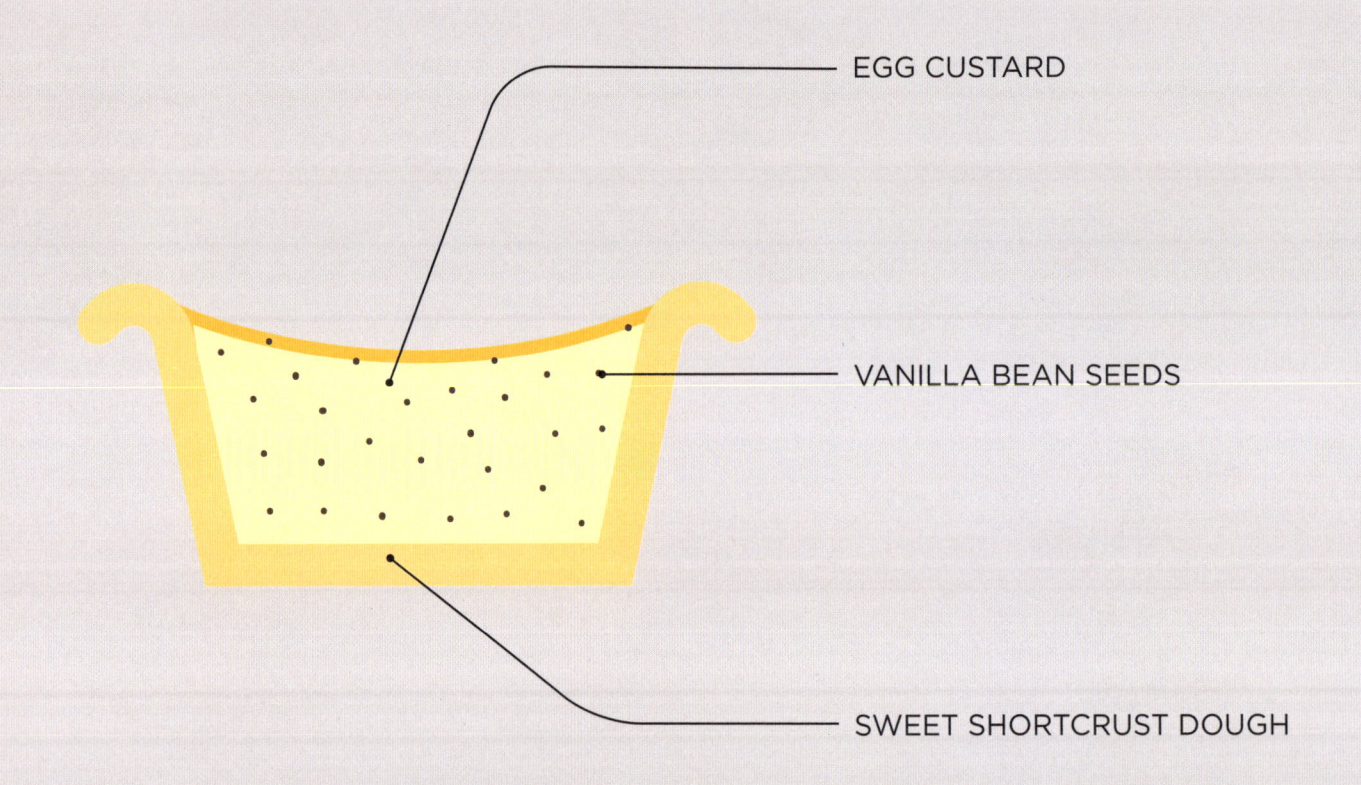

- EGG CUSTARD
- VANILLA BEAN SEEDS
- SWEET SHORTCRUST DOUGH

WHAT IS IT?
A sweet pastry filled with custard.

ORIGIN
Traditionally, a puff pastry base made with lard is used. This version uses a sweetened shortcrust dough, which allows the tartlets to be stored longer. This pastry, along with the mai la go (page 254), is the most popular pastry in Canton. The tartlet is a result of two influences: The *pasteis de nata* of the Portuguese in Macau, and the egg custard tarts of the British in Hong Kong.

COMPLETION TIME
Preparation time: 1 hour
Resting time: 4 hours 40 minutes
Cooking time: 25 minutes
Storage: 24 hours in the refrigerator

SPECIAL EQUIPMENT
Stand mixer + paddle attachment and dough hook
12 *pasteis de nata* or small brioche molds (flared molds 2 inches / 4.5 cm at the base, 2¾ inches / 7 cm at the top, and 1 inch / 3 cm high)

Learning

EGGS
Choose medium size.

VANILLA BEANS
Choose plump vanilla beans that are as moist as possible.

EVAPORATED MILK
Found in the baking aisle of grocery stores.

SOFTENED BUTTER
Remove the butter from the refrigerator at least 2 hours before using it so that it is soft enough to work with.

MAKES 12 TARTLETS

SWEET SHORTCRUST DOUGH
- ½ cup / 55 g confectioners' sugar
- 8½ tablespoons / 120 g unsalted butter, softened
- 1 medium / 45 g egg
- 2 cups / 250 g all-purpose flour

CUSTARD FILLING
- 1 cup / 240 ml water
- 1 to 2 vanilla beans
- ⅔ cup / 130 g sugar
- 4 medium / 180 g eggs
- Scant ½ cup / 100 ml evaporated milk or whole milk

Making

DAN TAT

1 **2** **3**

4 **5** **6**

1 In the bowl of a stand mixer fitted with the paddle attachment, combine the confectioners' sugar and butter. Add the egg and combine. Add the flour and combine. Mix to a homogeneous dough; do not overmix.

2 Cover with plastic wrap and refrigerate for at least 4 hours.

3 Make the custard filling: In a saucepan, add the water. Split and scrape the vanilla bean. Add the pod and seeds to the saucepan. Bring the water to a low boil. Add the sugar, turn off the heat, and stir until the sugar is completely dissolved. Whisk together the eggs and evaporated milk. When the syrup is warm but not hot, add it slowly to the egg mixture while whisking. Strain, and set aside in the refrigerator for at least 4 hours.

4 Lightly dust the work surface with flour. Roll the dough into a sausage shape and cut it widthwise into twelve pieces 1½ ounces / 40 g each. Roll out the dough pieces using a rolling pin and line the molds, lightly pressing them using your fingers to about ¼ inch / 5 mm above the rim of the pan. Decorate the edge of the dough by scoring it all around with the tip of a chop stick.

5 Refrigerate for 40 minutes, then fill each one with the cold custard filling. Preheat the oven to 350°F / 180°C. Bake for about 25 minutes.

6 Let cool before unmolding. Serve warm.

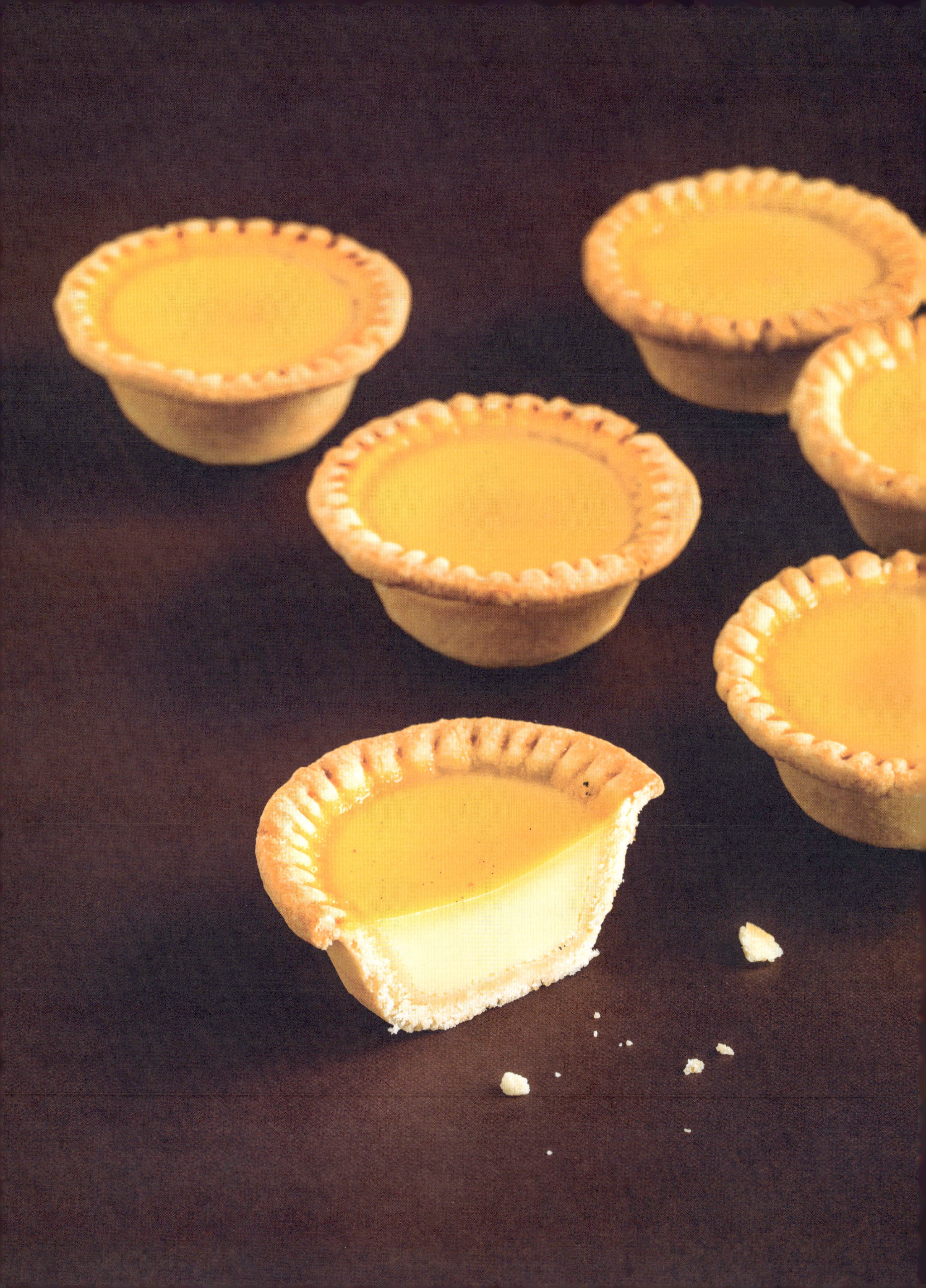

Understanding
YUÈBĬNG MOONCAKES

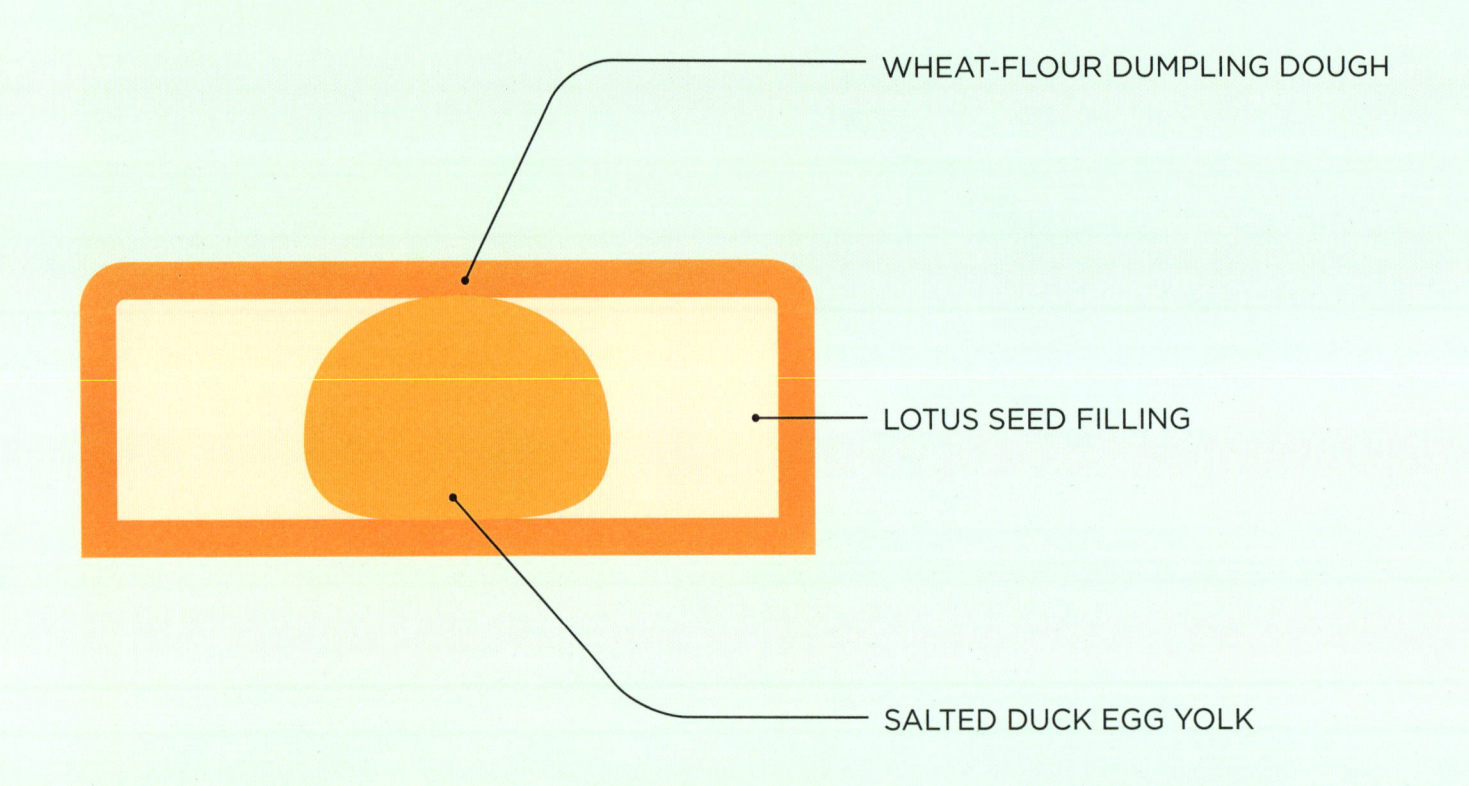

— WHEAT-FLOUR DUMPLING DOUGH

— LOTUS SEED FILLING

— SALTED DUCK EGG YOLK

WHAT IS IT?
A Cantonese version of a traditional pastry filled with lotus and a salted duck egg yolk center.

ORIGIN
Made for the Moon Festival in mid-autumn, these pastries celebrate the end of the harvest season and symbolize family unity with their round shape. Each region has its version of mooncake (red bean paste, taro paste, five-nut filling, mung bean cream, ham and nuts, etc.), but the most famous version is from Canton.

COMPLETION TIME
Preparation time: 2½ hours
Resting time: 3½ hours + 3 days
Cooking time: 17 minutes
Storage: These can be enjoyed up to 3 days later (they will be shinier and softer) and can be kept for 1 to 2 weeks in the refrigerator.

SPECIAL EQUIPMENT
Mooncake cake press, for a 3½-ounce / 100 g cake

SKILL TO MASTER
Rehydrating lotus seeds (page 280)

CHALLENGE
Thoroughly dry out the lotus cream, otherwise the cakes will be misshapen when baked. The texture should look like modeling clay.

USEFUL TIPS
Golden syrup is an invert sugar used in this case to give the dough a soft, shiny, and moist character. The syrup extends the cake's shelf life and allows the dough to retain its shape despite its thinness. Alkaline kansui water (lye water) helps neutralize acidity provided by the golden syrup and tenderizes the dough as well as provides color. Maltose helps retain moisture and lends softness to lotus cream.

Learning

LYE WATER
Alkaline water (page 43).

MALTOSE
A sugar made from the starch of barley or corn in the form of a viscous liquid. It lends shine, facilitates caramelization, and stabilizes certain pastry preparations.

DRIED LOTUS SEEDS
Rehydrate them in 4 cups / 1 L water, then remove the bitter germ from the center before use.

SALTED DUCK EGG YOLK
Sold in the frozen section of grocery stores. It is a prized ingredient in Chinese cuisine. The duck eggs are immersed in a saline solution for 20 to 30 days. The yolks take on a bright orange color. They become denser and their texture becomes slightly grainy.

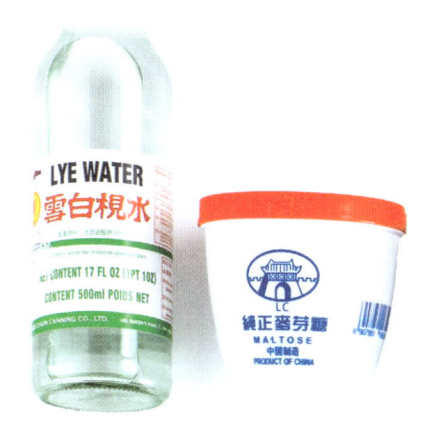

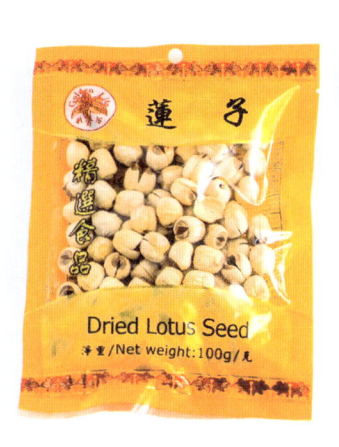

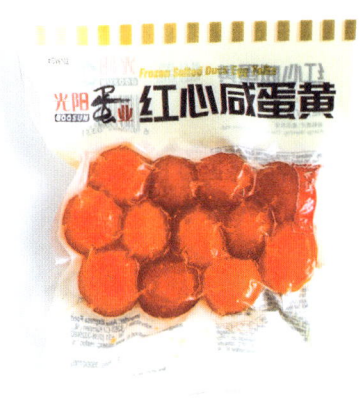

MAKES 12 CAKES 100 G EACH

LOTUS SEED FILLING
- 6⅔ cups / 200 g lotus seeds
- ¾ cup / 150 g sugar of your choice (organic cane sugar, brown sugar, etc.)
- 2 tablespoons honey
- ⅔ cup / 150 ml peanut oil
- ¾ ounce / 20 g maltose
- ⅓ teaspoon salt

DOUGH
- ¼ cup plus 1 tablespoon / 75 ml peanut oil
- ½ cup / 120 ml golden syrup
- 1 tablespoon plus 1 teaspoon / 20 ml lye water (kansui water; page 43)
- About 2 cups / 255 g pastry or all-purpose flour, divided
- 12 salted duck egg yolks

FINISHING
Cornstarch, for dusting the cake pan
Egg yolk, for the egg wash

1 The day before, soak the lotus seeds (page 280). The next day, open the seeds and remove the germ from the center. Cook the seeds in water for 45 minutes. They must be soft enough to crush with a fork. Drain, reserving a scant ½ cup / 100 ml of the cooking liquid.

2 Make the filling: Blend the seeds with the reserved cooking water to a smooth dough. In a nonstick skillet over medium heat, place the dough and dry it while stirring using a spatula. Add the sugar and honey. When the sugar is incorporated, stir in the oil in thirds. Add the maltose and salt and stir to combine. Cook the mixture to dry it, stirring until it is the texture of modeling clay. Remove from the heat and cover the surface with plastic wrap.

Making

YUÈBĬNG

3 Make the dough: Whisk together the oil, golden syrup, and lye water. Add 1 cup plus 3 tablespoons / 145 g of the flour, whisk to combine, then knead by hand for 3 to 4 minutes. Cover with plastic wrap and set aside at room temperature for 3 hours. Add an additional ¾ cup plus 1 teaspoon / 110 g of flour and knead to a homogeneous dough that no longer sticks to your hands. Set aside for 30 minutes.

4 Steam the duck egg yolks for 10 minutes. Let cool.

5 Make 1⅔-ounce / 45 g balls of filling and 1½-ounce / 40 g balls of dough. Set the balls aside under a piece of plastic wrap.

6 Spread a ball of lotus filling between two pieces of parchment paper (3 to 3½ inches / 8 to 9 cm in diameter). Place 1 egg yolk in the center. Fold the dough over the filling to enclose it. Using a rolling pin, roll out the dough between two sheets of parchment paper to a 4- to 4⅓-inch / 10 to 11 cm disc. Place the ball of filling in the center and fold the dough over to enclose it, pressing out any air. Place on a baking sheet lined with parchment paper. Repeat these steps for each cake.

7 Lightly dust the cake press and the cake balls with cornstarch using a pastry brush. Place the cake balls into the press placed on the baking sheet. Press the mold to shape the cake. Lift the mold and push down again to loosen the cake.

8 Preheat the oven to 350°F / 180°C. Bake for 5 minutes. Beat the egg yolk with 2 tablespoons water to make the egg wash. Brush the cakes twice with the egg wash. Reduce the oven temperature to 325°F / 160°C and bake for an additional 12 minutes. Let cool, then refrigerate in airtight containers for 3 days before serving.

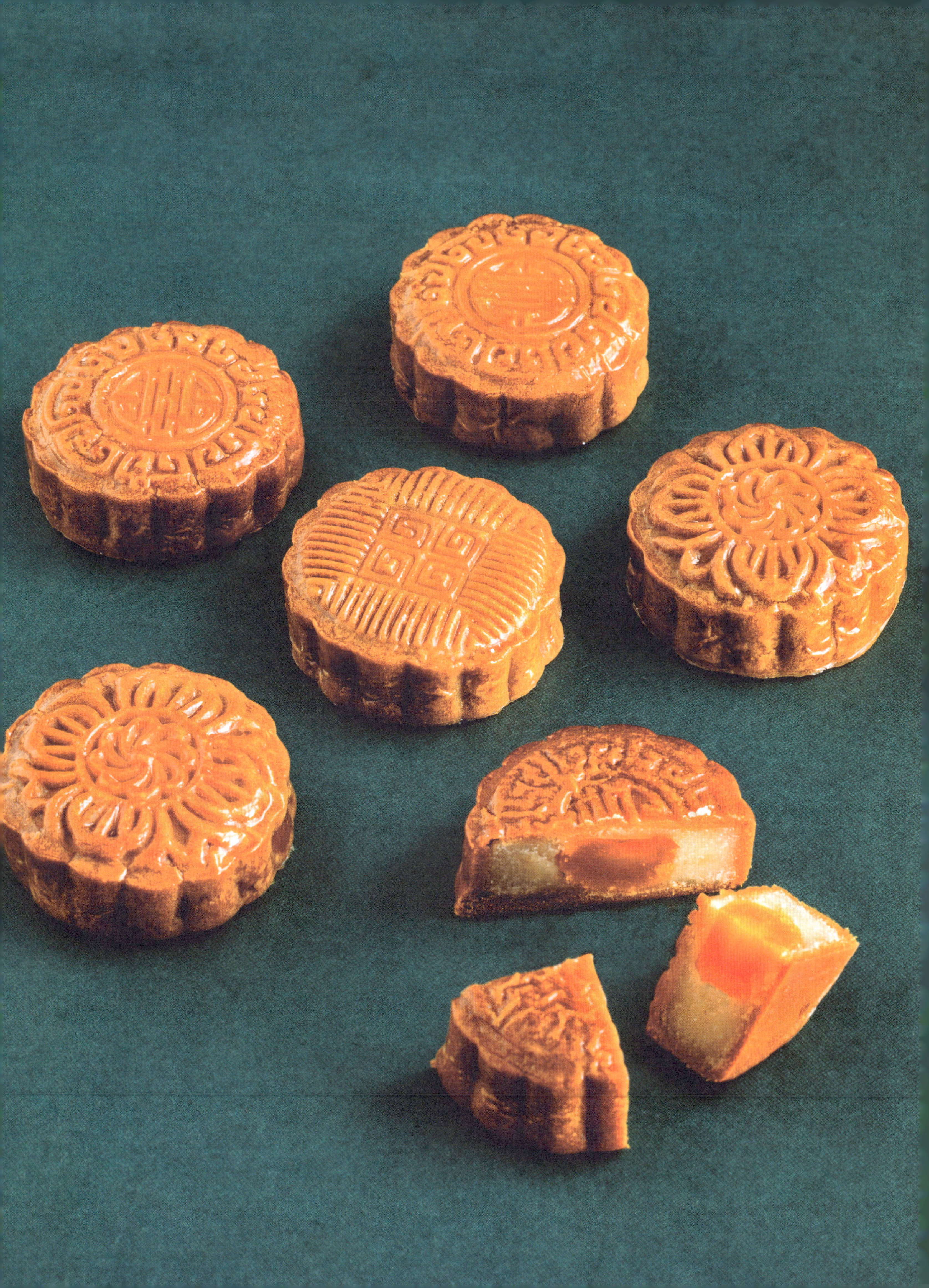

Understanding
TĀNGYUÁN
WITH BLACK SESAME

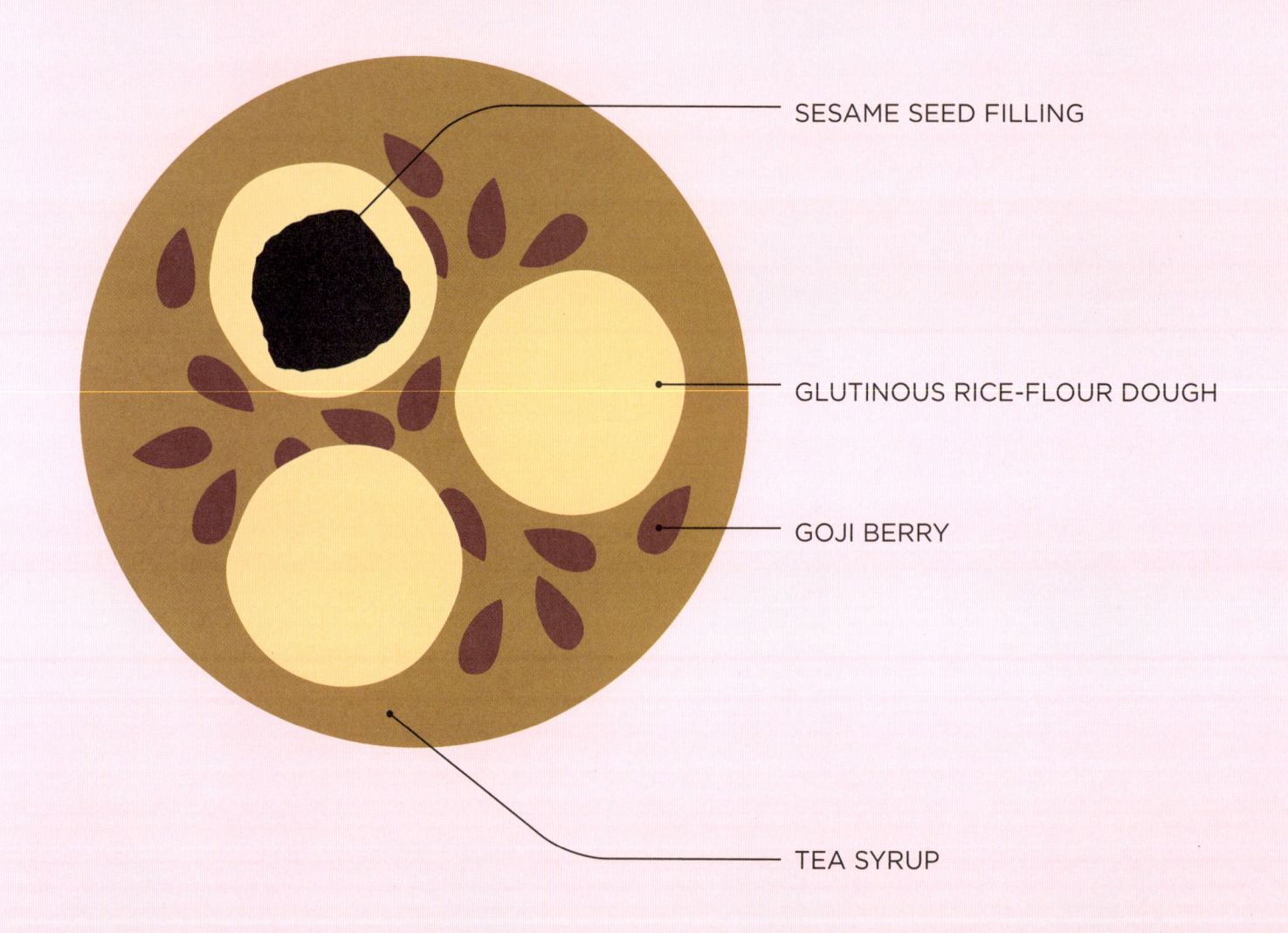

- SESAME SEED FILLING
- GLUTINOUS RICE-FLOUR DOUGH
- GOJI BERRY
- TEA SYRUP

WHAT IS IT?

Balls made from glutinous rice flour filled with black sesame, poached in water, then served hot in a syrup.

ORIGIN

These are enjoyed during the Lantern Festival, which marks the end of the Chinese New Year celebrations (winter solstice). They are also served at weddings. Their shape and sweet filling symbolize reunion and family unity. The tāngyuán filling can be made of red bean paste or a mixture of peanuts, walnuts, and sugar. There are also versions where smaller rice balls are not filled but instead accompanied with meat and vegetable soup.

COMPLETION TIME

Preparation time: 1 hour
Resting time: 30 minutes
Cooking time: about 8 minutes
Storage: You can freeze the filled and uncooked balls. Cook them without thawing them.

VARIATIONS

For a traditional version, replace the butter with lard. For a vegan version, replace the butter with coconut oil. Tāngyuán can also be served with a little cooking water or ginger-infused syrup in place of the tea syrup.

Learning

JASMINE TEA
A green tea flavored with dried jasmine flowers. Choose loose tea leaves over tea bags.

GLUTINOUS RICE FLOUR
Made from round glutinous rice with opaque grains. It becomes very sticky after cooking.

BLACK SESAME SEEDS
These have a more intense taste, slight bitterness, and crisper texture than white sesame seeds. Toasting them lends a more intense and grilled flavor.

MAKES 20 TĀNGYUÁN

FILLING
- ⅔ cup / 80 g black sesame seeds
- 2½ packed tablespoons / 35 g brown sugar or sugar of your choice
- 2 tablespoons unsalted butter, softened

DOUGH
- 1⅔ cups / 240 g glutinous rice flour
- ¼ cup plus 2 tablespoons / 90 ml boiling water
- ½ cup / 120 ml water, room temperature

TEA SYRUP (OPTIONAL)
- 4 cups / 1 L water
- ⅔ cup / 150 g organic cane sugar
- ⅜ ounce / 12 g jasmine tea
- ¾ ounce / 20 g goji berries

Making

TĀNGYUÁN

1 Preheat the oven to 325°F / 160°C. Make the filling: Toast the sesame seeds for several minutes in the oven. Let cool, then combine with the brown sugar. In a food processor, process the mixture to a fine powder. Add the butter and continue mixing to a paste. Transfer the paste to a container and refrigerate for 20 to 30 minutes.

2 Make the tea syrup, if desired: Bring the water and sugar to a boil. Add the tea leaves and steep for 3 minutes over low heat. Strain, and add the goji berries. Let cool.

3 Shape the filling into twenty balls about ¼ ounce / 7 g each. Set aside in the refrigerator.

4 Make the dough: In a mixing bowl, add the flour. Combine the boiling water and room temperature water. Add the water to the flour and stir to combine. Knead to a smooth, homogeneous dough. Divide the dough into twenty balls weighing about ¾ ounce / 22 g each. Set aside, covered with plastic wrap to prevent them from drying out. Press each ball with your thumbs while turning them to shape them into a disc of about 1⅓ inches / 3.5 cm. Place the sesame balls in the middle and fold the edges of the dough over to enclose them. Avoid touching the filling to prevent staining the outside of the balls.

5 Bring a large pot of water to a boil. Cook the balls in two or three batches, depending on the size of the pot, dropping the balls into the boiling water. Stir gently with a spoon to prevent the balls from sticking together or sticking to the bottom. Reduce the heat to medium, and cook until the balls rise to the surface. Once this happens, cook for an additional 3 minutes. Using a slotted spoon, remove the balls. If you made the syrup, place them in the syrup as each one finishes. Serve warm.

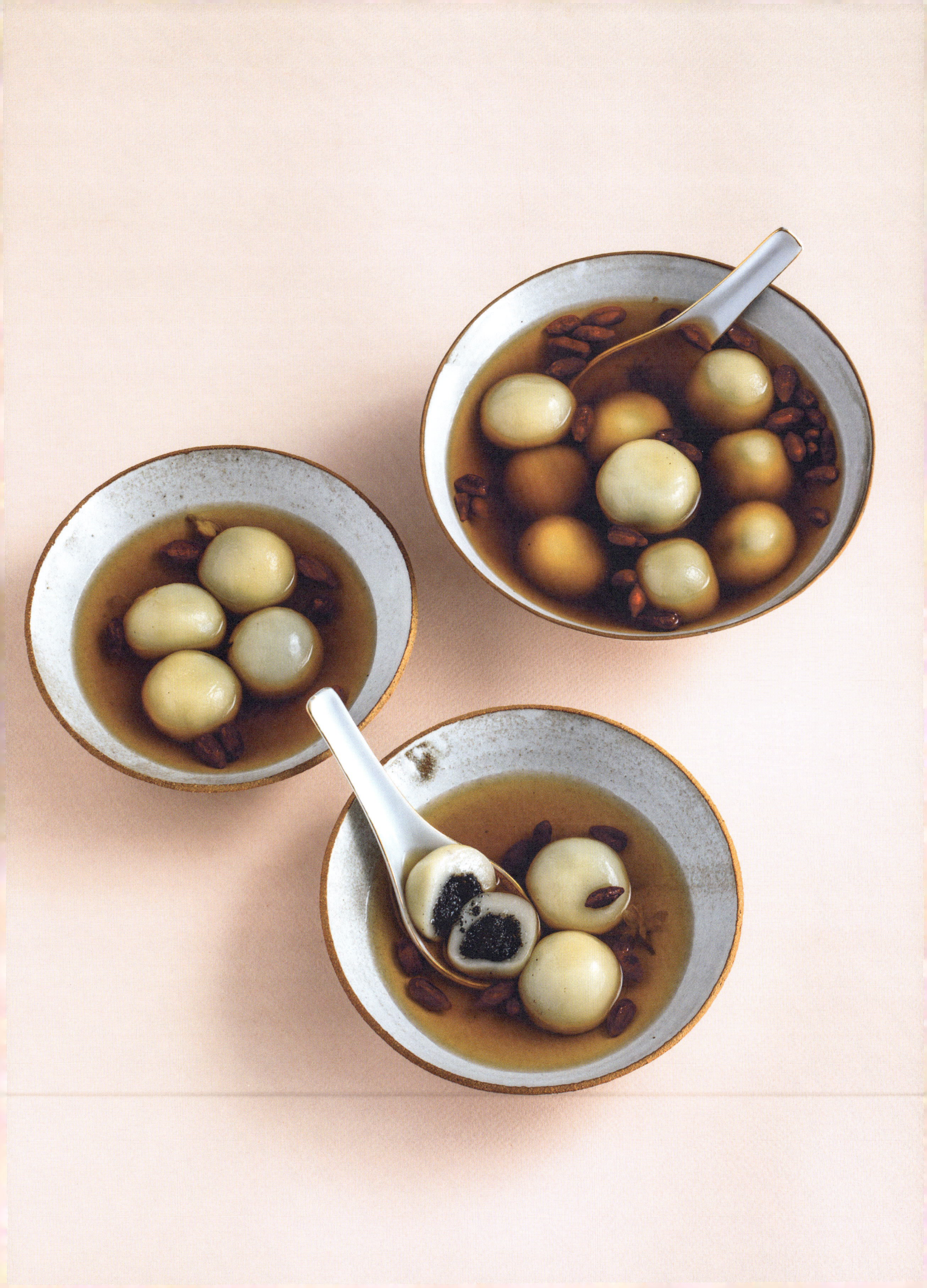

Understanding

LIÚSHĀ BĀO
LAVA BAO

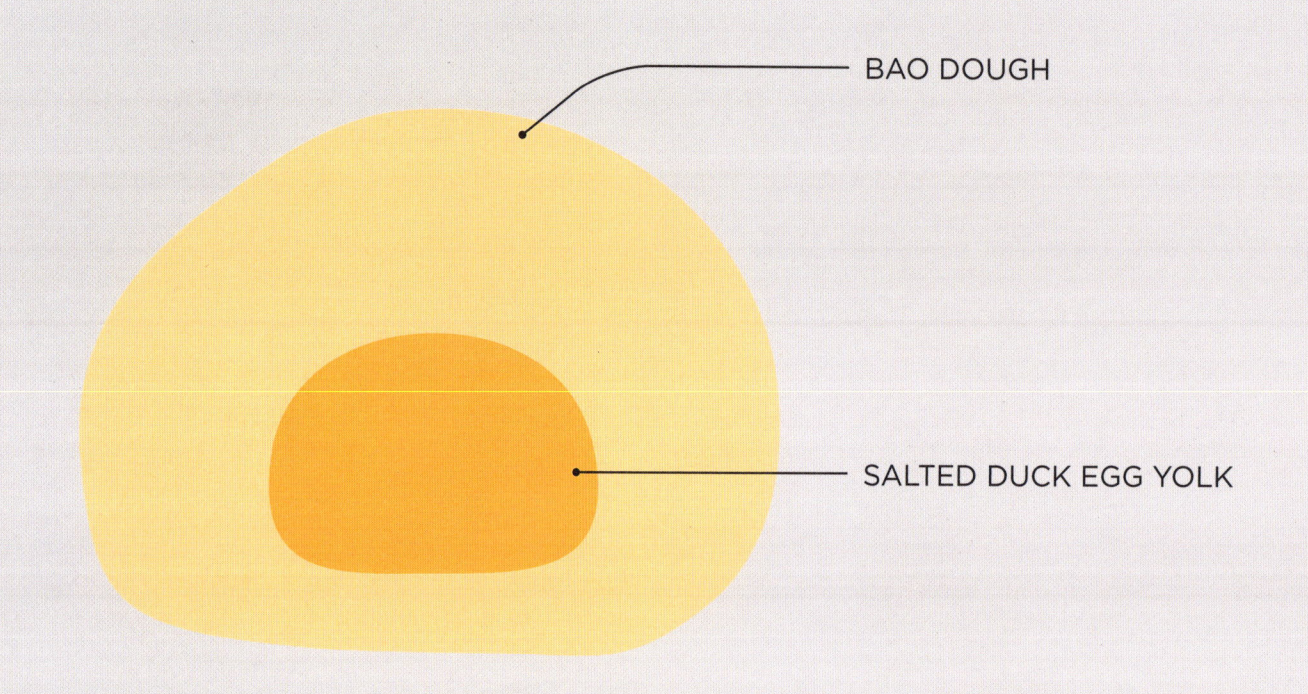

BAO DOUGH

SALTED DUCK EGG YOLK

WHAT IS IT?
A steamed bun filled with a flowing cream made from salted duck egg yolk.

ORIGIN
Its name in Chinese means "flowing sand bao." It is a recent creation (from 2009) in Hong Kong. It has been very popular in dim sum restaurants since its introduction.

COMPLETION TIME
Preparation time: 1½ hours
Resting time: 7 hours
Cooking time: 12 minutes
Storage: Once cooked, they can be stored for 5 to 6 days in the refrigerator. Steam for about 8 minutes.

SPECIAL EQUIPMENT
2 silicone molds with twelve half-sphere cavities 1⅓ inches / 3.5 cm in diameter
Paper baking cups
Steamer
Steamer basket
Bowl scraper
Stand mixer + dough hook

SERVING
Because the filling is runny, it is best not to bite it but to tear it in half.

USEFUL TIPS
If using whole salted eggs, separate the whites from the yolks and reserve the whites for another use. Rinse the yolks in water.

Learning

CHINESE LOW-GLUTEN FLOUR

Bleached wheat flour with a low-gluten content (9–10 percent). It can be replaced with pastry flour.

SALTED DUCK EGG YOLK

Sold in the frozen section. It is a prized ingredient in Chinese cuisine. The duck eggs are immersed in a saline solution for 20 to 30 days. The yolks take on a bright orange color. They become denser and their texture becomes slightly grainy.

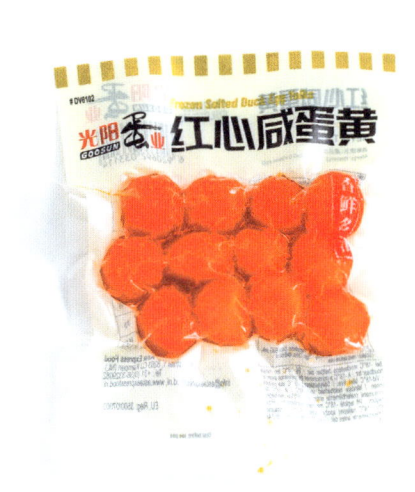

MAKES 12 BAOS

FILLING

¼ ounce / 7 g 200 bloom gelatin sheets or gelatin powder

3⅛ ounces / 90 g salted duck egg yolks

2 tablespoons custard powder or cornstarch

⅓ cup / 80 ml whole milk

¼ cup plus 2 teaspoons / 70 g organic cane sugar

6 tablespoons / 90 g unsalted butter

1 tablespoon pure vanilla extract

DOUGH

2¾ cups / 350 g low-gluten flour

1½ teaspoons / 6 g active dry yeast

2 tablespoons unsalted butter, softened and cubed

1 large / 30 g egg white

¼ cup plus 2 teaspoons / 70 g organic cane sugar

⅔ cup / 150 ml whole milk

1 Make the filling: Rehydrate the gelatin sheets in a bowl of cold water. If using gelatin powder, sprinkle the gelatin powder in a few tablespoons of cold water. Let the mixture sit for 5 to 10 minutes until the gelatin has absorbed all of the water and has a gelatinous appearance. Place the egg yolks in a steamer basket and steam them for 10 minutes. Crush the yolks using a plastic bowl scraper. Combine them with the custard powder.

Making

LIÚSHĀ BĀO

2 Bring the milk and the sugar to a boil. Add the butter and whisk to combine. When the butter is melted, add it to the egg yolk mixture while whisking. Scrape the mixture back into the saucepan and cook over low heat for 1 minute, whisking until smooth. Add the vanilla. Whisk the hydrated gelatin into the mixture (if using gelatin sheets, squeeze the excess water from the sheets and microwave for 5 seconds to melt it first).

3 Pour the mixture into the half-sphere molds and let cool. Once cooled, freeze for at least 6 hours.

4 Make the dough: In the bowl of a stand mixer fitted with the dough hook, combine the flour, yeast, butter, egg white, and sugar. Add the milk and knead for 10 minutes on low speed. The dough should be soft but not sticky. Adjust the texture by adding a little milk or flour, as needed. Turn the dough out onto a work surface. Knead by hand for 1 minute. Shape it into a ball and set aside in a warm place for 1 hour to rise.

5 Unmold the frozen inserts and stick two of them together to make spheres.

6 Shape the dough into twelve balls 1¾ ounces / 50 g each. Set aside under a clean kitchen towel. Dust the work surface with flour, if necessary. Roll out a ball of dough. When it starts to take on a round shape, focus on rolling out the edges more so that the center is thicker. Roll out to a disc measuring 3½ to 4 inches / 9 to 10 cm in diameter. Place a ball of filling in the center. Fold the dough over, enclosing the filling, and pinch the edges together to seal it. Gently roll the bao between your hands to form a nice ball shape.

7 Place the baos seam side down in paper baking cups. Place in a steamer basket and let rise for 1 hour, covered. Bring the water in the steamer to a boil. Once the water is boiling, reduce the heat to medium. Cook the baos for 10 minutes. Turn off the heat and let rest for 2 minutes without opening the lid to prevent the dough from sagging. Let cool for 5 minutes before serving.

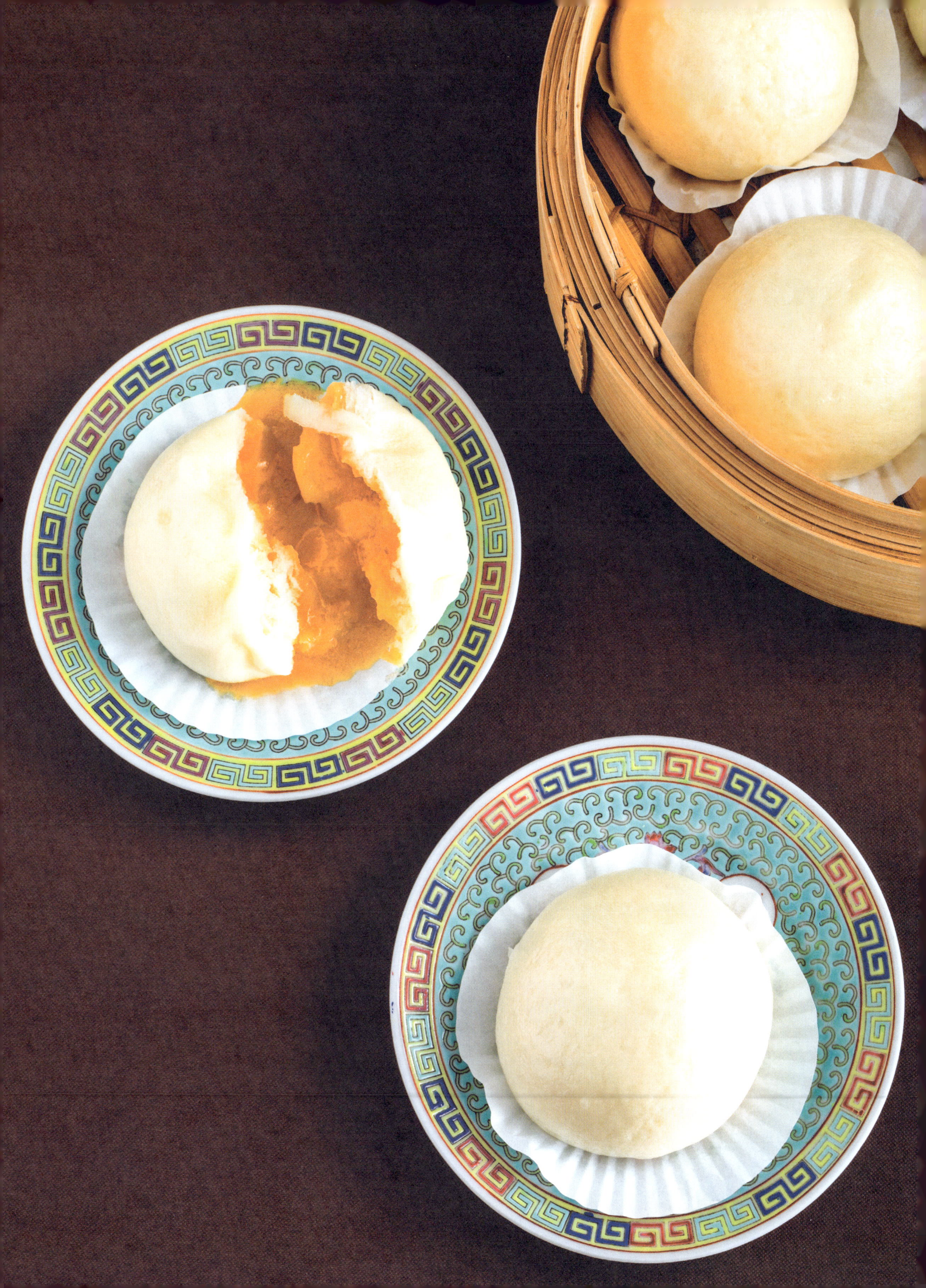

Understanding

MÁHUĀ
BLACK SESAME TWISTS

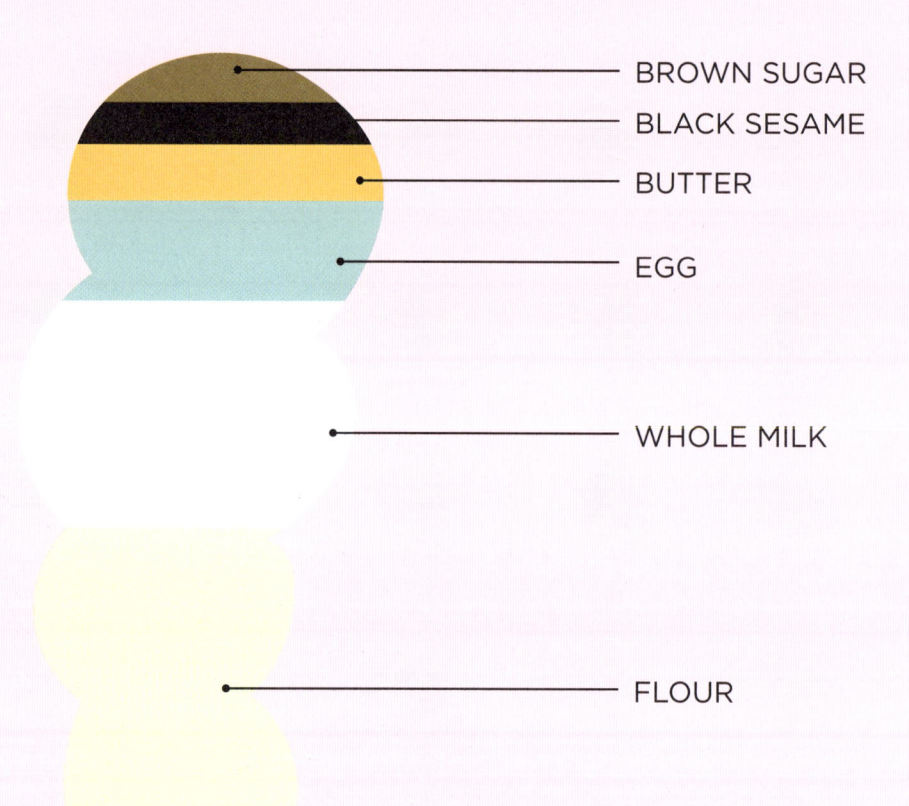

- BROWN SUGAR
- BLACK SESAME
- BUTTER
- EGG
- WHOLE MILK
- FLOUR

WHAT IS IT?
A leavened black sesame dough, shaped into twists, fried, and coated with sesame sugar.

ORIGIN
This is an interpretation of the Tianjin doughnut.

COMPLETION TIME
Preparation time: 1½ hours
Resting time: 3 hours 40 minutes
Cooking time: 5 minutes

SPECIAL EQUIPMENT
Stand mixer + dough hook

Learning

BLACK SESAME SEEDS

These have a more intense taste, slight bitterness, and crisper texture than white sesame seeds. Toasting them lends a more intense and grilled flavor.

MAKES ABOUT 20 TWISTS

DOUGH

3¼ cups / 400 g pastry flour

1 large / 50 g egg

- 3½ tablespoons / 25 g toasted black sesame seeds

2 tablespoons plus 2 teaspoons / 35 g sugar

¾ teaspoon / 3 g active dry yeast

⅔ teaspoon / 3 g baking powder

⅓ teaspoon salt

Just over ¾ cup / 200 ml whole milk

2⅔ tablespoons / 40 g unsalted butter, softened

COATING

½ cup / 100 g sugar

- ⅓ cup / 50 g toasted black sesame seeds

COOKING

Oil, for frying

Making

MÁHUĀ

1 In the bowl of a stand mixer fitted with the dough hook, combine the flour, egg, sesame seeds, sugar, yeast, baking powder, and salt. Begin kneading while adding the milk a little at a time until the dough forms a ball and pulls away from the sides of the bowl.

2 Add the butter and continue kneading until fully incorporated. Shape the dough into a ball, cover with plastic wrap, and set aside in the refrigerator for 3 hours to rise.

3 Make the coating: In a food processor, blend together the sugar and sesame seeds to a fine powder.

4 Cut the dough into balls weighing 1 ounce / 30 g each.

5 Roll out the dough balls to sticks about 4¾ inches / 12 cm long.

6 Secure the ends of each stick with the palms of your hands. Roll the dough with the left hand moving forward and the right hand moving backward. You should feel tension when the strand becomes twisted.

7 Lift the strand and join the two ends. The twist should now be formed naturally when the tension is released. Readjust the twist, if needed. Seal the ends by pinching them together. Transfer them to a baking sheet lined with parchment paper. Cover with a kitchen towel and set aside at room temperature for 30 to 40 minutes to rise.

8 Heat the oil to 340°F / 170°C. Fry the twists for about 5 minutes, turning them occasionally.

9 When golden brown, transfer them to paper towels to drain. Immediately coat them with the sesame sugar.

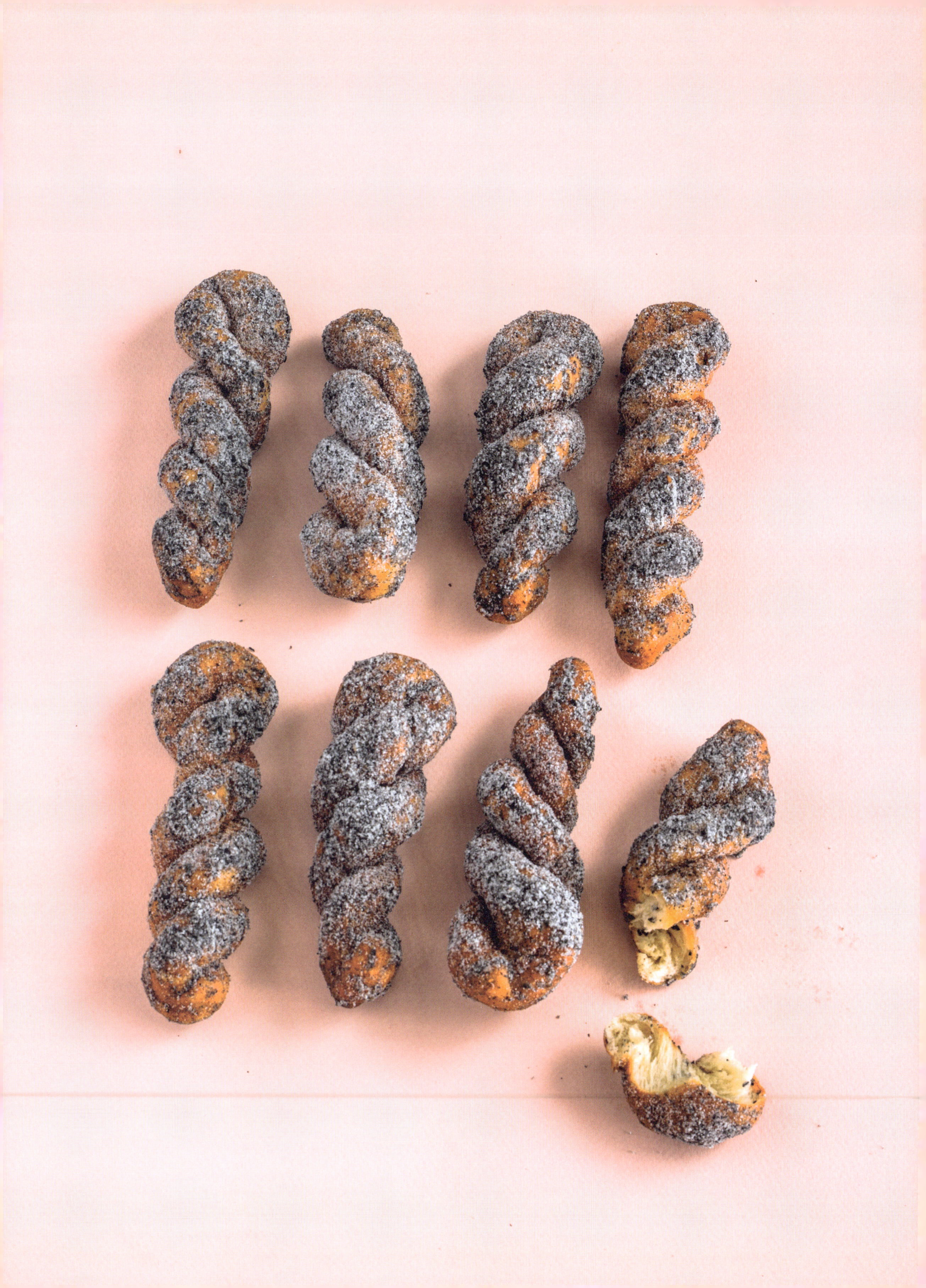

CHAPTER 3
ILLUSTRATED GLOSSARY

EQUIPMENT

Earthenware pot.................278
Vegetable cleaver...............278
Soup skimmer /
spider skimmer.................278
Cleaver or chef's knife..........278
Raised rack 278
Wok + raised rack...............278
Steamer 278
Pasta machine..................278
Mandoline......................278
Mooncake press / mold 279
Pasteis de nata molds..........279
Silicone half-sphere mold.......279
Bamboo steamer basket 279
Strainer........................279
Nonstick rectangular
baking sheet 279
Vegetable peeler (for julienne)..279
Instant-read thermometer 279
Wok............................279

ESSENTIAL TECHNIQUES

Softening lotus leaves......... 280
Softening bamboo leaves...... 280
Rehydrating lotus seeds....... 280
Rehydrating
shiitake mushrooms........... 280
Rehydrating
black mushrooms............. 280
Rehydrating mung beans
vermicelli noodles 280
Rehydrating sweet potato
vermicelli noodles 280
Rehydrating tofu skins 280
Rehydrating dried shrimp 280
Crushing garlic 281
Blanching bamboo shoots...... 281
Cutting into julienne 281
Lacquered duck 281
Carving duck................... 281

INGREDIENTS

Red clay 282
Thai basil 282
Enoki..........................282
Century eggs..................282
Fermented mustard greens.....283
Fermented black soybeans 283
Chinese sesame sauce 283
Red pepper (chile) flakes.......283
Fresh red chile pepper 283
Golden syrup..................283

Equipment

1 Lidded earthenware pot
(or use a cast-iron pot)

2 Vegetable cleaver
(or use a large chef's knife)

3 Soup skimmer, spider skimmer

4 Cleaver

5 Raised rack

6 Wok + raised rack for steaming

7 Steamer

8 Pasta machine

9 Mandoline

Equipment

10 Mooncake press / mold

11 *Pasteis de nata* molds
Base diameter: 2 inches / 5 cm;
Top diameter: 4⅓ inches / 11 cm;
Height: 1⅛ inches / 3 cm

12 Silicone half-sphere mold
(diameter: 1⅓ inches / 3.5 cm)

13 Bamboo steamer basket

14 Strainer

15 Nonstick rectangular baking sheet

16 Vegetable peeler

17 Laser instant-read thermometer

18 Wok

Essential Techniques

REHYDRATING AND SOFTENING DRY INGREDIENTS

1 Lotus leaves Place the leaves in a bowl or sink of hot water for 30 to 40 minutes to soften them. Place a weight on them to keep them submerged completely, such as a steamer rack, bowl, or saucepan filled with water.

2 Bamboo leaves Place the leaves in a bowl or sink of hot water for 20 minutes to soften them. Cut off the base of the leaves where the stem becomes tough.

3 Lotus seeds Rehydrate the seeds in cold water for about 3 hours. Open them and remove the bitter germ from the center.

4 Shiitake mushrooms Rehydrate shiitake mushrooms in a bowl of cold water for 2 to 4 hours. If the preparation of the recipe is long, soak them the day before to ensure they are fully hydrated. Remove the tough portion of the stems, if necessary.

5 Black mushrooms Rehydrate the mushrooms for 20 minutes to 1 hour in a bowl of cold water. Remove the tough portion of the stems, if necessary.

6 Mung bean vermicelli noodles Rehydrate them in a bowl of cold water for 20 to 30 minutes.

7 Sweet potato vermicelli noodles Rehydrate them in a bowl of cold water according to the instructions on the package.

8 Tofu skins Rehydrate the skins for about 2 hours in a large dish of cold water. Place a weight on them to submerge them completely. The curved parts (where the skin is suspended to be dried) can take longer to rehydrate.

9 Dried shrimp Rehydrate the shrimp in a bowl of warm or cold water for 30 to 40 minutes.

Essential Techniques

10

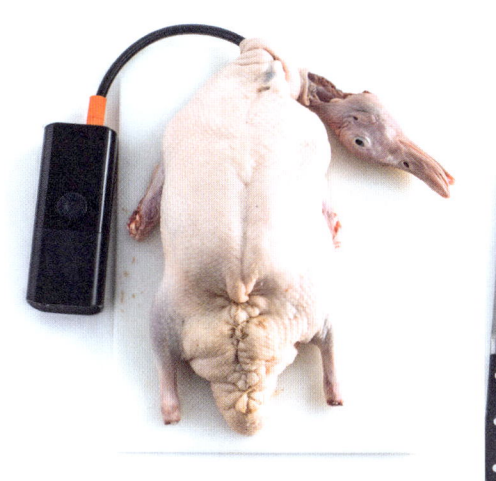

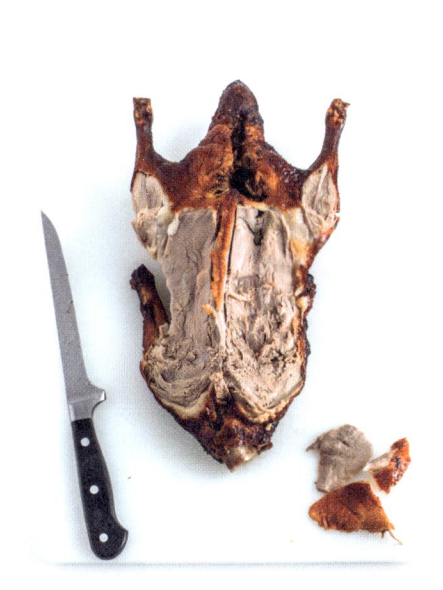

11

12

13

14

10 CRUSHING GARLIC

Crush the garlic clove by pressing it hard with the flat side of a knife blade or the bottom of a saucepan.

11 BLANCHING BAMBOO SHOOTS

Bring a pot of water to a boil and blanch the shoots for 1 to 2 minutes. Drain before using. This helps remove their strong odor.

12 CUTTING INTO JULIENNE

Cut the vegetable widthwise into sections and then into thin slices. Layer the slices on top of each other and cut them lengthwise into very thin strips.

13 MAKING LACQUERED DUCK

Peel off the skin using a small air compressor. Insert the tip of the compressor under the neck between the skin and meat to peel the skin off the breasts. Move toward the bottom to peel off the skin from the thighs. Turn the duck over and repeat. The goal is to peel the skin off the fat so that the skin can crisp during cooking. Without a compressor, skip this step and thoroughly dry the duck for 48 to 72 hours in a very cold, ventilated refrigerator.

14 CARVING A DUCK

Remove the neck. Make an incision along the breasts, following the central bone. Cut slices slightly at an angle starting from the neck down to the thighs. Place the slices on a plate. Turn the duck over and cut slices at the thighs. Detach the small tips of the wings. Cut the neck into pieces, if preferred. The Chinese do eat the neck meat. Otherwise, reserve the neck and bones to make a broth. Serve the slices with rice, noodles, or pancakes (chun bing).

Ingredients

1 RED CLAY

Use fresh, untreated clay. This can be found at a potter's studio or fine art supply store.

2 THAI BASIL

It has a slight aniseed and refreshing taste.

3 ENOKI

An Asian mushroom with a slightly sweet and fruity taste. They need little cooking time (30 seconds maximum).

4 CENTURY EGG

The century egg is a duck egg that is fermented in an alkaline environment (high pH) made of clay, salt, ash, lime, and rice or tea bran.

After several weeks, the fermentation process raises the pH of the egg, which causes the proteins to denature and gelatinize the egg white. The white becomes a translucent, dark brown with a firm and elastic texture.

The yolk becomes creamy, dark green or gray, with a cheese-like taste rich in umami. The egg becomes chemically transformed, making it edible without needing to be cooked.

The high alkalinity (high pH) creates conditions in which pathogens cannot survive, therefore presenting no risk from harmful bacteria.

Sometimes crystalline striations, resembling pine needles, appear in the egg white. These are referred to as "pine flowers" and are the sign of a quality fermentation resulting in optimal chemical transformation.

The origin of these eggs dates back centuries. They are a culinary curiosity and a must-try.

They are often eaten with congee or topped with sauce (soy sauce, sugar, black rice vinegar, sesame oil, or chile oil), silken tofu, or herbs (scallions and cilantro).

Ingredients

5

6

7

8

9

10

5 FERMENTED MUSTARD GREENS (SUI MI YA CAI)

Originally Szechuan. This is a fermented vegetable made from chopped brown mustard greens. After fermentation with salt and spices, its texture is slightly crunchy, and its taste is intense, very salty, and sour. It can be rinsed briefly to reduce its strong taste. It is indispensable in dan dan noodles and stuffed rice-flour balls. It is also eaten in small quantities with rice and can be used as a wrapper or bao filling. It is sold vacuum-packed. Another leaf can be substituted, or use fermented mustard bulbs.

6 FERMENTED BLACK SOYBEANS

This is an ancient and traditional Chinese condiment. It has a salty and intense taste, a sort of "umami bomb." They are used to season dishes. Rinse them before use to remove the salt crystals.

7 CHINESE TOASTED SESAME SAUCE

This is made from unshelled and heavily toasted white sesame seeds, which gives it a very toasted flavor with a hint of bitterness. You will often find them in Asian grocery stores as a version that is 50 percent peanut, also suitable for use in recipes. The flavor of this version will be rounder and sweeter.

If you have trouble finding it, you can replace it with ¼ cup / 60 g of tahini mixed with 1½ tablespoons of Chinese sesame oil.

8 RED PEPPER (CHILE) FLAKES

Considered to have medium intensity compared to chile peppers from China or Korea. Considered very spicy compared to those from Thailand.

9 FRESH RED CHILE PEPPER

Hot Thai chile. It can be replaced by milder long red chiles, usually from Morocco.

10 GOLDEN SYRUP

An invert sugar, similar to honey in texture.

Table of Contents

THE BUILDING BLOCKS

FLOURS & STARCHES

Wheat flour	10
Starches	11

RICE

Rice (jasmine)	12

DIM SUM DOUGH

Translucent dumpling dough	14
Wheat-flour dumpling dough	16
Bao dough	20

NOODLES & PANCAKES

Rice-flour noodles	22
Egg noodles	26
Biang Biang noodles	28
Steamed wheat-flour pancakes	32

TECHNIQUES

Deboning a chicken thigh	34
Preparing shrimp	36

BROTHS

Basic broth	38
Vegan broth	40

INGREDIENTS

Baking soda	42
Kansui	43
Lye water	43
Chile oil	44
Rice vinegar	46
Soy sauce	47
Oyster sauce	48
Wine and spirits	49

THE RECIPES

DIM SUM

Ha kao / Shrimp dumplings	54
Fun guo / Vegetable dumplings	58
Xiǎo lóng bāo / Soup dumplings	60
Guō tiē / Grilled pork dumplings	64
Shu mai / Pork and shrimp bites	68
Char siu bao	72
Mama's bao	76
Lo bak go / Daikon cake	80
Wu gok / Taro croquette	84
Cheung fun / Rice noodle rolls with shrimp	88
Jiǔcài hézǐ / Flat steamed garlic chive dumplings	92
Lo mai gai / Glutinous rice with chicken in lotus leaf	96

MEAT

Kǎoyā / Cantonese lacquered duck	100
Lor ark / 5-flavor braised duck	104
Zhāngchá yā / Tea-smoked duck	108
Jiàohuā jī / Beggar's chicken	110
Zuì jī / Drunken chicken	114
Gōng bǎo jī dīng / Kung pao chicken	118
Sān bēi jī / Three-cup chicken	120
Char siu / Lacquered pork	122
Siu yuk / Crispy pork	124
Dōng pō ròu / Dong po pork	128
Gūlǔ ròu / Sweet and sour pork	132
Chǐ zhī niúròu / Stir-fried beef with black soybeans	136
Yángròu bāo / Braised lamb casserole	138

FISH & SEAFOOD

Jiāng cōng yú / Steamed turbot with ginger and scallion sauce	142
Shuǐ zhǔ yú / Szechuan poached fish	144
Yú shēng / Prosperity salad	148
Sōngshǔ yú / Sweet and sour fish	152
Jiāoyán xiā / Salt-and-pepper shrimp	156
Steamed prawns, vermicelli noodles, and fried garlic	158
Chǎo lóngxiā / Sautéed langoustine	162

TOFU

Mápó dòufu / Mapo tofu	164
Jiāng chǎo dòufu / Stir-fried tofu with ginger	168

VEGETABLES

Háoyóu jiè lán / Gai lan in oyster sauce	170
Luóhàn zhāi / Buddha's delight	172
Pāi huángguā / Pressed cucumber salad	176
Hóngshāo qiézi / Braised eggplant	178
Shǒu sī bāo cài / Cabbage stir-fry in vinegar	180
Dìsānxiān / Three Treasures from the earth	182
Suān là tāng / Hot and sour soup	186
Chūn bǐng / Spring pancake	190

NOODLES & RICE

Hǎixiān chǎomiàn / Seafood noodles	194
Sùcài chǎomiàn / Stir-fried noodles with vegetables	198
Yóu pō chě miàn / Biang biang noodles with spicy oil	200
Yángròu miàn / Biang biang noodles with lamb	202
Niúròu miàn / Beef noodle soup	206
Zhájiàng miàn	210
Dàndàn miàn / Dan dan noodles	214
Jiǎndāo miàn / Scissor-cut noodles	216
Gon chow ngau ho / Stir-fried beef noodles	220
Yángzhōu chǎofàn / Yangzhou stir-fried rice	224
Bāo zǎi fàn / Clay pot rice	228
Pídàn jīròu zhōu / Century egg chicken congee	232
Zòngzi / Stuffed glutinous rice	234
Xián yú chǎofàn / Salted fish fried rice	238

STREET FOODS

Gē bāo / Dong po pork gua bao	242
Cōng yóubǐng / Fried scallion pancake	244
Yè er bā / Stuffed dumplings wrapped in leaves	248
Yán sū jī / Popcorn chicken	250

DESSERTS

Ma lai go / Steamed sponge cake	254
Dan tat / Egg tarts	256
Yuèbǐng / Mooncakes	260
Tāngyuán with black sesame	264
Liúshā bāo / Lava bao	268
Máhuā / Black sesame twists	272

ILLUSTRATED GLOSSARY

Equipment	278
Building Blocks	280
Ingredients	282

Index of Chinese Ingredients

B

BAMBOO (LEAF)
Stuffed glutinous rice........................ 234

BAMBOO (SHOOT)
Braised lamb casserole 138
Hot and sour soup 186
Shrimp dumplings 54

BIANG BIANG NOODLES
Biang biang noodles with lamb............. 202
Biang biang noodles with spicy oil 200
Scissor-cut noodles 216

BLACK MUSHROOM
Buddha's delight............................. 172
Hot and sour soup 186
Mama's bao 76
Spring pancake.............................. 190
Vegetable dumplings........................ 58

BLACK SESAME
Black sesame twists......................... 272
Tāngyuán with black sesame 264

BLACK SOY (BEANS)
Stir-fried beef with black soybeans 136

BOK CHOY
Beef noodle soup 216
Scissor-cut noodles 206

C

CHILE PEPPER
Cabbage stir-fry in vinegar................... 180
Dong po pork gua bao 242
Hot and sour soup 186
Mapo tofu................................... 164
Sautéed langoustine 162
Steamed turbot with ginger and scallion 142

CHINESE BACON
Beggar's chicken............................. 110
Scissor-cut noodles 216

CHINESE BROCCOLI
Gai lan in oyster sauce....................... 170

CHINESE CABBAGE
Buddha's delight............................. 172
Grilled pork dumplings 64
Szechuan poached fish 144

CHINESE DOUGH STICKS
Century egg chicken congee 232

CHINESE EGGPLANT
Braised eggplant............................. 178
Three treasures from the earth 182

CHINESE SAUSAGES
Clay pot rice................................. 228
Daikon cake 80
Stuffed glutinous rice........................ 234
Yangzhou stir-fried rice...................... 224

CHINKIANG BLACK RICE VINEGAR
Biang biang noodles with lamb............. 202
Biang biang noodles with spicy oil 200
Cabbage stir-fry in vinegar................... 180
Dan dan noodles............................ 214
Hot and sour soup 186
Kung pao chicken........................... 118
Pressed cucumber salad..................... 176

D

DAIKON
Beef noodle soup 206
Daikon cake 80
Prosperity salad 148

DÒUBÀNJIÀNG
Szechuan poached fish 144

DRIED CHILE PEPPER
Kung pao chicken........................... 118
Mapo tofu................................... 164

E

EGG NOODLES
Seafood noodles............................. 194
Stir-fried noodles with vegetables 198

ENOKI
Szechuan poached fish 144

F

FERMENTED MUSTARD LEAF
Dan dan noodles............................ 214
Stuffed dumplings wrapped in leaves 248

FERMENTED RED SOYBEAN PASTE
Lacquered pork.............................. 122

FIVE-SPICE POWDER
5-flavor braised duck........................ 104
Beef noodle soup 206
Beggar's chicken............................. 110
Cantonese lacquered duck................... 100
Char siu bao................................. 72
Crispy pork.................................. 124
Fried scallion pancake....................... 244
Glutinous rice with chicken in lotus leaf...... 96
Lacquered pork.............................. 122
Mama's bao 76
Mapo tofu................................... 164
Popcorn chicken............................. 250
Prosperity salad 148
Stuffed glutinous rice........................ 234
Taro croquettes.............................. 84
Tea-smoked duck............................ 108

FRESH WHEAT-FLOUR NOODLES
Beef noodle soup 206
Dan dan noodles............................ 214
Zhájiàng miàn 210

G

GAI LAN
Gai lan in oyster sauce....................... 170
Salted fish fried rice.......................... 238

GALANGA
5-flavor braised duck........................ 104

GARLIC CHIVE
Flat steamed garlic chive dumplings 92

GINGER
5-flavor braised duck........................ 104
Beggar's chicken............................. 110
Biang biang noodles with lamb............. 202
Braised eggplant............................. 178
Braised lamb casserole 138
Buddha's delight............................. 172
Cabbage stir-fry in vinegar................... 180
Cantonese lacquered duck................... 100
Century egg chicken congee 232
Clay pot rice................................. 228
Drunken chicken............................. 114
Grilled pork dumplings 64
Hot and sour soup 186
Kung pao chicken........................... 118
Lacquered pork.............................. 122
Mapo tofu................................... 164
Pressed cucumber salad..................... 176
Prosperity salad 148
Soup dumplings 60
Steamed turbot with ginger and scallion 142
Stir-fried noodles with vegetables 198
Stuffed dumplings wrapped in leaves 248
Sweet and sour fish.......................... 152
Szechuan poached fish 144
Three-cup chicken........................... 120
Zhájiàng miàn 210

GLUTINOUS (STICKY) RICE
Glutinous rice with chicken in lotus leaf...... 96
Stuffed glutinous rice........................ 234

GLUTINOUS RICE FLOUR
Flat steamed garlic chive dumplings 92
Stuffed dumplings wrapped in leaves 248
Tāngyuán with black sesame 264

K

KWANTUNG MIJIU
Seafood noodles............................. 194

L

LOTUS (LEAF)
Beggar's chicken............................. 110

LOTUS (ROOT)
Buddha's delight............................. 172

LOTUS (SEED)
Glutinous rice with chicken in lotus leaf...... 96
Mooncakes.................................. 260

M

MUNG BEAN SPROUTS
Spring pancake.............................. 190
Stir-fried beef noodles....................... 220
Stir-fried noodles with vegetables 198
Szechuan poached fish 144
Zhájiàng miàn 210

MUNG BEAN VERMICELLI NOODLES
Buddha's delight............................. 172
Streamed prawns,
vermicelli noodles and fried garlic 158

R

RICE
Century egg chicken congee 232
Clay pot rice................................. 228
Salted fish fried rice.......................... 238
Yangzhou stir-fried rice...................... 224

RICE FLOUR
Daikon cake 90
Flat steamed garlic chive dumplings 92
Rice noodle rolls with shrimp................. 88

RICE NOODLES
Stir-fried beef noodles....................... 220

S

SALTED DUCK EGG YOLK
Lava bao.................................... 268
Mooncakes.................................. 260

SCALLIONS
Biang biang noodles with lamb............. 202
Biang biang noodles with spicy oil 200
Braised eggplant............................. 178
Braised lamb casserole 138
Cabbage stir-fry in vinegar................... 180
Century egg chicken congee 232
Clay pot rice................................. 228
Fried scallion pancake....................... 244
Kung pao chicken........................... 118
Mapo tofu................................... 164
Sautéed langoustine 162
Stuffed dumplings wrapped in leaves 248
Sweet and sour fish.......................... 152
Three treasures from the earth 182
Steamed prawns, vermicelli noodles,
and fried garlic 158
Yangzhou stir-fried rice...................... 224
Zhájiàng miàn 210

SHAOXING RICE WINE
5-flavor braised duck........................ 104
Beef noodle soup 206
Beggar's chicken............................. 110
Biang biang noodles with lamb............. 202
Braised lamb casserole 138
Clay pot rice................................. 228
Dan dan noodles............................ 214
Dong po pork 128
Drunken chicken............................. 114
Hot and sour soup 186
Kung pao chicken........................... 118
Mapo tofu................................... 164

286

Sautéed langoustine 162
Steamed turbot with ginger and scallion 142
Stir-fried beef with black soybeans 136
Stuffed dumplings wrapped in leaves 248
Stuffed glutinous rice. 234
Sweet and sour pork 132
Szechuan poached fish .144
Taro croquettes. 84
Tea-smoked duck 108
Three-cup chicken 120
Zhájiàng miàn 210

SHIITAKE
Beggar's chicken. 110
Braised lamb casserole .138
Buddha's delight. 172
Clay pot rice. 228
Daikon cake 80
Glutinous rice with chicken in lotus leaf. 96
Hot and sour soup 186
Mama's bao 76
Pork and shrimp bites 68
Stir-fried noodles with vegetables 198
Stuffed glutinous rice. 234
Taro croquettes. 84
Vegetable dumplings. 58

SHIMEJI
Szechuan poached fish .144

STAR ANISE
5-flavor braised duck. 104
Braised lamb casserole .138
Dong po pork 128
Drunken chicken. 114
Prosperity salad 148
Sweet and sour pork 132
Three-cup chicken 120
Zhájiàng miàn 210

SWEET POTATO VERMICELLI NOODLES
Spring pancake 190

SZECHUAN PEPPER
Beef noodle soup . . . .
Biang biang noodles with lamb. . . . .
Biang biang noodles with spicy oil 200
Cabbage stir-fry in vinegar. 180
Dan dan noodles. 214
Kung pao chicken. 118
Mapo tofu. 164
Popcorn chicken. 250
Stuffed dumplings wrapped in leaves 248
Szechuan poached fish .144
Tea-smoked duck 108

T

TAPIOCA STARCH
Flat steamed garlic chive dumplings 92
Shrimp dumplings 54
Vegetable dumplings. 58

TEA
Tāngyuán with black sesame 264
Tea-smoked duck 108

THAI BASIL
Popcorn chicken. 250
Three-cup chicken 120

TOFU
5-flavor braised duck. 104
Buddha's delight. 172
Hot and sour soup 186
Mapo tofu. 164
Spring pancake 190
Stir-fried tofu with ginger. 168
Vegetable dumplings. 58

TOFU SKINS
Braised lamb casserole .138
Buddha's delight. 172
Pressed cucumber salad 176

W

WATER CHESTNUT
Mama's bao 76
Pork and shrimp bites 68
Vegetable dumplings. 58

WONTON WRAPPERS
Pork and shrimp bites 68
Prosperity salad 148

Index of Ingredients

B

BEEF
Beef noodle soup 206
Stir-fried beef noodles. 220
Stir-fried beef with black soybeans 136

BELL PEPPER
Stir-fried beef with black soybeans 136
Sweet and sour pork 132
Three treasures from the earth 182

C

CABBAGE
Cabbage stir-fry in vinegar. 180
Dong po pork gua bao 242

CARROT
Spring pancake 190
Stir-fried noodles with vegetables 198
Vegetable dumplings. 58

CHICKEN
Beggar's chicken. 110
Century egg chicken congee 232
Clay pot rice. 228
Drunken chicken. 114
Glutinous rice with chicken in lotus leaf. 96
Hot and sour soup 186
Kung pao chicken. 118
Popcorn chicken. 250
Three-cup chicken 120

CUCUMBER
Pressed cucumber salad 176

CUTTLEFISH
Seafood noodles. 194

D

DUCK
5-flavor braised duck. 104
Cantonese lacquered duck. 100
Tea-smoked duck 108

E

EGG
5-flavor braised duck. 104
Egg tarts. 256
Lava bao 268
Steamed sponge cake 254
Yangzhou stir-fried rice. 224

EVAPORATED MILK
Egg tarts. 256

F

FISH
Prosperity salad 148
Salted fish fried rice. 238
Steamed turbot with ginger and scallion 142
Sweet and sour fish 152
Szechuan poached fish .144

L

LAMB
Biang biang noodles with lamb. 202
Braised lamb casserole .138

LANGOUSTINE
Sautéed langoustine 162

N

NOODLES
Beef noodle soup 206
Biang biang noodles with lamb. 202
Biang biang noodles with spicy oil 200
Dan dan noodles. 214
Scissor-cut noodles 216
Seafood noodles. 194
Stir-fried beef noodles. 220
Stir-fried noodles with vegetables 198
Zhájiàng miàn 210

P

PEAS
Yangzhou stir-fried rice. 224

PINEAPPLE
Sweet and sour pork 132

PORK
Char siu bao. 72
Clay pot rice. 228
Crispy pork. 124
Dan dan noodles. 214
Dong po pork 128
Dong po pork gua bao 242
Grilled pork dumplings 64
Lacquered pork. 122
Mama's bao 76
Mapo tofu. 164
Pork and shrimp bites 68
Soup dumplings 60
Stuffed dumplings wrapped in leaves 248
Sweet and sour pork 132
Taro croquettes. 84
Yangzhou stir-fried rice. 224
Zhájiàng miàn 210

POTATO
Three treasures from the earth 182

R

RICE
Century egg chicken congee 232
Clay pot rice. 228
Salted fish fried rice. 238
Stuffed glutinous rice. 234
Yangzhou stir-fried rice. 224

S

SCALLOPS
Seafood noodles. 194

SHRIMP
Shrimp dumplings 54
Pork and shrimp bites 68
Rice noodle rolls with shrimp. 88
Salt and pepper shrimp. 156
Seafood noodles. 194
Stuffed glutinous rice. 234
Steamed prawns, vermicelli noodles,
and fried garlic. 158
Yangzhou stir-fried rice. 224

T

TOMATO
Scissor-cut noodles 216

V

VANILLA
Egg tarts. 254
Steamed sponge cake 256

Hardie Grant

NORTH AMERICA

Hardie Grant North America
2912 Telegraph Ave
Berkeley, CA 94705
hardiegrant.com

Copyright © 2025 by Orathay Souksisavanh
Photographs Copyright © 2025 by Pierre Javelle
Illustrations Copyright © 2025 by Yannis Varoutsikos

All rights reserved. No part of this book may be reproduced in any form without written permission from the publisher.

Published in the United States by Hardie Grant North America, an imprint of Hardie Grant Publishing Pty Ltd.

Styling: Orathay Souksisavanh
Culinary assistant: Mélanie Philippo
Graphic design: Yannis Varoutsikos
Layout: Chimène De

Translation: Zachary R. Townsend
Typesetting: Mira Green

ISBN: 9781964786285
ISBN: 9781964786292 (ebook)
Printed by Toppan in China, in 2025.